EAST-WEST LITERARY IMAGINATION

EAST-WEST LITERARY IMAGINATION

CULTURAL EXCHANGES FROM YEATS TO MORRISON

Yoshinobu Hakutani

UNIVERSITY OF MISSOURI PRESS
Columbia

For
Jaeyeon Park Hakutani
and
Emiko Hakutani

CONTENTS

CONTENTS

ACKNOWLEDGMENTS

I am indebted to many writers and sources, as acknowledged in the notes and the works cited. I wish to thank, in particular, the late John M. Reilly, the late Robert L. Tener, the late Michiko Hakutani, and the anonymous readers for the University of Missouri Press, who read part or all of the manuscript and offered useful, constructive suggestions. I would also like to acknowledge my son Yoshiki Hakutani for his editorial and technical support, and Toru Kiuchi for making an index.

Over the years the Kent State University Research Council has provided several research leaves and travel grants. I am grateful for their support.

I have used in modified form my previously published essays "Ezra Pound, Yone Noguchi, and Imagism," *Modern Philology* 90 (August 1992); "W. B. Yeats, Modernity, and the Noh Play," in *Modernity in East-West Literary Criticism: New Readings* (Associated University Presses, 2001); and "Cross-Cultural Poetics: Sonia Sanchez's *Like the Singing Coming off the Drums*" and "James Emanuel's Jazz Haiku and African American Individualism," in *Cross-Cultural Visions in African American Modernism: From Spatial Narrative to Jazz Haiku* (Ohio State University Press, 2006).

ABBREVIATIONS

12M   Wright, Richard. *12 Million Black Voices: A Folk History of the Negro in the United States*. New York: Viking, 1941.

AW   Thoreau, Henry David. *A Week on the Concord and Merrimack Rivers*. Edited by Carl F. Hovde et al. Princeton, NJ: Princeton University Press, 1980.

B   Morrison, Toni. *Beloved*. New York: Knopf, 1987.

BB   Wright. *Black Boy: A Record of Childhood and Youth*. 1945. Reprint, New York: Harper and Row, 1966.

BOH   Kerouac, Jack. *Book of Haikus*. Edited by Regina Weinreich. New York: Penguin Books, 2003.

BP   Wright. *Black Power: A Record of Reactions in a Land of Pathos*. New York: Harper, 1954.

CNT   Pound, Ezra, and Ernest Fenollosa. *The Classic Noh Theatre of Japan*. New York: New Directions, 1959.

CEOE   Emerson, Ralph Waldo. *The Complete Essays and Other Writings of Ralph Waldo Emerson*. Edited by Brooks Atkinson. New York: Modern Library, 1940.

CP   Walker, Alice. *The Color Purple*. 1982. Reprint, New York: Pocket Books, 1985.

CPOED   Dickinson, Emily. *The Complete Poems of Emily Dickinson*. Edited by Thomas H. Johnson. Boston: Little, Brown, 1960.

CPOW   Whitman, Walt. *Complete Poetry and Selected Prose*. Edited by James E. Miller Jr. Boston: Houghton Mifflin, 1959.

DB   Kerouac. *The Dharma Bums*. New York: Viking, 1958.

EM   Wright. *Eight Men*. Cleveland: World, 1961.

HTOW   (A number following this abbreviation is that of Wright's haiku, not a page number.)
        Wright. *Haiku: This Other World*. Edited by Yoshinobu Hakutani and Robert L. Tener. New York: Arcade, 1998. Reprint, New York: Random House, 2000.

IM   Ellison, Ralph. *Invisible Man*. 1952. Reprint, New York: Vintage, 1995.

OTR   Kerouac. *On the Road*. New York: Viking, 1958.

POY   Yeats, W. B. *The Variorum Edition of the Plays of W. B. Yeats*. Edited by Russell K. Alspach. New York: Macmillan, 1966.

PRWE   Emerson. *The Poems of Ralph Waldo Emerson*. Edited by Louis Untermeyer. New York: Heritage, 1945.

PS   Wright. *Pagan Spain*. New York: Harper and Brothers, 1957.

SA   Ellison. *Shadow and Act*. New York: Random House, 1964.

SEWOYN Noguchi, Yone. *Selected English Writings of Yone Noguchi: An East-West Literary Assimilation*. Edited by Yoshinobu Hakutani. 2 vols. Rutherford, NJ: Fairleigh Dickinson University Press / London: Associated University Presses, 1990, 1992.

SJP   Noguchi. *The Spirit of Japanese Poetry*. London: John Murray / New York: Dutton, 1914.

SPLH   Hughes, Langston. *Selected Poems of Langston Hughes*. New York: Knopf, 1959.

TO   Wright. *The Outsider*. 1953. Reprint, New York: Harper and Row, 1965.

WOE   Emerson. *The Works of Emerson*. 4 vols. New York: Tudor, 1900.

EAST-WEST LITERARY IMAGINATION

INTRODUCTION

Cultural exchanges between the East and the West began in the early decades of the nineteenth century as American transcendentalists, whose ideas had originated from European philosophers and writers, such as Kant and Wordsworth, explored Eastern philosophies and arts. The works by New England transcendentalists—Emerson, Thoreau, Margaret Fuller, Bronson Alcott, and others—mark the influences of and responses to various Eastern religions, philosophies, and literatures. The impact of Eastern cultures on nineteenth-century American literature was in contrast to Edward Said's notion of Orientalism, in which West, the dominating, influenced East, the dominated. Unlike European literatures, such as British, French, German, Russian, and others, American literature has become a hybridization of Eastern and Western literatures as modern, postmodern, and postcolonial African American literature has demonstrated. The writings of Richard Wright, for example, take on their full significance only when they are read, not as part of a national literature, but as an index to an evolving literature of cultural exchanges.

In the New England 1880s, the intellectual climate was dominated by the transcendentalists' fascination with Eastern religions and philosophies. Bronson Alcott, a lesser-known transcendentalist, wrote in his memoir *Concord Days*, "Plainly, the drift of thinking here in New England, if not elsewhere, is towards a Personal Theism, inclusive of the faiths of all races, embodying the substance of their Sacred Books, with added forms and instrumentalities suited to the needs of our time. . . . The signs of our time indicate that we are on the eve of a recasting of old forms" (265). As Arthur Versluis has noted, some New England transcendentalists, such as Margaret Fuller, showed little interest in the East, but others, like Alcott, were interested in Hindu or Buddhist works because of Emerson's enthusiasm. "Emerson and Thoreau," Versluis notes, "wrote many of their works with the Bhagavad Gita, the Laws of Manu, the Puranas, and poets like Saadi for reference. In short, without 'Oriental religions,' many transcendentalist works could not exist in the same form, and much second-generation transcendentalist work would not exist at all."[1]

The influence of Eastern religions and philosophies on the New England transcendentalism caught the attentions of Frederic Ives Carpenter and Arthur Christy in the early 1930s. Both critics felt that Emerson's interest in Eastern thought was ambivalent. The young Emerson, Carpenter noted in *Emerson and Asia*, was drawn to as well as repulsed by the Oriental scriptures, and only later did he return to them and study the texts. Carpenter observed that Eastern philosophies had come much too late in shaping Emerson's philosophy. Christy, on the other hand, observed in *The Orient in American Transcendentalism* that Emerson had all along been interested in Confucianism and Persian poetry. "The entries in his journals," according to Versluis,

> show an ever-increasing fascination with Asiatic subjects, until by the end of his life we find that they comprise a large part of his reading and notation. But Emerson was not always so deeply immersed in the Upanishads and the Bhagavad-Gita; early on he was introduced to the Orient through articles in popular journals, and not surprisingly, he did not care for the 'ritualism,' the 'superstitious cruelties' depicted as characteristic of Hinduism and Buddhism.[2]

Unlike his followers in the nineteenth century, Thoreau and Whitman, Emerson was fascinated by Middle Eastern thought and tradition as his lifelong interest in Persian poetry suggests. As shown by Wai Chee Dimock, Emerson's interest in Islam is indicated by his reading of Gibbon's *Decline and Fall of the Roman Empire*. In particular, Emerson was struck by Gibbon's high praise for the Islamic language and poetry. Emerson's subsequent readings included such books as *Oriental Geography* (1800) by Ibn Haukal, *Annales Muslemici Arabice et Latine* (1837) by Abulfeda, and Simon Ockley's *Conquest of Syria, Persia, and Egypt by the Saracens* (1708–1718). What impressed Emerson about Islam was the scope, the long duration, the ability to find people across space and time. Emerson was especially impressed with the work of the fourteenth-century poet Hafiz. To Emerson, Hafiz's poetry poignantly reflects one's religious belief and heresy. Emerson believed that religious writing is the only record by which the early ages of any nation are remembered. Emerson was struck by Hafiz's poetry, for it sounded least divine. For example, he found Hafiz's poem with a portrayal of bottled spiders that did not bow their heads before the Koran.

On the other hand, Emerson was also reading books on Buddhism. He, however, responded to its religious philosophy with caution. While he saw a similarity between his theory of transcendentalism and his understanding of Buddhist philosophy that both emphasize the primacy of the spiritual over the material, he was adamantly opposed to the Buddhist conception of nirvana. He found the definition of nirvana as an undisciplined state of oblivion to the self and the world antithetical to his theory of the self and the oversoul. Although Emerson was not read in any of the writings on Zen, such as those by Dogen, or was not familiar with the sects of Zen, such as Soto and Rinzai, there is some affinity between his theory of transcendentalism and Zen doctrine. Emerson stressed the independence of the self from God's power and influence: an individual must attain enlightenment by self rather than by reliance on God. The Rinzai sect, on one other hand, urged its followers to achieve Buddhahood even by "annihilating" Buddha. Emersonian transcendentalism, however, ultimately differs from Zen, for Zen admonishes against self-consciousness and validates the concept of *mu*, the state of nothingness, whereas Emerson's theory upholds that self is capable of intuitive knowledge.

Although Thoreau, Emerson's famous disciple, grew up in New England as a devout Christian, he was open-minded and interested in other religions. Walter Harding wrote of Thoreau, "It is obvious to any serious student of Thoreau that a sympathy with, and knowledge of, the great works of Oriental literature permeates his writings."[3] Well versed in the Bible, he was even more curious about Hebrew and Hindu scriptures than Emerson. He also was much more fascinated with Buddhism than was his mentor Emerson. Thoreau's neighbors in Concord, Massachusetts, thought that he loved his Buddha more than they did their Christ. Among the transcendentalists of the nineteenth century, including Whitman, Thoreau was perhaps the most tolerant with all ancient philosophies, "Atomists, Pneumatologists, Atheists, Theoists,—Plato, Aristotle, Leucippus, Democritus, Pythagoras, Zoroaster and Confucius." "It is the attitude of these men," Thoreau observed, "more than any communication which they make, that attracts us. Between them and their commentators, it is true, there is an endless dispute. But if it comes to this that you compare notes, then you are all wrong" (*AW*, 152).

As "Song of Myself" intimates, Walt Whitman, a young generation transcendentalist hailing from New York, was more interested in Buddhism than in Christianity. Fascinated with Buddhist ontology, he believed in the Buddhist theory of transmigration and reincarnation. Whitman's interest in the East has been considered one of the legacies he received from Emerson. But Beongcheon Yu has not found supporting evidence for this observation. He, however, acknowledges that Emerson was the first to recognize Whitman's Orientalism by describing *Leaves of Grass* as "a remarkable mixture" of the Bhagavad Gita and the *New York Herald*. In *The Great Circle: American Writers and the Orient*, Yu minutely traces Eastern thought intertwined with the American concepts of democracy and freedom in the texts of Whitman's writings, especially "Passage to India" and "Song of Myself."

More recently, Shoji Goto, in *The Philosophy of Emerson and Thoreau: Orientals Meet Occidentals*, has challenged some of the earlier observations of the influence of Eastern thought on New England transcendentalism. Goto argues that while Emerson theorized the concept of the over-soul worldview in transcendentalism in terms of his own worldview, he also incorporated into his thought the ideas and visions he acquired from Eastern philosophies, such as Confucian Mencius, Hindu Vishnu, and Persian Zoroaster. Although Emerson did not directly read Chinese or Japanese Buddhist texts, Goto demonstrates that Emerson was knowledgeable of Zoroastrian and Zen thought.

Goto also shows that Confucian ethics buttressed Thoreau's political thought, especially in "Civil Disobedience." Thoreau's ethics of conscious and conscientious withdrawal from the state derived from Confucius. All in all, Goto demonstrates, as has Wai Chi Dimock, that while Emerson and Thoreau were eager to incorporate Eastern thoughts and visions into their philosophies, their American interpreters have long failed to see the globalization and hybridization of American transcendentalism.

In the early decades of the twentieth century in the West, modernism was characterized by a synchronic and nonnarrative mode of thinking: the modernistic temperament underscored a reaction against and a release from Victorian literature. Modernist writing often created a microcosmic world that thrives on self-referentiality and moral relativism. William Faulkner, himself an influential modern novelist, called modernists such artists and writers as Picasso, Stravinsky, Proust, Yeats, Pound, Eliot, Joyce, Lawrence, and Woolf. While Western modernists stressed impersonality to suppress human subjectivity, a vestige of romanticism, they developed the autonomous mode of expression as an aesthetic commitment to disrupt the mimetic and descriptive method characteristic of realism and naturalism.

The essence of modernism—how modernism distinguishes itself from romanticism and realism—is a sense of independence and autonomy, an awareness of the self-contained, self-referential realm of art. Modernists thus challenged both the realist's concern with correspondence through reflection and the romanticist's preoccupation with vision. Instead they sought to realize autonomy in their writing, the impersonal essence of pure form in the work itself. But George Orwell, for instance, deplored modernists' indifference to content and their concentration on form. "Our eyes," he wrote, "are directed to Rome, to Byzantium, to Montparnasse, to Mexico, to the Etruscans, to the subconscious, to the solar plexus—to everywhere except the places where things are actually happening" (*Collected Essays*, 1:557). This formalism in the 1920s was regarded by many as the logical aesthetic for modernist writing. Modernists believed that their art offers a privileged insight into reality and at the same time that, because art creates its own reality, it is not at all concerned about commonplace reality: art is an autonomous activity.

The modernist's privileged insight into reality is best seen in Eliot, who is more concerned with discovering the relations between surface and depth than with those between appearance and reality. Unlike a layperson, a modernist writer is capable of deciphering some meaningful relation between the surface of everyday experience and the deep structure of truth. In reference to John Donne's poetry, Eliot writes, "When a poet's mind is perfectly equipped for its work, it is constantly amalgamating disparate experience; the ordinary man's experience is chaotic, irregular, fragmentary. The latter falls in love, or reads Spinoza, and these two experiences have nothing to do with each other, or with the noise of the typewriter or the smell of cooking; in the mind of the poet these experiences are always forming new wholes" (*Selected Essays*, 247).

Eliot's privileged insight into human experience is remindful of what Basho, the most celebrated haiku poet, said about the poet's sensibility. In his travelogue, *Manuscript in My Knapsack (Oi no Kobumi)*, Basho wrote:

One and the same thing runs through the waka of Saigyo, the renga of Sogi, the paintings of Sesshu, the tea ceremony of Rikyu. What is common to all these arts is their following nature and making a friend of the four seasons. Nothing the artist sees but is flowers, nothing he thinks of but is the moon. When what a man sees is not flowers, he is no better than a barbarian. When what he thinks in his heart is not the moon, he belongs to the same species as the birds and beasts. I say, free yourselves from the barbarism, remove yourself from the birds and beasts; follow nature and return to nature.[4]

This passage reveals not only that Basho had great confidence in his art but also that he believed that a Zen poet like him is privileged to see relations between human experience and natural phenomenon, appearance and reality, surface and depth.

The aesthetic world that modernists in Western literatures attained through their privilege and authority, however, displayed a proclivity toward fragmentation and despair. The worldview in modernist writing often conveys a bleak, devastated urban cityscape, as Eliot's *The Waste Land* depicts. "Hugh Selwyn Mauberley" by Ezra Pound, a poet often regarded as the harbinger of modernism, summarizes his disillusionment with the devastating war and with Western civilization: the world is filled with images of mendacities, liars, adulterers, prostitutes. The modernist landscape is in contrast to the Victorian world full of hopes and optimism. Joyce's Leopold Bloom finds such a world unfit for men and women to inhabit.

Despite the sentiments of fragmentation and alienation modernists generated, they tried to redeem themselves through the creation of art. "Man acts," Heidegger said, "as though he were the shaper and master of language, while in fact, language remains the master of man. Perhaps it is above all else man's subversion of this relation of dominance that drives his nature into alienation."[5] To overcome alienation, modernists shifted the burden of knowledge from the rational to the aesthetic; some of the modernists gauged their world in relation to past culture. To Eliot, present culture is an embodied experience of the present arising from the continuous transformation of the past. Above all, modernists are opposed to absolute polarities in human experience. Victorians, by contrast, had a penchant for the dichotomy of masculine and feminine, object and subject, the higher and the lower, the earlier and the later, present and past, time and place. Modernists, on the contrary, explore the notion of integrating the opposites. They view the opposites as convenient ways of discussing present phenomena, which, upon closer observation, reveal themselves to be related to one another or to be functions of one another.

Among the modernists in the twentieth century, Yone Noguchi (1875–1947) played the most vital role in disseminating Japanese poetics and haiku, in particular, to the West. As early as 1903 he met W. B. Yeats in London; in the 1920s and '30s Noguchi was the best-known interpreter of Japanese art in the West, especially in England. Beginning with *The Spirit of Japanese Art* (1915), he published ten books about celebrated artists, with colorful illustrations, on Hiroshige, Korin, Utamaro, Hokusai, and Harunobu. Yeats, whose interest in the noh play is well-known, became fascinated with these artists through Noguchi. Noguchi in return dedicated the collection of his own English haiku to Yeats.

In the modernist writing of this period, symbolism played a dominant stylistic role. Yeats, inspired by the primordial life force rather than by the contemporary political turmoil, was attracted to Japanese medieval symbolism. In his poetry and drama, the old Irish folk tradition provided him with expressionist vitalism. Yeats's fascination with Eastern arts came from his impression that simplicity and naturalness in Eastern arts derived from the cultural backgrounds of the arts rather than from the individual emotions of the artists. Yeats's interest in the symbolism of the noh theatre came from a desire to condense and simplify the action of his plays. This meant that action must be reduced to its essentials and that the characters involved in it must be freed from anything that may distract the viewer's attention from the meaning of the play. Simplicity and concentration are so essential to the performance of a noh play that the stage itself must be physically small and confined. Not only did Yeats adapt noh scenery to his play, but the use of masks also verified his concept of simplicity, impersonality, and profundity in symbolism. In place of surface realism, Yeats had long believed, a great dramatist would employ rituals and masks. When he was introduced to the noh theatre, he was at once impressed with such devices.

Through Yeats and other English writers, Noguchi also became well acquainted with Pound as early as 1911. In the meantime, Noguchi's later poetry, collected in *The Pilgrimage* (1908) and *Japanese Hokkus* (1920), and his literary criticism, *The Spirit of Japanese Poetry* (1914), in particular, were widely circulated in the West. In relating Japanese poetics to Western intentions in early modernism, Noguchi played a principal role. Among the various sources of influence and assimilation, the imagists responded directly to the example of their fellow poet Noguchi. In Japan, on the other hand, his associations with poets in the West had a considerable impact on such modernist Japanese poets as Shimazaki Toson (1872–1943), Takamura Kotaro (1883–1952), and Hagiwara Sakutaro (1886–1942).

In reference to Eastern philosophy, Noguchi attempted to explain the integration and reconciliation of oppositions in human life. To criticize the Victorian tendency to polarize oppositions, he wrote in 1914:

> Japanese poetry, at least the old Japanese poetry, is different from Western poetry in the same way as silence is different from a voice, night from day; while avoiding the too close discussion of their relative merits, I can say that the latter always fails, naturally enough through being too active to properly value inaction, restfulness, or death; to speak shortly, the passive phase of Life and the World.

As if to support Pound's modernist thinking in poetry, Noguchi urged poets in the West to depict the sensitiveness of the human heart "influenced by the night and silence, as well as by the day and voice" (*SEWOYN*, 2:59). In Japanese poetics, Noguchi argued, an intensified art can be created not from action but from inaction.

In the development of modernism, one of the bridges built between East and West was a poetic movement, imagism, spearheaded by Pound. Like symbolism, imagism was a form of representation that arose in reaction to realism and naturalism. Because modernism emphasized the writer's attention to the smallest segment, which would reveal the depth of the world rather than the surface of the macrocosmic world, modernist writing did concentrate on the precise and exact word and on the concrete image. To Pound the immediate model for this principle was nineteenth-century French prose. He was adamantly opposed to Victorian poetry, which he called wordy and rhetorical. Instead, he urged his contemporary poets to emulate such novelists as Flaubert and de Maupassant, who raised the level of prose to that of a finer art.

Another source of Pound's vorticist theory was Chinese characters, which Pound called ideograms. Ernest Fenollosa's essay "The Chinese Written Character as a Medium of Poetry" shows that Chinese characters, derived from visual rather than aural experiences, form images. The Chinese character, Fenollosa noted, signifies an observable action rather than an abstract notion. In contrast to a Western word, a phonetic sign, a Chinese character denotes a concrete, natural phenomenon. The Chinese character, he wrote, "is based upon a vivid shorthand picture of the operations of nature. In the algebraic figure and in the spoken word there is no natural connection between thing and sign: all depends upon sheer convention. But the Chinese method follows natural suggestion."[6]

Above all, Pound's acquaintance with the art of haiku through Yone Noguchi had a strong influence on the theory and practice of imagism. Pound's definition of imagism differs from Nietzsche's view of metaphor. Nietzsche conceived metaphor to be an ingenious fiction imposed upon the senses. Nor is Pound's concept of imagism akin to Fenollosa's view of metaphor. Fenollosa considered metaphor as a representation of nature; for him, the metaphors embedded in our consciousness objectively represent phenomena and relations in nature itself. Pound's imagism, on the other hand, is neither Nietzschean fiction nor Fenollosan fact; it is a hermeneutic activity and construct. Because Pound's image generates its own life, it conforms to the twin principles of modernism: impersonality and autonomy.

Imagism, furthermore, betrays an affinity with Noguchi's interpretation of haiku. In haiku there is little division between the perceiver and the perceived, spirit and matter, human and nature. In poetry, Noguchi argues, there is no strict boundary between what is called subjective and objective. Some haiku that appear to be objective turn out to be "quite subjective through the great virtue of the writers having the fullest identification with the matter written on" (*SEWOYN*, 2: 73). In Noguchi's poetry, then, as in traditional haiku, poetry and sensation are spontaneously joined in one and the same, so that there is scarcely any room left for rationalism or moralism, a mode of writing characteristic of Victorian poetry.

The absence of rationalism and moralism, which haiku and Pound's image share, entails that the poet is capable of escaping the confinement of the poem. The sense of liberation in haiku is usually accomplished through impersonal references to time and place. A classic haiku contains not only a reference to a season, an indication of time, but also an impersonal image of nature, that of place. Pound's haiku-like poems, such as "In a Station of the Metro" and "Alba," indeed have references to time and place. Pound called the metro emotion objective and the image of the petals subjective, but this image is nevertheless a natural object in contrast to the image of the faces in the crowded station, a human object. Both the haiku and Pound's image, functioning as independent, hermeneutic metaphors, are not governed by external forces other than their own. Though autonomous, their existence is not controlled by the author's will or emotion. They both avoid the ornamental, ancillary functions of metaphor and use what Pound calls "the language of exploration" ("Vorticism," 466).

In 1913, a year before Pound's essay "Vorticism" appeared, Noguchi published an essay, "What Is a Hokku Poem?," in the journal *Rhythm*. Noguchi demonstrated that the brevity and intensity of wording makes haiku composition most expressive. Pound, in his earlier career, also tried to apply the principle of terseness and intensity to the construction of a single image. It is well known that Eliot's *The Waste Land* is dedicated to Pound and that the final manuscript was meticulously edited, but how much Pound's principle of imagism influenced the editing has been a matter of speculation.

In any event, Pound found images in haiku to be depictions of concrete, autonomous objects in nature and life rather than symbols. Pound regarded symbolism as "a sort of allusion, almost of allegory." The symbolists, he thought, "degraded the symbol to the status of a word. . . . Moreover, one does not want to be called a symbolist, because symbolism has usually been associated with mushy technique" ("Vorticism," 463). For Pound, symbolism is inferior to imagism, because in symbolism one image is used to suggest another or to represent another whereby both images would be weakened. Pound's theory of imagism was derived from haiku, which shuns metaphor and symbolism, rather than from the noh play, which Yeats considered "indirect and symbolic." If Yeats's ideal language has the suggestiveness and allusiveness of symbolism as opposed to the directness and clearness of imagism, then his sources certainly did not include Pound. Even though Yeats dedicated *At the Hawk's Well* (1917) to Pound, Yeats was not enthusiastic about Pound's theory. Yeats, a symbolist and spiritualist poet, was fascinated by the noh play while Pound, an imagist, was influenced by Japanese poetry and by haiku in particular.

A few years later, haiku also had an impact on modernist poets such as William Carlos Williams and Wallace Stevens. Just like Pound's definition of an image, an image in a phenomenological poem such as Williams's "The Red Wheel Barrow," an object found in the environment rather than in one's mind, is autonomous and exists on its own power:

so much depends
upon

a red wheel
barrow

glazed with rain
water

beside the white
chickens.

Like Pound's image, Williams's, endowed with energy, becomes an artistic, poetic image rather than a picture in a photograph. To the reader, such an image appears fresh and dynamic rather than stale and static. The image of the wheel barrow becomes fresh and real because of the word "red" that lights up the scene. The word "glazed" evokes another painterly image; the rain transforms the image as well, giving it a newer fresh look, just as Pound's Metro poem thrives on the image of the faces in the crowd, which in turn transforms into the image of petals on a wet, black bough: "The apparition of these faces in the crowd: / Petals, on a wet, black bough."

Another modernist influenced by East-West cross-culturalism was Marcel Proust, whose writing is also considered postmodern. Whereas a typical modernist in the West, like Eliot, is characterized by autonomy and self-referentiality, Proust is not. If modernist writing is called existential and Western, Proust's writing can be read as animistic and Eastern. The souls of the dead, Proust writes in *Remembrance of Things Past* (1913–1927), "are held captive in some inferior being, in an animal, in a plant, in some inanimate object, and thus effectively lost to us until the day (which to many never come) when we happen to pass by the tree or to obtain possession of the object which forms their prison" (*Remembrance*, 47). Unlike the Victorian novel, Proust argued, the modern novel must aim at discovering what he called "a different self." The purpose of the novel, he believed, is not to tell a story, expound a moral, or, as in realism and naturalism, describe a social environment, though he certainly did the latter. It is to accomplish the creation of a different self that one's experience in the environment has failed to reveal. The self sought is a re-creation, a construct entirely different from the ordinary, mundane self—a familial, social, and political being known in daily life. What Proust called "our social personality" is "a creation of the thoughts of other people. Even the simple act which we describe as 'seeing someone we know' is to some extent an intellectual process. We pack the physical outline of the person we see with all the notions we have already formed about him, and in the total picture of him which we compose in our minds those notions have certainly the principal place" (*Remembrance*, 20).

To Proust, then, self in the novel is a re-creation by removing the ego that has created a world of illusion. At the outset of this novel, Proust gives an account of his own consciousness after a sleep. Upon waking at midnight, he fails to locate himself and regain human identity. He has "only the most rudimentary sense of existence, such as may lurk and flicker in the depths of an animal's consciousness." After traversing ages of civilization, he "would gradually piece together the original pieces of [his] ego," (*Remembrance*, 5–6). Once his ego is destroyed, what it masks below—the essence of life—will emerge. This self-realization, as McKay Jenkins has observed, is remindful of the Buddhist nirvana.[7] Along with Yeats and Pound, Proust was another major modernist in the West who crossed the paths of Eastern cultures in the early decades of the twentieth century.

In the aftermath of World War II, existentialism as a literary movement, originated in France, became influential the world over. Existentialist writing gathered momentum with the works of Camus, Sartre, and de Beauvoir, and their novels became the models for their contemporaries in the West as well as in the East. *No Longer Human* [*Ningen Shikkaku*] (1948) by Osamu Dazai, a Japanese writer, was an impressive existentialist novel. In America, Richard Wright's *Black Boy* (1945), one of the greatest autobiographies in American literature, can be read as an existentialist work. In midcentury, Ralph Ellison and Wright wrote *Invisible Man* (1952) and *The Outsider* (1953), respectively, in response to European existentialism.

In the development of modern African American fiction, the early 1950s marks an important turning point. Ellison's *Invisible Man* thrives on a set of symbols with conscious allusions to American history and ideology. Ellison's vision, like Wright's, is not that of Invisible Man, the subject, but is representative of others. Like Wright's *Black Boy*, *Invisible Man* is deeply concerned with the development of an African American youth into maturity. Evoking the name of Ralph Waldo Emerson suggests Ellison's serious concern with W. E. B. Du Bois's sense of double-consciousness, what Ellison calls his "mixed background as American, as Negro American, and as a Negro from what in its related way was a pioneer background" (*SA*, xix). In search of identity in American society, however, Ellison's vision focuses not only on broader culture and history but also on deeper self-realization, reflecting the modernist principles of self-referentiality and moral relativism.

Invisible Man also reflects the crossroads of Eastern and Western cultures. To envision the latent consciousness of the invisible man, Ellison relies on the techniques of French writers like André Malraux and Paul Valéry. Among the European existential works, Malraux's *Man's Fate* had an influence on Ellison's characterization of the invisible man. In commenting on the psychological makeup of Wright's *Black Boy*, Ellison points out in *Shadow and Act* that "all men possess the tendency to dream and the compulsion to make their dreams reality . . . and that all men are the victims and the beneficiaries of the goading, tormenting, commanding and informing activity of that imperious process known as the Mind—the

Mind, as Valéry describes it, 'armed with its inexhaustible questions.'" Ellison considers *Black Boy* and *Invisible Man* not merely accurate representations of African American life but typical twentieth-century works that poignantly reflect humanity's quest of meaning for its existence.

Invisible Man is also a representation of Eastern ideology and point of view. Ellison expresses Eastern thought through Trueblood and the invisible man himself. Like Wright's haiku "It Is September," Trueblood's observation of human life is not based on thought but upon his spontaneous response to natural spirituality. In Zen-inspired art, nature is the mirror of humanity. Zen practice calls for self-effacement; one should not allow oneself to control action. Lao Tze said, "Man takes his law from the earth; the Earth its law from Heaven; Heaven its law from *Tao*; but the law of Tao in its own spontaneity" (*SJP*, 43). The twin deeds of humanity—naturalness and spontaneity—are, in Zen, the means by which human beings can be connected with the absolute, the achievement of satori.

In midcentury, Richard Wright's fiction served as an example of the East-West crossroads as well. One of the existential works of fiction to which *Invisible Man* bears a striking resemblance is Wright's novella "The Man Who Lived Underground" (1945). In both stories the protagonist's identity is withheld throughout; the invisible man is anonymous just as is Wright's protagonist, whose name is neither mentioned nor referred to. Wright's underground man once spells his name on a typewriter in lower keys as "freddaniels." Alienation from society, a dominant theme in existential writing, is also characteristic of both works; initially the invisible man is convinced, as is Daniels, that being an African American is responsible for his alienation from society. The two men, who try to be good, law-abiding citizens, both suffer from the oppression that stems from what they consider a lawless, amoral, corrupt, and chaotic world with little human value and little hope for renewal. Fred Daniels's underground life has shown that he is liberated from desire, greed, and hatred and, more significantly, that he is free even of thoughts. His state of mind at the end of his life has an affinity with Zen enlightenment; his state of mind is reminiscent of that of Wright, who composed this haiku shortly before his death:

> It is September
> The month in which I was born
> And I have no thoughts.
> (*HTOW*, 127)

It is difficult to conjecture whether Wright had Zen philosophy in mind when he wrote "The Man Who Lived Underground." But in the late 1950s he borrowed R. H. Blyth's four-volume history and study of haiku from Sinclair Beiles, a poet from South Africa living in Paris and associating with other poets of the Beat Generation, such as Jack Kerouac, Allen Ginsberg, William Burroughs, and Gary Snyder. Like these Beat poets, Wright studied not only the techniques and aesthetics of haiku composition but also Eastern philosophies and religions, such as Taoism, Confucianism, Mahayana Buddhism, and Zen, by reading, in particular, the first volume of Blyth's book, subtitled *Eastern Culture.*

Wright's *The Outsider* (1953), on the other hand, is considered an existential novel as well. Portraying the highly educated, mature intellectuals Cross Damon and Invisible Man, both novels express the goal of modern African American novelists whose efforts is to make their characters representative of others and universalize their cultural visions. The worldviews of these characters were influenced by those of an early existentialist like Kierkegaard, and French existential novelists like Sartre and Camus. Critics have noted distinct parallels between Wright and European existentialist novelists in the treatment of the metaphysical rebel, calling Cross Damon's philosophy nihilistic. Wright lived and wrote *The Outsider* in France, where he maintained a close contact with Camus, Sartre, and de Beauvoir. Moreover, these French existentialists can conveniently be placed side by side with Wright's protagonist, who contemplates human existence through his exhaustive reading of Nietzsche, Hegel, Kierkegaard, and Dostoevsky. Despite the differences in ideology and action between the two protagonists, Wright's *The Outsider* and Camus's *The Stranger* (1946) both serve as eloquent social criticisms in the twentieth century. A comparison of the two novels of distinct characters and traditions reveals that both Wright and Camus are writing ultimately about a universal human condition in modern times.

The conclusion of *The Stranger* furthermore serves as another example of the East-West crossroads. After Meursault is sentenced to death, he realizes for the first time that his life has been enveloped in the elusive beauty of the world. Having compassion on his mother for the first time in his life, he says, "With death so near, Mother must have felt like someone on the brink of freedom, ready to start life all over again. No one, no one in the world had any right to weep for her. And I, too, felt ready to start life all over again." This is an expression of karma instead of nirvana. Only at the very end of his life is he conscious of an epiphany: "To feel it so like myself, indeed, so brotherly, made me realize that I'd been happy, and that I was happy still" (154). Despite his death sentence, he remains calm and happy, for he has cleansed his mind of materialistic desire and fear. The prisoner, though alone and trapped by a society without human values, is freed from within. Meursault's state of mind at the end of his life is akin to Zen enlightenment.

One of the most popular East-West artistic, cultural, and literary exchanges that have taken place in modern and postmodern times was reading and writing of haiku in the West. The end of World War II provoked an outpouring of interest in Japanese haiku. In the late 1940s and 1950s, a number of important books in English on haiku were published. Among them, R. H. Blyth's four volumes of Japanese haiku with his translations and analyses, mentioned earlier, inspired many English speakers to write haiku in English. Many of the poets of the Beat Generation, most notably Allen Ginsberg, Jack Kerouac, and Gary Snyder, tried their hand at composing haiku. Among them, Jack Kerouac, who captured a huge audience when his first book, *On the Road*, appeared in 1958, wrote numerous haiku throughout his career and played a central role in the literary movement he named the Beat Generation. His second novel, *The Dharma Bums* (1958), gave an intimate biographical account of himself in search of the truths in life. In San Francisco he met Gary Snyder, and the two dharma bums explored the thoughts and practices of Buddhism. As Snyder left for Japan to study at a Zen monastery, Kerouac's search reached an apogee on a desolate mountaintop in the Sierras. Through his friendship with such Beat poets as Allen Ginsberg and Gary Snyder, as well as through his studies of Buddhism, Zen, and R. H. Blyth's volume *Haiku: Eastern Culture*, in particular, Kerouac firmly established his poetics. His haiku reflect his fascination with Mahayana Buddhism as well as with Zen philosophy. What is remarkable about his haiku is that not only was he influenced by the books he read, but he also was inspired by his own experiences in wandering and meditating in the fields and on the mountains in America.

Richard Wright also distinguished himself as a haiku poet by writing over four thousand haiku in his last eighteen months of his life while in exile in Paris. Back in 1955 Wright attended the Bandung Conference of the Third World; two years later he was a member of the First Congress of Negro Artists and Writers, which met in Paris in September. During the same period, he liked to work in his garden on his Normandy farm, an activity that supplied many themes for his haiku. Like Kerouac's haiku, many of Wright's depict the vivid memories of his experiences in America. Of his experience in exile, Wright's travels to the newly independent Ghana, in West Africa, also had a great impact on his writing of haiku. The African philosophy of life Wright witnessed among the Ashanti, "the African primal outlook upon life" (*BP*, 266), as he called it, served as an inspiration for his poetic sensibility. Ezra Pound's theory that the poet's use of an image is not to support "some system of ethics or economics" ("Vorticism," 464) coincides with a theory that haiku express the poet's intuitive, impersonal worldview. Wright, then, found the haiku poet's intuitive worldview akin to that of the African.

Kerouac's and Wright's haiku, inspired by R. H. Blyth, have in turn inspired some of the contemporary American poets, most notably Robert Hass (1941–), Sonia Sanchez (1935–), James A. Emanuel (1921–2013), and Lenard D. Moore (1958–). Hass, US Poet Laureate 1995–1997, wrote in *The Washington Post*, "Here's a surprise, a book of haiku written in his last years by the fierce and original American novelist Richard Wright. . . . What an outpouring!" There appeared numerous reviews praising Wright's unexpected achievement, such as "*Haiku: This Other World* is an outstanding addition to Wright's literary and humanist achievements and stands as a beacon to this other world,"[8] and "The only full collection of haiku by a major American writer to remotely suggest both the range and depth possible in the genre."[9]

As some of the haiku and tanka (short song) collected in *Like the Singing Coming Off the Drums* (1998) and *Morning Haiku* (2010) reflect, Sonia Sanchez follows the poetic tradition in which human action emulates nature and the poet suppresses human subjectivity. In portraying nature, Sanchez is at times puzzled by its spontaneous imagery. In such poems, she is reluctant to draw a distinction between human beings and animals, animate and inanimate objects. Not only do many of Sanchez's haiku follow Zen doctrine, but they also share the aesthetic principles that underlie classic haiku, such as *yugen*, by which to express the sense of loss. From time to time, her blues haiku figure a brightened sense of *yugen*. As aesthetic principles, *yugen* and the blues share the sentiments derived from private and intensely personal feelings. Unlike *yugen*, the blues in Sanchez's haiku confines its attention solely to the immediate and celebrates the bodily expression. Most importantly, Sanchez tries to link the blues message with sexually charged language so as to liberate black bodies from the distorted images slavery inflicted.

In *Jazz from the Haiku King* (1999), James A. Emanuel tries to conflate haiku with jazz. His intention is to translate the musical expressions of

African American life, its pain and joy, into the traditional form of haiku. While adhering to the five-seven-five syllabic pattern, he has widened its sensory impact beyond its single impression by including narrative and rhyme. On the surface, jazz and haiku have much in common. As jazz performance thrives on an endless improvisation that the composer fashions from traditional materials, such as spirituals and the blues, so does haiku composition thrive on an infinite improvisation with beautiful objects in nature and humanity. Because of improvisation, the composer in both genres must efface identity and subjectivity. In jazz, play changes on ideas as well as on sounds to create unexpected sensations. In haiku, the poet spares no pains to capture unexpected sensations. In both genres, the composer and the composed, subject and object, coalesce as the identity of the composer disappears in the wake of creation. As Zen stresses self-reliance, not egotism, and nature, not materialism, so does jazz. Just as jazz challenges listeners to hear sounds and rhythms they have not heard or recognized before, so does haiku challenge readers to see images of nature and humanity they have not seen or visualized before. For Emanuel, a postmodern and postcolonial poet, haiku and jazz enable readers to open their minds and imagine ways of reaching a higher ground in their present lives.

Postmodernist critics in the West, such as Roland Barthes and Jacques Derrida, have viewed Japanese culture as decentered. Because they define modernist writing as structural, systematic, and rational, they theorize that Japanese culture is essentially postmodern. Barthes argues that Japan is a decentered society in which the Buddhist state of *mu*, nothingness, represents the lack of a privileged signified behind what he calls the "empire of signs." For Barthes, the brevity and closure of each haiku is to divide and classify the world infinitely; haiku achieves this worldview without human subjectivity. "In the West," he observes, "the mirror is an essentially narcissistic object: man conceives a mirror only in order to look at himself in it; but in the Orient, apparently, the mirror is empty."[10]

As most critics have noted, postmodernism is characterized by the decentered text. The postmodern text thrives on oppositions, what Jacques Derrida calls *différance* (*Writing and Difference*). In each signifying text, internal conflicts develop independently of the author, the supposedly central informant. Consequently, the text deconstructs itself because of the oppositional and conflictual nature of language. Because the *différance* is at work in the text, the author, let alone the reader, can scarcely claim absolute authority over a given text; there arises a structural impossibility of imposing a central idea, a summary, or a conclusion to the text. This is the reason that many postmodern texts incorporate segments of mass culture and late capitalism and draw on parodic and ludic forms in order to minimize autonomy, self-referentiality, and centralized vision. Postmodern texts, then, are said to denote a fundamental loss of rational and ontological certainty.

The lack of center and the recognition of gaps and oppositions that characterize the postmodern text suggest that postmodernists are bent on abolishing marginality and extending referentiality in their text. As postmodern texts such as Richard Wright's *The Color Curtain* (1956) and Salman Rushdie's *The Satanic Verses* (1989) reveal, cultural discourse and dialogue have come to include relations not only between East and West, Old and New, but also between the First, Second, and Third Worlds within as well as across national cultures. The conflict between Rushdie's postmodern satirism and the ancient Muslim dogma, as fictionalized in *The Satanic Verses*, and the clash between left and right, race and religion, as portrayed in *The Color Curtain*, exemplify the postmodern East-West crossroads of cultures.

This cross-culturalism, however, finds its origin in a much earlier period. One of the idiosyncrasies of Victorian thought was Western chauvinism. As late as the middle of the twentieth century, as Richard Wright declared in *Black Power: A Record of Reactions in a Land of Pathos* (1954), the West was perceived as an advanced culture while Africans were regarded as primitives. Victorian intellectuals respected Chinese and Indian societies, which represented ancient cultures, but they considered these societies decadent and backward. Rudyard Kipling deemed it the moral duty of the West to help the nonwhite races of the world.

The very margins that were suppressed in modernism, as well as in romanticism, have come to gain power in postmodernist writing. Such margins are converted to signs of power, and these signs are used to reshape the ostensibly fixed material world of history and produce new and more humane identities for human beings. To illustrate the power of postmodern signs, Rushdie writes in *Shame*:

> So-called Islamic 'fundamentalism' does not spring, in Pakistan, from the people. It is imposed on them from above. Autocratic regimes find it useful to espouse the rhetoric of faith, because people respect that language, are reluctant to oppose it. This is how religions shore up dictators; by encircling them with words of power, words which the people are reluctant to see discredited, disenfranchised, mocked. (251)

In *Midnight's Children* (1980), Rushdie intensifies the power of signs by the postmodern concept of history influenced by Buddhism. "Rushdie's narrative world," McKay Jenkins has noted, "is far richer and less pessimistic than the 'literature of exhaustion' that has become the paradigm of West postmodern writing."[11]

The power of language in postmodernism is in singular contrast to the function of language in realism. Realistic language, which functions as a mirror, conveys a common view by suppressing contradictory voices; it reflects the commonly experienced world outside the text. That is, experience is prior to language. In postmodernism, language, though often derived from experience, has its own power and development independent of experience. In Alice Walker's *The Color Purple* (1982), Celie's voice realistically echoes racist experience but simultaneously reflects what Richard Wright calls in *Black Power* "a primal African attitude" (266). Celie laments that cutting a young tree is like cutting her own arm. Walker's text is remindful of Wright's: Wright was fascinated by the African reverence for nonhuman beings, a primal African philosophy that corresponds to the Buddhist ontology. *The Color Purple* and *Black Power* as postmodern texts both poignantly express the cross-cultural vision that humankind is not at the center of the universe.

Another postmodern text conducive to a cross-cultural reading is Wright's *Pagan Spain* (1957). In this text, anomalies appear on the surface of the text: Spain looks like a Christian as well as a pagan society. Wright's discourse conveys such a message on the surface, but on the same surface it contains anomalies, or what Derrida calls "gaps," which, when taken into account, are found to conflict and put into question what is signified. These gaps exist on the virtual margins of the text, but as the reader focuses on the gaps, the text begins to deconstruct itself. The gaps spread and immerse themselves throughout the text. For example, the Black Virgin at Montserrat, an established symbol of Catholicism, becomes a powerful signifier, a text that systematically deconstructs itself before the reader's expectant eyes. Wright's discourse indeed defines the genesis of the Virgin as non-Western. In contrast to the male principle of life, for which Christianity stands, Spanish religiosity underscores the female principle of life the Virgin signifies. Such a reading leads to the basic assumption of feminism that there are crucial differences between men and women, and further, that women, as some feminists have argued, are inherently superior. The latter argument might be supported by Wright's observation in *Pagan Spain* that

Spanish women are the pillar of Spanish culture. A postmodern reading of this text, then, is bent on restoring the matriarchal power in an earlier culture, which merely existed in the margins of the premodern text.

Not only has postmodernism subverted the premodern text by shifting the margins to the center of the text, but the decentric mode of writing has also produced the effect of collapsing and destroying the time-honored oppositions: male and female, fact and fiction, civilized and indigenous, colonial and postcolonial, East and West, America and Europe. For instance, Akira Kurosawa's film *The Seven Samurai* (1954) and John Sturges's *The Magnificent Seven* (1960), based on the same narrative premise, as Shawn St. Jean has noted, depict the commonalty of East and West as well as that of modernism and postmodernism.[12] Theresa Hak Kyung Cha's *Dictee* (1982), Nicole Cooley has argued, "deploys strategies of the avant-garde, specifically, of postmodernism, in order to challenge the limits of conventional narrative for a representation of radical difference."[13] *Dictee*, then, can be read as metafiction just as Rushdie's *Shame* and *Midnight's Children* can; in such novels, the author deploys postmodern textual strategies to invoke the experience of postcoloniality. In contrast to a modernist like James Joyce, Theresa Hak Kyung Cha as a postmodernist regards Western mythology as the construction of an inadequate linguistic system. For Cha, myth, like history, is problematic rather than recoverable as foregrounding discourse.

In the postmodern forms of writing, aesthetics no longer functions as a hegemonic model that occupies an autonomous realm of its own. It has a tendency to integrate itself with the real world of flesh and blood. In this process, the old psychological polarities are diminished and abandoned. The art of postmodern haiku, as Bruce Ross shows in "North American Versions of Haibun and Postmodern American Culture," is characterized by the mode of writing that has entered a new world of knowledge and ethics in an attempt to integrate mind with body, thought with desire, self with world.[14] Contemporary American haiku poet Rich Youmans's "For My Wife on Our First Anniversary" ends with a passage with a postmodern haiku:

> Slowly, the sky brightens; sunlight washes our room, breaks through window prisms into tiny rainbows. I search them out as if on an Easter hunt: one on the frame of the standing mirror; another on my chest of drawers, under the photos of us laughing and hugging. And others—on my nightstand, the cedar chest, the Japanese lantern hanging over our bed. . . .

prisms in
early light:
we make love
(15)

Haiku written in English, and American haiku in particular, have evolved as a form of modernist poetry under the influence of Zen philosophy, but some of the contemporary haiku in English bear a striking resemblance to postmodern poetry.

On the one hand, an Eastern culture such as Japan is perceived to be a culture buttressed by its unique national philosophy and arts. On the other hand, contemporary Japan, in its economic power and materialistic culture, is considered an international leader of postmodern society. This contradictory image of an Eastern society can be seen in the light of East-West cross-culturalism. In the early decades of the twentieth century, Western modernism partly evolved under the influence of Eastern philosophy and aesthetics. But in the later decades, some of the postmodern novelists in the East, in turn, emulated the modernists in the West such as James, Twain, Hemingway, Faulkner, Camus, and Sartre.

In the nineteenth century, American transcendentalists took interest in Eastern religions and philosophies. As Thoreau read Confucius's writings with great enthusiasm through French translation, Emerson was acquainted with Islamic poetry, translated into German. In the early decades of the twentieth century, Eastern philosophy, literature, and art had a great impact on the development of modernism in the West. In the aftermath of World War II, existentialism, which influenced many of the novelists in the West, as well as in the East, was partly derived from Zen philosophy. In midcentury, as a Beat writer such as Jack Kerouac and an African American writer such as Richard Wright were deeply influenced by Whitman, another American transcendentalist, who had earlier been fascinated with Buddhism, they both directly studied that religion in earnest.

I hasten to add that what I have tried to demonstrate in this book represents some preliminary markers for more detailed future studies. My attempts here are heuristic and my observations are not conclusive. There are also several omissions in reading contemporary American writers whose works thrive on their cross-cultural visions, such as Amiri Baraka, Ishmael Reed, Charles Johnson, and haiku poets such as Robert Hass, William J. Higginson, Rich Youmans, and Lenard D. Moore.

PART ONE
TRANSCENDENTALISTS

1

HENRY DAVID THOREAU
AND CONFUCIAN ETHICS

In *A Week on the Concord and Merrimack Rivers* (1849), his first book, Thoreau wrote:

> We can tolerate all philosophies, Atomists, Pneumatologists, Atheists, Theoists,—Plato, Aristotle, Leucippus, Democritus, Pythagoras, Zoroaster and Confucius. It is the attitude of these men more than any communication which they make, that attracts us. Between them and their commentators, it is true, there is an endless dispute. But if it comes to this that you compare notes, then you are all wrong. (152)

The statement reflects Thoreau's interest in and respect for these philosophers. Not only does Thoreau's observation indicate his fascination with all these philosophies, however variant they may be, but Thoreau considered these philosophers eminently superior to their commentators and to him. *A Week on the Concord and Merrimack Rivers* also admonishes the reader against an intolerance of other religions. Growing up a Christian, Thoreau was well versed in the Bible, but he was impatient with such a ritual as keeping the Sabbath.[1] He studied Hebrew and Hindu scriptures with open mind. He was fascinated by Buddhism. "It is necessary not to be Christian," Thoreau argued, "to appreciate the beauty and significance of the life of Christ. I know that some will have hard thoughts of me, when they hear their Christ named beside my Buddha, yet I am sure that I am willing they should love their Christ more than my Buddha" (*AW*, 67).

Among Thoreau's references to ancient philosophies and religions, his quotations from Confucius's sayings signify Thoreau's ethical principles.[2] Throughout his writing career, Thoreau edited selections from "ethical scriptures" outside the Christian tradition, including "Sayings of Confucius" and "Chinese Four Books," both published in *The Dial*. It is legendary that Thoreau spent a night in the Concord jail in 1846 for refusing to pay his poll tax. It is also well known that the essay he wrote on this symbolic act of civil disobedience has become the text of American social and political activism. The essay "Civil Disobedience" inspired Mahatma Gandhi and Martin Luther King Jr. In the conclusion of "Civil Disobedience," Thoreau evoked Confucius: "The progress from an absolute to a limited monarchy, from a limited monarchy to a democracy, is to a progress toward a true respect for the individual. Even the Chinese philosopher was wise enough to regard the individual as the basis of the empire" (*Variorum Civil Disobedience*, 55).

Thoreau's stronger interest in Confucius than in Christ suggests that Thoreau was inspired by the ethics of Confucius rather than by the religious revelations of Christ. He was intrigued by Confucian ethics, a code of moral principles that is based upon the human mind and spirit rather than the religious thought and sentiment. *The Analects*, from which Thoreau read through French translation, consists of Confucius's maxims and parables, which have more to do with human life than to do with the life of a religious figure such as Christ and Buddha.

Confucian ethics may be defined as a code of honor by which the individual must live in society. It consists of four virtues written in Chinese characters: 仁 (humanity), 義 (justice), 忠 (loyalty), and 孝 (filial piety). Basho, the eminent Japanese haiku poet, who read *The Analects*, wrote many haiku that express Confucian virtues. Basho wrote such haiku as:

> Shake, O grave!
> My wailing voice
> Is the autumn wind.

> Should I take it in my hand,
> It would disappear with my hot tears,
> Like the frost of autumn.

> The dew of the Camphor tree
> Falls in tears
> On the pinks.
> (Blyth, *Haiku: Eastern Culture*, 82)

In the first haiku, Basho expresses an affinity between his wailing voice and the autumn wind. The second haiku focuses on his tears for his dead mother; the tears are so hot that his mother's hair would disappear like autumn frost. The third haiku draws an analogy between the virtue of loyalty and the dew of the camphor tree. This haiku, R. H. Blyth notes, "refers to Kusunoki and his son Masatsura, when they parted, in 1336, before the father's defeat and suicide" (82).

These haiku suggest that, for Basho, Confucian virtues are derived from human sentiments as well as from natural phenomena. "This simple Confucianism," Blyth observes, "developed into something deeper and wider, embracing all nature in its scope, without losing its human feeling:

> Nothing intimates
> How soon they must die,—
> Crying cicadas.

> The morning
> After the gale too,
> Peppers are red.

> The first snow
> Just enough to bend
> The leaves of the daffodils."
> (Blyth, *Haiku: Eastern Culture*, 82–83)

The Confucian worldview, reflected in Basho's haiku, is also echoed by Nakae Toju (1608–1648), one of the greatest thinkers in Japanese history. Toju said that "Heaven and Earth and man appear to be different, but they are essentially one. This essence has no size, and the spirit of man and the infinite must be one" (80).

The unity of humanity and nature is also stressed in the *Saikontan*, said to be written by Kojisei, a collection of 359 short passages and poems, which was widely known in the Ming Dynasty in China. One of the passages reads:

Water not disturbed by waves settles down of itself. A mirror not covered with dust is clear and bright. The mind should be like this. When what beclouds it passes away, its brightness appears. Happiness must not be sought for; when what disturbs passes away, happiness comes of itself. (Blyth, *Haiku: Eastern Culture*, 75)

Not only does this epigram demonstrate an affinity that exists between humanity and nature, it suggests that ethics is sanctioned by fact of nature rather than by human subjectivity. Another passage provides an illustration of the way in which the human mind learns from nature:

The song of birds, the voices of insects, are all means of conveying truth to the mind; in flowers and grasses we see messages of the Way. The scholar, pure and clear of mind, serene and open of heart, should find in everything what nourishes him. (76)

This maxim admonishes the reader against human subjectivity; the less subjective the mind is, the more objective it becomes. The mind that is sanctioned by nature thus enables ethics to be established.

In a later passage Kojisei states, "If your heart is without stormy waves, everywhere are blue mountains and green trees. If our real nature is creative like nature itself, wherever we may be, we see that all things are free like sporting fishes and circling kites" (Blyth, *Haiku: Eastern Culture*, 79). The human mind, as Kojisei observes, is often influenced by excessive emotion, like anger. Once the mind is overwhelmed by such emotion and loses its control, it becomes alienated from ethics. Kojisei's observation suggests that if human nature becomes destructive, instead of creative like nature, it ceases its function.

Creation of ethics is possible, as Kojisei demonstrates, only if the mind is capable of seeing the truth in nature—the universal truth. "The just man," Kojisei sees, "has no mind to seek happiness; Heaven, therefore, because of this mindlessness, opens its inmost heart." On the other hand, he sees, "the man busies himself with avoiding misfortunes; Heaven therefore confounds him for this desire." Contrasting nature with humanity, he says, "How unsearchable are the ways of Heaven! How useless the wisdom of men!" (Blyth, *Haiku: Eastern Culture*, 75). What Kojisei calls "the ways of Heaven" are "unsearchable" and infinite; therefore, they constitute the universal truth, the absolute values. Chapter 16 of *The Doctrine of the Mean*, a medieval Chinese text, quotes Confucius: "Confucius said, 'The power of spirits, how abundant! We look, but do not see them; we listen, but do not hear them; yet they sustain all things, and nothing is neglected by them'" (73).

In Confucius, the universe consists of 天 (heaven), 地 (earth), and 人 (human). Some of the passages in *The Analects* express Confucius's thoughts and observations on the relationships among heaven, human, and God:

> How can a man conceal his nature? How can a man conceal his nature (*Analects*, 2. 10).
>
> He who offends against Heaven has none to whom he can pray (*Analects*, 3. 12).
>
> He sacrificed to the spirits [God] as if the spirits were present (*Analects*, 3. 12).
>
> A virtuous man finds rest in his virtue (*Analects*, 4. 2).
> (Blyth, *Haiku: Eastern Culture*, 73)

For Confucius, God is not a living being like a human being; God is a concept that originates from a human being. The individual living in society thus formulates this concept by apprehending the ways of nature in Heaven and Earth. God, then, reflects the conscience, a code of ethics established by the individual. Confucius sees that one who is endowed with ethics, "a virtuous man," is able to achieve one's peace of mind. If a man is without virtues, on the other hand, neither can he conceal his nature nor can he rest peacefully in his life.

As Blyth has noted, "Confucianism is a much more poetical thing than most people suppose. In fact, as of Christianity and all other religions, one may say that what in it is poetical is true, using the word true in the sense of something that feeds the life of man, which can be absorbed into our own life and yet have a life of its own, which is organic and growing" (*Haiku: Eastern Culture*, 71). In *Analects* 8. 8, Confucius urges the reader to:

> Arise with poetry;
> Stand with propriety;
> Grow with music.

"The mind," Blyth remarks, "is roused by poetry, made steadfast by propriety, and perfected by music" (72). *Analects* 9. 16 reads, "Standing by a stream, Confucius said, 'It ceases not day or night, flowing on and on like this'" (72). Not only is Confucius's description of the scene poetic and beautiful to look at, it conveys the universal truth.[3]

Confucian thought is said to have inspired Japanese poets, such as Basho. At the beginning of *The Analects*, Confucius says, "Is it not delightful to have a friend come from afar?" This saying, Blyth notes, inspired Basho to compose this haiku:

> A paulownia leaf has fallen;
> Will you not come to me
>   In my loneliness?
> (*Haiku: Eastern Culture*, 71)

The haiku was addressed to his fellow haiku poet Ransetsu. Basho's wish to share his poetic vision with others suggests that one can model one's life after a code of ethics best defined in poetic words. That Confucius's advice "Stand with propriety" is mediated between "Arise with poetry" and "Grow with music" defines the meaning of the word "propriety." This word in Confucius means, as Blyth explains, "a harmonious mode of living . . . a poetical way of doing everything . . . a deep, inward rightness of relation between ourselves and all outward circumstances" (72). In Confucius, an individual must establish himself or herself by adhering to universal ethics. Once this ethics becomes the foundation of the individual, no other ideas and facts are to undermine that foundation.

Confucius's admonition for the individual to establish the moral principle for society to follow influenced Thoreau's argument in "Civil Disobedience." Thoreau came to agree with Confucius, who regarded "the individual as the basis of the empire," as noted earlier (*Variorum Civil Disobedience*, 55). Thoreau's definition of the conscience of the individual has an affinity with a parable Thoreau quoted from *The Analects* in *A Week on the Concord and Merrimack Rivers*. Thoreau wrote, "They say that Lieou-hia-hoei and Chao-lien did not sustain to the end their resolutions, and that they dishonored their character. Their language was in harmony with reason and justice; while their acts were in harmony with the sentiments of men" (*AW*, 132–33). For Confucius and Thoreau, while Lieou-hia-hoei and Chao-lien were familiar with the ethical principles, their conduct followed the unethical sentiments of society and therefore their character was dishonorable.

In "Civil Disobedience" Thoreau characterizes the individual, unlike Lieou-hia-hoei and Chao-lien, as a person who is endowed with ethical principles and is capable of putting them into practice. Considering such an individual a superior man, Thoreau quotes, in *Walden*, Confucius as saying, "The virtues of a superior man are like the wind; the virtues of a common man are like the grass; the grass, when the wind passes over it, bends" (172). Thoreau took pride in being such an individual and urged the government to heed his conscience. The American government, Thoreau argued "has not the vitality and force of a single living man; for a single man can bend it to his will." Although he recognized that the American people were endowed with a conscience, the government "sometimes got in its way" to prevent them from fully realizing their conscience. It is the moral responsibility of an individual like Thoreau to exercise the collective conscience of the American people (*Variorum Civil Disobedience*, 31–32).

But his fellow citizens marched "in admirable order over hill and dale to the wars, against their wills, ay, against their common sense and consciences" (*Variorum Civil Disobedience*, 33). With respect to his fellow neighbors, "a distinct race from me," he took pains to remind them of "their prejudices and superstitions" (*Variorum Civil Disobedience*, 49). His conscience urged him to shake the American people up from their moral amnesia. He wrote in *Walden*, "I do not propose to write an ode to dejection, but to brag as lustily as chanticleer in the morning, standing on his roost, if only to wake my neighbors up" (84).

Thoreau's motive for reminding his neighbors of their consciences is derived from the French translation of the book, *Confucies et Mencius*, which Thoreau read. The aim of Confucian thought and ethics, M. G. Pauthier writes in his introduction, is:

> l'amélioration constante de soi-même et des autres hommes; de soi-même d'abord, ensuite des autres. L'amélioration ou le perfectionnement de soi-même est d'une nécessité absolue pour arriver à l'amélioration et au perfectionnement des autres.[4]

Shoji Goto has translated the passage: "The constant amelioration of oneself; of oneself to begin with, and then the others. The amelioration or the perfection of oneself is absolutely necessary in order to arrive at the amelioration or the perfection of the others."[5] For Thoreau, the passage means that a single living man like him must first establish his own moral principles and then help others acquire them. "Virtue," Thoreau observes in *Walden*, "does not remain as an abandoned orphan; it must of necessity have neighbors" (134). What is most important in the life of an individual, according to Confucius, is for one to establish oneself before helping others do the same. In *Walden* Thoreau quotes Confucius as saying, "Renew thyself completely each day; do it again, and again, and forever again" (88).

"Civil Disobedience" also teaches the imperative of individual conscience. Conscience must originate in the mind of an individual. "We are accustomed to say," Thoreau admits, "that the mass of men are unprepared; but improvement is slow, because the few are not materially wiser or better than the many. It is not so important that many should be as good as you, as that there be some absolute goodness somewhere; for that will leaven the whole lump." For Thoreau, "some absolute goodness" constitutes justice, on which individual conscience rests. This individual conscience, signified by a biblical metaphor "a little leaven," will enlighten "the whole lump," "the mass of men" (*Variorum Civil Disobedience*, 36). In the conclusion of *Walden*, Thoreau illustrates how powerful and influential the conscience of the individual is by quoting a parable from *The Analects*: "From an army of three divisions one can take away its general and put it in disorder; from the man the most abject and vulgar one cannot take away his thought" (328).

The primacy of individual conscience thus underlies Thoreau's argument in "Civil Disobedience" that the individual has the right to dissociate with the government if it is not based on justice. This principle is also derived from *The Analects*, chapter 8, book 13. Thoreau quoted Confucius as saying, "If a state is governed by the principles of reason, poverty and misery are subjects of shame; if a state is not governed by the principles of reason, riches and honors are the subjects of shame" (*Variorum Civil Disobedience*, 44). Thoreau also observed that the government was not based on the principles of reason while the governed, represented by an individual like Thoreau, were endowed with their consciences. "Civil Disobedience" begins with the motto "That government is best which governs least." "Carried out," Thoreau asserts, "it finally amount to this, which also I believe,—The government is best which governs not at all" (31). If the government does not govern at all, the individual must govern his or her own life. In *Walden* Thoreau declares, "Every man is the lord of a realm" (321).

Whereas Thoreau has trust and confidence in the individual with conscience, he is critical of those who lack their conscience. He complains that his neighbors fail to see reality because their minds are corrupted by their emotion and desire. Thoreau urges them to see things before them, not things "in the outskirts of the system, behind the farthest star. . . . God himself culminates in the present moment" (*Walden*, 96–97). To Thoreau, they refuse to "penetrate the surface of things" and to see things with "a true gaze . . . stand right fronting and face to face to a fact" (96–98). Thoreau urges the reader not to lose sight of the moral principles, "a true law and relations" (96).

In Confucius's "Commonplace Book," which Thoreau translated, he read a dialogue between Confucius and his disciples. Confucius observed that the approach of Yeou to life is for an individual to have courage. Confucius then asked Tian, another disciple, to express his approach to life. Tien replied:

> Spring time being no more, my robe of spring laid aside, but covered with the bonnet of manhood, accompanied by five or six men, and six or seven young people, I should love to go and bathe in the waters of the-Y-, to go and take the fresh air in those woody places where they offer sacrifices to heaven to obtain rain, to modulate some airs, and then return to my abode.[6]

Hearing these words, Confucius was impressed with Tian's thoughts on life. He said, "I am of [the opinion of] Tian['s mind]." He further said, "One ought to administer a kingdom according to the established law and customs; the words of Yeou were not modest; this is the reason I smiled."[7]

Thoreau interpreted what Confucius called "the established law and customs" to mean "the essential facts of life" or "all the marrow of life" (*Walden*, 90, 91). "The established law and customs," Shoji Goto remarks, means "the silence rooted in virtue and God's voice" and what "Confucius called 'A sovereign principle'" in Thoreau's "Sayings of Confucius," which Thoreau read (141).[8] Thoreau's interpretation of the Confucian principles finds a similar expression in *A Week on the Concord and Merrimack Rivers*:

> The man enjoyeth not freedom from action from the non-commencement of that which he hath to do; nor doth he obtain happiness from a total inactivity. No one ever resteth a moment inactive. Every man is involuntarily urged to act by those principles which are inherent in his nature. The man who restraineth his active faculties, and sitteth down with his mind attentive to the objects of his senses, is called one of an astrayed soul, and the practiser of deceit. So the man is praised, who, having subdued all his passions, performeth with his active faculties all the functions of life, unconcerned about the event. (139)

What such a passage suggests is that, for Confucius and Thoreau, a human being must conduct his or her life according to nature's law, but that the individual is free to choose how to live under that law.

Thoreau and Confucius agree that human nature is characteristic of self-discipline and self-control and that the ultimate goal of human life is the liberation of the mind. They share the thought that on the strength of the human mind there exists a fundamental difference between the life of human beings and that of other living beings. This difference, in particular, makes Thoreau, like Emerson, a transcendentalist. Thoreau believed that human nature is universal and that it is consonant with nature regardless of a particular religion one believes in. In *Walden* Thoreau describes a storm vehemently hitting his hut: he says it sounds like "Aeolian music to a healthy and innocent ear" (131). Shoji Goto points out that "only the transcendental ear enables the storm to be transformed into Aeolian music." A storm Thoreau is describing, Goto notes, "is not a simple, ordinary storm, because it is only when the sense extends, and the being expands that the nonexistent sound comes to hit the inward ear and the inward sight." This transformation of the sound, Goto sees, takes place by intuition; it is called "pure apperception," or "primitive apperception" in transcendentalism, and it is distinguished from the empirical in Kantian philosophy.[9]

For Thoreau, intuition is a sensibility generated by the uniquely human faculty. Defining the human mind and spirit, Thoreau wrote in *A Week on the Concord and Merrimack Rivers*:

> I see, smell, taste, hear, feel, that everlasting Something to which we are allied, at once our maker, our abode, our destiny, our very Selves; the one historic truth, the most remarkable fact which can become the distinct and uninvited subject of our thought, the actual glory of the universe; the only fact which a human being cannot avoid recognizing, or in some way forget or dispense with. . . . What are ears? What is Time? that this particular series of sounds called a strain of music. . . . It is the flower of language, thought colored and curved, fluent and flexible, it crystal fountain tinged with the sun's rays, and its purling ripples reflecting the grass and the clouds. . . . It teaches us again and again to trust the remotest as the divinest instinct, and makes a dream our only real experience. (173–75)

As Thoreau's episode of the cock-crowing song suggests, the cock's sound constitutes human's voice as well as God's and reflects the human soul as well as God's soul. That intuition is human and divine leads Thoreau to argue in his journal, "It is in vain to write on the seasons unless you have the seasons in you" (*Journal*, 10:253).

Thoreau today is best known as the author of *Walden* and "Civil Disobedience," in both of which he offered ethical examples. Many of his illustrations were influenced by reading, among other ancient philosophers,

Confucius. What is so compelling about Thoreau's writings on ethical principles is that Thoreau himself put these principles into practice. To understand the individual in nature instead of society, he deliberately lived in the woods for two years. In so doing, he discovered that society was fundamentally corrupt. To protest against slavery and unjust wars, he refused to pay his poll tax and spent a night in the Concord jail.

A foremost ethical principle Thoreau learned from Confucius is that justice originates from the individual. In the outset of "Civil Disobedience" Thoreau states:

> Can there not be a government in which majorities do not virtually decide right or wrong, but conscience?—in which majorities decide only those questions to which the rule of expediency is applicable? Must the citizen ever for a moment, or in the least degree, resign his conscience to the legislator? Why has every man a conscience, then? I think that we should be men first, and subjects afterward. It is not desirable to cultivate a respect for the law, so much as for the right. The only obligation which I have a right to assume is to do at any time what I think right. (*Variorum Civil Disobedience*, 32–33)

At the very end of the essay, as noted earlier, Thoreau remarks, "Even the Chinese philosopher was wise enough to regard the individual as the basis of the empire" (55). Thoreau concludes his protest by declaring, "There will never be a really free enlightened State until the State comes to recognize the individual as a higher and independent power, from which all its own power and authority are derived, and treats him accordingly" (55). Not only does Thoreau consider the individual conscience a higher power, he calls it an innate human virtue. "Heaven," he quoted a passage from "Chinese Four Books": "'The She King says, 'Heaven created all men having their duties and the means or rules of performing them. It is the natural and constant disposition of men to love beautiful virtue'" (*Early Essays and Miscellanies*, 152).

One of the cardinal virtues Thoreau sees the individual possess is his or her inborn ability to listen to nature's sounds, a range of sounds from celestial music to silence. *Walden* records, for example, the distant lowing of a cow in the horizon over the hill in the evening that sounded sweet and melodious; to Thoreau it was "one articulation of Nature" (123). The whippoorwills sang their songs for half an hour in the evening on a stub by the door or on the edge of the roof. These birds "would begin to sing almost with as much precision as a clock, within five minutes of a particular time, referred to the setting of the sun, every evening" (123–24). When the cattle train went by the woods, Thoreau was annoyed and said, "I will not have my eyes put out and my ears spoiled by its smoke and steam and hissing" (122). He would call this sound one articulation of society. For him a sound of nature restores an individual to the self and, in turn, restores the self to God.

In living in the midst of nature away from society, Thoreau found silence to be the virtue that reflects God's voice. In his earlier essays he wrote on the meaning of various sounds and distinguished silence, the absence of sound, from the rest of the sounds:

> There is as much music in the world as virtue. In a world of peace and love music would be the universal language, and men greet each other in the fields in such accents, as a Beethoven now utters at rare intervals from a distance. All things obey music as they obey virtue. It is a herald of virtue. It is God's voice. . . . When we listen to it we are so wise that we need not to know. All sounds, and more than all, silence, so file and drum for us. (*Reform Papers*, 10)

Not only did silence enable Thoreau to hear God's voice, it created a space where and when he felt lonely but friendly. "To be alone," he wrote in *Walden*, "was something unpleasant. But I was at the same time conscious of a slight insanity in my mood, and seemed to foresee my recovery" (131). Solitude to him was a necessary virtue for the individual to live in society. When he was alone in the woods, he wrote:

> I was suddenly sensible of such sweet and beneficent society in Nature . . . an infinite and unaccountable friendliness all at once like an atmosphere sustaining me, as made their fancied advantages of human neighborhood insignificant. . . . Every little pine needle expanded and swelled with sympathy and befriended me.[10] I was so distinctly made aware of the presence of something kindred to me, even in scenes which we are accustomed to call wild and dreary, and also that the nearest of blood to me and humanest was not a person nor a villager, that I thought no place could ever be strange to me again. (*Walden*, 132)

To Thoreau, silence and solitude are not only signifiers of God and nature but also harbingers of death and eternity, the ultimate truth. Silence in solitude, like the cock-crowing sound Thoreau depicts in *Walden*, "is an expression of the health and soundness of Nature, a brag for all the world—healthiness as of a spring burst forth, a new fountain of the Muses, to celebrate this last instant of time" (*Portable Thoreau*, 628). Thoreau indeed envisions nature's connection to eternity. Not only does nature exist in opposition to society, but it is also akin to the universe, what Confucius called "Heaven." Wilderness, which Thoreau witnessed in his life in the woods, is a signifier of Heaven; it signifies eternity, infinity, timelessness— the ultimate truth of the universe.[11] The wilderness of nature reminds him of the highest state of the mind. "My most essential progress," he realized, "must be to me a state of absolute rest. So in geology we are nearest to discovering the true causes of the revolutions of the globe, when we allow them to consist with a quiescent state of the elements. We discover the causes of all past change in the present in variable order of the universe" (*Journal*, 1:191).

Thoreau's concept that silence, the sound of the universe, leads to wisdom and virtue has an affinity to Confucian ethics. In "Sayings of Confucius," he quotes Confucius as stating:

Silence is absolutely necessary to the wise man. Great speeches, elaborate discourses, pieces of eloquence, ought to be a language unknown to him; his actions ought to be his language. As for me, I would never speak more. Heaven speaks; but what language does it use to preach to men? That there is a sovereign principle from which all things depend; a sovereign principle which makes them to act and move. Its motion is its language; it reduces the seasons to their time; it agitates nature; it makes it produce. This silence is eloquent. (*Early Essays and Miscellanies*, 141–42)

In the *Saikontan*, which conveys Confucian thoughts, Kojisei quotes Confucius as saying, "The shadow of the bamboo sweeps over the stairs, but the dust does not move. The disc of the moon passes through water of the lake, leaving no trace." Kojisei thus quotes one of the Confucians as explaining, "The stream rushes down swiftly but all is silent around. The flowers fall incessantly, but we feel quiet." "If you have grasped the meaning of this in all your relations with things," Kojisei writes, "you are free in mind and body" (Blyth, *Haiku: Eastern Culture*, 78–79).

"The wise man," Thoreau quoted Confucius as saying, "never hastens, neither in his studies nor his words; he is sometimes, as it were, mute" (*Early Essays and Miscellanies*, 141). Like Emerson, who wrote in his essay "Nature," "To go into solitude, a man needs to retire as much from his chamber as from society. I am not solitary whilst I read and write, though nobody is with me. But if a man would be alone, let him look at the stars" (*Selections from Emerson*, 23). Thoreau wrote in his journal, "To be alone I find it necessary to escape the present—I avoid myself. How could I be alone in the Roman emperor's chamber of mirrors? I seek a garret. The spiders must not be disturbed, nor the floor swept, nor the lumber arranged" (*Journal*, 1:5). In a similar vein, Basho, who wrote haiku under the influence of the Confucian worldview, gave advice for his disciples: "You must not take a needle or blade of grass that belongs to another. Mountains, streams, rivers, marshes,—all have an Owner; be careful about this" (Blyth, *Haiku: Eastern Culture*, 85).

It is only the silence of solitude that makes the individual mind conscious of the real world. Thoreau lived most of his life in Concord, Massachusetts, a small village near Walden Pond. But he never felt isolated from the world of learning. He argued:

> It is time that villages were universities, and their elder inhabitants the fellows of universities, with leisure—if they are indeed so well off—to pursue liberal studies the rest of their lives. Shall the world be confined to one Paris or one Oxford forever? Cannot students be boarded here and get a liberal education under the skies of Concord? Can we not hire some Abelard to lecture to us? . . . This town has spent seventeen thousand dollars on a town-house, thank fortune or politics, but probably it will not spend so much on living wit, the true meat to put into that shell, in a hundred years. . . . Why should our life be in any respect provincial? (*Walden*, 109).

The reason for his disparaging remarks about well-respected universities like Sorbonne and Oxford is that professors of philosophy who lectured at such universities, to Thoreau, lacked wisdom and were not really philosophers. "To be a philosopher," he argued, "is not merely to have subtle thoughts, nor even to found a school, but so to love wisdom as to live according to its dictates, a life of simplicity, independence, magnanimity, and trust. It is to solve some of the problems of life, not only theoretically, but practically" (*Walden*, 14–15).

Thoreau's Walden Pond venture had a twofold goal. Thoreau wanted to acquire the wisdom to solve the mystery of life and wanted to put the wisdom into practice. He wrote:

I went to the woods because I wished to live deliberately, to front only the essential facts of life, and see if I could not learn what it had to teach, and not, when I came to die, discover that I had not lived. I did not wish to live what was not life, living is so dear. . . . I wanted to live deep and suck out all the marrow of life . . . as to put to rout all that was not life, to cut a broad swath and shave close, to drive life into a corner, and reduce it to its lowest terms. (*Walden*, 90–91)

On a previous page he wrote what he used to do on a good morning with a quotation from a commentary on the *Great Learning of Confucius*: "I got up early and bathed in the pond; that was a religious exercise, and one of the best things which I did. They say that characters were engraven on the bathing tub of King Tching-thang to this effect: 'Renew thyself completely each day; do it again, and again, and forever again'" (*Walden*, 88). For Confucius and Thoreau, to live on earth is to renew yourself until death. One of the Confucian admonitions in the *Rules of Pilgrimage* (1760), ascribed to Basho, reads, "Apart from poetry, do not gossip about all things and sundry. When there is such talk, take a nap and recreate yourself" (Blyth, 85).

For Thoreau to put into practice "a life of simplicity, independence, magnanimity, and trust" (*Walden*, 15), has a strong affinity with Confucian ethics. Nakane Tori, a seventeenth-century Japanese Buddhist monk, who converted to Confucianism, wrote, "The universe and humanity are one, and my parents, brothers, and all men are my self. Sun, moon, rain, dew, mountains, rivers, birds, animals and fish are also my self. Therefore I should love and sympathize with others, because they are my self, and not separate from me" (Blyth, *Haiku: Eastern Culture*, 81). Just as Thoreau lived on the twin virtues of magnanimity and trust, Tori saw others with sympathy and trust. Thoreau, too, saw others with sympathy, but he regarded others as friends only if they had virtue.

Thoreau's definition of friendship is derived from Confucius. In *A Week on the Concord and Merrimack Rivers*, Thoreau quotes Confucius as saying, "Never contract Friendship with a man that is not better than thyself" (271). Thoreau characterizes a friend as an individual who possesses at least as good qualities as you do. He quotes Confucius again as saying, "To contract ties of Friendship with any one, is to contract Friendship with his virtue. There ought not to be any other motive in Friendship." "But," Thoreau laments, "men wish us to contract Friendship with their vice also" (*AW*, 281–82). Thoreau's concept of friendship is also remindful of the

Confucian virtue of filial piety. To Confucius, filial piety means not only a child's respect for his parents but also one's respect for age—elders and teachers—as well.[12] Basho gave advice for his disciples: "Be grateful to a man who teaches you even a single word. Do not try to teach unless you understand fully. Teaching is to be done after you have perfected yourself" (Blyth, *Haiku: Eastern Culture*, 85).

Thoreau's treatment of another individual in terms of virtue was put into practice in his own life. While living in the woods, Thoreau was a good fisherman and hunter, but in later years he came to detest such sports. Not only did preparing his meals with fish and birds fill the house with "all ill odors and sights," he felt guilty of killing his fellow living beings. He refrained from using animal food, tea, coffee, etc., "not so much because of any ill effects which I had traced to them, as because they were not agreeable to my imagination" (*Walden*, 214). His imagination, indeed, reflects the Confucian worldview. Confucius believed in the unity of the universe and humanity, a world made of all the animate and the inanimate, as Confucian Nakane Tori said, "Sun, moon, rain, dew, mountains, rivers, birds, animals and fish are also my self" (Blyth, *Haiku: Eastern Culture*, 81). Reflecting on his own concept of virtue, Thoreau also stated, "Whatever my own practice may be, I have no doubt that it is a part of the destiny of the human race, in its gradual improvement, to leave off eating animals, as surely as the savage tribes have left off eating each other when they came in contact with the more civilized" (*Walden*, 216). In the *Rules of Pilgrimage*, Basho also admonishes his disciples against eating animal food: "The desire for the flesh of fish, fowl, and beast is not good. Indulging in tasty and rare dishes leads to baser pleasures. Remember the saying 'Eat simple food, and you can do anything'" (Blyth, *Haiku: Eastern Culture*, 84).

Walden also teaches the virtue of drinking pure water. Drinking tea, coffee, wine, or smoking tobacco, opium, etc., would harm not only one's physical health but also one's mental health. Thoreau remarks:

> I am glad to have drunk water so long, for the same reason that I prefer the natural sky to an opium-eater's heaven. I would fain keep sober always; and there are infinite degrees of drunkenness. I believe that water is the only drink for a wise man; wine is not so noble a liquor; and think of dashing the hopes of a morning with a cup of warm coffee, or of an evening with a dish of tea! Ah, how low I fall when I am tempted by them! Even music may be intoxicating. Such apparently slight causes destroyed Greece and Rome, and

will destroy England and America. Of all ebriosity, who does not prefer to be intoxicated by the air he breathes? (*Walden*, 217)

In the *Rules of Pilgrimage*, Basho, Confucianist as well as Zen Buddhist, warned his disciples against drinking alcohol: "Do not be fond of wine. If it is difficult to refuse at banquets, stop after you have had a little. 'Restrain yourself from all rowdiness.' Because drunkenness at the *matsuri* [festival] is disliked, the Chinese use unrefined saké. There is an admonition to keep away from saké; be careful!" (Blyth, *Haiku: Eastern Culture*, 84).

With respect to sexuality, Thoreau finds virtue in regarding one's body as a gift of God, a part of nature. Abusing one's body would lead to vice. "Every man," he argues, "is the builder of a temple, called his body, to the god he worships, after a style purely his own, nor can he get off by hammering marble instead. We are all sculptors and painters, and our material is our own flesh and blood and bones. Any nobleness begins at once to refine a man's features, any meanness or sensuality to imbrute them" (*Walden*, 221). Thoreau believed, as did Benjamin Franklin, that the nobility of human sexuality lies in procreation.[13] Unless sex is for producing offspring, it would lead to vice. Thoreau's thoughts on sexuality suggest a dialectical solution to this human dilemma: "If you would be chaste, you must be temperate" (*Walden*, 220). For Thoreau, to be temperate is to mediate between celibacy, a virtue, and sexuality, an innate human nature. Basho gave advice on the teaching of haiku: "Do not become intimate with women *haiku* poets; this is good for neither teacher nor pupil. If she is in earnest about *haiku*, teach her through another" (Blyth, *Haiku: Eastern Culture*, 85). Like Thoreau and Franklin, Basho believed that sexuality is "the duty of men and women" and that it is for "the production of heirs." As Thoreau regarded indulgence in sensuality as vice, Basho considered "dissipation" what "prevents the richness and unity of the mind" (Blyth, *Haiku: Eastern Culture*, 85).

In sum, Thoreau's writings, based on his own life, offer lucid, eloquent illustrations of "a life of simplicity, magnanimity, and trust" (*Walden*, 15). Not only are his essays a splendid rendition of Emersonian transcendentalism, but they also thrive on Thoreau's unique moral vision, which has inspired contemporary thinkers of environment, society, and politics the world over. Although he had faith in Christian doctrine, he was eager to read scriptures of various religions as well as ancient books of philosophy. And his writings strongly reflect, among other influences, the principles of Confucian ethics.

2

THE POETICS OF SUBJECTIVITY:
EMERSON, ZEN, AND LACAN

In their works, both Ralph Waldo Emerson and Jacques Lacan, two of the most influential Western thinkers in the nineteenth and twentieth centuries, respectively, encountered what might loosely be called Buddhist ontologies. Intrigued by the mysticism of the East, Emerson adapted to his own poetics many allusions to Eastern religions. From time to time, however, one is surprised to find in his essays an aversion to Buddhism. This "remorseless Buddhism," he wrote in *Journals*, "lies all around, threatening with death and night. . . . Every thought, every enterprise, every sentiment, has its ruin in this horrid 'Infinite' which circles us and awaits our dropping into it" (318). Such a disparaging remark may betray the young Emerson's unfamiliarity with the religion, as Frederic Ives Carpenter suggested,[1] but the passage may also betray Emerson's aversion to the Buddhist conception of nirvana. For Emerson, the association of nirvana with an undisciplined state of oblivion to the self and the world is uncongenial to his theory of subjectivity.

When he stated elsewhere, "The Buddhist . . . is a Transcendentalist" (*CEOE*, 91–92), he meant that Buddhism, unlike a religion, is a philosophy that emphasizes the primacy of the spiritual and transcendental over the material and empirical. Zen Buddhists, unlike the believers of other sects in Buddhism, are urged to achieve Buddhahood within them, an advice that sounds much like the one given by Emerson, who urges his readers to think not for the sake of accomplishing things but for the sake of realizing their own world. In analyzing the mystery of God, Emerson stresses human's independence from God's power and influence: an individual must attain enlightenment by self even at the risk of losing the sight of God. This is somewhat akin to Zen doctrine. Unlike the other sects of Buddhism, Zen is not a religion that teaches the follower to have faith in a monolithic deity.

Like American transcendentalism, represented by Emerson, Thoreau, and Whitman, Zen teaches a way of life completely different from what one has been conditioned to lead. The instructional tenet inherent in Zen is manifested in a form of a colloquy used by a Zen master and disciples.

In Zen, every individual possesses Buddhahood, and all one must do is to realize it. One must purge one's mind and heart of any materialistic thought or emotion and appreciate the wonder of life here and now. Zen is a way of self-discipline and self-reliance. Its emphasis on self is derived from the prophetic admonishment Gautama Buddha is said to have given to his disciples: "Seek within, you are the Buddha." Self-enlightenment in Zen is indeed analogous to self-reliance in Emersonian transcendentalism, in which one is taught to discipline oneself and look within because divinity resides not only in nature but also in human.

But there are certain differences between Zen and Emersonian transcendentalism. Satori in Zen is an enlightenment that transcends time and place, the twin human constructions, and even the consciousness of self. It is a state of *mu*, nothingness. The state of nothingness is absolutely free from human thoughts and feelings, so that such a consciousness corresponds to that of nature. *Mu*, however, is not synonymous with a state of void, but functional. And its function is perceived by the senses. If, for example, the enlightened person sees a tree, that person is able to see it from a perspective to which the person has not been accustomed. The tree is no longer an ordinary tree; it now exists with different meaning. Only when the viewer is enlightened does the tree contain satori. Buddha exists in nature only if one achieves the Buddha in oneself. For Emerson, on the contrary, God exists in nature regardless of whether human is capable of such intuition.

What Emerson and Zen share is this revelatory and emulating relationship nature holds for human. The basis of such a comparison is the enlightenment one achieves in relating one's spirit to that of nature. Yet a striking difference between the two philosophies concerns the definition of human enlightenment. Zen calls the enlightenment "satori," while Emerson defines it as one's consciousness of the over-soul. In his essay "The Over-Soul," Emerson describes this state of mind as a boundless sphere in which "there is no screen or ceiling between our heads and the infinite heavens." No sooner does the consciousness of self disappear than the over-soul appears on the scene, as Emerson writes, "man, the effect, ceases, and God, the cause, begins." For Emerson, the over-soul is so pervasive "a light" that it "shines through us upon things and makes us aware that we are nothing, but the light is all" (*CEOE*, 263–64). In his essay "Nature," this light is so powerful that one becomes "a transparent eyeball" that cannot see beyond one's state of mind.

In Zen, on the other hand, one is taught to annihilate this eyeball before satori is attained. It seems as though Emerson would empower God to conquer the faithful while allowing them to cling to their subjectivity. For Emerson, because God resides in each and all, human subjectivity has a divine sanction. Zen, on the contrary, does not rely on such a sanction. In contrast to the other sects of Buddhism, Zen is not a monolithic religion. Its ontology calls for the follower to annihilate self to reach the state of *mu*. For Emerson, one destroys neither God nor subjectivity; one believes not only in God but in oneself. Emerson's self-reliance, then, is opposed to Zen's concept of *mu*. Unlike Zen, Emerson believes that his vision of life not only emanates from God but also derives from human reasoning.

Lacan, as a postmodern psychoanalyst, came to challenge this traditional concept of human subjectivity. Based on his own experience, Lacan defined human subjectivity merely as a concept that concerns neither the autonomy of the self nor the ability to influence the other. Subjectivity, as he demonstrated, is deficient because of the deficiencies inherent in language:

> The effects of language are always mixed with the fact, which is the basis of the analytic experience, that the subject is subject only from being subjected to the field of the Other, the subject proceeds from his synchronic subjection in the field of the Other. That is why he must get out, get himself out, and in the *getting-himself-out*, in the end, he will know that the real Other has, just as much as himself, to get himself out, to pull himself free. (*Four Fundamental Concepts*, 188)

Because the subject, an infinitesimal fraction in time and space, is isolated from the world, the subject is only capable of imagining the other: society, nature, and life. Only when the subject is conscious of the deficiencies of language, as Lacan theorizes, does the subject of the unconscious emerge. Only then is the subject able to approach and encounter the truth of life, what Lacan calls "the real" and "the unsymbolizable."

In his first published seminar, Lacan, fascinated by Zen ontology, emulated the practice of a Zen master:

> The master breaks the silence with anything—with a sarcastic remark, with a kick-start. That is how a Buddhist master conducts his search for meaning,

according to the techniques of Zen. It behooves the students to find out for themselves the answer to their own questions.[2]

Lacan's aim in his work was to become the ultimate master of psychoanalysis, as many critics have suggested,[3] but he was absolutely critical of any kind of human mastery. Although there is no written evidence for Lacan's commentary on Emerson, one might assume that Lacan's theory of subjectivity is diametrically opposed to Emerson's.

Lacan's interest in Zen, as evident throughout his writing, suggests that Lacan is as highly critical of human egotism as is a Zen master. Along with Lacan, Roland Barthes, who traveled to Japan, was also fascinated by Zen ontology, as shown in his *Empire of Signs*. Barthes demonstrated that haiku, a Zen-inspired poetic genre, is a decentered writing in which the poet is dethroned, or Lacan would have thought that the Zen master is "kicked out," let alone expressing the ego.[4]

One of the salient characteristics of haikū is the poet's utmost attention paid to what Lacan calls "the Other," the most visible of which are natural objects. Unlike Western romantic poetry and even the earlier Japanese poetry called *waka*, haiku, as R. H. Blyth observed, "is as near to life and nature as possible, as far from literature and fine writing as may be, so that the asceticism is art and the art is asceticism" (*History*, 1:1). Blyth's definition of haiku as an ascetic art means that classic haiku by such masters as Basho, Buson, and Issa are strictly concerned with objects in nature. A haiku is not a haiku if it is an expression or representation of human subjectivity. In a haiku the poet, the subject, is absent.[5]

In contrast to haiku, many of Emerson's poems show that the poet, while attempting to coalesce his vision and God's into one, still retains his. In Emerson's poetics, then, this vision buttresses his concept of subjectivity. In his essay "Self-Reliance," Emerson posits human subjectivity as part of divinity. This essay consists of a series of instructions in a form of command:

Insist on yourself; never imitate. Your own gift you can present every moment with the cumulative force of a whole life's cultivation; but of the adopted talent of another you have only an extemporaneous half possession. That which each can do best, none but his Maker can teach him. No man yet knows what it is, nor can, till that person has exhibited it. Where is the master who could have taught Shakespeare? Where is the master who could have instructed Franklin, or Washington, or Bacon, or Newton? Every great man is a unique. (*Selections*, 166)

Just as a Zen master suppresses subjectivity, Emerson empowers it. For Emerson, all one has to do to attain one's subjectivity is to "[abide] in the simple and noble regions of [one's] life, obey [one's] heart, and [one] shall reproduce the Foreworld again" (*Selections*, 165). Only when one acquires the divinity that already exists in one's life, "the Foreworld," which is "simple" and "noble," can human subjectivity become reliable.

To Emerson this is not a contradiction, for he believes that God resides in human as well as in nature, as depicted in his poem "The Rhodora":

> Why thou wert there, O rival of the rose!
> I never thought to ask, I never knew;
> But, in my simple ignorance, suppose
> The self-same Power that brought me there brought you.
> (*WOE*, 4:111)

In another poem, "All for Love," the consciousness of self, Emerson's concept of subjectivity, has a corollary to such disciplines as stoicism and self-reliance. "All for Love" is an admonition that can be given in opposition to that of a Zen master. Stoical self-reliance, as Emerson urges, must be kept alive underneath one's passion:

> Heartily know,
> When half-gods go,
> The gods arrive.
> (*WOE*, 4:157)

As long as the subject relies on the other, "half-gods," the subject is not able to attain enlightenment. Lacan would have argued that only when the subject relies on the other and undermines subjectivity can the subject attain enlightenment. In Zen doctrine, self-reliance would preclude the attainment of satori, for the consciousness of self means that the subject is not completely free of self-centered thought and emotion and has not identified the self with the absolute truth.

Some of Emerson's poems, on the other hand, show that the poet attempts to underplay the role of the subject in deference to the other. In common with Zen art, such poems thrive on images of peace and tranquility that suggest not only silence but also freedom from the thinking ego, the agitation of human subjectivity. Even "The Rhodora" opens with a scene of nature, a vision of nonhuman objectivity:

> In May, when sea-winds pierced our solitudes,
> I found the fresh Rhodora in the woods,
> Spreading its leafless blooms in a damp nook,
> To please the desert and the sluggish brook.
> (*WOE*, 4:111)

"Hymn" (*WOE*, 4:213), in its quiet compactness, alludes to death and eternity. In "The Humble-Bee," Emerson leads himself to "gulfs of sweetness without bound / In Indian wilderness found" (*WOE*, 4:112).[6] "Wood-Notes, I" also abounds in images of infinity and death:

> For Nature ever faithful is
> To such as trust her faithfulness.
> When the forest shall mislead me,
> When the night and morning lie,
> When sea and land refuse to feed me,
> 'Twill be time enough to die;
> (*WOE*, 4:119)

Both "Sea-Shore" (*WOE*, 4:282–83) and "Two Rivers" (*WOE*, 4:286–87) present symbols of the boundless other that, transcending time and space, flows through all things.

Emerson's poems, such as "Wood-Notes, I," that depict the continuity of life and death as does Philip Freneau's "Indian Burying Ground" are mindful of Zen's emphasis on transcending the dualism of life and death. Zen master Dogen (1200–1254), whose work *Shobogenzo* is known in Japan for his practical application rather than his theory of Zen doctrine, observed that since life and death are beyond human control, there is no need to avoid them. Dogen's teaching, as is Emerson's in "Wood-Notes, I," is a refutation of the assumption that life and death are entirely separate entities as are seasons or day and night.[7] To Freud, the unconscious includes a death instinct, an instinct in opposition to libido—an instinct to turn into elements in opposition to reproduction of organisms.

To Lacan, who believes in the continuity of life and death, the death instinct is not "an admission of impotence, it isn't a coming to a halt before an irreducible, an ineffable last thing, it is a concept" (*Seminar*, 70). Lacan takes issue with Freud, for Freud defines death as the opposite of life; the pleasure principle underlying life is opposed to the death wish, which "tends to reduce all animate things to the inanimate things" (*Seminar*, 80). Lacan, on the other hand, defines this change from life to death as "human experience, human interchanges, intersubjectivity" (*Seminar*, 80). Lacan's concept of death, then, has a strong resemblance to Dogen's.

As his poem "Wood-Notes, I" betrays, Emerson, too, believes in the continuity of life and death. But, to describe a vision of life after death, he uses the language mediated by subjectivity, the human-made categories of logic and social definition. He concludes "Wood-Notes, I" with these lines:

> Then will yet my mother yield
> A pillow in her greenest field
> Nor the June flowers scorn to cover
> The clay of their departed lover.
> (*WOE*, 4:119)

The six previous lines, quoted earlier, depict nature with its metonymic signifiers: "the forest," "the night and morning," and "sea and land." The last four lines above, on the other hand, thrive on a set of images that signify human as strongly as they do nature. The image of "my mother," while alluding to Mother Nature, also expresses human sentiments. "A pillow in her greenest field" becomes another hybrid image of humanity and nature, as represented by the words "pillow" and "field." So does the image of "the June flowers," for the word "June" is a human term while "flowers" are objects in nature. The last line begins with the word "clay" that describes an object in nature but ends with "lover," a distinctly human, personal expression. For Emerson, the fulfillment of spirituality is to include subjectivity in his consciousness of life and death; in Zen, it is to establish a state of *mu*, a concept that is no longer mediated by subjectivity.

Another way of looking at Emerson's view of life after death is to compare his nature poems with Emily Dickinson's poems on life after death. In her poem 280, "I felt a Funeral, in my Brain," the state of nothingness is signified by the collapsing of the floor of reason:

And then a Plank in Reason, broke,
And I dropped down, and down—
And hit a World, at every plunge,
And finished knowing—then—
(*CPOED*, 129)

In poem 465, "I heard a Fly buzz—when I died—," the state of nothingness is suggested by the disappearance of the windows:

With Blue—uncertain stumbling Buzz—
Between the light—and me—
And then the Windows failed—and then
I could not see to see—
(*CPOED*, 224)

Whereas Emerson remains highly conscious of life after death, Dickinson becomes unconscious as she approaches death.

Dickinson in these poems is more Lacanian and Zen-like than is Emerson in his poems on life after death. One might also argue that Emerson's concept of death is similar to Freud's rather than to Lacan's. From a Zen point of view, Emersonian transcendentalism, as expressed in poetry, conveys an objective vision of natural objects but at the same time retains an insistent subjective view of the poet. In terms of Lacan's psychoanalysis, Emerson's poetry takes the role of the imaginary on the part of the subject rather than that of the unconscious. In this respect, Dickinson's poems on death and eternity, such as "I felt a Funeral, in my Brain" and "I heard a Fly buzz—when I died—," thrive not only on the imaginary but on the unconscious.

This interchange and interaction between the imaginary and the unconscious can also be seen in modernist poetics. In Zen poetics, as Basho's haiku show, there is little distinction between human and nature, the subjective and the objective, or, in Lacanian terms, between the imaginary and the unconscious. Ezra Pound's imagism, for example, in its philosophical aspect considerably differs from Basho's poetics. Pound cannot genuinely be called a Zen poet, for he declared, "An 'Image' is that which presents an intellectual and emotional complex in an instant of time" (*Literary Essays*, 4). For a Zen poet, nature is a mirror of the enlightened self; one must see and hear things as they really are by making one's consciousness pure and clear. Pound seems to have been able to appreciate this state of mind, but he did not always seek it in his work, just as Emerson, while affirming pure nature, the state of *mu*, instead reaffirms the self, his subjectivity.

In Pound's early poetics, an image, though created by the subject, is based on a Zen-like, instantaneous response to pure nature. Pound writes, "It is the presentation of such a 'complex' instantaneously which gives that sense of sudden liberation; that sense of freedom from time and space limits; that sense of sudden growth, which we experience in the presence of the greatest works of art" (*Literary Essays*, 4). This sense of liberation suggests an impersonal conception of poetry, for it focuses attention not upon the poet, the subject, but upon the other, the image that represents nature.

By contrast, Emerson's poem "Days," for example, expresses a personal rather than an impersonal vision of nature:

> Damsels of Time, the hypocrite Days,
> Muffled and dumb like barefoot dervishes,
> And marching single in an endless file,
> Bring diadems and fagots in their hands.
> To each they offer gifts after his will
> Bread, kingdoms, stars, and sky that holds them all.
> I, in my pleached garden, watched the pomp,
> Forgot my morning wishes, hastily
> Took a few herbs and apples, and the Day
> Turned and departed silent. I, too late,
> Under her solemn fillet saw the scorn.
> (*WOE*, 4:275–76)

This poem abounds in images of nature, but each image is constructed with reference to subjectivity. The "Days," a representation of nature, is likened to "barefoot dervishes." The objects in nature, such as "stars" and "sky," appear side by side with "Bread" and "kingdoms," human objects. In a similar vein, "the pomp," a signifier of nature, becomes a provoking contrast to "my pleached garden," a humble human construction. In creating the final image of nature, "the Day," Emerson, chiding himself, imposes a personal, subjective view on the image: the fillet the Day wears looks solemn as she scorns him.

Pound's theory of imagism in poetry suggests that the imagistic depiction of a natural object or event is always through the mediation of language. In Emerson's poems, describing nature ultimately merges into expressing human subjectivity. Such an expression more closely reflects the poet's point of view than does the imagistic description that directly derives from a natural object or event itself without the mediation of language, as seen in classic haiku and some of Pound's imagistic poems.

On the other hand, the instantaneity and spontaneity in the construction of haiku images fend off the interference of subjectivity. Traditionally, the principle of instantaneity and spontaneity is as fundamental for the composition of haiku as the same principle is applied to Zen-inspired painting and calligraphy. In Zen-inspired painting, one must efface subjectivity; the longer it takes for one to compose one's work, the more likely it is for subjectivity to take over the composition. Although Pound's imagism and haiku poetics are not the same, both poetics and Emerson's are diametrically opposed in terms of subjectivity. From a Lacanian perspective, Emersonian poetics represents the imaginary function of the subject instead of the subject's encounter with the unconscious, the unsymbolizable, and the real.

3

EMERSON, WHITMAN, AND ZEN AESTHETICS

1

It is well known that Emerson's interest in Eastern religions and cultures is evident in his writings. Fascinated by Buddhism, Emerson considered the Buddhist a transcendentalist. But, unlike Thoreau, he was hesitant to embrace the Buddhist theory and practice. In a journal he wrote, "Buddhism. Winter, Night, Sleep are all the invasions of eternal Buddh, and it gains a point everyday. Let be, *laissez-faire*, so popular now in philosophy and in politics, that is bold Buddhism; and then very fine names it has got to cover up its chaos withal, namely, trances, raptures, abandonment, ecstasy,—all Buddh, naked Buddh" (*Journals*, 382). What Emerson calls "abandonment, ecstasy" alludes to the Buddhist nirvana. For him, the association of nirvana with an undisciplined state of oblivion to the self and the world is uncongenial to his stoicism and self-reliance.

But Emerson's detestation of nirvana does not necessarily imply that he felt greater affinity with Hinduism than with Buddhism. It is true that he used Hindu ideas as material for his poetry even though he did not accept their conclusions. When he regarded a Buddhist as a transcendentalist, he meant that Buddhism, unlike a religion, is a philosophy that emphasizes the primacy of the spiritual and transcendental over the material and empirical. Although Emerson was not familiar with the various sects of Buddhism that had flourished in China, Korea, and Japan, what united them was the doctrine of satori, the realization that material phenomena are not concrete facts but inane thoughts.

Among the chief Buddhist sects that existed in medieval Japan,[1] the Zen sect was the only one that advocated the doctrine that truth, concealed in the soul of an individual, cannot be spoken or written, and that satori can be achieved only through contemplative introspection, called zazen.[2] In Zen Buddhism, human is urged to achieve Buddhahood within the self. This sounds a great deal like Emerson, who urges one to think not for the sake of accomplishing things but for the sake of realizing one's own world.[3] The achievement of godhead within human rather than its discovery elsewhere is echoed in Whitman's poetry as well. In "Song of Myself" Whitman admonishes the reader, "Not I, not any one else can travel that road for you, / You must travel it for yourself" (*CPOW*, 64). In "Passage to India," too, Whitman defines God not as the wonder of the world but as a journey:

> Passage to you, your shores, ye aged fierce enigmas!
> Passage to you, to mastership of you, ye strangling problems!
> You, strew'd with the wrecks of skeletons, that, living, never reach'd you.
> (*CPOW*, 294)

As does Whitman, Zen teaches one a way of life completely different from any other one has been conditioned to lead.[4]

However superficial such a comparison may be, what is common among Zen, Emerson, and Whitman is that they are relatively free from dogma as a religion is not. Zen appeals to deed rather than word as Emerson and Whitman portray the human deed in terms of real life instead of the scripture. What Zen, Emerson, and Whitman share in principle is a detraction from, if not a denial of, Buddha, Christ, or any other deity or prophet as a supreme being. Their aim is to teach how God, whose definition varies, resides in every individual and every animate or inanimate being in nature. Despite such parallels between Zen and American transcendentalism, there are certain fundamental differences. The chief difference lies in the achievement of satori. Satori in Zen is an enlightenment that transcends time and place, and even the consciousness of self.[5]

2

In any culture, religion is often mixed with supernaturalism. Religions are at least tinged with myths and legends that cannot be comprehended in terms of nature; the traditional Buddhism and New England Calvinism both fall in this category of religion. The dissatisfaction of American writers, such as Emerson and Whitman, with religion suggests that they were able to express themselves most effectively in the form of poetry. In this endeavor, the farther they departed from the religious conceits, the deeper they delved into their natural, social, or philosophical concerns. This partly accounts for the fact that Emerson left the pulpit and that Whitman never attended church as a worshiper. It is not surprising, then, that Zen Buddhism, an unconventional Buddhist doctrine, found its aesthetic expression in the arts as American transcendentalism found its expression in poetry. In Japan, more than in China, where Zen Buddhism originated, it had a pervasive influence on painting, drama, music, poetry, and living custom in general.[6] Among the various arts, Zen found a congenial mode of expression in haiku, the quintessence of Japanese poetry.[7]

The aim of a Zen poet is to understand human's relationship to the spirit of nature. Observing the silent rites of a Zen priest, Yone Noguchi, the most influential interpreter of Japanese arts for the West, once wrote, "Let the pine tree be green and the roses red. We have to observe the mystery of every existence. . . . The language of silence cannot be understood by the way of reason, but by the power of impulse, which is abstraction."[8] Based on the philosophy of Zen, a Japanese haiku often is an expression of sensation rather than of human emotion or thought. One of the reasons for the opposition of Zen poetry to the use of symbols and metaphors is that figurative language might lessen the intensity and spontaneity of a newly perceived sensation. Such a language would not only undermine originality in the poet's sensibility but also resort to intellectualization and what Noguchi calls "a criticism of life," which traditionally Japanese poetry was not (*Through the Torii*, 159). The best haiku poems, because of their linguistic limitation (they consist of only seventeen syllables each), are inwardly extensive and outwardly infinite. A severe constraint imposed on one aspect of haiku poetry must be balanced by a spontaneous, boundless freedom on the other. From a Zen point of view, such a vision is devoid of any thought or feeling.

Whether a Zen artist regards his work as impersonal or Ezra Pound defines his poem as a personal complex, what underlies a Zen work of art is the naturalness of human sensibility. In Zen art, nature is the mirror of human. Zen practice thus calls for the austerity of the human mind; one should not allow his individuality to control one's actions. "Drink tea when you are thirsty," maintains Noguchi, "eat food in your hunger. Rise with dawn, and sleep when the sun sets. But your trouble will begin when you let desire act freely; you have to soar above all personal desire" (*Story*, 242). This tenet of Zen, which teaches human to emulate nature, was one of the Taoist influences upon Zen Buddhism. Lao Tze said, "Man takes his law from the earth; the Earth its law from Heaven; Heaven its law from Tao; but the law of Tao in its own spontaneity"

(*SJP*, 43). The twin deeds of human—naturalness and spontaneity—are, in Zen, the means by which one can be connected with the absolute, the achievement of satori.

Human's fascination with and emulation of nature is amply reflected in Zen art. Japanese haiku, in particular, do not treat such subjects as physical love, war, beasts, earthquakes, and floods just as Japanese paintings shun eroticism, ugliness, hatred, evil, and untruth. Unlike certain arts in the West, Zen-inspired art abhors sentimentalism, romance, and vulgarity. While Zen art refrains from the negative aspects of life, it seeks a harmony between human and nature. If human's affinity with nature is considered a Chinese contribution to the development of Zen Buddhism in Japan, an attempt to harmonize human and nature is historically a Japanese practice.

As does a Japanese poet, Whitman inspires the reader to immerse the self in nature. In the opening stanza of "Song of Myself," while celebrating himself and singing himself, he says, "I loaf and invite my soul, / I lean and loaf at my ease observing a spear of summer grass." He closes the stanza with these lines:

> Creeds and schools in abeyance,
> Retiring back a while sufficed at what they are, but never forgotten,
> I harbor for good or bad, I permit to speak at every hazard,
> Nature without check with original energy.

As an American poet like Emerson, on the other hand, Whitman also inspires the reader to seek enlightenment in the self as he says in the second stanza, "I am mad for it to be in contact with me" (*CPOW*, 25). The "I" consists of all the senses that the person possesses, as well as his or her emotional and intellectual faculties; the "me" is his soul, the spiritual, essential identity, as opposed to the physical, actual "I." As Emerson calls this identity divine, describing it as an all-powerful light, Whitman regards it as mystical. Although Emerson's divine light permeates each and all in the universe, Whitman's is not as abstruse as Emerson's. What Whitman finds in himself can be found in anyone else.

Unlike Emerson, Whitman finds an affinity with the common people. The humanistic and democratic spirit in Whitman rejects the Calvinistic antitheses of body and soul, good and evil, man and woman, as the following lines in "Song of Myself" express his belief:

I am the poet of the Body and I am the poet of the Soul.
The pleasures of heaven are with me and the pains of hell are
    with me,
. . . .
I am the poet of the woman the same as the man,
(*CPOW*, 39)

Whitman also rejects the conventional antitheses of bride and prostitute:

The bride unrumples her white dress, the minute-hand of the clock moves
    slowly,
. . . .
The prostitute draggles her shawl, her bonnet bobs on her tipsy
    and pimpled neck,
The crowd laugh at her blackguard oaths, the men jeer and wink
    to each other,
(Miserable! I do not laugh at your oaths nor jeer you;)
(*CPOW*, 35)

Even though Whitman's means of reaching this state of mind differ from that of Zen, his motto remains similar to what Zen indoctrinates its followers: only by severing oneself from the mundane world of good and evil, love and hate, life and death, can one reach the essential self.

Another striking similarity between Zen and Whitman is that the state of enlightenment is not as "intuitively" realized as it is in Emerson's approach. In the tradition of Zen instruction, one's attainment of satori is as practical as is his actual life. When the young Bassui, who later became a celebrated Zen priest in Japan in the fourteenth century, asked his master, "What's the highway to self-elevation?" the master replied, "It's *never stop*." Failing to understand, Bassui persisted: "Is there some higher place to go on to?" The master finally answered, "It's just underneath your standpoint."[9] The Zen master's pronouncement, "*never stop*," recalls Whitman's last lines in "Song of Myself":

Failing to fetch me at first keep encouraged,
Missing me one place search another,
I stop somewhere waiting for you.
(*CPOW*, 68)

It is also reminiscent of the last lines in "Passage to India":

> O my brave soul!
> O farther farther sail!
> O daring joy, but safe! are they not all the seas of God?
> O farther, farther, farther sail!
> (*CPOW*, 294)

The Zen master's final statement, "It's just underneath your standpoint," reverberates Whitman's in the last stanza of "Song of Myself": "If you want me again look for me under your boot-soles" (*CPOW*, 68).

Whether an individual can achieve Godhead through intuition, as Emerson emphasizes, or through deed and discipline, as do Whitman and the Zen master, the ultimate goal of an individual is to discover his or her place in the totality of the universe. Emerson, in a moment of exaltation, can envision a transparent eyeball merging into a divine light, an image of infinity and oneness. "Passage to India" is likewise Whitman's demonstration of monism: the world is one, spirit and matter is one, humanity and nature is one. In "Crossing Brooklyn Ferry," the people separated by time and space are united in an image of sea gulls:

> Watched the Twelfth-month sea-gulls, saw them high in the
> air floating with motionless wings, oscillating their bodies,
> . . . .
> Saw the slow-wheeling circles and the gradual edging toward the
> south,
> . . . .
> Looked at the fine centrifugal spokes of light round the shape
> of my head in the sunlit water,
> (*CPOW*, 117)

This concept of unity and infinity is also the basis for Zen's emphasis on transcending the dualism of life and death. Zen master Dogen is known for his refutation of the assumption that life and death are entirely separate entities as seasons are. Whitman similarly seeks a reconciliation between life and death; his feat of turning the solemn sense of bereavement in "When Lilacs Last in the Dooryard Bloom'd" into a celebration of death is well known, but less known is his idea of death given in "A Sight in Camp in the Daybreak Gray and Dim." In this poem, after seeing two of his comrades lying dead, one old and another young, Whitman comes upon a third—"a face nor child nor old, very calm, as of beautiful yellow-white ivory." The third dead soldier is identified with "the Christ himself, / Dead and divine and brother of all, and here again he lies" (*CPOW*, 219). For Whitman, the dead soldier is no less divine than the savior Christ and they both represent the living Godhead. Whitman and a Zen Buddhist thus refuse to believe in the dualism of human and God, life and death.

3

From this comparison of Zen Buddhism and American transcendental-ism, the justification of their otherwise inexplicable stylistic similarities and differences readily unfolds. Basho's famous haiku on a frog leaping into the water evokes an image of unity and infinity. Basho is said to have awakened into his enlightenment when he heard the sound bursting out of silence; he realized, in Noguchi's words, "life and death were mere change of condition" (*Selected English Writings*, 2:74). Chinese painter Liang K'ai's *Buddha Leaving the Mountains*[10] or Japanese painter Sesshu's *Landscape*[11] also exhibits a Zen artist's concept of infinite silence. "In the best 'Noh,'" Ezra Pound notes, "the whole play may consist of one image. I mean it is gathered about one image. Its unity consists in one image, enforced by movement and music."[12] The music in noh plays, though consisting of the sounds of the flute and the drum, has the quality of sound that calms one's nerves and settles one's mind. In these arts Zen doctrine permeates every element of their style and structure.

In some of Whitman's poems, calm imagery dominates their form as well. "When Lilacs Last in the Dooryard Bloom'd" abounds in quiet passag-es and subdued music: the poet's song and the bird's song, as if in a musical recitation, lead one's heart to a sense of infinity and peace, to "Dark mother" and "lovely and soothing death" (*CPOW*, 237). Some of Whitman's lesser-known poems, such as "A Noiseless Patient Spider," "When I Heard the Learn'd Astronomer," and "On the Beach at Night," are buttressed by pre-dominantly tranquil imagery. In "When I Heard the Learn'd Astronomer," Whitman, critical of the astronomer's method of analysis, stares at the stars "in perfect silence" and succeeds in relating himself to the universe. "On the Beach at Night" shows how a child's awe at the vast universe is mitigated by the idea of immortality and infinity. Interestingly, "A Noiseless Patient Spider" can easily be compared to a haiku, which has a single, concentrated image, such as a bird perching on a withered branch. In Whitman's poem a spider noiselessly spreads his gossamer thread in "measureless oceans of space,/ . . . seeking the spheres to connect them, / Till the bridge you will need be form'd, till the ductile anchor hold" (*CPOW*, 314).

Other poems by Whitman, however, are not entirely conducive to the sense of calmness and liberation found in Zen poetry. "Crossing Brooklyn Ferry" thrives partly on the passages that suggest peace of mind, but the theme of the poem is the mystical unity of the people who have crossed and will cross the East River over the generations. Uniting the people separated in time and space is accompanied by robust passages in contrast with the subdued ones that dominate "When Lilacs Last in the Dooryard Bloom'd." Actions portrayed in "Crossing Brooklyn Ferry," in particular, are propelled by the scenes that suggest trumpets and trombones:

> Come on, ships from the lower bay! pass up or down, white-
> sail'd schooners, sloops, lighters!
> Flaunt away, flags of all nations! be duly lower'd at sunset!
> Burn high your fires, foundry chimneys! cast black shadows at
> nightfall! cast red and yellow light over the tops of the houses!
> (*CPOW*, 120)

The music to which such passages allude are the opposite of the kind heard in a noh play or haiku. If Emerson's motto of life is self-reliance, Whitman's is reliance upon tradition and fellowship. In Zen discipline, liberation means freedom from any vestiges of worldliness by which one may cling to the Buddha or the ancestry.

Emerson's poetry, on the other hand, manifests an ambivalent attitude toward the concept of liberation inherent in Zen Buddhism. "Wood-Notes, I," for instance, is characteristic of a sprightly mood and a sense of liberation. The poem centers around a personage reminiscent of Thoreau, who "roamed, content alike with man and beast . . . / So long he roved at will the boundless shade" (*Poems of Emerson*, 33–34). In "Grace," however, Emerson replaces wild freedom with divine grace; human needs "the defenses thou hast round me set; / Example, custom, fear, occasion slow" (228). The weakness and helplessness of human is indicated by the "scorned bondmen" (line 4) as it is also implied by the final lines in "Days": ". . . I, too late, / Under her solemn fillet saw the scorn" (154). "Brahma," in which Emerson uses the god Brahma to explain the concept of the universal soul, is indeed Hinduism and thus antithetical to Zen's idea of liberation.

The liberation in Zen, moreover, implies one's liberation from human-made laws, rules, and authorities. "America, My Country," in which Emerson airs his disparaging remarks about England while singling out America's lacks, expresses this spirit of liberation. The argument against his own priesthood in "The Problem" is also based on the spirit of liberation, a desire in him that remains unstated in the course of the argument. For Emerson, liberation results from one's desire to adhere to nature's laws: how a woodbird weaves her nest, how a shellfish outbuilds her shell, how a pine tree adds new needles to her old leaves.

Liberation in Zen also requires that an individual liberate self from normality, equilibrium, or perfection. This definition of liberation accounts for the aesthetic principles that Zen art shuns—full circles, even numbers, balanced squares. The Zen-styled calligraphy calls for uneven strokes and rugged lines that reflect simplicity, spontaneity, and uncouthness found in nature. In the traditional Chinese and Japanese paintings, the only color used is black in various shades, for such a coloring reflects the simplicity of nature and the lack of polish. Black ink, moreover, implies oneness if it is dark, and nothingness if it is light. Such characteristics of style in Zen art are clearly visible in Lian Kai's portrait of Buddha or Sesshu's landscape, mentioned earlier.[13] Emerson's poetic form and style, on the other hand, are somewhat more akin to those of Zen art than Whitman's. "Crossing Brooklyn Ferry," for example, is full of round or symmetrical shapes and figures: "beads," "slow-wheeling circles," "round masts," "slender serpentine pennants," "the quick tremulous whirl of the wheels," "scallop-edg'd waves," "sea-gulls oscillating their bodies," "sea birds! fly sideways," "wheel in large circles high in the air," "fine spokes of light, from the shape of my head, or any one's head" (*CPOW*, 117–20).

By contrast, Emerson's poetry is aphoristic in its conception and truncated in its form. Its rhythm, despite the prevailing rhymes, is sometimes uneven. "Days," one of his briefest but richest poems, consists of intriguing images, mysterious events, and sudden movements. In the "Wood-Notes" poem, Emerson encounters nature, puzzles over her workings, and leaves them alone:

> Boughs on which the wild bees settle,
> Tints that spot the violet's petal,
> Why Nature loves *the number five*,
> And why *the star-form* she repeats:

Lover of all things alive,
Wonderer at all he meets,
Wonderer chiefly at himself,—
(*Poems of Emerson*, 32; emphasis added)

That Emerson accepts nature as it is with all its enigmas is the perspective of Zen. Such an attitude clearly is conveyed in his poems; his lines are often short and cryptic as Whitman's are long and avowed. Emerson's style is markedly in common with *yugen*, an aesthetic principle derived from Zen. *Yugen* has all the connotations of modesty, concealment, depth, and darkness. In Zen painting, woods and bays, as well as houses and boats, are hidden; hence these objects suggest infinity and profundity. Detail and refinement, which would mean limitation and temporariness of life, destroys the sense of permanence and eternity.

Whitman also expounds on the idea of infinity in various ways. In "Song of Myself," it appears as a continuous cycle of life and death, for which "grass" and "dirt" are used as a pair of symbols. In "Out of the Cradle Endlessly Rocking," the child discovers the meaning of life, which is death. In "Passage to India," God is discovered within one's soul, which defies time and space. In each poem Whitman chooses various symbols in reaching a central idea of his own. As his approach is expansive as well as refined, Emerson's is concentrated on a single scene, a single image, a single object. "The Rhodora," for example, is about a flower found in the American forest in contrast with "the rose," admired in English poetry. Emerson's flower lacks splendor and grandeur because "its leafless blooms" are "in a damp nook" and "the purple petals" are fallen in "the sluggish brook" (*Poems of Emerson*, 28). This scene provides Emerson with a "fresh" picture just as Basho's famous haiku about a crow perching on a barren branch on a desolate hill would lead the reader to the world of infinity.[14]

In his essay "Nature," Emerson seems to agree with the Zen artist on the method of concentrating on one dominant object: "A single object is only so far beautiful as it suggests this universal grace. The poet, the painter, the sculptor, the musician, the architect, seek each to concentrate this radiance of the world on one point, and each in his several work to satisfy the love and beauty which stimulates him to produce." Emerson also agrees with the Zen principle on the definition of beauty: "But beauty in nature is not ultimate. It is the herald of inward and eternal beauty, and is not alone a solid and satisfactory good. It must stand as a part, and not as yet the last or highest expression of the final cause of Nature." Emerson and the Zen artist, however, do not agree on the role the artist must assume in creating beauty, for in Zen practice the artist must annihilate any vestiges of self that might interfere with the artist's vision of what Emerson calls "the universal grace." "Thus," Emerson says, "is Art a nature passed through the alembic of man. Thus in art does Nature work through the will of a man filled with the beauty of her first works" (*CEOE*, 13–14).

The idea of infinity and eternity in Zen art is also represented by the imagery of age. Buddha's portrait hung in Zen temples shows the Buddha as an old man—as Lian Kai's *Buddha Leaving the Mountains* well indicates— in marked contrast to the young figure typical of the Buddha statue in other temples. Zen's Buddha looks emaciated, his environment barren; his body, his tattered clothes, the aged tree standing nearby, the pieces of dry wood strewn around—all indicate the fact that they have passed the prime of their life and function. In such a painting, the old man with thin body is nearer to his soul as the old tree with its skin and leaves fallen is to the essence of nature.

This aesthetic principle, based on agedness, leanness, and dimness, can be applied to Emerson's poetry. His use of paradox and irony, evident in such poems as "Brahma" and "Hamatreya," is not entirely characteristic of Zen poetics, but it has an affinity with the Zen artist's predilection for the ideas and images that suggest age and maturity. Emerson's use of aphorism and understatement in "Days" and "Grace" betrays a manner of imparting wisdom and restraint to his words. "Each and All" and "The Problem," despite his rhetorical eloquence, which is uncharacteristic of Zen poetry, both abound in abstractions and exhibit his emphasis on experience and wisdom. Among his poems, "Give All to Love" is perhaps the closest to the spirit of Zen in form and content, since the poem resembles the colloquy practiced in Zen Buddhism, in which the master gives his disciples advice, and since Emerson's outlook on life is stoical.

If Emerson's style has the elements of age, leanness, and dimness, Whitman's has a distinct taste for youth, robustness, and brightness. As in "Song of Myself," the people depicted in his poetry generate the optimism apparent in his ideas and attitudes. His style mirrors his mood of expansion and exuberance in striking contrast to Emerson's austerity and stoicism. The cataloguing method that typifies "Song of Myself" comes from his penchant for the spirit of the common man and the sense of freedom and abandonment. Some of Whitman's later poems, however, express the meaning of the experience and trial in one's life that matures with age. "Prayer of Columbus" is focused on the great admiral stranded on the island of Jamaica, with whom Whitman identifies himself. His hands and limbs growing "nerveless," the poet-speaker declares, "Let the old timbers part, I will not part" (*CPOW*, 296).[15] "The Dismantled Ship," one of Whitman's last and shortest poems, is an unrhymed, five-line poem reminiscent of Japanese *tanka*.[16] This poem catches a glimpse of "An old, dismasted, gray and batter'd ship . . . / . . . / rusting, mouldering." The battleship, stripped of its technology and power, is now sunk "In some unused lagoon, some nameless bay / On sluggish, lonesome waters" (*CPOW*, 367–68). The admiral and the battleship, whose long careers have met their challenges and accomplished their great deeds, and whose bodies now turn into nature, both provide the poem with concise images of age and experience. As in Zen art, Whitman's fascination with age and fulfillment is expressed with grace and humility.

4

American transcendentalism, as epitomized by Emerson and Whitman, and Zen Buddhism seem to have in their teaching similar manifestations about human life. Both philosophies instruct their followers how to find peace of mind and happiness on earth. To explain the method of self-reliance, Emerson puts it in a form of command: "Insist on yourself; never imitate" (*CEOE*, 166). His poem "Give All to Love" is an advice given to a young man like a Zen master's admonition: a young man whose love has deserted him can still regain happiness by believing in himself. In expounding a theory of happiness, Whitman insists in "Song of Myself" that one must reject the conventional dualism of soul and body, good and evil, man and woman, friend and foe. Zen masters would not disagree with such teachings, because they believe that human's model of life can be found in the world of human and nature rather than in religious dogma.

A Zen Buddhist, Emerson, and Whitman all agree that human responsibility rests on the self, as Socrates said, "Know thyself," or Plato disparaged books. From Zen's point of view, human can be happier by adhering to nature's laws than by clinging to human's. To Emerson, because God resides in human as well as in nature, one can rely on self to be happy. The Zen discipline in which one must sever self from human laws is a severe one just as Emerson's stoicism is a frustrating experience as shown in "Give All to Love": ". . . the palest rose she flung . . . her parting dims the day" (*Poems of Emerson*, 65). For Whitman, as his exuberant attitude to nature demonstrates, human is inferior to nature where one can achieve godhead more readily. The Zen Buddhist and the American transcendentalists seem to share the belief that an individual has a capacity to participate fully in real life and that life is what an individual makes here and now.

Zen Buddhism and the philosophy of Emerson and Whitman, however, differ in the means by which an individual can attain the state of mind called peace and happiness. Zen's doctrine of satori stipulates that one annihilate self to reach the state of *mu* where one can be liberated from the habitual way of life. In Zen, not only does one annihilate self but one must also destroy God, or Buddha, because it is only the self, not God or Buddha, that can deliver an individual to the state of *mu*. To Emerson and Whitman, on the contrary, one destroys neither God nor self; one believes not only in God but also in self. Emerson's self-reliance, therefore, is opposed to Zen's concept of the state of nothingness. Whitman's denial of dualism in human life, on the other hand, while it resembles Zen's indifference to good and evil, life and death, human and nature, is similar to Emerson's self-reliance. For both Emerson and Whitman, unlike Zen, believe that their vision of life not only emanates from God but derives from human intuition and reasoning as well.

This procedural difference between the two doctrines has a direct corollary to the way in which the artist's attitude to enlightenment is expressed. In Zen, human strives to live in accordance with the laws of nature, to which the individual finds no parallels in society. For Emerson and Whitman, the individual strives to pattern human laws after natural laws by means of, in Emerson's words, "intellect," "will," and "affection" (*Complete Essays*, 263). This is why Emerson and, more so, Whitman, find enlightenment to be a passionate and emotional experience, whereas attaining enlightenment in Zen practice is a calm and unemotional one. To call for reason and self-discipline, as does Emerson, often accompanies frustration and agony, just as to appreciate the sense of freedom and abandonment, as does Whitman, often results in joy and ecstasy. Emerson seeks guidance in human and so does Whitman in nature, but Zen remains indifferent to such efforts.

Zen's approach to life is free, as it were, of any kinds of hardship for human. Zen Buddhism, however, requires severe discipline on the part of its follower, as zazen testifies. In terms of psychology, Zen's enlightenment is regarded as "release," liberation from any of the human materials or moralistic thoughts and feelings. Unlike Emerson and Whitman, the Zen practitioner asserts that one's consciousness of self-discipline or happiness is no guarantee that it truly is the enlightenment one has sought. As long as one is proud of the past glory or dreams of a better future, never can one achieve enlightenment.

It is this view of life that is reflected in Zen art. The aim of the Zen-inspired artist is to express the individual's response to the experience through which the artist has attained enlightenment. The suppression of pride, for instance, is conveyed through the imagery of modesty the Zen artist creates. Although one cannot exactly say that Emerson's poem represents the sense of modesty in the way a Zen poem does, it is true that Emerson's style is characterized by modesty in a larger degree than is Whitman's. Whitman's poetry, on the other hand, strikes one as youthful, robust, passionate. But insofar as the poet's desire to be natural and spontaneous, indispensable elements in Zen poetry, is concerned, Whitman's style bears greater resemblance to the style of Zen poetry. Emerson would rather resort to reasoning and planning in a desire to demonstrate his principles of self-reliance and restraint. His poetry, as a result, has a tendency to become metaphorical, ironical, and paradoxical; Emerson is indeed less natural and spontaneous than Whitman. Small wonder Whitman called Emerson "unspeakably serviceable and precious as a stage," but deplored his cold intellectuality (*Democratic Vistas*, 2:155).

Emerson is least Zen-like in his poetic style if one looks for the elements of naturalness and spontaneity. But if one had a taste for the style of age and grace, an Emersonian poem might sound like a noh play or haiku. Similarly, Whitmanesque verse sounds like a haiku in one way but not in another. Emerson and Whitman are both considered transcendentalists, but they are not cut from the same cloth. If one can say that they do share many views but do not share their poetic style, one cannot say that Emersonian or Whitmanesque poetry has great affinity with Zen poetry.

PART TWO
MODERNISTS

4

W. B. YEATS'S POETICS IN THE NOH PLAY

Since childhood, Yeats felt in his heart that "only ancient things and the stuff of dreams were beautiful" (*Reveries*, 82). It was the rise of science and realism in the Victorian age that directed his attention to the Middle Ages and the world of myths and legends. As he read *Certain Noble Plays of Japan*, translated by Ezra Pound and Ernest Fenollosa in 1916, he found in them what he would emulate in reshaping his own poetic drama. "In fact," he wrote, "with the help of these plays . . . I have invented a form of drama, distinguished, indirect and symbolic, and having no need of mob or press to pay its way—an aristocratic form" (*CNT*, 151). Although there is no controversy over who introduced Yeats to the noh play, critics have overlooked other sources on which he might have relied.[1]

Having lived many years in Japan as an art historian, Fenollosa became well versed in Japanese art and literature, but his actual knowledge of the language was not profound.[2] Pound, on the other hand, who edited Fenollosa's notes, had no knowledge of Japanese, either. Since he did not visit Japan, he was unable to see the actual performance of a noh play in Japanese. Nor did he have firsthand knowledge of the drama and its cultural background. The most likely source of information available to Yeats, besides Fenollosa and Pound, was Yone Noguchi, who had, by the mid-1910s, published not only such widely read books of criticism in England and America as *The Spirit of Japanese Poetry* (1914) and *The Spirit of Japanese Art* (1915) but also several collections of his own poems in English.[3] In *The Spirit of Japanese Poetry*, in particular, Noguchi included a long discussion of noh entitled "No: The Japanese Play of Silence" with his own composition of a noh play in English, "The Morning Glory: A Dramatic Fragment"

(54–70). Noguchi was also invited to contribute another English noh play, "The Everlasting Sorrow: A Japanese Noh Play" (1917), and an article, "The Japanese Noh Play" (1918), to *The Egoist*.[4]

1

Not only through Noguchi's writings did Yeats learn about Japanese art and literature, and the noh play in particular, but he also made much of his acquaintance with Noguchi in person. Noguchi, in fact, delivered in England several lectures on Japanese art and literature. Among them, "The Japanese *Hokku* Poetry" was a lecture given at Oxford's Magdalen College in January 1914 at the invitation of Robert Bridges, the poet laureate, and Dr. T. H. Warren, president of the college.[5] In the same month, Noguchi gave another lecture, "Japanese Poetry" at the Japan Society of London.[6] It seems as though Yeats's interest in Japanese painting and noh coincided with the publication of Noguchi's essays and lectures on these subjects during this period.

But Yeats's personal acquaintance with Noguchi goes back a decade earlier. Yeats first met Noguchi in 1903. In 1921 Yeats wrote, in part, to Noguchi, who was in Japan:

> When a Japanese, or Mogul, or Chinese painter seems to say, "Have I not drawn a beautiful scene," one agrees at once, but when a modern European painter says so one does not agree so quickly, if at all. . . . The old French poets were simple as the modern are not, & I find in Francois Villon the same thoughts, with more intellectual power, that I find in the Gaelic poet [Raftery]. I would be simple myself but I do not know how. I am always turning over pages like those you have sent me, hoping that in my old age I may discover how. (Noguchi, *English Letters*, 220–21)

As this letter suggests, Yeats's introduction to the noh came after his fascination with the oriental paintings he had seen in England. His interest in Japanese visual arts was intensified by Noguchi's *The Spirit of Japanese Art* and later by his *Hiroshige* (1921), which was produced with numerous collotype illustrations and a colored frontispiece.[7] What seemed to have inspired Yeats was the "simplicity" of the artists, a century-old form of beauty that transcends time and place. Irked by modern ingenuity and science, he was adamantly opposed to realism in art and literature. For him realism failed to uncover the deeply ingrained human spirit and character. He later discovered that noble spirits and profound emotions are expressed with simplicity in the noh play. His statement about the simple beauty of Japanese arts echoes how Noguchi characterizes the noh drama. "It was the time," Noguchi writes, "when nobody asked who wrote them, if the plays themselves were worthy. What a difference from this day of advertisement and personal ambition! . . . I mean that they are not the creation of one time or one age; it is not far wrong to say that they wrote themselves, as if flowers or trees rising from the rich soil of tradition and Buddhistic faith" (*SJP*, 63).

Yeats and Noguchi thus shared the notion that simplicity and naturalness in Japanese arts came from the cultural backgrounds of the arts rather than the personal emotions of artists. Yeats clearly implied in his letter to Noguchi that contemporary arts in the West were "infected with egotism" while classical works of art in Japan, as Noguchi observed, were created as if anonymously. "The names of the authors, alas," Noguchi writes, "are forgotten, or they hid their own names by choice. Even when some of their names, Seami and Otoami for instance, are given, it is said by an authority that they are, in fact, only responsible for the music, the dance, and the general stage management" (*SJP*, 63).

Among the classic arts in Japan, the noh drama had the strongest appeal to Yeats because it was buttressed by a spiritual and philosophical foundation. Initially he was attracted to noh, which had developed from religious rites practiced in the festivals of the Shinto gods, as Fenollosa notes in *The Classic Noh Theatre of Japan*. Although Yeats was introduced to noh through Fenollosa's historical accounts of the genre, first published in 1916, he might have acquired further knowledge from Noguchi's *The Spirit of Japanese Poetry*. In it Noguchi reminds the reader that as the Japanese tea ceremony grew out of Zen, the noh drama had an intimate connection with Buddhism. Among the three hundred existing noh plays, he points out, there is no play in which a priest does not appear to offer prayers so that the ghost of a warrior, a lady, a flower, or a tree may attain nirvana. The purpose of a noh play is to recount "the human tragedy rather than comedy of the old stories and legends seen through the Buddhistic flash of understanding" (63). To Yeats, such a form of beauty as seen in the classic art of Japan, which lasts for centuries, changes no more than the Lord's Prayer or the crucifix on the wall portrayed in the classic art of Europe.

The spiritual foundation of the noh drama also has a corollary to the abhorrence both Yeats and Noguchi felt about realism and sensationalism in contemporary arts. In place of surface realism, a great dramatist would employ rituals and masks. When Yeats was introduced to the noh theatre, he was at once impressed with such devices. In the performance of *At the Hawk's Well*, he used masks to present intensified, time-honored expressions as the Roman theatre "abandoned 'make-up' and used the mask instead. He thought the use of the mask is "to create once more heroic or grotesque types that, keeping always an appropriate distance from life." The images created by the mask can convey "those profound emotions that exist only in solitude and in silence" rather than in actual scenes and personages (*POY*, 416). His idea about the mask, in fact, repeats Noguchi's: "the mask," Noguchi argues, "is made to reserve its feeling, and the actors wonderfully well protect themselves from falling into the bathos of the so-called realism through the virtue of poetry and prayer" (*SJP*, 60).

The comments Yeats made after the performance of *At the Hawk's Well* in 1917 are foreshadowed in a passage written in the previous year:

> A mask never seems but a dirty face, and no matter how close you go is still a work of art; nor shall we lose by staying the movement of the features, for deep feeling is expressed by a movement of the whole body. In poetical painting and in sculpture the face seems the nobler for lacking curiosity, alert attention, all that we sum up under the famous word of the realists 'vitality.' It is even possible that being is only possessed completely by the dead, and that it is some knowledge of this that makes us gaze with so much emotion upon the face of the Sphinx or Buddha. . . . Let us press the popular arts on to a more complete realism, for that would be their honesty; and the commercial arts demoralise by their compromise, their incompleteness, their idealism without sincerity or elegance, their pretence that ignorance can found a true theatre of beauty. (*CNT*, 155–56)

In *The Spirit of Japanese Poetry*, published a few years earlier than Yeats's essay, Noguchi, as if to call for Yeats's response, had written:

> When the Japanese poetry joined its hand with the stage, we have the *No* drama, in which the characters sway in music, soft but vivid, as if a web in the air of perfume; we Japanese find our joy and sorrow in it. Oh, what a tragedy and beauty in the *No* stage! I always think it would be certainly a great thing if the *No* drama could be properly introduced into the West; the result would be no small protest against the Western stage, it would mean a real revelation for those people who are well tired of their own plays with a certain pantomimic spirit underneath. (*SJP*, 11)

2

The salient feature of noh that must have held a strong appeal for Yeats is the structure of a noh play. Unlike a realistic, mimetic play in the West, the noh play thrives on its unity and concentration. It was Pound again who called Yeats's attention to this play as a concentrated image. In "Vorticism," an essay on imagism published in *The Fortnightly Review* in 1914, Pound included a note: "I am often asked whether there can be a long imagiste or vorticist poem. The Japanese, who evolved the hokku, evolved also the Noh plays. In the best 'Noh' the whole play may consist of one image. I mean it is gathered about one image. Its unity consists in one image, enforced by movement and music" (471). Pound's statement, however, was derived from Fenollosa, who wrote:

> The beauty and power of Noh lie in the concentration. All elements—costume, motion, verse, and music—unite to produce a single clarified impression. Each drama embodies some primary human relation or emotion; and the poetic sweetness or poignancy of this is carried to its highest degree by carefully excluding all such obtrusive elements as a mimetic realism or vulgar sensation might demand. The emotion is always fixed upon idea, not upon personality. (*CNT*, 69)

Fenollosa's notes, moreover, made Pound realize that a series of different noh plays presents "a complete service of life" (11). Visions of life portrayed on the noh stage are not segmented; they are continuous and unified. "We do not find," Pound reminds the reader, "as we find in Hamlet, a certain situation or problem set out and analyzed. The Noh service presents, or symbolizes a complete diagram of life and recurrence" (11–12). In some ways noh resembles the Greek play, for the individual plays deal with well-known legends and myths. As an Oedipus play treats the character of Oedipus in a known predicament, *Suma Genji*, for example, features Shite, an old woodcutter who appears as the ghost of the hero Genji at the seashore of Suma.

To present a cycle of life and death, the noh play often employs spirits and ghosts. Such a structural device, obviously different from the Western convention of plot, accounts for a different philosophy of life that underlies noh. As if to explain this difference, Noguchi made a modest proposal for Western writers. "I think," he urged, "it is time for them to live more of the passive side of Life and Nature, so as to make the meaning of the whole of them perfect and clear, to value the beauty of inaction so as to emphasize action, to think of Death so as to make Life more attractive" (*SJP*, 24). The concept of unity and continuity expressed in Japanese literature primarily stemmed from Zen Buddhism, which teaches its believers to transcend the dualism of life and death. Zen master Dogen (1200–1254), whose work *Shobogenzo* is known in Japan for his practical application rather than his theory of Zen doctrine, said that because life and death are beyond human control, there is no need to avoid them,[8] as noted earlier. Dogen refuted the assumption that life and death are entirely distinct human constructs.

Among the fifteen noh plays translated by Fenollosa and Pound, seven of them present characters that appear as spirits and ghosts to interact with living persons. In *Nishikigi*, the priest has a dream in which the unrequited love of a dead man for a living woman is consummated through the priest's prayer. Yeats's *The Dreaming of the Bones* (1919) has a plot structure strikingly similar to that of *Nishikigi*: the lovers Diarmuid and Dervorgilla as spirits brought the Norman invaders into Ireland after seven centuries to consummate their love by an Irish revolutionary taking the role of a noh priest. The image of human and spirit recurs frequently in Yeats's later poem "Byzantium" (1930):

> Before me floats an image, man or shade,
> Shade more than man, more image than a shade;

Yeats's attempt to reconcile life and death also extends to other opposites in human life: body and soul, human and spirit:

> A mouth that has no moisture and no breath
> Breathless mouths may summon;
> I hail the superhuman;
> I call it death-in-life and life-in-death.
> (*POY*, 248)

There is nothing new in the West, however, about the poet's bringing the rich opposites into a unified vision. Whitman seeks a reconciliation between life and death, human and God, and other oppositions. He turns the bereavement in "When Lilacs Last with the Dooryard Bloom'd" into a celebration of death. In "A Sight in Camp in the Daybreak Gray and Dim," the poet, after seeing two of his comrades lying dead, one old and another young, comes upon a third—"a face nor child nor old, very calm, as of beautiful yellow white ivory." The third dead soldier is identified with "the Christ himself, / Dead and divine and brother of all, and here again he lies" (*CPOW*, 219).

But the problem with Western poetry and drama, Yeats felt, was the lack of intensity and artistry in presenting the image of unity and continuity.

One of the disagreements between Pound and Yeats was that Pound regarded symbolism as "a sort of allusion, almost of allegory." The symbolists, Pound thought, "degraded the symbol to the status of a word. . . . Moreover, one does not want to be called a symbolist, because symbolism has usually been associated with mushy technique" ("Vorticism," 463). For Pound, symbolism is inferior to imagism because in symbolism one image is used to suggest another or to represent another, whereby both images would be weakened. His theory of imagism was derived from haiku, which traditionally shuns metaphor and symbolism, rather than from the noh play, which Yeats considered "indirect and symbolic." If Yeats's ideal language has the suggestiveness and allusiveness of symbolism, as opposed to the directness and clearness of imagism, then his sources certainly did not include Pound. Even though Yeats dedicated *At the Hawk's Well* to Pound, Yeats was not enthusiastic about Pound's theory. "My own theory of poetical or legendary drama," Yeats wrote to Fiona Macleod, "is that it should have no realistic, or elaborate, but only a symbolic and decorative setting. A forest, for instance, should be represented by a forest pattern and not by a forest painting."[9] In short, Yeats, a symbolist and spiritualist poet, was fascinated by the noh play while Pound, an imagist, was influenced by Japanese poetry and by haiku in particular.

For this technique of symbolism on the noh stage, the notes by Pound and Fenollosa were of great use to Yeats, who was eager to adapt an image that unifies the play or an action that foreshadows the outcome. The well in *At the Hawk's Well*, the birds in *Calvary*, and Cuchulain lying on his deathbed in *The Only Jealousy of Emer* were all consciously modeled on the noh play. In 1920 Arthur Waley, who translated with success the monumental *Tale of Genji*, also published *The No Plays of Japan*, a translation of over twenty well-known plays, with lengthy notes, but his writings were of no particular interest to Yeats. Waley's introduction is primarily a historical survey of the genre with well-detailed biographical and textual notes on Zeami, the most celebrated noh dramatist. The only native scholar writing in English was Yone Noguchi, who not only wrote about noh but even tried his hand at composing noh plays in English.

Yeats's interest in the symbolism used on the noh stage came from a desire to condense and simplify the action of his plays. This means that action must be reduced to its essentials and that the characters involved in it must be freed from anything that may distract the viewer's attention from the meaning of the play. The stage does not show any elaborate scenery, nor do subsidiary persons appear on the scene. The stage for the well-known *Takasago*, for instance, contains a painted old pine tree that, Noguchi describes, "looms as if a symbol of eternity out of the mist." The word "pine-tree," signifying "the hosts of pine-trees in the shapes of an old man and woman singing deathlessness and peace," is repeated throughout the performance. On the gallery connected with the stage, Noguchi says, "*No* actors move as spectres and make the performance complete, the passage of a beginning and ending, I might say Life and Death" (*SJP*, 58).

Simplicity and concentration are so essential to the performance of a noh play that the stage itself must be physically small and confined. "There is no other stage like this *No* stage," Noguchi emphasizes. "The actors and audience go straight into the heart of prayer in creating the most intense atmosphere of grayness, the most suggestive colour in all Japanese art, which is the twilight soared out of time and place." As Yeats would wholeheartedly have agreed, "It is a divine sanctuary where the vexation of the outer world and the realism of modern life" are left behind (*SJP*, 55–58). Anything that gets in the way of concentration, such as scenery, is eliminated. In the notes to *At the Hawk's Well*, Yeats writes:

> I do not think of my discovery as mere economy, for it has been a great gain to get rid of scenery, to substitute for a crude landscape painted upon canvas three performers who, sitting before the wall or a patterned screen, describe landscape or event, and accompany movement with drum and gong, or deepen the emotion of the words with zither or flute. Painted scenery, after all, is unnecessary to my friends and to myself, for our imagination kept living by the arts can imagine a mountain covered with thorn-trees in a drawing-room without any trouble, and we have many quarrels with even good scene-painting. (*POY*, 415–16)

Equally effective is the use of the mask that enables the actors and audience alike to concentrate on the meaning of the play. "*No*," as Noguchi reminds the English reader, "is the mask play to speak directly . . . which, marvellously enough, seems to differentiate the most delicate shades of human sensibility; we should thank our own imagination which turns the mood to a spirit more alive than you or I, when neither the actors nor the mask-carvers can satisfactorily express their secret" (*SJP*, 59–60). The mask, a permanent work of art, is made to preserve its feeling so that the actors, uninfluenced by the superficial actuality, protect themselves from falling into what Noguchi calls "the bathos of reality which would, in nine cases out of ten, alienate them from the rhythmical creation of beauty" ("Japanese Noh Play," 99). Yeats was convinced of the notion that the mask can convey legendary emotions far more artistically than the actual face of an actor. For his Cuchulain, a legendary figure, can show with the mask "a face, not made before the looking-glass by some leading player . . . but moulded by some distinguished artist." For Yeats, the device of the mask is a culmination of the joint effort by a poet and an artist to keep "an appropriate distance from life" (POY, 416).

Another structural device is the dance performed at the climax. Dance in noh is not choreographic movement as in the ballet, but, as Yeats cautions, "a series of positions and movements which may represent a battle, or a marriage, or the pain of a ghost in the Buddhist purgatory." While the Western dance often presents mimetic movements of arms or body to express physical beauty, dancers in noh, always keeping the upper part of their body still, "associate with every gesture or pose some definite thought." The focus of attention in the noh dance is not on the human form, but on the rhythm to which it moves. "The triumph of their art," Yeats recognizes, "is to express the rhythm in its intensity." The aim of such dance is to intensify the deep meaning of the play, and the deeper the meaning is, the fewer and simpler are the gestures of the dance. As Yeats observed, dances in the noh stage "pause at moments of muscular tension." The dancers walk on the stage "with a sliding movement, and one gets the impression not of undulation but of continuous straight lines" (CNT, 158).

The function of dance in noh was later adapted to Yeats's poetry. In "Among School Children," for example, Yeats uses the metaphor of the dance to suggest a unity of oppositions in human life:

> Labour in blossoming or dancing where
> The body is not bruised to pleasure soul,

In Yeats's vision the body and the soul become indistinguishable because of the unifying image of the dance:

> O chestnut tree, great rooted blossomer,
> Are you the leaf, the blossom or the bole?
> O body swayed to music, O brightening glance,
> How can we know the dancer from the dance?
> (POY, 217)

In a similar vein, Noguchi as a Japanese poet goes to nature to make life more meaningful; he, too, tries to bring the opposition of humanity and nature into a unified vision.[10]

The reconciliation of oppositions also occurs with the image of a flower in Noguchi's noh play "The Morning-Glory," as is the consummation of love between the estranged lovers symbolized by the climactic dance of the Rainbow Skirt and Feather Jacket in his other noh play "The Everlasting Sorrow."[11] In "The Morning-Glory," the Priest at the end of the play speaks to the Lady, the personification of a flower:

> Poor child, there is no life where is no death:
> Death is nothing but the turn or change of note.
> The shortest life is the sweetest, as is the shortest song:
> How to die well means how to live well.
> Life is no quest of Longevity and days:
> Where are the flowers a hundred years old?
> O, live in death and Nirvana, live in dissolution and rest,
> Make a life out of death and darkness;
> Lady or flower, be content, be finished as a song that is sung!
> (*SJP*, 70)

3

Yeats's adaptation from the noh play is not only in structure and technique but also in style. His borrowing of the conventions and devices from noh are apparent in his stage directions included in the text, as well as in the notes written separately, but the stylistic influences of the Japanese poetics upon Yeats's writing are subtle. To define Japanese characteristics in his style would be to find fine distinctions between his earlier style and that of his later period as a result of his familiarity with the noh drama.

His *Autobiography* (1938) makes it clear that his early poetry was aesthetic. His poetical style was the product of the emotionalism associated with the fin de siècle, as well as of late nineteenth-century impressionism. Because he was not altogether content with the conventional refinement and genteelness of English aestheticism, he was eager to vitalize his style as he was introduced to the noh play. The language of noh is consistently devoid of embellishment and tautology; the aim of a great noh dramatist like Zeami is to seek the profound beauty in expression influenced neither by the wishful thinking of the writer nor by the fashion of the day. Yeats recognized this mode of expression when he studied certain of the noh dances with Japanese players.[12] What he noticed was "their ideal of beauty, unlike that of Greece and like that of pictures from Japan and China" (*CNT*, 158).

In writing *At the Hawk's Well*, Yeats attempted to adapt a style of tension and intensity that is characteristic of the noh structure and of the noh dance in particular. The dramatic power of this play lies in the opening lines sung by the musicians while they unfold a piece of cloth symbolizing the well. The verse is direct and taut, the image clear, and the song rhythmic:

> I call to the eye of the mind
> A well long choked up and dry
> And boughs long stripped by the wind,
> And I call to the mind's eye
> Pallor of an ivory face,
> A man climbing up to a place
> The salt sea wind has swept bare.
> (*POY*, 399)

The vividness and intensity of imagery can also be seen in Yeats's later poetry, such as "Byzantium":

> Where blood-begotten spirits come
> And all complexities of fury leave,

Passion and violence thus coalesce into the unified and intensified image of a dance:

> Dying into a dance,
> An agony of trance,
> An agony of flame that cannot singe a sleeve.
> (*POY*, 248)

The symbolic use of a dance also occurs in Noguchi's English poem "Hagoromo," a summary translation of the well-known noh *Hagoromo*.[13] Pound made a poetic translation of the play into English, based on Fenollosa's notes, and incorporated it into his *Cantos*.[14] Noguchi, on the other hand, renders the scene of the dance in a prose poem:

> The fisherman blushed hugely from shame, and restored the robe to
> the angel. The angel in her waving robe, with every secret and charm

of clouds and sky, with Spring and beauty, began to dance: the fisherman cried in rapturous delight, "Behold! Behold!" The angel sung: "And then in the Heavens of melody and peace, a place of glory and Love was built by magic hands: it bears the name of Moon. . . . I now stray from the golden sphere, and show the heavenly dance to Mankind. . . ."

The air overflowed with dreams: the Heavens and earth joined their arms and hearts. O angel, dance on through the purple hours: Oh, dance on, fair maiden, while the heavenly flowers crown thy tresses in odorous breeze: O beauteous angel, dance on in Life and Love! (*Summer Cloud*, 1–4)

The metaphor of dance used by Yeats and Noguchi, an increased dramatic intensity in poems of dialogue, is adapted from the noh play.

The element of style most pervasive in the language of noh is called, in Japanese, *yugen*—an aesthetic principle originated in Zen metaphysics. *Yugen*, as noted earlier, designates the mysterious and dark, what underlies the surface. The mode of expression is subtle as opposed to obvious, suggestive rather than declarative. The fisherman in Noguchi's "Hagoromo," watching the complete performance of a dance as promised by the angel, is left with the feeling of *yugen*:

The angel abruptly stopped, and looked on the fisherman, and with a pretty little bow (like that of a drowsy rose) said: "'Tis the time I have to return home; farewell, dear man!" She soon caught the zephyr from Paradise: her feather robe winged Heavenward. What a strangely splendid sight! And she vanished beyond the clouds and mortal reach. The fisherman stupidly looked round over the empty sea. The singing wind passed amid the pines of the dreamy shore. (*Summer Cloud*, 4–5)

Such a scene conveys a feeling of satisfaction and release, as does the catharsis of a Greek play, but *yugen* differs from catharsis because it has little to do with the emotional stress caused by tragedy. *Yugen* functions in art as a means by which one can comprehend the course of nature; it is an enlightenment that transcends time and place and even the consciousness of self. The style of *yugen* can express either happiness or sorrow. Cherry blossoms, however beautiful they may be, must fade away; love between man and woman is inevitably followed by sorrow.

This mystery and elusion, which surrounds the order of the universe, had a strong appeal to Yeats. The hawk at the climax of Yeats's noh play performs an enigmatic dance, luring away the young man and inducing the old man to sleep. The dance is a symbol of the mysterious and elusive forces of the universe that thwart desire for immortality and knowledge. When Cuchulain hears the cry of the hawk for the first time, he utters, "It sounded like the sudden cry of a hawk, / but there's no wing in sight." During the dance, while he is mesmerized by the hawk's demeanor, the chorus sings on his behalf, "O god, protect me / From a horrible deathless body / Sliding through the veins of a sudden" (*POY*, 406–10). As Noguchi's dancer in "Hagoromo" "vanished beyond the clouds and mortal reach," Yeats's bird "seemed to vanish away" whenever Cuchulain approached her.

Noguchi attributes the principle of *yugen* to the ghostliness of Buddhism. "The *No*," he says, "is the creation of the age when, by virtue of sutra or the Buddha's holy name, any straying ghosts or spirits in Hades were enabled to enter Nirvana" (*SJP*, 66). As an illustration he cites a Japanese noh play called *Yama Uba*, or *Mountain Elf*, in which the author, a learned Buddhist priest, portrays how mortals are confused in "a maze of transmigration."[15] Noguchi describes the ending of the play, "after making her prayer to the Elf, the dancer disappears over mountains and mountains, as her life's cloud of perplexity is now cleared away, and the dusts of transmigration are well swept," and adds, "This little play would certainly make a splendid subject for a modern interpretation" (*SJP*, 66–67).

Although Yeats's noh play at times carries religious overtones as does the Japanese noh, his mode of perception seldom reflects the religious belief. In *Calvary*, where the two principal dialogues of Christ with Lazarus and of Christ with Judas are presented, the focus of the play is upon the story of human beings. In the notes, Yeats writes, "I have used my bird-symbolism in these songs to increase the objective loneliness of Christ by contrasting it with a loneliness, opposite in kind, that unlike His can be, whether joyous or sorrowful, sufficient to itself." Yeats's emphasis is not on Christ but on "the images of those He cannot save"; the birds thus signify "Lazarus and Judas and the Roman soldiers for whom He has died in vain." Departing from the scripture, Yeats deliberately uses birds as symbols of subjective life: "Certain birds, especially as I see things, such lonely birds as the heron, hawk, eagle, and swan, are the natural symbols of subjectivity, especially when floating upon the wind alone or alighting upon some pool or river, while the beasts that run upon the ground, especially those that run in packs, are the natural symbols of objective man" (*POY*, 789–90).

For Yeats, then, *yugen* is a purely aesthetic principle with which the natural symbols of subjectivity are presented. "Subjective men," Yeats further comments, "are the more lonely the more they are true to type, seeking always that which is unique or personal" (789). This manner of perception about the lonely flight of the bird exactly corresponds to the style of expression reminiscent of noh, a kind of veiled, melancholic beauty full of mystery and depth. In Yeats's *The Dreaming of the Bones*, which in its structure closely resembles the noh play *Nishikigi*, a young man describes the dance performed by the lovers Diarmuid and Dervorgilla at the climax:

> So strangely and so sweetly. All the ruin,
> All, all their handiwork is blown away
> As though the mountain air had blown it away
> Because their eyes have met. They cannot hear,
> Being folded up and hidden in their dance.
>
> They have drifted in the dance from rock to rock.
> They have raised their hands as though to snatch the sleep
> That lingers always in the abyss of the sky
> Though they can never reach it. A cloud floats up
> And covers all the mountain-head in a moment;
> And now it lifts and they are swept away.
> (*POY*, 774–75)

The consummation of love celebrated in this play epitomizes the poetics of *yugen*, for "the aim of the Noh play," Noguchi asserts in *The Egoist*, "is to express a desire of yearning, not for beauty, but for the beauty we dream" ("Everlasting Sorrow," 99). The success of the noh play, therefore, depends not so much upon the truth of history or humanity as upon the attainment of what Edgar Allan Poe called "a portion of that Loveliness whose very elements, perhaps, appertain to eternity alone" (*Selected Writings*, 470).

4

This concept of beauty was instrumental in drawing Yeats's interest to Japanese poetics. Historically, the influences of noh on Yeats's style was inevitable. Yeats was deeply impressed with the noh drama because he found himself in the age of realism. "I am bored and wretched, a limitation I greatly regret," he complained when the artist seemed to him "no longer a human being but an invention of science" (*CNT*, 152). Yeats did not merely attempt to imitate noh plays but succeeded in adapting the form to his own purposes. His aim was to restore the Irish legends as Zeami yearned for the lost world of the Heian period when Japanese literature achieved its elegance.

Yeats, however, was not the earliest writer in modern times who came in close contact with Japanese literature. Lafcadio Hearn, disheartened by the onslaught of modern civilization, was inspired by the mysticism of Japanese Buddhism. Ernest Fenollosa, originally interested in Japanese visual arts, was the first to interpret the noh play for the West. And Ezra Pound, strongly influenced by Japanese poetry and by haiku in particular, launched the movement of imagism. These predecessors of Yeats, whose writings had, undoubtedly, a significant role in Yeats's introduction to Japanese art and literature, were, as was Yeats himself, all looking in from outside. But Yone Noguchi, whose prolific writings in English as well as in Japanese have made a lasting contribution to the East-West literary confluence in modern times, was the only writer deeply ingrained in both traditions.

Whether or not Yeats learned more from Noguchi than from any other contemporary is debatable. What is well understood, however, is that Noguchi, throughout his career as a poet and a critic, had a stronger affinity for Yeats than for any other poet in the West. In "A Japanese Note on Yeats," published in 1922 as a testimony to Yeats's poetry, Noguchi wrote, "When I admire the Irish literature as I do, it is in its independent aloofness from the others, sad but pleasing like an elegy heard across the seas of the infinite. . . . In its telling of visions and numberless dreams, I see the passionate flame burning to Eternity and deathlessness" (*Through the Torii*, 114–15). This bringing of the rich oppositions of joy and sorrow, life and death, into a unified and eternal vision that Noguchi saw in Yeats was also what Yeats discovered in the Japanese noh play.

$$5$$

YONE NOGUCHI, EZRA POUND, AND IMAGISM

1

Among the modernists in the twentieth century, Yone Noguchi (1875–1947) played the most influential role in disseminating Japanese poetics and haiku, in particular, to the West. As early as 1903 he met W. B. Yeats in London; in the 1920s and 1930s Noguchi was the best-known interpreter of Japanese art in the West, especially in England. Beginning with *The Spirit of Japanese Art*, he published ten books about celebrated artists, with colorful illustrations, on Hiroshige, Korin, Utamaro, Hokusai, and Harunobu. Yeats, whose interest in the noh play is well known, became fascinated with these artists through Noguchi. Noguchi, in return, dedicated to Yeats the collection of his own English haiku, published in 1920, the largest collection of haiku written in English until Richard Wright's *Haiku: This Other World* appeared in 1998.

Through Yeats and other English writers, Noguchi also became well acquainted with Ezra Pound as early as 1911. In the meantime, Noguchi's later poetry, collected in *The Pilgrimage* and *Japanese Hokkus*, and his literary criticism, *The Spirit of Japanese Poetry*, in particular, were widely circulated in the West. In relating Japanese poetics to Western intentions in early modernism, Noguchi played a principal role. Among the various sources of influence and assimilation, the imagists responded directly to the example of their fellow modernist poet Noguchi. In his essay "Vorticism," published in *The Fortnightly Review* in 1914, Pound acknowledged for the first time in his career his indebtedness to Japanese poetics in general and the art of haiku in particular. In this essay, his famous haiku-like poem, "In a Station of the Metro," appeared. Pound's interest in Japanese haiku imagery influenced his theory of imagism.

In Japan, on the other hand, his associations with poets in the West had a considerable impact on such modernist Japanese poets as Shimaza-ki Toson (1872–1943), Takamura Kotaro (1883–1952), and Hagiwara Sakutaro (1886–1942). Noguchi published many books in Japanese and English, ranging from poetry collections, including a collection of haiku written in English, to books of literary and art criticisms dealing with Japanese poetry, noh play, and visual arts. Not only did he write books on Japanese poetry and drama, but he also published many critical biographies of Japanese painters such as Hiroshige, Utamaro, Hokusai, Korin, and Harunobu. He wrote more books in English than any other Japanese writer in history.

Noguchi was born near Nagoya, attended a middle school there, and became interested in English texts used in the school. But, in any case, he was dissatisfied with his public school instruction and withdrew from the middle school in Nagoya and went to Tokyo in 1890. At a prep school there, he diligently read such Victorian writings as Thomas Macaulay's, exactly the type of reading many a literary aspirant was doing on the other side of the Pacific. A year later, detesting the national university that an ambitious young man of his circumstances would be expected to attend, Noguchi entered Keio University, where he studied Herbert Spencer and Thomas Carlyle, whose hero worship, in particular, made an impact on him. At the same time, he devoured such American classics as Washington Irving's *Sketch Book*. He even tried to translate into Japanese eighteenth-century English poems, such as Oliver Goldsmith's "The Deserted Village" and Thomas Gray's "Elegy Written in a Country Churchyard." On the other hand, he did not ignore his native culture. His lifelong interest in haiku and Zen philosophy dates from this period, and the frequent visits he made to Zen temples while in college established a practice he continued later in his career in Japan.[1]

Although two years of college provided him with omnivorous reading in English, the young aspiring poet was not content with his education. Dreaming of living and writing in an English-speaking country, Noguchi took a voyage to San Francisco in 1893. The turning point of his life in America came three years later, when, twenty-one years old and already an aspiring poet in English, he paid homage to the Western poet Joaquin Miller (1837–1913). Miller, in turn, admired Noguchi's youth and enthusiasm. Except for a few occasions when Noguchi had to travel to Los Angeles partly on foot, or walk down the hills to see his publishers in San Francisco, he led a hermit's life for three years in Miller's mountain hut in Oakland.

Through Miller he became acquainted with Edwin Markham, Dr. Charles Warren Stoddard, and the publishers Gelett Burgess and Porter Garnett.

Within a year of meeting Miller, Noguchi published some of his earliest poems in three ephemeral journals of the day, *The Lark*, *The Chap Book*, and *The Philistine*. These poems attracted critical attention, and in the following year he brought out his first collections of poetry: *Seen and Unseen or, Monologues of a Homeless Snail* and *The Voice of the Valley*.[2] These, too, received praise. Willa Cather, for instance, commenting on Yone Noguchi and Bliss Carman, the Canadian poet, wrote, "While Noguchi is by no means a great poet in the large, complicated modern sense of the word, he has more true inspiration, more melody from within than many a greater man."[3] Despite initial success, however, his literary production became erratic, and his fragile reputation was not sustained for long. Like the wandering bard traditional in Japan, the young Noguchi spent his energy walking and reading in the high mountains and in the fields. Of this experience he wrote in his journal: "I thank the rain, the most gentle rain of the Californian May, that drove me into a barn at San Miguel for two days and made me study 'Hamlet' line after line; whatever I know about it today is from my reading in that haystack" (*Japan and America*, preface).

Noguchi's wandering journey came to an end when he returned to Japan in 1904, the year Isamu Noguchi, who was to become a famous sculptor, was born and left behind in America with the mother. The elder Noguchi became a professor of English at Keio University in Tokyo, the same college from which he had withdrawn eleven years earlier. Among the more than ninety books he wrote in Japan, many of them in English, four are genuine collections of English poetry.[4] The rest range from books of literary and art criticism to travelogues. In the midst of his burgeoning literary career in Japan, he sometimes came back to America, and once visited England to deliver a lecture at Oxford's Magdalen College.

His role in East-West literary relations can scarcely be overestimated. The significance of his work should become even more evident when one tries to determine his influence on such major poets in Japan as Toson Shimazaki, Sakutaro Hagiwara, and Kotaro Takamura, as mentioned earlier, as well as on W. B. Yeats, Ezra Pound, and Rabindranath Tagore, but above all on the imagist poets of the day. In particular, Noguchi's writings on Japanese poetics and haiku made an impact on Pound's theory and practice of imagism.

Noguchi first corresponded with Pound and then met Pound, along with Yeats, when he gave a series of lectures on Japanese poetry in England in early 1914. The relationship between Pound and Noguchi began in 1911, when Noguchi sent his fifth collection of English poems, *The Pilgrimage*, in two volumes (1908 and 1909), to Pound with a note: "As I am not yet acquainted with your work, I wish you [would] send your books or books which you like to have me read. This little note may sound quite business-like, but I can promise you that I can do better in my next letter to you." Noguchi also wrote as a postscript, "I am anxious to read not only your poetical work but also your criticism."[5] Pound acknowledged receipt of the books and note and thanked him in a letter postmarked September 2, 1911. Pound further wrote, in part:

> I am reading those you sent me but I do not yet know what to say of them except that they have delighted me. Besides it is very hard to write to you until I know more about you, you are older than I am—I gather from the dates of the poems—you have been to New York. You are giving us the spirit of Japan, is it not? very much as I am trying to deliver from obscurity certain forgotten odours of Provence & Tuscany (my works on Guido Cavalcanti, & Arnaut Daniel, are, the one in press, the other ready to be printed.)
>
> I have sent you two volumes of poems. I do not know whether to send you "The Spirit of Romance" or not: It treats of mediaeval poetry in southern Europe but has many flaws of workmanship. . . .
>
> Of your country I know almost nothing—surely if the east & the west are ever to understand each other that understanding must come slowly & come first through the arts.
>
> You ask about my "criticism". There is some criticism in the "Spirit of Romance" & there will be some in the prefaces to the "Guido" & the "Arnaut". But I might be more to the point if we who are artists should discuss the matters of technique & motive between ourselves.
>
> Yours very sincerely
>
> Ezra Pound[6]

Although Noguchi did not write again to Pound, Noguchi published his essay "What Is a Hokku Poem?" in London in January 1913. In the mean-time, three books of criticism by Noguchi appeared during this period: *The Spirit of Japanese Poetry* (1914), *Through the Torii* (1914), and *The Spirit of Japanese Art* (1915).[7] Noguchi was also invited to contribute "The Everlasting Sorrow: A Japanese Noh Play" in 1917 and an article, "The Japanese Noh Play," in 1918 to *The Egoist*.[8] Pound's encouragement was perhaps responsible for the publication of some of Noguchi's own hokku poems in *The Egoist* and in *Poetry*.[9]

Because his essays and lectures during this period also dealt with Japanese art, Yeats, who was interested in Japanese painting and the noh play, became interested in Noguchi's work as well.[10] As Pound's and Yeats's letters to Noguchi indicate, Pound and Yeats not only were close associates themselves but also were both well acquainted with Noguchi. Despite the active dialogues that occurred between Pound and Noguchi, critics have not seriously considered their relationship. The only critic who has mentioned Noguchi in discussing the imagist movement regarded Noguchi not as a poet and critic from whose ideas Pound might have benefited, but as one of the poets whom Pound himself influenced.[11] Such a preposterous connection is undermined by the simple fact that most of Noguchi's English poems, as Pound noted in his letter to Noguchi, had been published in America and England long before the early 1910s, when Pound and his fellow poets began to discuss imagism among themselves. It is more accurate historically to say that Noguchi influenced Pound rather than the other way around.

2

Through his books published and a number of lectures delivered in London in the 1910s, Noguchi was intent on disseminating to the modernist poets what he called the spirit of Japanese poetry. By publishing the essay "What Is a Hokku Poem?," he emphasized that haiku imagery is direct instead of symbolic. Above all, he argued that haiku is a depiction of nature unlike Western lyric that expresses personal emotion. He realized that whereas lyric in the West is an expression of the spirit of humanity, haiku is a depiction of the spirit of nature.

Like transcendentalists such as Emerson and Whitman, Japanese haiku poets were inspired by nature, especially its beautiful scenes and seasonal changes. Poetry by Emerson and Whitman has an affinity with Japanese haiku in terms of their attitude toward nature. Although the exact origin of haiku is not clear, the close relationship haiku has with nature suggests the ways in which the ancient Japanese lived on those islands. Where they came from is unknown, but they must have adapted their living to ways of nature. Many were farmers, others hunters, fishermen, and warriors. While they often confronted nature, they always tried to live in harmony with it; Buddhism and Shintoism constantly taught them that the soul existed in them as well as in nature, the animate and the inanimate alike, and that nature must be preserved as much as possible. Haiku traditionally avoided such subjects as earthquakes, floods, illnesses, and eroticism—ugly aspects of nature. Instead, haiku poets were attracted to such objects as flowers, trees, birds, sunset, the moon, genuine love. Those who earned their livelihood by labor had to battle with the negative aspects of nature, but noblemen, priests, writers, singers, and artists found beauty and pleasure in natural phenomena. Since the latter group of people had the time to idealize or romanticize nature and impose a philosophy on it, they became an elite group of Japanese culture. Basho was an essayist, Buson was a painter, and Issa was a Buddhist priest, and each of them was an accomplished haiku poet.

The genesis of haiku can be seen in the *waka* (Japanese song), the oldest verse form of thirty-one syllables written vertically in five lines (five-seven-five-seven-seven). As an amusement at the court, one would compose the first three lines of a *waka* and another person was challenged to provide the last two lines to complete the verse. The haiku form, a verse of seventeen syllables arranged five-seven-five (with such exceptions as five-seven-six and five-eight-five, etc.), corresponds to the first three lines of the *waka*. *Hyakunin Isshu* (*One Hundred Poems by One Hundred Poets*, A.D. 1235), a *waka* anthology compiled by Fujiwara no Sadaiye, contains haiku-like verses. Sadaiye's "Chiru Hana wo" ("The Falling Blossoms"), for example, reads:

Chiru hana wo	The falling blossoms:
Oikakete yuku	Look at them, it is the storm
Arashi kana	That is chasing them.[12]

The focus of this verse is the poet's observation of a natural object, the falling blossoms. To a beautiful picture Sadaiye adds his feeling about this phenomenon: it looks as though a storm is pursuing the falling flower petals.

This seventeen-syllable verse form had been preserved by noblemen, courtiers, and high-ranked samurai for over two centuries since the publication of *Hyakunin Isshu*. Around the beginning of the sixteenth century, however, the verse form became popular among the poets. It constituted a dominant element of another popular verse form called *renga*, or linked song. *Renga* was a continuous chain of fourteen (seven-seven) and seventeen (five-seven-five) syllable verses, each independently composed but connected as one poem. The first collection of *renga*, *Chikuba Kyogin Shu* (*Chikuba Singers' Collection*) contains over two hundred *tsukeku* (adding verses) linked with the first verses of another poet. As the title of this *renga* collection suggests, the salient characteristic of *renga* was a display of ingenuity and coarse humor. *Chikuba Kyogin Shu* also collected twenty hokku (starting verses). Because the hokku was considered the most important verse of a *renga* series, it was usually composed by the senior poet attending a *renga* session. The fact that this collection included a much fewer number of hokku in proportion to *tsukeku* indicates the poets' interest in the comic nature of the *renga*.[13]

By the 1680s, when Matsuo Basho (1644–1694) wrote the first version of his celebrated poem on the frog jumping into the old pond, haikai, an older poetic genre from which haiku evolved, had become a highly stylized expression of poetic vision. Basho's poem was totally different from most of the haikai poems written by his predecessors; it was the creation of a new perception and not merely an ingenious play on words. As most scholars observe, the changes and innovations brought about in haikai poetry were not accomplished by a single poet.[14] Basho's contemporaries, and Basho as their leader, attempted to create the serious haikai, a verse form known in modern times as haiku.[15] The haiku, then, was a unique poetic genre that was short but could give more than wit or humor; a haiku late in the seventeenth century became a crystallized expression of one's vision and sensibility.

To explain Basho's art of haiku, Noguchi once quoted "Furu Ike ya" ("The Old Pond"):[16]

Furu ike ya	The old pond!
Kawazu tobi komu	A frog leapt into—
Mizu no oto	List, the water sound!

One may think a frog an absurd poetic subject, but Basho focused his vision on a scene of desolation, an image of nature. The pond was perhaps situated on the premises of an ancient temple whose silence was suddenly broken by a frog plunging into the deep water. As Noguchi conceived the experience, Basho, a Zen Buddhist, was "supposed to awaken into enlightenment now when he heard the voice bursting out of voicelessness, and the conception that life and death were mere change of condition was deepened into faith" (*SEWOYN*, 2:74). Basho was not suggesting that the tranquility of the pond meant death or that the frog symbolized life. Basho here had the sensation of hearing the sound bursting out of soundlessness. A haiku is not a representation of goodness, truth, or beauty;

there is nothing particularly good, true, or beautiful about a frog's leaping into the water.

It seems as though Basho, in writing the poem, carried nature within him and brought himself to the deepest level of nature where all sounds lapse into the world of silence and infinity. Though his vision is based upon reality, it transcends time and space. What a Zen poet like Basho is showing is that one can do enough naturally, enjoy doing it, and achieve one's peace of mind. This fusion of humanity and nature is called spontaneity in Zen. The best haiku, because of their linguistic limitations, are inwardly extensive and outwardly infinite. A severe constraint imposed on one aspect of haiku must be balanced by a spontaneous, boundless freedom on the other.

From a Zen point of view, such a vision is devoid of intellectualism and emotionalism. Since Zen is the most important philosophical tradition influencing Japanese haiku, the haiku poet aims at understanding the spirit of nature. Basho strives to realize little division between humanity and nature, the subjective and the objective; he is never concerned with the problems of good and evil. A Zen poet seeks satori, a Japanese term for enlightenment, as noted earlier. This enlightenment is defined as the state of *mu*, nothingness, which is absolutely free of any thought or emotion; it is so completely free that such a state corresponds to that of nature. For a Zen-inspired poet, nature is a mirror of the enlightened self; one must see and hear things as they really are by making one's consciousness pure and clear. Classic haiku poets like Basho, Buson, and Issa avoided expressions of good and evil, love and hate, individual feeling and collective myth; their haiku indeed shun such sentiments altogether. Their poetry was strictly concerned with the portrayal of nature—mountains, trees, flowers, birds, waterfalls, nights, days, seasons. For the Japanese haiku poet, nature reflects the enlightened self; the poet must always make his or her consciousness pure, natural, and unemotional. "Japanese poets," Noguchi wrote, "go to Nature to make life more meaningful, sing of flowers and birds to make humanity more intensive" (*SEWOYN*, 2:69).

The haiku poet may aim not only at expressing sensation but also at generalizing and hence depersonalizing it. This characteristic can be shown even by one of Basho's lesser-known haiku:

Hiya hiya to   How cool it is,
Kabe wo fumaete   Putting the feet on the wall:
Hirune kana[17]   An afternoon nap.

Basho was interested in expressing how his feet, anyone's feet, would feel when placed on a wall in the house on a warm summer afternoon. His subject was none other than this direct sensation. He did not want to convey any emotion, any thought, any beauty; there remained only poetry, only nature.

Because of their brevity and condensation, haiku seldom provides the picture with detail. The haiku poet delineates only an outline or highly selective parts, and the reader must complete the vision. Above all, a classic haiku, as opposed to a modern one, is required to include a clear reference to one of the four seasons. In Basho's "The Old Pond," said to be written in the spring of 1686, a seasonal reference to spring is made by the frog in the second line: the plunging of a single frog into the deep water suddenly breaks the deadly quiet background. Although the frog traditionally is a *kigo*, seasonal reference, to spring, Noguchi interprets "The Old Pond" as an autumnal haiku:

> The Japanese mind turns it into high poetry (it is said that Basho the author instantly awoke to a knowledge of the true road his own poetry should tread with this frog poem; it has been regarded in some quarters as a thing almost sacred although its dignity is a little fallen of late). . . because it draws at once a picture of an autumnal desolation reigning on an ancient temple pond. (*SEWOYN*, 2:74)

As a result, the poet's perception of the infinitely quiet universe is intensified. It is also imperative that a haiku be primarily concerned with nature; if a haiku deals with human life, that life must be viewed in the context of nature rather than society.

The predilection to portray human life in association with nature means that the poet is more interested in genuinely human sentiments than in moral, ethical, or political problems. That haiku thrives upon the affinity between humanity and nature can be illustrated by this famous haiku by Kaga no Chiyo (1703–1775), a foremost woman poet in her age:

Asagao ni	A morning-glory
Tsurube torarete	Has taken the well-bucket:
Morai mizu[18]	I'll borrow water.

Since a fresh, beautiful morning glory has grown on her well-bucket overnight, Chiyo does not mind going over to her neighbor to borrow water.

Not only does her action show a desire to preserve nature, but also the poem conveys a natural and tender feeling one has for nature. A classic haiku, while it shuns human-centered emotions, thrives upon such a nature-centered feeling as Chiyo's. Nor can this sensibility be explained by logic or reason. Longer poems are often filled with intellectualized or moralized reasoning, but haiku avoids such language.

Because haiku is limited in its length, it must achieve its effect by a sense of unity and harmony within. Feelings of unity and harmony, indicative of Zen philosophy, are motivated by a desire to perceive every instant in nature and life—an intuition that nothing is alone, nothing is out of the ordinary. One of Basho's later haiku creates a sense of unity and relatedness:

> Aki fukaki   Autumn is deepening:
> Tonari wa nani wo   What does the neighbor do
> Suru hito zo[19]   For a living?

Though a serious poet, Basho was enormously interested in commonplace and common people. As autumn approaches winter and he nears the end of his life, he takes a deeper interest in his fellow human beings. His observations of the season and his neighbor, a total stranger, are separate and yet both observations intensify each other. His vision, as it is unified, evokes a deeply felt sentiment. In haiku, two entirely different things are joined in sameness: spirit and matter, present and future, doer and deed, word and thing, meaning and sensation. Basho's oft-quoted "A Crow" depicts a crow perching on a withered branch, a moment of reality:

> Kare eda ni   A crow
> Karasu no tomari taruya   Perched on a withered tree
> Aki no kure[20]   In the autumn evening.

This image is followed by the coming of an autumn nightfall, a feeling of future. Present and future, thing and feeling, humanity and nature, each defining the other, are unified.

The unity of sentiment in haiku is further intensified by the poet's expression of the senses. Basho's "Sunset on the Sea," for instance, shows the unity and relatedness of the senses:

Umi kurete	Sunset on the sea:
Kamo no koe	The voices of the ducks
Honoka ni shiroshi[21]	Are faintly white.

The voices of the ducks under the darkened sky are delineated as white as well as faint. The chilled wind after dark evokes the whiteness associated with coldness. The voices of the ducks and the whiteness of the waves refer to two entirely different senses, but both senses, each reinforcing the other, create a unified sensation. The transference of the senses may occur between color and mood, as shown in a haiku by Usuda Aro, a contemporary Japanese poet:

Tsuma araba	Were my wife alive,
Tozomou asagao	I thought, and saw a morning-glory:
Akaki saku[22]	It has blossomed red.

The first line conveys a feeling of loneliness, but the red morning glory reminds him of a happy life they spent when she was living. The redness, rather than the whiteness or blue color of the flower, is transferred to the feeling of happiness and love. The transference of the senses, in turn, arouses a sense of balance and harmony. His recollection of their happy marriage, a feeling evoked by the red flower, compensates for the death of his wife, a reality.

Well-wrought haiku thrive upon the fusion of humanity and nature, and upon the intensity of love and beauty it creates. A haiku by Takarai Kikaku (1661–1707), Basho's first disciple and one of the most innovative poets, is exemplary:

Meigetsu ya	The harvest moon:
Tatami no uye ni	Lo, on the tatami mats
Matsu no kage[23]	The shape of a pine.

The beauty of the moonlight here is not only humanized, since the light is shining on the human-made object, but also intensified by the shadows of a pine tree that fall upon the mats. The beauty of the shadow reflected on the human-made object is far more luminous than the light itself, for the intricate pattern of an ageless pine tree as it stamps the dustless mats intensifies the beauty of the moonlight. Not only does such a scene unify the image of humanity and that of nature, but also humanity and nature do interact.

3

That haiku imagery is based on the poet's objective, impersonal depiction of nature, and that an image in haiku is endowed with what Noguchi called "the spirit of nature," influenced Ezra Pound's theory and practice of imagism. In his celebrated essay on imagism, "Vorticism," published in *Fortnightly Review* in September 1914, Pound acknowledged for the first time in his career his indebtedness to the spirit of Japanese poetry in general and the technique of hokku, an older term of haiku, in particular.

As Pound explained in his essay, the image is not a static, rational idea: "It is a radiant node or cluster; it is what I can, and must perforce, call a VORTEX, from which, and through which, and into which ideas are constantly rushing. In decency one can only call it a VORTEX. And from this necessity came the name 'vorticism'" ("Vorticism," 469–70). A year later Pound defined the form of an image by stating that the image "may be a sketch, a vignette, a criticism, an epigram or anything else you like. It may be impressionism, it may even be very good prose" ("As for Imagisme," 349). An image, he argued, does not constitute simply a picture of something. As a vortex, the image must be "endowed with energy" ("As for Imagisme," 349). Imagism, in turn, is likened to the painter's use of pigment. "The painter," Pound wrote, "should use his colour because he sees it or feels it. I don't much care whether he is representative or non-representative. . . . It is the same in writing poems, the author must use his *image . . . not* because he thinks he can use it to back up some creed or some system of ethics or economics" ("Vorticism," 464).

To demonstrate his poetic theory, Pound thought of an image not as a decorative emblem or symbol but as a seed capable of germinating and developing into another organism. As an illustration he presented what he called "a *hokku*-like sentence" he had written:

> The apparition of these faces in the crowd:
>> Petals, on a wet, black bough.

"In a poem of this sort," he explained, "one is trying to record the precise instant when a thing outward and objective transforms itself, or darts into a thing inward and subjective" ("Vorticism," 467). The image of the faces in the crowd is based in immediate experience at a metro station in Paris; it was "a thing outward and objective." Not only did Pound actually see the "thing," but it also generated such a sensation that he could not shake it out of his mind. This image, he emphasizes, "transforms itself, or darts into a thing inward and subjective"—that is, the image of the "Petals, on a wet, black bough." Imagism is further contrasted to symbolism: "The symbolist's *symbols* have a fixed value, like numbers in arithmetic, like 1, 2, and 7. The imagiste's images have a variable significance, like the signs a, b, and x in algebra" ("Vorticism," 463).

Although Pound's definition is clear enough, the sources for his ideas are hard to determine. Most discussions about the genesis of the imagist movement are speculative at best. Pound's insistence that an image in poetry must be active rather than passive suggests that a poem is not a description of something but, as Aristotle had said of tragedy, an action. Pound approaches Aristotelianism in his insistence that the image of the faces in the crowd in his metro poem was not simply a description of his sensation at the station but an active entity capable of dynamic development. According to his experience, this particular image instantly transformed itself into another image, the image of the petals on a wet, black bough. To Pound, the success of this poem resulted from his instantaneous perception of the relatedness between the two entirely different objects.

But Pound's note on the genesis of "In a Station of the Metro" in the "Vorticism" essay makes it clear that there was nothing instantaneous about the composition of this poem. It was in 1911 that Pound, having seen those "beautiful faces" at La Concorde, wrote a thirty-line poem, "and destroyed it because it was what we call work 'of second intensity'" (467). Six months later he reduced the longer text to a poem half the length, and still a year later he wrote the final version, a two-line poem. Pound's insistence on the instantaneous perception of the metro images drove him to repeated attempts at recreating the instantaneous images he had perceived a year and a half earlier. Traditionally, the principle of instantaneity and spontaneity is as fundamental for the composition of hokku as the same principle is when applied to Zen-inspired painting and calligraphy. In any event, his discovery of hokku in 1913–1914 was, as he says, "useful in getting out of the impasse in which I had been left by my metro emotion" (467). To Pound, the most important thing he learned about hokku was "this particular sort of consciousness," which he was unable to identify with any version of impressionist art.[24]

Another equally important tenet of imagism calls for directness in expression. The immediate model for this principle was nineteenth-century French prose. Pound did not mention specific English poets but seemed adamantly opposed to Victorian poetry, which he characterized as wordy and rhetorical. Instead, he urged his fellow poets "to bring poetry up to the level of prose." "Flaubert and De Maupassant," he believed, "lifted prose to the rank of a finer art, and one has no patience with contemporary poets who escape from all the difficulties of the infinitely difficult art of good prose by pouring themselves into loose verses" ("Vorticism," 462).

If Pound's ideal poetry has the directness and clarity of good prose as opposed to the suggestiveness and vagueness of symbolist poetry, then his sources, as pointed out earlier, did not include Yeats. Even though Yeats dedicated the noh play *At the Hawk's Well* to Pound, as noted earlier, Yeats was not enthusiastic about Pound's poetics. "My own theory of poetical or legendary drama," Yeats wrote to Fiona Macleod, "is that it should have no realistic, or elaborate, but only a symbolic and decorative setting. A forest, for instance, should be represented by a forest pattern and not by a forest painting."[25] The difference between Pound and Yeats reveals itself in the two poets' differing views of the Japanese noh play.

This disagreement between Pound and Yeats over whether poetic images should be suggestive or active also involves what Noguchi, a poet and critic well acquainted with both poets, felt compelled to write in "What Is a Hokku Poem?," published in London in 1913.[26] In that essay, Noguchi first defined hokku as an expression of Japanese poets' "understanding of Nature," or, better put, as a song or chant of "their longing or wonder or adoration toward Mother Nature" that is "never mystified by any cloud or mist like Truth or Beauty of Keats' understanding." Noguchi differentiated between the "suggestive" and subjective coloration of English poetry and the Japanese hokku, "distinctly clear-cut like a diamond or star." "I say," he argued, "that the star itself has almost no share in the creation of a condition even when your dream or vision is gained through its beauty. . . . I value the 'hokku' poem, at least some of them, because of its own truth and humanity simple and plain." Noguchi then analyzed the aim of hokku: the hokku poet expresses the spirit of nature rather than the will of man or woman. Noguchi would agree that hokku is "suggestive" only if the word "suggestive" means that "truth and humanity are suggestive." He added, "But I can say myself as a poet . . . that your poem would certainly end in artificiality if you start out to be suggestive from the beginning" ("What Is a Hokku Poem?" 355).

Finally, Noguchi based his definition and analysis of aim in Zen philosophy, understood as discipline of the mind: one should not allow one's individuality to control action. Zen does not, indeed, recognize human reality, the existence of good and evil, because this reality is but the creation of human will rather than the spirit of nature. Noguchi thus observed that "there is no word in so common use by Western critics as suggestive, which makes more mischief than enlightenment." Although Western critics "mean it quite simply . . . to be a new force or salvation, . . . I say that no critic is necessary for this world of poetry" ("What Is a Hokku Poem?" 355).

Pound had apparently known little about Japanese poetry before he became acquainted with Noguchi's writings and before he attended the April 1909 meeting of the Poets' Club. This group, headed by T. E. Hulme, was succeeded by another group called "Les Imagistes," or "Des Imagistes," which Pound led from 1912 to 1914.[27] Although Pound, in fact, joined the Poets' Club, its sessions did not prove of much inspiration to him. Richard Aldington, who joined in 1911, was more interested in the color prints by Utamaro, Hokusai, and others found in the British Museum than in Japanese poetry.[28] The fact that Pound was more seriously interested than Aldington was in Japanese poetry is indicated by a parody of Pound's metro poem that Aldington published in the January 1915 issue of *The Egoist*.[29] Allen Upward, another member of the "Les Imagistes" group, whom Pound had met in 1911, had some importance for Pound because Upward used the term "whirl-swirl" in his book *The New Word* (New York, 1908). Upward, a self-styled intellectual and a poet, had "a powerful and original mind clearly and trenchantly concerned with matters that bear directly on what Pound meant by 'vortex.'"[30] But Upward, who was well-read in Confucius and perhaps familiar with Chinese poetry, did not have sufficient knowledge of Japanese poetry, let alone of hokku, to influence Pound.[31]

The degree of Pound's initial interest in hokku, therefore, was not entirely clear, for he was much occupied with Provençal poetry and criticism, as his letter to Noguchi, quoted earlier, indicates. It is quite possible that Pound learned about hokku from T. E. Hulme and F. S. Flint, who were experimenting with hokku and tanka, the thirty-one-syllable Japanese poetic form.[32] The difficulty with this assumption, however, is that Hulme and Flint studied hokku through French translators and critics who used the terms haiku and haikai, more modern words, rather than hokku. Most strikingly, neither Pound nor Noguchi referred to the Japanese poem as haiku or haikai; both consistently called it hokku in their writings.

However coincidental this might have been, there are two more pieces of evidence suggesting that Pound might have learned about hokku in Noguchi's work. First, as noted earlier, the essay "What Is a Hokku Poem?"—in which Noguchi declared that poetic images must be active instead of suggestive, direct instead of symbolic, and that the aim of a hokku is to understand the spirit of nature rather than to express the will of an individual—was published in *Rhythm* (London) in January 1913, almost two years before Pound's essay "Vorticism." Even Pound's essay "A Few Don'ts," the earliest manifesto on imagism, appeared in the March 1913 issue of *Poetry* (Chicago) two months after Noguchi's essay. Second, Noguchi's book of criticism, *The Spirit of Japanese Poetry*, was published in London by John Murray in March 1914, half a year before Pound's "Vorticism" essay.[33]

Moreover, the key chapter of Noguchi's book, entitled "The Japanese Hokku Poetry," was a lecture delivered in the Hall of Magdalen College, Oxford, on January 28, 1914, at the invitation of Robert Bridges, the poet laureate, and T. H. Warren, president of the college and professor of poetry in the university. The first chapter, "Japanese Poetry," was also based on a lecture Noguchi gave at the Japan Society of London on January 14. The rest of the book had been presented as other lectures to such audiences as the Royal Asiatic Society and the Quest Society in England before April 1914, when Noguchi left London for Tokyo by way of Paris, Berlin, and Moscow. It is altogether possible that Pound heard Noguchi lecture at the Quest Society since Pound, Wyndham Lewis, and T. E. Hulme all lectured there in 1914.[34] During this stay in England, *Through the Torii*, another collection of essays that included a variety of commentary on William Rossetti, James Whistler, W. B. Yeats, and Oscar Wilde, and his autobiography, *The Story of Yone Noguchi Told by Himself*, also appeared in print.

It is most intriguing that Pound's "Vorticism" essay quoted a famous hokku by Moritake (1452–1540) just before discussing the often-quoted metro poem:

The fallen blossom flies back to its branch:
A butterfly.
("Vorticism," 467)

This hokku in Japanese has three lines:

Rak-ka eda ni
Kaeru to mireba
Kocho-o kana

Noguchi translated this poem in three lines:

I thought I saw the fallen leaves
Returning to their branches:
Alas, butterflies were they.
(*SJP*, 50)

Pound must have reconstructed the hokku in two lines simply because he had in mind "a form of super-position" in which his metro poem was to be composed. The similarities between Pound's and Noguchi's versions of the poem in question do not seem coincidental, because the superpository division is indicated by a colon in both constructions. Both translations have identical key words: "fallen," "branch," and "butterfly." The only difference in diction is between Pound's "blossom" (*ka* in Japanese) and Noguchi's "leaves." In syntax, however, these translations are different: Noguchi's version is subjective from the start and ends objectively; the reverse is true in Pound's rendering. Syntactically, Noguchi's version is closer to the Japanese original than Pound's. A literal translation of Moritake's first two lines, "Rak-ka eda ni / Kaeru to mireba," would read: "The fallen blossom appears to come back to its branch."

What appealed to Pound was the terseness and intensity of imagery in a hokku. Irked by the decorative and superfluous style of much Victorian poetry, he urged his fellow poets to eliminate words that do not contribute to the central meaning of the poem. "All poetic language," Pound insisted, "is the language of exploration. Since the beginning of bad writing, writers have used images as ornaments" ("Vorticism," 466). By saying, "Great literature is simply language charged with meaning to the utmost possible degree," he meant to elaborate the imagist principle that using fewer words maximizes and intensifies meaning.[35] In "What Is a Hokku Poem?" Noguchi wrote, "I always thought that the most beautiful flowers grow close to the ground, and they need no hundred petals for expressing their own beauty; how can you call it real poetry if you cannot tell it by a few words?" (355).

Pound, furthermore, applied the principle of terseness and intensity to the construction of a single image in his poetry. "The 'one image poem,'"

Pound noted, "is a form of super-position, that is to say it is one idea set on top of another. I found it useful in getting out of the impasse in which I had been left by my metro emotion" ("Vorticism," 467). Noguchi pointed out the same technique: "*Hokku* means literally a single utterance or the utterance of a single verse; that utterance should be like a 'moth light playing on reality's dusk,' or 'an art hung, as a web, in the air of perfume,' swinging soft in music of a moment" (*SJP*, 39). To illustrate his point, Noguchi quoted a hokku by Buson:

> The night of the Spring,—
> Oh, between the eve
> And the dawn.

This hokku was placed against the opening passage of *Makura no Soshi* (*Pillow Sketches*) by Sei Shonagon (965–1025?), a celebrated prose writer in medieval Japan: "I love to watch the dawn grow gradually white and whiter, till a faint rosy tinge crowns the mountain's crest, while slender streaks of purple cloud extend themselves above." Noguchi considered Buson's image far more vivid and intensive than Sei Shonagon's, remarking, "Buson is pleased to introduce the night of the Spring which should be beautiful without questioning, since it lies between those two beautiful things, the eve and the dawn" (*SJP*, 48–49).

4

What a Japanese hokku and Pound's image share, besides their brevity and intensity, is the poet's ability to escape the confinement of the poem. The sense of liberation in hokku is usually accomplished through references to time and space. A Japanese hokku contains not only a reference to a season, an indication of time, but also an image of nature, that of space. Pound's hokku-like poems, such as "In a Station of the Metro" and "Alba," indeed have references to time and space. Pound called the metro emotion, which came from the image of the faces in the crowd, "a thing outward and objective," and the image of the "petals, on a wet, black bough" "a thing inward and subjective." The image of the petals, nevertheless, is a natural object in contrast to that of the faces in the crowded station, a human object.

In Pound's mind—in the realm of subjective perception—the image of the faces, an objective image, transforms into the image of the petals, a subjective image. This perception also means that the image of the faces, an image of people, transforms into that of the petals, an image of nature.

The shifting of objective and subjective images in Pound's poem is depicted in terms of a vortex, in which an image is not only active in itself but also capable of merging into another image that appears in its wake. Because Pound's image has this tendency, it is often as difficult to separate the mental vision from the external as it is to separate mind from matter, the perceiver from the perceived, in Japanese hokku.

In *The Spirit of Japanese Poetry*, Noguchi is as critical as Pound of the Western poet's tendency to wordiness. Noguchi's emphasis on the Japanese hokku as "the real poetry of action" entails that a hokku aims to narrow the distance between humanity and nature, the perceiver and the perceived. The narrower the distance, the better the hokku becomes. Based upon "Lao Tze's canon of spiritual anarchism" and Zen's principle of controlling the mind, Noguchi declares:

> To attach too closely to the subject matter in literary expression is never a way to complete the real saturation; the real infinite significance will only be accomplished at such a consummate moment when the end and means are least noticeable, and the subject and expression never fluctuate from each other, being in perfect collocation; it is the partial loss of the birthright of each that gains an artistic triumph. . . . I do never mean that the *Hokku* poems are lyrical poetry in the general Western understanding; but the Japanese mind gets the effect before perceiving the fact of their brevity, its sensibility resounding to their single note, as if the calm bosom of river water to the song of a bird. (34)

To illustrate what he calls "the sense of mystical affinity between the life of Nature and the life of man, between the beauty of flowers and the beauty of love," he quotes his own poem:

> It's accident to exist as a flower or a poet:
> A mere twist of evolution but from the same force;
> I see no form in them but only beauty in evidence;
> It's the single touch of their imagination to get
>   the embodiment of a poet or a flower:
> To be a poet is to be a flower,
> To be the dancer is to make the singer sing. (37)

Pound, on the other hand, views the affinity between humanity and nature differently. What Pound calls "a thing inward and subjective" does not necessarily correspond to a vision of a person; nor is "a thing outward and objective" the same thing as a vision of nature.

This fusion of humanity and nature is called spontaneity in Zen. The best hokku poems, because of their linguistic limitations, are inwardly extensive and outwardly infinite. A severe constraint imposed on one aspect of hokku must be balanced by a spontaneous, boundless freedom on the other. From a Zen point of view, such a vision is devoid of thought and emotion. Since Zen is the most important philosophical tradition influencing Japanese hokku, the hokku poet aims at understanding the spirit of nature. Basho, a Zen-inspired poet, recognizes little division between humanity and nature, the subjective and the objective; he is never concerned with the problems of good and evil. Placed against this tradition, Pound's poetics in its philosophical aspect considerably differs from Basho's. Pound cannot be called a Zen poet because he declared, "An 'Image' is that which presents an intellectual and emotional complex in an instant of time" (*Literary Essays*, 4). A Zen poet seeks satori, an enlightenment that transcends time and place, and even the consciousness of self. This enlightenment is defined as a state absolutely free of any thought or emotion, a state that corresponds to that of nature. For a Zen-inspired poet, nature is a mirror of the enlightened self; one must see and hear things as they really are by making one's consciousness pure and clear. Pound seems to be able to appreciate this state of mind, but obviously he does not necessarily try to seek it in his own work.

In fact, Japanese traditional haiku seldom take physical love, war, beasts, earthquakes, floods, and the like for their subjects. And while Pound's poetry does express good and evil, love and hatred, individual feeling and collective myth, Basho's shuns such sentiments and emotions altogether. Pound and a Zen poet, however, do agree that their poetic vision is spontaneous and capable of attaining enlightenment. Pound maintained, "It is the presentation of such a 'complex' instantaneously which gives that sense of sudden liberation; that sense of freedom from time and space limits; that sense of sudden growth, which we experience in the presence of the greatest works of art" (*Literary Essays*, 4). Pound's observation, however, is very much a Western formulation of an experience familiar to Zen-inspired artists.

This sense of liberation suggests an impersonal conception of poetry, for it focuses attention not upon the poet but upon the image. T. S. Eliot, whom most observers agree Pound influenced, held the same view (*Selected Essays*, 8–10). Japanese poets such as Basho, Buson, and Issa held the same principle. Their poetry seldom dealt with dreams, fantasies, or concepts of heaven and hell; it was strictly concerned with the portrayal of nature—mountains, trees, flowers, birds, animals, insects, waterfalls, nights, days, seasons. For the Japanese hokku poet, nature is a mirror of the enlightened self; the poet must see and hear things as they really are by making his or her consciousness pure, natural, and unemotional. "Japanese poets," Noguchi wrote, "go to Nature to make life more meaningful, sing of flowers and birds to make humanity more intensive" (*SJP*, 37).

As opposed to his later poetry, Pound's early poetry, and his hokku-like poems in particular, have little to do with his personal emotion or thought. In such poetry, Pound is not really concerned with thought and emotion. If Pound's hokku sounded intellectual or emotional, it did so only to an English reader who was still Arnoldian in his or her taste and unfamiliar with the imagist movement of the 1910s, not to mention with "the spirit of Japanese poetry" Noguchi tried to introduce to the English audience. Japanese poetry shuns symbols and metaphors because figurative language might lessen the intensity and spontaneity of a newly experienced sensation. Such expressions would not only undermine originality in the poet's sensibility but also resort to intellectualization—as well as what Noguchi, perhaps echoing Matthew Arnold, called "a criticism of life," which traditionally Japanese poetry was not (*Through the Torii*, 159).

As partly suggested in the remarks on super-position quoted above, the hokku also provided a structural model for Pound's version of imagism. Acknowledging that the Japanese had evolved this short form of poetry, Pound seized upon the unique form of "super-position" that, he observed, constitutes a hokku. To him, the hokku often consists of two disparate images in juxtaposition, and yet it appears as a single image. Lacking the copula "is" or the preposition "like," the image cannot be metaphoric or analogical. As Pound's account of the composition of the metro poem shows, he had no intention of likening the image of the beautiful faces in the crowd to the image of petals on a wet, black bough or of making one image suggestive or representative of the other.[36] If one image is used to suggest another or to represent another, both images would be weakened. But if one image is used to generate or intensify another, and the other image, in turn, intensifies the first one, then the whole poem as one image would be intensified.

The key to the superpository structure of Pound's image is a coalescence of two unlike images. Such an image must be generated "in an instant of time," as Pound cautions in his essay "A Few Don'ts" (*Literary Essays*, 4).

Creating such an image needs no preparations, no explanations, no qualifications; Pound calls "the 'natural course of events' the exalted moment, the vision unsought or at least the vision gained without machination" (*Spirit of Romance*, 97). In *The Spirit of Japanese Poetry* and *The Spirit of Romance*, Noguchi and Pound respectively emphasized this revelatory moment when high poetry must be written. But such a parallel in their poetics does not necessitate that one's ideas came from the other's. Pound's observations might have been made independently.

To illustrate the energy latent in this transformation of images, Pound provided an anecdote: "I once saw a small child go to an electric light switch and say, 'Mamma, can I *open* the light?' She was using the age-old language of exploration, the language of art" ("Vorticism," 466). Although he later became interested in Fenollosa's explanation that written Chinese characters denote action, he was first attracted to the poetics of the hokku, what he called "the sense of exploration . . . the beauty of this sort of knowing" ("Vorticism," 466–67). Noguchi expounded this poetics in terms of an intensive art by referring to Kikaku's celebrated hokku, as discussed earlier:

> Autumn's full moon:
> Lo, the shadows of a pine tree
> Upon the mats!

The beauty of the harvest moon is not only humanized but also intensified by the shadow of a tree Kikaku saw on the tatami mats. "Really," Noguchi wrote, "it was my first opportunity to observe the full beauty of the light and shadow, more the beauty of the shadow in fact, far more luminous than the light itself, with such a decorativeness, particularly when it stamped the dustless mats as a dragon-shaped ageless pine tree" ("What Is a Hokku Poem?" 357). The situation here, shared by Pound and Noguchi, is one of finding, discovering, and hence of inventing the new.

As if to bear out Pound's vorticist thinking in poetry, Noguchi made a modest proposal for English poets. "I think," he wrote, "it is time for them to live more of the passive side of Life and Nature, so as to make the meaning of the whole of them perfect and clear." To the Japanese mind, an intensive art can be created not from action but from inaction. Noguchi thus argued that the larger part of life "is builded upon the unreality by the strength of which the reality becomes intensified" (*SJP*, 24–25). Noguchi's paradox was echoed in Pound's statement about vorticism. To Pound, an intensive art is not an emphatic art. By an intensive art, Pound meant that "one is concerned with the relative intensity, or relative significance, of different sorts of expression. . . . They are more dynamic. I do not mean they are more emphatic, or that they are yelled louder" ("Vorticism," 468).

Pound illustrated this intensive art with a hokku-like sentence in his essay "Affirmations," first published in the *New Age* in 1915:

> The pine-tree in mist upon the far hill looks
> like a fragment of Japanese armour.

The images appear in simile form, but Pound has no intention of intensifying the beauty of either image by comparing it to that of the other. "In either case," he points out, "the beauty, in so far as it is beauty of form, is the result of 'planes in relation.' . . . The tree and the armour are beautiful because their diverse planes overlie in a certain manner." Unlike the sculptor or the painter, the poet, who must use words to intensify his art, Pound says, "may cast on the reader's mind a more vivid image of either the armour or the pine by mentioning them close together . . . for he works not with planes or with colours but with the names of objects and of properties. It is his business so to use, so to arrange, these names as to cast a more definite image than the layman can cast" (*Gaudier-Brzeska*, 120–21).

Critics have shown over the years that Pound's idea of vorticism underlies not only his short imagistic poems but also his longer pieces, such as the *Cantos, Cathay*, and his translation of noh plays. Noguchi, on the other hand, attempted to intensify an image in a poem longer than the hokku by endowing it with action and autonomy. "The Passing of Summer" (1909), for instance, reads:

> An empty cup whence the light of passion is drunk!—
> To-day a sad rumour passes through the trees,
> A chill wind is borne by the stream,
> The waves shiver in pain;
> Where now the cicada's song long and hot?
> (*Pilgrimage*, 1:68)

Such visual images as an empty cup, the chilly wind blowing over the stream, and the shivering waves do not simply denote the passing of summer; they constitute its action. Similarly, experiences, or memories of experiences, like drinking "the light of passion" and hearing "the cicada's song long and hot" do not merely express the poet's nostalgia or sentiment about the summer; these images, rather than being metonymies, recreate the actions of the summer itself.[37] In Noguchi's poetry, as in the hokku, poetry and sensation are spontaneously conjoined and intensified, to leave no room for rationalism or moralism.

Much of Pound's early work and Noguchi's clearly reflects this accord between the imagists and Noguchi. It is true that while Pound was fascinated by Japanese poetics, he was also interested in vorticism as applied to visual arts, as his commentary on such artists as Gaudier-Brzeska, Brancusi, and Picasso indicates. Through the Poets' Club, Pound was also closely associated with Hulme, Flint, Aldington, Upward, and others, some of whom were initially attracted to Japanese color prints by such painters as Utamaro and Hokusai exhibited in the British Museum. There is clear evidence that Pound's associates also tried their hand at hokku with various degrees of seriousness and success.

By the mid-1910s, imagism had indeed become the literary zeitgeist, and any poet living in London would have received some influence from the Japanese sources. Noguchi's English poems had been widely circulated in London well before September 1914, when Pound's "Vorticism" essay appeared, and Noguchi's essay on hokku in *Rhythm* and his book *The Spirit of Japanese Poetry* were published in January 1913 and March 1914, respectively. The material in the essay and the book was delivered as a series of lectures during his stay in England from December 1913 to April 1914. In these circumstances, it is hardly conceivable that the imagists did not acquaint themselves with Noguchi's ideas. Even though Pound's modernist theory might partly have derived from other sources, one can scarcely overlook the direct link between Japanese poetics and Pound's imagism through Noguchi.

6

ALBERT CAMUS'S *THE STRANGER*
AND RICHARD WRIGHT'S *THE OUTSIDER*

1

Critics have largely regarded the Harper edition of *The Outsider* published in 1953 as existential. They have also noted parallels between Wright and European existentialist novelists in the treatment of the metaphysical rebel, calling Cross Damon's philosophy nihilistic.[1] It is well-known that Wright lived and wrote *The Outsider* in France, where he maintained a close contact with such influential writers as Camus, Sartre, and de Beauvoir. Moreover, these French existentialists can conveniently be placed side by side with Wright's protagonist, who contemplates human existence through his exhaustive reading of Nietzsche, Hegel, Kierkegaard, and Dostoevsky.

But Arnold Rampersad's edition of *The Outsider*, published by the Library of America in 1991, suggests that Wright's original intention for *The Outsider* was not as existential as critics have thought. The Harper edition, as Rampersad has shown, the original length of 741 typescript pages was shortened to 620 pages, a 16.3 percent deduction of the original manuscript. The difference between the two versions is partly stylistic, but it also has to do with Wright's intention for the book as racial discourse. Most of the block cuts suggest that the novel as originally conceived is not as avowedly existentialist as critics have characterized the Harper edition. The original version suggests that Cross Damon is not a black man in name only. Not only is his plight real, but all the incidents and characters he is involved with, which at times appear to be clumsily constructed symbols, nonetheless express well-digested ideas. He is not "pathetically insane" as a reviewer described him.[2] The novel bewildered black reviewers as well, not because of Wright's novel philosophy, but because Wright seemed to have lost contact with his native soil.[3] But a detailed comparison of the two versions will show not only that Cross Damon as originally portrayed is not simply an embodiment of a half-baked philosophy, but also that he is a genuine product of American society.

Wright's intention in the Harper edition of *The Outsider* is to express a version of existentialism in which human action is taken as the result of an individual's choice and will. Early in the novel Damon's wife Gladys complains to her husband that white people intimidate her. He in turn admonishes her that one must exert one's will to exist. "It's up to us to make ourselves something," he argues. "A man creates himself" (*TO*, 51). Initially Damon is attracted to his Communist mentor Gil Blount for his ideology and action. After his death, Damon realizes that Blount epitomized "a modern man." "Life, to him," Damon reflects, "was a game devoid of all significance except that which he put into it" (370). Damon, however, killed Blount because Blount had attempted to wield the Communists' power over Damon's will.

Corollary to Damon's idea of self-creation is his abhorrence of human dependency on others. Damon loses his interest in Gladys because, as Wright observes, "it was the helplessness of dependence that made her fret so. Men made themselves and women were made only through men" (*TO*, 51). In order to characterize modern man as self-reliant and autonomous, Wright deleted a number of passages in which people are portrayed as passive and dependent on others. Both editions of the novel begin with a scene where Damon, tired with his long work at the post office, tries to rest his body on one of his companions. But his friend, a short man, chides him, saying, "Hell, naw! Stand on your own two big flat feet, Cross!" (*TO*, 1, *Later Works*, 369). The opening scene is, indeed, identical between the two versions except for the three sentences allusive to a racial feature of the black men: "Tiny crystals trembled whitely between their dark faces. The shoulders of their overcoats were laced with icy filigrees; dapples of moisture glowed diamondlike on their eyebrows where the heat of their blood was melting the snow" (*Later Works*, 371). This passage is deleted, since Damon and his black friends, conscious of their racial background, give the impression that having been born black is responsible for their plight. Such an implication is in contrary to Wright's portrait of a self-made man.

Among the sequences and incidents cut out of the original manuscript, the extended Hattie episode, which runs fourteen pages in two scenes, is the longest. Hattie is a young black widow who is lost in her life and is trying to cling to others for help. Damon finds himself easily tempted by this lonely woman but he staves off her temptation. Even before this event,

Wright also deletes a sentence from Damon's conversation with Ely Houston, a district attorney he happens to meet on the train; Damon says to Houston, "The American Negro, because of his social and economic situation, is a congenital coward" (*Later Works*, 505). Even though Damon characterizes the African American as a helpless victim of society rather than a courageous, self-sufficient individual, he is not aware that he himself remains a coward. The irony in Wright's portrayal of Cross Damon rests in the fact that while Damon disparages African American women like Gladys and Hattie as weak and dependent, he himself does not always act like a strong man. The original manuscript includes an episode in which Damon, pursued by the Communist agents, desperately tries to save his life by begging Hattie to hide him in her apartment and promising to give her $250 for her help. An existentialist like Meursault in Camus's *The Stranger* and Raskolnikov in Dostoevsky's *Crime and Punishment* would not stoop to such an action as does Wright's protagonist.

Cross Damon as originally conceived strikes one as an egotist, a selfish individual, rather than an indifferent, audacious human being compelled to do nothing in the face of the void and meaningless universe. For this reason, Wright seems to have excised the two opening paragraphs of book four, entitled "Despair." In this passage Damon confesses his selfish motive for murdering Blount and Herndon. Damon accomplished his goal, Wright observes, "as much for a dawning reverence for her as for the protection of his own self-love" (*Later Works*, 618).

In the original version of the novel, the character of Eva Blount, Damon's love, is strikingly similar to that of Damon. He falls in love with Eva because both have suffered from a loveless marriage. In stark contrast to an existentialist, Eva is as passionately in search of meaning in existence as is Damon. "Her sense of guilt," Wright says, "was throwing her on his side; she had long been wanting to be free of Gil and now that she was free she wants to unburden her guilt on to someone else, on to Herndon" (*Later Works*, 642). In fact, Wright eliminates this passage to make Eva as selfless and passive a person as Damon; she is portrayed "as calm as marble. Balling a handkerchief in her right fist, she sat looking bleakly in front of her. His eyes caught hers and he saw in them a glint of recognition. Yes, she's with me. She thinks I'm a victim too" (*TO*, 253–54).

Despite the fact that Eva has fallen prey to the Communists as has Damon, Wright's aim in the Harper version is to endow her character with courage and autonomy. To strengthen her individualism, Wright omits two sentences from Eva's diary in which she expresses an outrage against the

Communists: "The Party lifted me up in its hands and showed me to the world, and if I disown them, they'll disown me. . . . What a trap!" (*Later Works*, 594). Such a passage intimates that she has been deprived of freedom and independence and become a helpless victim of the Communists. Omitting this passage makes Eva akin to Damon and hence more attractive to him. His affinity for her, in turn, whets his craving for freedom and independence from a totalitarian philosophy. While his intimate relationship with Eva constitutes a credible event in *The Outsider* as a realistic protest novel, it also plays a crucial role in Wright's dialectics between oppression and freedom.

Wright's chief interest in *The Outsider* lies in an exposition of what freedom means to certain individuals. As Damon disparages Gladys and Hattie, he repudiates his own mother not only because she is the product of the traditional Christianity in the South but also because she failed to challenge the lack of freedom and individualism that prevailed in African American life. To make Mrs. Damon freer of a religious dogma, Wright cuts out a long speech by her in which she admonishes her son to abide by God's law. "If you feel you can't master yourself," she warns him, "then take your problem to God. . . . Life is a promise, son; God promised it to us and we must promise it to others. Without that promise life's nothing. . . . Oh, God, to think that at twenty-six you're lost" (*Later Works*, 391). It is only natural that he should find his peace of mind in a liberal woman like Eva. Wright also tries to show how religion gets in the way of achieving freedom. In his flight to New York, he meets a priest he regards as "a kind of dressed-up savage intimidated by totems and taboos that differed in kind but not in degree from those of the most primitive of peoples." The priest's demeanor shows Damon as if good and evil are not discovered by "the edicts of any God" but by human actions, for it is only the individual who is responsible for the consequences of the actions (*Later Works*, 494).

To Damon, law, like religion, is created to inhibit human actions. A truly liberated individual does not control the actions under the law. Instead, one creates one's own law and abides by it. For this reason, Wright deletes a long passage in which Damon discusses how law has the capacity to inhibit individuality and creativity in human life but at the same time provide the freedom of choice. "Implied in law," Damon asserts, "is a free choice to each man living under the law; indeed, one could almost say a free challenge is embedded in the law" (*Later Works*, 700). Since this ambivalence in Damon's interpretation of law is embodied in Houston, Wright also deletes several sentences that specifically refer to Houston: "Cross shrewdly suspected that Houston, a self-confessed outlaw, knew this, felt it; and it was what had made him become an active defender of the law; he *had* to represent the law in order to protect himself against his own weakness and fear" (*Later Works*, 700). Wright makes such an omission to strengthen his argument that one's moral obligation is to the individual and not to society, as well as to justify his murder of the men who had deprived him of individual freedom.

Wright's emphasis on the autonomy of human action is also reflected in the style of the novel. While Wright partly intended the book to be a social protest, his chief aim was to mold an African American man's life upon existential tenets. As Damon's statement in the original manuscript that the African American is a victim of the social and economic environment is excised from the Harper edition, other descriptions of naturalistic determinism are also deleted. The subway accident in which he is involved makes him feel as if he were imprisoned in himself. He was "so swamped . . . by himself with himself that he could not break forth from behind the bars of that self to claim himself" (*Later Works*, 488). A stranger who witnessed the accident tells Damon, "Brother, your blood is the tomato sauce. Your white guts is the spaghetti. And your flesh is the meat, see? You'd be surprised how like a plate of meatballs and spaghetti you look when you get minced up in one of those subway wrecks" (*Later Works*, 470). Such a description is omitted, for it is a cynical remark about the gruesome condition of a human being.

To make *The Outsider* akin to existential novels by Sartre and Camus, Wright also eliminated much of the profane and sexually allusive language. The Harper edition, for instance, deletes an expression Eva writes in her diary as she accuses the Communists of having deceived her into marrying her husband: "Goddam this deception!" (*Later Works*, 595). In describing the ground where Joe, a friend of his Damon kills, lies, Wright originally wrote, "some of the grounds spilled over a bloodstained Kotex which still retained the curving shape of having fitted tightly and recently against the lips of some vagina; there was a flattened grapefruit hull whose inner pulpy fibres held a gob of viscous phlegm" (*Later Works*, 485). The quoted passage was changed to "some of the grounds spilled over a flattened grapefruit hull" (*TO*, 115). Similarly, the passages including such sentences as "Sarah's breasts heaved" and "her lips hung open and she breathed orgiastically" are deleted (*Later Works*, 556).

At a crucial point in the development of the story, Wright is at the pains of revising the original manuscript to express an existential philosophy. On the one hand, Wright comes to recognize a close relationship between Damon's actions and his social and psychological backgrounds; on the other hand, he tries to demonstrate in Damon's life a nihilistic view of the world stated earlier in the book that "man is nothing in particular" (*TO*, 135). As the story progresses, however, the feeling of isolation and loneliness increasingly dictates Damon's action. Reading Eva's diary makes him realize that Eva's love for him came out of her sympathy for his oppressed life just as his love for her was intensified by his compassion for her personal predicament. This revelation leads to his statement on his deathbed—"To make a bridge from man to man" (*TO*, 439)—a clear contradiction to his earlier view of human beings.

Though Damon's final vision makes the Harper version of *The Outsider* less existential than originally intended, it suggests that Wright is ambivalent in expressing his view of human existence. In both versions, he intended to portray an outsider as an individual with courage and audacity, but as the story unfolds, Damon finds himself increasingly alienated and realizes that, however imperfect society may be, he cannot live without relating to others. It is ironic that Wright's hero is determined to be an outsider but in his heart he wants to be an insider. A character like Cross Damon is sometimes larger than the author's occasional philosophy, and he is able to speak for himself. Wright the philosopher only gets in his way; Wright the artist remains true to him. In the end, the interest of the story lies not in Wright's mind but in his heart, in the genuine feelings Wright himself had experienced in American society.

2

A comparison of *The Outsider* with Camus's *The Stranger*, a typical French existentialist novel, further suggests that *The Outsider* is not as existential as it appears. Although the likeness in theme, character, and event between *The Outsider* and *The Stranger* has been pointed out, it has not been studied in any detail. In general, critics have regarded Wright's philosophy in *The Outsider* as nihilistic, as noted earlier. Charles I. Glicksberg, in "Existentialism in *The Outsider*" and "The God of Fiction," saw parallels between Wright and Camus in the treatment of the metaphysical rebel, calling Cross Damon's philosophy most consistently nihilistic.[4] More recently, critics have demonstrated Camus's influences on Wright in his conception of Cross Damon. According to Michel Fabre, Wright read *The Stranger* in the American edition at a very slow pace, "weighing each sentence, 'admiring' its damn good narrative prose," and remarked:

It is a neat job but devoid of passion. He makes his point with dispatch and his prose is solid and good. In America a book like this would not attract much attention for it would be said that he lacks feeling. He does however draw his character very well. What is of course really interesting in this book is the use of fiction to express a philosophical point of view. That he does with ease. I now want to read his other stuff.[5] (qtd. Fabre, "Wright," 191)

Edward Margolies, in his comparison of Damon and Meursault, pointed out that "both men kill without passion, both men appear unmoved by the death of their mothers; both men apparently are intended to represent the moral and emotional failure of the age."[6] (135).

It would be quite tempting to compare the two works if they were the products of the same age and the particular philosophy they dealt with was in vogue. Moreover Camus's indifferent philosopher can conveniently be placed side by side with Wright's protagonist, a self-styled existentialist. One suspects, however, that the comparison of the two novels would never have been made unless the two novelists were both caught up in the philosophical context of existentialism. This meant that the literary likeness was taken for granted. Meursault kills a man; he is charged with a murder, tried, and convicted in a world of court, jury, and judge. But Damon kills more than one man, not only an enemy but also a friend, a mentor, and an ally, and is responsible for the suicide of a woman he loves. But he is never charged with a crime, brought to a trial, or convicted. Unlike Meursault, who encounters his death in the world of daylight in Algiers, Damon is himself murdered by two men, the agents of the Communist Party, on a dimly lit street in New York. Such a comparison makes *The Outsider* fiction of a different order, brought together with *The Stranger* in an assumed definition of human existence in the modern world. Although the two novels are regarded largely as existentialist, giving attention to the crucial details that differentiate the narratives would make Meursault and Damon radically different in their ideology and action.

It is time to reexamine *The Outsider* as a discourse on race; that is, it is important to redefine the African American tradition and experience that underlies this work. Comparing this novel with an avowedly existentialist novel like Camus's *The Stranger* will reveal that Wright's novel is not what critics have characterized. A detailed comparison of this novel with *The Stranger*, a novel of another culture and another tradition, will show not only that Wright's hero is not simply an embodiment of a half-baked philosophy, but also that he is a genuine product of the African American experience. Such a reevaluation of the book will also clarify misconceptions about his other books.

The disparity of the two books becomes even more apparent if it is seen in the light of the less fashionable literary philosophy, naturalism. To some American writers, such as Stephen Crane and Theodore Dreiser, naturalism is a doctrine that asserts the indifference of the universe to the will of human beings. The indifference of the universe is most poignantly described by Stephen Crane in "The Open Boat": "When it occurs to a man that nature does not regard him as important, and that she feels she would not maim the universe by disposing of him, he at first wishes to throw bricks at the temple, and he hates deeply the fact that there are no bricks and no temples. Any visible expression of nature would surely be pelleted with his jeers" (Crane, 294). Dreiser describes the forces of nature in *Sister Carrie*:

> Among the forces which sweep and play throughout the universe, untutored man is but a wisp in the wind. Our civilisation is still in a middle stage, scarcely beast, in that it is no longer wholly guided by instinct; scarcely human, in that it is not yet wholly guided by reason. . . . As a beast, the forces of life aligned him with them; as a man, he has not yet wholly learned to align himself with the forces. In this intermediate stage he wavers—neither drawn in harmony with nature by his instincts nor yet wisely putting himself into harmony by his own free-will. (83)

Although his naturalistic vision is not conveyed with Dreiser's massive detail or analyzed by Zola's experimental method, Camus nevertheless constructs his novel to dramatize a climactic assertion of universal indifference. Wright's novel, on the other hand, is filled with the events and actions that exhibit the world's concerns with human affairs. The outside world is indeed hostile to Damon, a man of great will and passion. Refusing to be dominated by it, he challenges its forces. But Meursault, remaining much of a pawn, is not willing to exert himself against the forces that to him have no relation to existence.

Heredity and environment, the twin elements in naturalistic fiction, are more influential to human action in *The Stranger* than they are in *The Outsider*. Though heredity has little effect on Meursault's behavior, environment does play a crucial role. Meursault is consistently shown as indifferent to any of society's interests and desires: love of God, marriage, friendship, social status. He is averse to financial success or political power;

he receives only what is given or acts when acted upon. He is, like Dreiser's Sister Carrie, "a wisp in the wind"; he is more drawn than he draws (*Carrie*, 83–84). This explains his passivity. Camus painstakingly accounts for human action just as Zola or Dreiser demonstrates the circumstances under which it occurs.

Camus shows that Meursault, who had no desire to kill the Arab, merely responded to pressures applied by natural forces. The blinding sun and the glittering knife held by the Arab caused Meursault to fear and forced him to pull the trigger. If the man with the knife had been a Frenchman, Meursault would not have acted with such rashness. Given the history of Arab-French colonial relations in the background, Meursault's antagonism toward the Arabs might have subconsciously triggered his action. Camus's emphasis in this narrative, however, is placed on the elements of chance— that is, the blinding sun and the glittering knife—rather than on the social elements such as the disharmony between the French and the Arabs.

This idea of chance and determinism is absent in Wright's concept of human action shown in *The Outsider*. Each of the four murders committed by Damon is premeditated, the suicide of a woman is directly related to his actions, and his own murder is a reprisal to the actions he could have avoided. In each case it is made clear that Damon had control over his action; in each murder he was capable of exerting his will or satisfying his desire. In marked contrast to Meursault, Damon exerts himself to attain the essences of his own existence. They are the very embodiments of the abstract words of society—friendship, love, marriage, success, equality, and freedom—to which he cannot remain indifferent. Wright takes pains to show that they are not empty dreams. The fact that Damon has been deprived of them at one time or another proves that they constitute his existence.

The Outsider represents a version of existentialism in which human action is viewed as the result of an individual's choice and will. To Wright, the individual's action must be assertive and, if need be, aggressive. This is perhaps why he was more attracted to Sartre and de Beauvoir than to Camus. In an unpublished journal Wright wrote, "Sartre is quite of my opinion regarding the possibility of human action today, that it is up to the individual to do what he can to uphold the concept of what it means to be human. The great danger, I told him, in the world today is the very feeling and conception of what is a human might well be lost. He agreed. I feel very close to Sartre and Simone de Beauvoir."[7]

If Wright's protagonist is considered an existentialist actively in search of an essence in the meaningless existence, Meursault seems a passive existentialist compelled to do nothing in the face of the void and meaning-less universe. Focused on the definition of existence, their views are alike; Damon at one time says, perhaps uncharacteristically, "Maybe man is nothing in particular" (*TO*, 135). The point of disparity in their worldview, however, is the philosophy of the absurd. While Meursault is convinced of the essential absurdity of existence, Damon is not. If one considers human life inherently meaningful, as does Damon, then it follows that his action to seek love, power, and freedom on earth is also meaningful. Conversely, however, if one judges life absurd, as does Meursault, then it follows that his action is also absurd.

What is absurd is this dilemma of Meursault between his recognition of chaos and his search for order. It is the conflict between his awareness of death and his dream of eternity. It is the disparity between the essential mystery of all existence and one's demand for explanation. The fundamen-tal difference in attitude between Meursault and Damon is that Meursault seeks neither order nor a dream of eternity nor explanation, while Damon is passionately in search of such an essence. Meursault's passivity, more-over, stems from Camus's attitude toward his art. Camus tries to solve the existentialist dilemma by arguing that an artist is not concerned to find order, to have a dream of eternity, or to demand explanation, but to experi-ence all things given. The artist describes; he does not solve the mystery of the universe that is both infinite and inexplicable.

Whereas Camus's hero resists action, Wright's is compelled to act. Wright endows his hero with the freedom to create an essence. Damon's revolt is not so much against the nothingness and meaninglessness of existence as it is against the inability of human beings' attempt to make illogical phe-nomena logical. In the eyes of the public, Damon is as guilty of his murder of the fascist as Raskolnikov is guilty of his murder of the pawnbroker in *Crime and Punishment*. As Damon's murder is analogous to Raskolnikov's, Damon's killing of his friend Joe is similar to Raskolnikov's killing of the pawnbroker's sister, Lizaveta. In the case of Joe or Lizaveta, the murderer has no malice toward the victim but intentionally kills the victim to protect himself from prosecution. Both crimes result from premeditated actions; Meursault's killing of the Arab is accidental.

Readers may find a contradiction in Damon's view of the world. Ear-lier in the story Damon considers human beings "nothing in particular" (135), but at the end of his life he asserts, "We must find some way of be-ing good to ourselves. . . . Man is all we've got. . . . I wish I could ask men to meet themselves" (439). Likewise, his inaction initially makes him see nothingness and meaninglessness in human existence, but in the end his action results in his realization of loneliness and "horror" on earth (440). In short, what appears to be a contradiction in Damon's view of existence is rather a reflection of activeness and aggressiveness in his character.

The chief difference in philosophy between the two books derives from the differing philosophies of the two novelists, Wright and Camus. Though both men are regarded as rebels against society, the motive behind the rebellion differs. Damon rebels against society because it oppresses him by depriving him of the values he and society share, such as freedom in association and opportunity for success. Meursault is aloof to society because he does not believe in such values. In fact, he does not believe in marriage or family loyalty. His obdurate attitude toward society is clearly stated in Camus's preface to the American edition of *The Stranger*:

> I summarized *The Stranger*—a long time ago, with a remark that I admit was highly paradoxical: "In our society any man who does not weep at his mother's funeral runs the risk of being sentenced to death." I only meant that the hero of my book is condemned because he does not play the game. In this respect, he is foreign to the society in which he lives; he wanders, on the fringe, in the suburbs of private, solitary, sensual life. And this is why some readers have been tempted to look upon him as a piece of social wreckage. A much more accurate idea of the character, at least one much closer to the author's intentions, will emerge if one asks just how Meursault doesn't play the game. The reply is a simple one: he refuses to lie. To lie is not only to say *more* than is true, and, as far as the human heart is concerned, to express more than one feels. This is what we all do, every day, to simplify life. He says what he is, he refuses to hide his feelings, and immediately society feels threatened.[8]

If Meursault is characterized by his refusal to play society's game, Damon is a type of person who cannot resist playing such a game. If society is threatened by Meursault's indifference to it, it is Damon, rather than society, that feels threatened.

This estranged personality of Meursault is reflected in his relationship with his mother. Some critics have used his calm acceptance of the bereavement as evidence for his callousness.[9] But the fact that he does not cry at his mother's funeral would not necessarily suggest that he is devoid of emotions. Had Meursault thought her death would have spared her the misery of her life or that death would be a happier state for human beings, he should not have been aggrieved by the passing away of his mother. What makes him a peculiar character, however, is the fact that an experience that would be a traumatic one for others is for him devoid of any meaning. *The Stranger* opens with the protagonist's unconcerned reaction to his mother's death: "Mother died today. Or, maybe, yesterday; I can't be sure" (1). But as the story progresses, he becomes a more sensitive individual. He is indeed disturbed during the vigil by the weeping of his mother's friend. And every detail, whether it is the driving home of the screws in the coffin lid or the starting of the prayers by the priest, is minutely described. Throughout the story there is no mention of Meursault's disliking his mother. He fondly reflects on her habits and personality; he affectionately calls her *Maman*.

By contrast, Damon's relationship with his mother betrays not only the estrangement between them but also his hostility to the racist society that had reared her. He rejects his mother not only because she reminds him of southern black piety but also because she is an epitome of racial and sexual repression:

> He was conscious of himself as a frail object which had to protect itself against a pending threat of annihilation. This frigid world was suggestively like the one which his mother, without knowing it, had created for him to live in when he had been a child. . . . This God's NO-face had evoked in his pliable boy's body an aching sense of pleasure by admonishing him to shun pleasure as the tempting doorway opening blackly onto hell; had too early awakened in him a sharp sense of sex by thunderingly denouncing sex as the sin leading to eternal damnation. . . . Mother love had cleaved him: a wayward sensibility that distrusted itself, a consciousness that was conscious of itself. Despite this, his sensibilities had not been repressed by God's fearful negations as represented by his mother; indeed, his sense of life had been so heightened that desire boiled in him to a degree that made him afraid. (17–18)

The young Damon's desire to free himself from such a bondage is closely related to his inability to love any black woman, as shown by his relationship with Gladys, his estranged wife, or Dot, his pregnant mistress. The only woman he loves is the white woman Eva. He feels an affinity with her, for he discovers that she, too, is a fearful individual and that she had been deceived into marrying her husband because of a political intrigue. He is, moreover, tormented by the envenomed abstraction of racial and political myths. Unlike the white phonograph salesman, who seduces the wife of a black man in "Long Black Song," he is permanently frustrated. Since *The Outsider* portrays a rich variety of racial and political animosities, his love life is defined in terms of the forces beyond his control. To him, the consummation of his love for Eva means the ultimate purpose of his new existence. It is understandable that when that goal appears within reach and yet is taken away from him, he finds only "the horror" that he has dreaded all his life (440).

Meursault's relationship with women, on the contrary, is totally uninhibited socially and psychologically. His relationship with Marie is free from the kinds of racial and political entanglements that smother Damon's relationship with Eva. Meursault, the perfectly adjusted man, does not suffer from any kind of repression. His action for love is motivated from within according to logic, rather than convention or sentiment. In his life, love of woman is a natural instinct, as is eating or resting; love is more akin to friendship than to marriage. He helps Raymond, for he says, "I wanted to satisfy Raymond, as I'd no reasons not to satisfy him" (41). Meursault is kind and benevolent as Damon is not; he is relaxed and content as Damon is tense and frustrated.

Meursault's indifference to existence is epitomized by his love life. His attitude toward Marie bears a sort of impersonal, superhuman mode of thought. To the public such an attitude is inhuman, unconventional, and unethical. His view of love is no different from that of death; his sexual relations with Marie begin immediately after his mother's death. If death occurs beyond human control, so does love. His meeting with her takes place by mere coincidence, and the relationship that develops is casual and appears quite innocent:

> While I was helping her to climb on to a raft, I let my hand stray over her breasts. Then she lay flat on the raft, while I trod water. After a moment she turned and looked at me. Her hair was over her eyes and she was laughing. I clambered up on to the raft, beside her. The air was pleasantly warm, and, half jokingly, I let my head sink back upon her lap. She didn't seem to mind, so I let it stay there. I had the sky full in my eyes, all blue and gold, and I could feel Marie's stomach rising and falling gently under my head. We must have stayed a good half-hour on the raft, both of us half asleep. When the sun got too hot she dived off and I followed. I caught up with her, put my arm round her waist, and we swam side by side. She was still laughing. (23–24)

Even when a marriage proposal is made by Marie, his indifference remains intact: "Marie came that evening and asked me if I'd marry her. I said I didn't mind; if she was keen on it, we'd get married" (52).

Meursault's indifference is also reflected in his reaction to the crime of which he is accused. Partly as a corollary to the nature of the crime, he is passive rather than active. Unlike Damon, he commits a crime without malice or intention. He kills the Arab not because he hates the victim but partly because he sympathizes with his friend Raymond, whose life has been threatened. Given this situation, it would be more natural for him to defend his friend than the hostile stranger. Meursault's crime is a crime of logic; it is not a murder. Camus's purpose for using crime in *The Stranger* is to prove that society, rather than the criminal, is in the wrong. Camus's intention is to prove that his hero is innocent, as well as to show that Meursault's logic is far superior to society's. When crime appears innocent, it is innocence that is called upon to justify itself. In *The Stranger*, then, it is society, not the criminal, that is on trial.

Because Meursault is convinced of his innocence, he attains at the end of his life his peace of mind, a Buddhist-like enlightenment. Despite the death sentence, he achieves a nirvana, through which he has liberated himself from the materialistic and egotistic pursuit of life:

> With death so near, Mother must have felt like someone on the brink of free-dom, ready to start life all over again. No one, no one in the world had any right to weep for her. And I, too, felt ready to start life all over again. It was as if that great rush of anger had washed me clean, emptied me of hope, and, gazing up at the dark sky spangled with its signs and stars, for the first time, the first, I laid my heart open to the benign indifference of the universe. (154)

Damon is also convinced of his innocence at the end of his life. What the two novels share is not only that the hero is prosecuted by society but also that society—the prosecutor, jurors, and judge—seems to him to be always in the wrong. Because Camus's hero refuses to play society's game, he is sentenced to death by society. Society expects him to grieve over his mother's death and refrain from having a casual affair with a woman during the mourning. But Wright's hero, induced to play society's game, loses in the end. He is tempted to participate in the normal activities of society such as a love affair and a political association. Tasting his agonizing defeat and dying, he utters:

I wish I had some way to give the meaning of my life to others. . . . To make a bridge from man to man . . . Starting from scratch every time is . . . is no good. Tell them not to come down this road. . . . We must find some way of being good to ourselves. . . . We're different from what we seem. . . . Maybe worse, maybe better . . . But certainly different . . . We're strangers to ourselves. (439)

The confession at the end of his life suggests that he, unlike Meursault, has always felt obliged to justify his actions. He has finally realized that they always collided with society's interests and values. As an outsider, he trusted no one, not even himself, nor did society trust him. While maintaining in his last breath that "in my heart . . . I'm . . . innocent" (440), he is judging society guilty. While Meursault is a victim of his own crime, Damon is a victim not only of his own crime but also of society's. Meursault, who refuses to justify his actions, always feels innocent: "I wasn't conscious of any 'sin'; all I knew was that I'd been guilty of a criminal offense" (148).

Although both novels employ crime as a thematic device, the focus of the author's idea differs. Camus's center of interest is not crime but its consequences—its psychological effect on his hero. Before committing his crime, Meursault is presented as a stranger who finds no meaning in life. After he is sentenced to death, he realizes for the first time that his life has been enveloped in the elusive beauty of the world. "To feel it so like myself, indeed, so brotherly," he says, "made me realize that I'd been happy, and that I was happy still" (154). In *The Outsider* crime is used, like accidental death or suicide, to create a new life for the hero. He murders the fascist Herndon as a reprisal; he intentionally kills the Communist Blount out of his desire for a white woman. In contrast to Camus's hero, to whom death has brought life and happiness, Wright's hero in the end is once more reminded of his own estrangement and horror. The kind of fear Damon suffers at the end of his struggle is clearly absent in Meursault's life. A critic, in comparing Meursault to Clyde Griffiths, the hero of Theodore Dreiser's *An American Tragedy*, comments, "Passivity in *L'Étranger* is strength, and only the strong can be indifferent. When Meursault receives this almost Buddhist illumination, he loses the two great distractions from life: hope and fear. He becomes happy, rather than terrified, in the face of his expected execution; he no longer hopes for some wild chance to deliver him from it. This prisoner is alone and freed, from within."[10]

The two novelists' divergent attitudes toward the problems of crime and guilt are also reflected in the style and structure of their works. *The Stranger* is swift in pace and dramatic in tone, and displays considerable subjectivity, involving the reader in the consciousness of the hero. The reader's involvement in the hero's dialectics is intensified because the book consists of two parts dealing with the same issue. The first part involves the reader in a few days of Meursault's life, ending with his crime; the second reinvolves the reader in the same experiences through the trial in court. Since the hero's experiences are viewed from different angles, they never strike one as monotonous or repetitious. The chief reason for the juxtaposition is for the hero, and for Camus, to convince the reader that what appears to society to be a crime is not at all a crime in the eyes of an existentialist.

This juxtaposition also elucidates the discontinuity and unrelatedness of Meursault's experiences in the first half of the story despite the reordering and construing of those experiences in the second half. As the incidents and actions in the first half are discontinuous, so is time. No days are referred to in Meursault's life except for Saturday and Sunday, his days off. Of the months, only August is mentioned since Meursault, Mason, and Raymond plan to have their vacation together; of the seasons, only summer. By the same token, there is no mention of the day of the month. And Meursault's age is unknown; he is merely "young."[11] As there is nothing unique about his concept of time, there is nothing unique about his experience. As points in time are discontinuous, so are the experiences. At his trial the prosecutor accuses him of moral turpitude, for Meursault shed no tears at his mother's funeral and casually started an affair with Marie immediately after. To Meursault, his mother's death, his behavior at the funeral, and his love affair are not only devoid of meaning in themselves but also discontinuous, unrelated incidents.

Similarly, the threatening gesture of the Arab, the sweating in Meursault's eyebrows, the flashing of the sun against his eyes, and the firing of his revolver occur independently of one another. If his eyes were blinded by the sun and the sweating of his eyebrows, his pulling the trigger on the revolver would not have been a logical reaction. When he is later asked by the prosecutor why he took a revolver with him and went back to the place where the Arab reappeared, he replies that "it was a matter of pure chance" (110). If he does not believe that he is "morally guilty of his mother's death" (128), as charged by the prosecutor, it would be impossible for him to admit that he is morally guilty of the Arab's death. This is precisely the reason why he tells the priest that he is guilty of a criminal offense but that he is not a sinner (148).

Swift and intensive though Camus's probing of Meursault's character is, the reader is deliberately kept from coming to an easy conclusion about Meursault's guilt. By contrast, the reader is instantly made aware of Damon's guilt in unambiguous terms. In *The Outsider*, truly heinous crimes are constructed in advance with all the plausible justifications. Before the reader is made aware of Damon's guilt, the author has defined in unequivocal terms the particular traits in Damon's character and the particular forces in society that had led to his crimes. In so doing, Wright creates a clear pattern by which Damon's motives for crime are shown. Whereas there is no such relatedness in Meursault's motives for action, there emerges in *The Outsider* a chain of events that can scarcely be misinterpreted. The murder of the fascist is committed side by side with that of the Communist. Another example of this relatedness in Damon's actions is, as Edward Margolies observes, the pattern in which Damon rejects the African American women as he destroys the Communists and fascist:

> When Cross murders two Communists and a fascist, his motives seem to derive more from what he regards as his victims' desire to enslave him psychologically, rather than from any detached, intellectualized, conscienceless 'compulsion' on his part. What the Communists and fascist would do to Cross if they had him in their power is precisely what his mother, wife, and mistress had already done to him. In a sense, Cross murders his women when he crushes his enemies. (133)

Damon kills both men with malice: he murders Herndon because of his hatred for the racist as he does Blount because of his passion for the white woman. Unlike Meursault, Damon is conscious of his guilt in the instant of committing the crime.

Because Damon's actions are predetermined and interrelated, Damon is constantly made conscious of the passage of time. The problems in his manhood and marriage, for example, are related to those of his childhood. His desertion of his wife is analogous to his rejection of his mother, just as the Communists' rule over workers in modern times is akin to slavery in the past. *The Outsider* opens with a scene at dawn in which Damon and his friends "moved slowly forward shoulder to shoulder and the sound of their feet tramping and sloshing in the melting snow echoed loudly" (1). Like Jake Jackson in *Lawd Today*, Damon, bored with routine work, finds the passage of time unendurable. In *The Stranger*, Meursault is least concerned with time; he never complains about the monotony of his work. In fact, he dislikes Sundays because he is not doing his routine job. Damon, on the contrary, wishes every day were Sunday, or reminisces about Christmas-time in a certain year. Damon's friend Joe Thomas reminds Damon of their happy days in the past. Joe speaks, "Remember that wild gag he pulled at Christmastime in 19 . . . ? . . . When the hell was that now? Oh, yes! It was in 1945. I'll never forget it. Cross bought a batch of magazines, *Harper's, Atlantic Monthly, Collier's, Ladies' Home Journal,* and clipped out those ads that say you can send your friends a year's subscription as a Christmas gift" (*TO*, 5). More importantly, Meursault says whether he dies at thirty or at seventy it doesn't matter. For him, life has no more significance than death.

For Damon, life is all that matters. If his earlier life is not worth living, a new one must be created. A freak subway accident, in which he is assumed dead, offers him another life and another identity. All his life he plans his action with hope for the future and with denial of the past. Such attitude is emblematic of the African American tradition, the deep-seated black experience, as expressed in the spirituals. While Edgar Allan Poe's writings sometimes smack of morbid romanticism, that erotic longing for death, the spirituals reverberate with energy and vitality and convey the sense of rejuvenation. However violent and destructive Damon may appear, he inherently emerges from this tradition. Meursault, on the other hand, is the very product of the nihilistic spirit that hovered over Europe, particularly France, after World War II.

Despite Wright's effort to relate Damon's actions to his social and psychological backgrounds, *The Outsider* remains an imperfect work as a novel, but as a racial discourse it closely reflects American social reality. Some of its faults are structural rather than philosophical. Given the kind of life Damon has lived, it is not difficult to understand his nihilistic view of the world stated earlier in the book that "man is nothing in particular" (135), or his conciliatory vision that man "is all we've got. . . . I wish I could ask men to meet themselves" (439). But, as some critics have pointed out, it is difficult to believe that a young man with such mundane problems, renewing his life through a subway accident, suddenly emerges as a philosopher discussing Nietzsche, Heidegger, and Kierkegaard. Saunders Redding considers *The Outsider* "often labored, frequently naive, and generally incredible." Another reviewer finds it impossible to relate Wright's "passionless slayer" to the Cross Damon of book one and says, "We can identify with the first Cross Damon, but not the later one. Wright goes out of his way to make this identification impossible."[12] While in *The Stranger* the two parts of the story are so structured that each enlightens the other, those in *The Outsider*, the hero's life before and after the accident, are constructed as though they were two tales.

This weakness notwithstanding, *The Outsider* is unquestionably a powerful statement made by an outsider who refuses to surrender his will to live. One can scarcely find among African American heroes in fiction such a courageous and tenacious, albeit violent, man. As compared to Bigger Thomas, Wright's celebrated hero, Damon stands taller and poles apart simply because Damon is endowed with an intellectual capacity seldom seen in African American fiction. Small wonder that when the novel came out, critics in general, both white and black, who were unfamiliar with such a character, failed to appreciate Wright's intention and execution in the book. Orville Prescott's *New York Times* review was a typical white critic's reaction to *The Outsider*. With due respect for Wright's previous successes, Prescott politely insisted that Wright must have deplored Damon's moral weakness and irrational behavior at the end of the book, and further remarked, "That men as brilliant as Richard Wright feel this way is one of the symptoms of the intellectual and moral crisis of our times." Saunders Redding, quoted earlier, noted that Wright's brand of existentialism, instead of being a device for the representation of truth, "leads away from rather than toward reality." Arna Bontemps was even sarcastic: "The black boy from Mississippi is still exploring. He has had a roll in the hay with the existentialism of Sartre, and apparently he liked it."

The strengths of *The Outsider* become even clearer as this novel is compared with *The Stranger*. Although Damon professes to be a nihilist, as does Meursault, he is never indifferent to human existence as is Meursault. Camus's hero is called a stranger to society as well as to himself; he is indifferent to friendship, marriage, love, success, freedom. Ironically, Damon, who seeks them in life, fails to obtain them. It is ironic, too, that Meursault, at whose disposal they are, is indifferent to them. Wright's hero, an outsider racially as well as intellectually, struggles to get inside. Damon wants to be treated as an individual, not as a second-class citizen or a person whose intellectual ability is not recognized. By contrast, Camus's hero, an insider but a stranger, strives to get outside.

It is hardly coincidental that both novels are eloquent social criticisms in our times. *The Outsider* is an indictment against American society, for not only does Wright demonstrate Damon's innocence, but he also shows most convincingly that men in America "hate themselves and it makes them hate others" (439). *The Stranger*, on the other hand, is an indictment against French society, for Camus proves that while the criminal is innocent, his judges are guilty. More significantly, however, comparison of the two novels of differing characters and traditions reveals that both Wright and Camus are writing ultimately about a universal human condition in modern times.

7

RICHARD WRIGHT'S HAIKU
AND MODERNIST POETICS

One of the most visible East-West artistic, cultural, and literary exchanges that has taken place since the end of World War II was reading and writing haiku in the West. Among others in the West, Richard Wright (1908–1960), the very influential African American writer known for *Native Son* (1940) and *Black Boy* (1945), distinguished himself as a haiku poet by writing over four thousand haiku in the last eighteen months of his life in exile in France. After his death, the Richard Wright estate deposited, in Yale's Beinecke Rare Book and Manuscript Library, his two haiku manuscripts: "This Other World: Projections in the Haiku Manner" and "Four Thousand Haiku."[1] The former was first published in 1998 as *Haiku: This Other World*, edited by me and Robert L. Tener.[2] This edition of the 817 out of four thousand haiku Wright himself had selected has been the largest collection of haiku written in English.

Before trying his hand at writing haiku, Wright had read and studied R. H. Blyth's seminal book of haiku, especially the first volume, *Haiku: Eastern Culture.*[3] Blyth, a foremost Japanologist and Sinologist, was the eminent and most influential haiku scholar and critic who introduced haiku to the West after World War II. Wright—as was Jack Kerouac, a Beat Generation writer known for *On the Road* (1957) and *The Dharma Bums* (1958)—was deeply influenced by the theory and technique of haiku composition that Blyth demonstrated with many of the well-known haiku by the four great masters—Matsuo Basho (1644–1694), Yosa Buson (1721–1783), Kobayashi Issa (1763–1827), and Masaoka Shiki (1867–1902). Reading the haiku by these masters, Wright became familiar with the classic Japanese poetics, as well as with modernist poetics.

131

The modernist movement of haiku, which took placed toward the end the nineteenth century, was spearheaded by a young poet, Masaoka Shiki. He assailed the tradition of haiku established in the seventeenth century by publishing his controversial essay "Criticism of Basho." He urged his fellow poets to express their subjective thoughts and feelings in haiku. He advised his followers that haiku should be a depiction not only of nature but also of humanity, and that humanity should be represented by the author of a haiku himself or herself. In short, he urged his followers to write haiku to please themselves.

Yone Noguchi, who played the central role in introducing haiku to the West and to W. B. Yeats and Ezra Pound, in particular, was not entirely persuaded by Shiki's manifesto but was nonetheless drawn to his modernist techniques of haiku. Shiki was in opposition to the classic tradition of suppressing subjectivity but was in agreement with such aesthetic principles as *yugen*, *sabi*, and *wabi*.

As haiku has developed over the centuries, it has established certain aesthetic principles. To define and illustrate them is difficult since they refer to subtle perceptions and complex states of mind in the creation of poetry. Above all, these principles are governed by the national character developed over the centuries. Having changed in meaning, they do not necessarily mean the same today as they did in the seventeenth century. Discussion of these terms, furthermore, proves difficult simply because poetic theory does not always correspond to what poets actually write. It has also been true that the aesthetic principles for haiku are often applied to other genres of Japanese art such as noh play, flower arrangement, and the tea ceremony.

One of the most delicate principles of Eastern art is *yugen*. Originally *yugen* in Japanese art was an element of style pervasive in the language of noh. In reference to the *Works* by Zeami, the author of many of the extant noh plays, Arthur Waley expounds this difficult term *yugen*:

> It is applied to the natural grace of a boy's movements, to the gentle restraint of a nobleman's speech and bearing. "When notes fall sweetly and flutter delicately to the ear," that is the *yūgen* of music. The symbol of *yūgen* is "a white bird with a flower in its beak." "To watch the sun sink behind a flower-clad hill, to wander on and on in a huge forest with no thought of return, to stand upon the shore and gaze after a boat that goes hid by far-off islands, to ponder on the journey of wild-geese seen and lost among the clouds"—such are the gates to *yūgen*.[4]

Such scenes convey a feeling of satisfaction and release as does the catharsis of a Greek play, but *yugen* differs from catharsis because it has little to do with the emotional stress caused by tragedy. *Yugen* functions in art as a means by which human beings can comprehend the course of nature. Although *yugen* seems allied with a sense of resignation, it has a far different effect on the human psyche. A certain type of noh play like *Takasago* celebrates the order of the universe ruled by heaven. The mode of perception in the play may be compared to that of a pine tree with its evergreen needles, the predominant representation on the stage. The style of *yugen* can express either happiness or sorrow. Cherry blossoms, however beautiful they may be, must fade away; love between man and woman is inevitably followed by sorrow.

This mystery and inexplicability that surrounds the order of the universe had a strong appeal to a classic haiku poet like Basho. His "The Old Pond" shows that while the poet describes a natural phenomenon realistically, he conveys his instant perception that nature is infinitely deep and absolutely silent:

> The old pond
> A frog jumped in—
> The sound of the water.[5]

> Furu ike ya
> Kawazu tobi komu
> Mizu no oto

Such attributes of nature are not ostensibly stated; they are hidden. The tranquility of the old pond with which the poet was struck remained in the background. He did not write, "The rest is quiet"; instead he wrote the third line of the verse: "The sound of the water." The concluding image was given as a contrast to the background enveloped in quiet. Basho's mode of expression is suggestive rather than descriptive, hidden and reserved rather than overt and demonstrative. *Yugen* has all the connotations of modesty, concealment, depth, and darkness. In Zen painting, woods and bays, as well as houses and boats, are hidden; hence, these objects suggest infinity and profundity. Detail and refinement, which would mean limitation and temporariness of life, destroy the sense of permanence and eternity.

Sabi, another frequently used term in Japanese poetics, implies that what is described is aged. Buddha's portrait hung in Zen temples, as the Chinese painter Lian K'ai's *Buddha Leaving the Mountains* suggests, exhibits the Buddha as an old man in contrast to the young figure typically shown in other temples.[6] Zen's Buddha looks emaciated, his environment barren; his body, his tattered clothes, the aged tree standing nearby, the pieces of dry wood strewn around—all indicate that they have passed the prime of their life and function. In this kind of portrait, the old man with thin body is nearer to his soul as the old tree with its skin and leaves fallen is to the very origin and essence of nature.

Sabi is traditionally associated with loneliness. Aesthetically, however, this mode of sensibility is characteristic of grace rather than splendor; it suggests quiet beauty as opposed to robust beauty. Basho's oft-quoted "A Crow," best illustrates this principle:

> A crow
> Perched on a withered tree
> In the autumn evening.[7]

Loneliness suggested by a single crow on a branch of an old tree is reinforced by the elements of time indicated by nightfall and autumn. The picture is drawn with little detail and the overall mood is created by a simple, graceful description of fact. Furthermore, parts of the picture are delineated, by implication, in dark colors: the crow is black, the branch dark brown, the background dusky. The kind of beauty associated with the loneliness in Basho's poem is in marked contrast to the robust beauty depicted in a haiku by Mukai Kyorai (1651–1704), one of Basho's disciples:

> The guardians
> Of the cherry blossoms
> Lay their white heads together.

> Hanamori ya
> Shiroki kashira wo
> Tsuki awase
> (Blyth, *History*, 2:vii)

Some well-known haiku poets in the twentieth century also preserve the sensibility of *sabi*. The predicament of a patient described in this haiku by Ishida Hakyo (1913–1969) arouses *sabi*:

In the hospital room
I have built a nest box but
Swallows appear not.

Byo shitsu ni
Subako tsukuredo
Tsubame kozu[8]

Not only do the first and third lines express facts of loneliness, but also the patient's will to live suggested by the second line evokes a poignant sensibility. To a modernist poet like Hakyo, the twin problems of humanity are loneliness and boredom. He sees the same problems exist in nature, as this haiku by him shows:

The caged eagle;
When lonely
He flaps his wings.

Ori no washi
Sabishiku nareba
Hautsu ka mo
(Blyth, *History*, 2:347)

The feeling of *sabi* is also evoked by the private world of the poet, the situation others cannot envision as this haiku by Nakamura Kusatao (1901–1983), another modernist, shows:

At the faint voices
Of the flying mosquitoes
I felt my remorse.[9]

Ka no koe no
Hisoka naru toki
Kui ni keri
(Blyth, *History*, 2:322)

Closely related to *sabi* is a poetic sensibility called *wabi*. Traditionally *wabi* has been defined in sharp antithesis to a folk or plebeian saying, "*Hana yori dango*" (Rice dumplings are preferred to flowers). Some poets are inspired by the sentiment that human beings desire beauty more than food, what is lacking in animals and other nonhuman beings. *Wabi* refers to the uniquely human perception of beauty stemmed from poverty. *Wabi* is often considered religious, as the saying "Blessed are the poor" implies, but the spiritual aspect of *wabi* is based on the aesthetic rather than the moral sensibility.

Rikyu, the famed artist of the tea ceremony, wrote that food that is enough to sustain the body and a roof that does not leak are sufficient for human life. For Basho, however, an empty stomach was necessary to create poetry. Among Basho's disciples, Rotsu (1649–1738), the beggar-poet, is well known for having come into Basho's legacy of *wabi*. This haiku by Rotsu best demonstrates his state of mind:

> The water-birds too
> Are asleep
> On the lake of Yogo?

> Toridomo mo
> Neitte iru ka
> Yogo no umi
> (Blyth, *History*, 2:viii–ix)

Rotsu portrays a scene with no sight or sound of birds on the desolate lake. The withered reeds rustle from time to time in the chilly wind. It is only Rotsu the beggar and artist who is awake and is able to capture the beauty of the lake.

The sensibilities of *yugen*, *sabi*, and *wabi* all derive from the ways in which Japanese poets have seen nature over the centuries. Although the philosophy of Zen, on which the aesthetics of a poet like Basho is based, shuns emotion and intellect altogether, haiku in its modernist development by such a poet as Shiki is often concerned with one's feeling and thought. A modernist poet, Shiki argued, should put more emphasis on humanity than on nature. A classic haiku poet like Basho, on the contrary, advocated the primacy of nature over humanity. To Shiki, the haiku poet's mission was to create beauty out of humanity, as well as out of nature. His argument bears a resemblance to the privilege in which a Western modernist such as T. S. Eliot took pride. Western modernists in the 1920s believed that their art offers a privileged insight into reality and at the same time, because art creates its own reality, it is not at all concerned with commonplace reality: art is an autonomous activity. In reference to John Donne's poetry, Eliot wrote,

When a poet's mind is perfectly equipped for its work, it is constantly amal-gamating disparate experience; the ordinary man's experience is chaotic, ir-regular, fragmentary. The latter falls in love, or reads Spinoza, and these two experiences have nothing to do with each other, or with the noise of the typewriter or the smell of cooking; in the mind of the poet these experiences are always forming new wholes.[10]

Much like Eliot, Shiki took pride in the privilege he had in creating art out of human reality.

Shiki is well-known in Japan for writing such haiku as "The Wind in Autumn" and "Yellow and White Mums":

The wind in autumn
As for me there are no gods,
There are no Buddhas.

Aki-kaze ya
Ware-ni kami nashi
Hotoke nashi[11]

Yellow and white mums
But at least another one—
I want a red one.

Kigiku shira-giku
Hito moto wa aka mo
Aramahoshi[12]

Because these haiku directly express subjectivity, they have not been con-sidered good haiku by all Japanese readers. On the other hand, Shiki wrote many haiku that thrive on the expression of the beauty the poet creates out of humanity. Subjectivity is expressed indirectly and subtly in such haiku as the following:

A small shop
Carving dolls,—
Chrysanthemums.[13]

Ningyō wo
Kizamu komise ya
Kiku no hana

At the bend of the road,
The temple in sight,—
Wild chrysanthemums.[14]

Tera miete
Komichi no magaru
Nogiku kana

Near the boat-landing,
A small licensed enclosure;
Cotton-plant flowers.[15]

Funatsuki no
Chisaki kuruwa ya
Wata no hana

The first two haiku, "A Small Shop" and "At the Bend of the Road," both depict images of beauty created out of humanity, as well as out of nature. In "A Small Shop," the carving of dolls, a human activity, complements the chrysanthemums, a product of nature. In "At the Bend of the Road," the temple, which represents religion, not only coexists with the wild chrysanthemums but also complements them. In both haiku, beauty is created by the interaction of humanity and nature.

The third haiku, "Near the Boat-Landing," depicts a house of prostitution with cotton-plant flowers. Not only did Shiki portray reality in society, but he also captured beauty in nature. The beautiful scene of nature compensates for the ugly feature of humanity. None of the words in this haiku directly expresses subjectivity, but the reader shares Shiki's feelings about the unfortunate women's livelihood. The reader also shares Shiki's appreciation of the beautiful cotton flowers. Such a haiku can indirectly convey the poet's thoughts and feelings. This haiku is reminiscent of Hawthorne's description in *The Scarlet Letter* of the wild rosebush growing by the door of the prison where Hester Prynne is doomed to wear the scarlet letter "A" for adultery. "Before this ugly edifice," Hawthorne wrote, and between it and the wheel-track of the street, was a grass-plot, much overgrown with burdock, pig-weed, apple-peru, and such unsightly vegetation, which evidently found something congenial in the soil that had so early borne the black flower of civilized society, a prison. But, on one side of the portal, and rooted almost at the threshold, was a wild rose-bush, covered, in this month of June, with its delicate gems, which might be imagined to offer their fragrance and fragile beauty to the prisoner as he went in, and to the condemned criminal as he came forth to his doom, in token that the deep heart of Nature could pity and be kind to him.[16]

Hawthorne's delineation of the scene not only indirectly express the compassion he felt for Hester but also thrives on the interaction of nature and humanity. It shows, as does Shiki's haiku, "Near the Boat-Landing," that the beauty of nature compensates for the ugliness of humanity.

Many of Wright's haiku reflect the features of modernist haiku, such as the expression of subjectivity and the interaction of humanity and nature. Although Wright emulated classic haiku, he consciously or unconsciously departed in many of his compositions from the classic poetics in which the poet effaces human subjectivity. Wright's "A Thin Waterfall," for example, is akin to Basho's "A Crow":

> A thin waterfall
> Dribbles the whole autumn night,—
>   How lonely it is.
> (*HTOW*, 569)

> A crow
> Perched on a withered tree
>   In the autumn evening.[17]
> (Basho)

Basho focuses on a single crow perching on a branch of an old tree, as does Wright on a thin waterfall. Both haiku create the kind of beauty associated with the aesthetic sensibility of *sabi* that suggests loneliness and quietude, the salient characteristics of nature, as opposed to overexcitement and loudness, those of society. As Basho expresses *sabi* with the image of autumn evening, so does Wright with the line "How lonely it is." Subjectivity, however, is absent in Basho's haiku while it is directly expressed by Wright's third line, "How lonely it is." The two haiku are different; while

Basho describes nature for its own sake, Wright interjects his own feelings. Whether Wright and Basho actually felt lonely when writing the haiku is moot.

Wright's "I Would Like a Bell" is comparable to Buson's well-known "On the Hanging Bell" in depicting a spring scene:

> I would like a bell
> Tolling in this soft twilight
> Over willow trees.
> (*HTOW*, 13)

> On the hanging bell
> Has perched and is fast asleep,
> It's a butterfly.[18]
> (Buson)

Wright and Buson take different approaches in terms of subjectivity; Wright's focus is on imagining a bell ringing softly over willow trees while Buson's is on a butterfly actually fast asleep on a hanging bell. The two haiku are quite different; subjectivity is present in Wright's haiku while it is absent in Buson's.

Buson was well-known in his time as an accomplished painter, and many of his haiku reflect his singular attention to color and its intensification. Wright's "A Butterfly Makes," for example, is reminiscent of Buson's "Also Stepping On":

> A butterfly makes
> The sunshine even brighter
> With fluttering wings.
> (*HTOW*, 82)

> Also stepping on
> The mountain pheasant's tail is
> The spring setting sun.[19]
> (Buson)

For a seasonal reference to spring, Buson links an image of the bird with a spring sunset, because both are highly colorful. As a painter he is also interested in the ambiguous impression the scene gives him; it is not clear whether the setting sun is treading on the pheasant's tail or the tail on the setting sun. In any event, Buson has made both pictures beautiful to look at, just as Wright draws pictures of a butterfly and the sunshine, themselves highly colorful and bright, which in turn intensify each other. But there are some differences between Buson's and Wright's haiku. While Buson abides by the traditional rule of including a seasonal reference, Wright does not. While Buson's perception is based solely on nature, Wright's haiku reflects a subjective perception. Wright is interjecting his view that a butterfly's action makes the sunshine brighter.

While classic haiku poets often tried to suppress subjectivity in depicting nature, some of Wright's haiku bring the poet to the fore:

> A wilting jonquil
> Journeys to its destiny
> In a shut bedroom.
> (*HTOW*, 720)

> Lines of winter rain
> Gleam only as they flash past
> My lighted window.
> (*HTOW*, 722)

While "A Wilting Jonquil" focuses on an object, "Lines of Winter Rain" insists on the importance of "my lighted window." None of the classic haiku Wright emulates expresses the poet's thoughts or feelings. The first haiku in Wright's *Haiku: This Other World* suppresses subjectivity by depicting the red sun that erases his name:

> I am nobody:
> A red sinking autumn sun
> Took my name away.
> (*HTOW*, 1)

And yet the poet is strongly present, even by negation.

In depicting the moon, for example, Wright and Kikaku write remarkably different haiku:

> A pale winter moon,
> Pitying a lonely doll,
>   Lent it a shadow.
> (*HTOW*, 671)

> The bright harvest moon
> Upon the tatami mats
>   Shadows of the pines.[20]
> (Kikaku)

In "A Pale Winter Moon," the second line, "Pitying a lonely doll," projects loneliness onto a doll; thereby Wright is indirectly expressing his sympathy for the doll. Subjectivity is entirely absent in "The Bright Harvest Moon"; Kikaku is simply depicting the intricate pattern of the shadow of the trees created on the dustless tatami mats under the bright harvest moon.

Absent subjectivity in composing haiku is akin to Lacan's concept of the subject. Lacan, as a postmodern psychoanalyst, challenges the traditional concept of subjectivity. On the basis of his analytic experience, he sees subjectivity as a concept that concerns neither the autonomy of the self nor the subject's ability to influence the other. Subjectivity is deficient because of the deficiencies inherent in language:

> The effects of language are always mixed with the fact, which is the basis of the analytic experience, that the subject is subject only from being subjected to the field of the Other, the subject proceeds from his synchronic subjection in the field of the Other. That is why he must get out, get himself out, and in the *getting-himself-out*, in the end, he will know that the real Other has, just as much as himself, to get himself out, to pull himself free.[21]

Because the subject, an infinitesimal fraction in time and space, is isolated from the world, the subject is only capable of imagining the other: society, nature, and life. Only when the subject is conscious of the deficiencies of language, as Lacan theorizes, does the subject of the unconscious emerge. Only then is the subject able to approach and encounter the truth of life—what Lacan calls "the real" and "the unsymbolizable."

To Lacan, the motive for subjectivity aims at the symbolic—what constitutes tradition, religion, law, and so on—whereas the motive for absence of subjectivity aims at the unconscious, a state largely derived from the other and partly derived from the imaginary on the part of the subject. The unconscious and the imaginary, then, are closer to the real than they are to the symbolic. Lacan posits, however, that "there exists a world of truth entirely deprived of subjectivity," universal truth, "and that . . . there has been a historical development of subjectivity manifestly directed towards the rediscovery of truth," historically subjective truth, "which lies in the order of symbols."[22] Lacan sees the door as language; the door is open either to the real or to the imaginary. He says that "we don't know quite which, but it is either one or the other. There is an asymmetry between the opening and the closing—if the opening of the door controls access, when closed, it closes the circuit."[23] He considers language either objective or subjective; the real is objective whereas the imaginary is subjective. Applied to traditional haiku composition, the language aims at the real through the imaginary rather than at the symbolic through the historically subjective.

The Lacanian distinction of the imaginary and the symbolic has an affinity with one of the disagreements between Pound and Yeats in reading Japanese poetry and drama. Pound regarded symbolism as "a sort of allusion, almost of allegory." The symbolists, Pound thought, "degraded the symbol to the status of a word. . . . Moreover, one does not want to be called a symbolist, because symbolism has usually been associated with mushy technique."[24] For Pound, symbolism is inferior to imagism, the imaginary in Lacan's theory, because in symbolism one image is used to suggest another or to represent another, whereby both images would be weakened. Pound's theory of imagism was derived from classic haiku, which shuns metaphor and symbolism, rather than from the noh play, which Yeats considered indirect and symbolic. If Yeats's ideal language has the suggestiveness and allusiveness of symbolism as opposed to the directness and clearness of imagism, then his sources certainly did not include Pound. Even though Yeats dedicated *At the Hawk's Well* (1917) to Pound, Yeats was not enthusiastic about Pound's theory. Yeats, a symbolist and spiritualist poet, was fascinated by the noh play, while Pound, an imagist, was influenced by Japanese poetry and by classic haiku in particular.

In any event, Lacan moreover envisions a domain of the real beyond "the navel of the dream, this abyssal relation to that which is most unknown, which is the hallmark of an exceptional, privileged experience, in which the real is apprehended beyond all mediation, be it imaginary or symbolic." Lacan equates this domain with "an absolute other . . . an other beyond all intersubjectivity." In Lacanian terms, the haiku poet is motivated to depict the real directly without using symbols. In this process the poet relies on the imaginary, a domain that is closer to nature, where subjectivity is suppressed as much as possible, or minimized. The poets avoid symbols in writing haiku in an attempt to be objective and yet creative. "If the symbolic function functions," Lacan laments, "we are inside it. And I would even say—we are so far into it that we can't get out of it."[25]

That symbolism is an obstacle in writing haiku can be explained in terms of Lacan's definition of the symbolic order. Lacan observes that language symbolizes things that do not exist, non-being: "The fundamental relation of man to this symbolic order is very precisely what founds the symbolic order itself—the relation of non-being to being. . . . What insists on being satisfied can only be satisfied in recognition. The end of the symbolic process is that non-being come to be, because it has spoken."[26] To Lacan, then, language makes non-being become being. Because haiku aim to represent being rather than non-being, what Lacan calls "language" or what is "spoken" does not apply to the language of haiku.

In Wright's haiku, as in Pound's imagistic poem, an image does not function as a symbol. In explaining the composition of the Metro poem ("The apparition of these faces in the crowd: / Petals, on a wet, black bough"), Pound stated that "the apparition of these faces" functions as an image that has generated another image, "petals, on a wet, black bough." Before this explanation Pound quoted Moritake's haiku ("The fallen blossom flies back to its branch: / A butterfly")[27] to demonstrate that "the fallen blossom" functions as an image that generates another image, "a butterfly." In a similar fashion, Wright composed the following haiku in which an image generates or transforms into another image as does it in Pound's and Moritake's haiku:

> Off the cherry tree,
> One twig and its red blossom
> Flies into the sun.
> (*HTOW*, 626)

> A leaf chases wind
> Across an autumn river
> And shakes a pine tree.
> (*HTOW*, 669)

Each moment or two
A long tongue of autumn wind
    Licks the river white.
(*HTOW*, 687)

The first haiku, "Off the Cherry Tree," like Moritake's "The Fallen Blossom," is a haiku of illusion. The image of a twig with its blossom generates an imaginary, illusionary image—that of a bird. Similarly, the image of a leaf chasing wind and shaking a pine tree in the second haiku transforms into an imaginary, illusionary image—again, that of a bird. The difference between Wright's haiku of illusion and Moritake's is that while Moritake identifies the imaginary image as that of a butterfly, Wright depicts the actions of a bird: chasing wind and shaking a pine tree. In the third haiku, "Each Moment or Two," the image of wind transforms into that of a long tongue. In this haiku, while the imaginary, illusionary image of a long tongue is identified as that of an actual tongue, the image of wind is identified not as that of actual wind that blows, but as an imaginary, illusionary image of wind that "licks the river white."

The unsymbolic characteristic of haiku, reflected in the imagistic haiku by Moritake, Pound, and Wright quoted above, also accounts for the absence of subjectivity in classic haiku. Those haiku by Wright that express subjectivity directly or indirectly might be considered modern rather than traditional. The first line in Wright's haiku 13 ("I would like a bell / Tolling in this soft twilight / Over willow trees."), quoted earlier, constitutes an expression of subjectivity, but the second line, "Tolling in this soft twilight," is an image created by the imaginary. In Pound's imagistic haiku-like poem "In a Station of the Metro," quoted earlier, the image of the apparition, as well as that of petals, as Pound explains in his "Vorticism" essay, is derived from the subject's experience at the metro station, so this poem indirectly expresses subjectivity. Pound also expresses subjectivity directly in another haiku-like poem, entitled "Alba":

As cool as the pale wet leaves
    of lily-of-the-valley
    She lay beside me in the dawn.[28]

As the image of "the pale wet leaves," a creation by the imaginary in Lacanian terms, indirectly expresses the subject's desire, the last line explicitly brings in the desiring subject. One of the disciplines in classic haiku composition calls for restraining the expression of desire. "Desire" as Lacan observes, "always becomes manifest at the joint of speech, where it makes its appearance, its sudden emergence, its surge forwards. Desire emerges just as it becomes embodied in speech, it emerges with symbolism."[29]

The following haiku by Wright bear a close resemblance to Pound's modernist haiku such as "Alba":

> As my delegate,
> The spring wind has its fingers
> In a young girl's hair.
> (*HTOW*, 209)

> While she undresses,
> A spring moon touches her breasts
> For seven seconds.
> (*HTOW*, 368)

In the first haiku, as the image of the spring wind with fingers in the middle line, a creation by the imaginary in Lacanian terms, indirectly expresses the subject's desire, the first and the third lines explicitly brings in the desiring subject. Similarly, in the second haiku, as the image of a spring moon while she undresses—another creation by the imaginary—indirectly expresses the subject's desire, the second and third lines depict the action of the desiring subject.

Another salient characteristic of modernist haiku is for the poet to depict the interactions between humanity and nature. As a classic haiku poet focuses on nature, a modernist like Shiki focuses on the relation of humanity to nature. The modernist's aim is to create images of humanity and relate them to those of nature. The modernist's vision of the world, however, was derived from Confucius's worldview. Confucius envisioned the universe consisting of heaven, earth, and humankind, united as one entity. Confucius theorized that God is a human concept and that, because humanity and nature are united, virtues are derived from human sentiments as well as from natural phenomena. The following haiku by Wright, for example, illustrate the interactions between humanity and nature:

Rotting yellow leaves
Have about them an odor
　　Both of death and hope.
(*HTOW*, 310)

　　Merciful autumn
Tones down the shabby curtains
　　Of my rented room.
(*HTOW*, 174)

The first haiku, "Rotting Yellow Leaves," shows that "hope," a human sentiment, is reflected on "rotting yellow leaves," an object in nature. Wright uses the technique of transference of the senses. Through transference of color and smell, the image of death and hope in the third line intensifies that of the rotting yellow leaves in the first. The second haiku, "Merciful Autumn," illustrates that the images of humanity and nature, "the shabby curtain" and "merciful autumn," reflect each other. Wright composed this haiku, as did Shiki, with the aesthetic sensibility of *wabi*, a beauty of poverty. Wright, while describing his poverty and isolation, intimated the transcendence of materialism and the creation of beauty. He captured a beautiful autumn scene in nature.

As classicist and modernist haiku poets were both influenced by Confucianism, so was Wright. Many of Wright's haiku reflect the Confucian thought that humanity and nature coexist and that humanity emulates nature. The following haiku show that humanity and nature are equal partners on earth:

　　When the school bell sounds
A momentary silence
　　Falls upon the birds.
(*HTOW*, 411)

　　A September fog
Mute upon the empty porch
　　Of an empty house.
(*HTOW*, 348)

The first haiku portrays a harmony between humanity and nature. Birds listen to the school bell just as do children; they both live on earth in peace.

The second haiku also exhibits the unity of humanity and nature. Silence in nature and silence in humanity complement each other; "a September fog," a silent image of nature, reflects "the empty porch of an empty house," a silent image of humanity, just as "the empty porch of an empty house" reflects "a September fog."

In the following haiku, Wright illustrates a Confucian cosmology in which humankind occupies the bottom of the universe:

> After the parade
> After all the flags are gone,
>   The snow is whiter.
> (*HTOW*, 262)

> Waving pennants gone,
> The white houses now belong
>   To a summer sky.
> (*HTOW*, 771)

"After the Parade" portrays a scene where "the parade" and "all the flags," representations of humanity, disappear and snow covers the earth. Wright is suggesting—as Emerson does in "The Snow-Storm," in which people and their properties are all buried helplessly by a powerful snowstorm—that even though humankind and nature coexist, nature is always above humankind. "Waving Pennants Gone" depicts a scene where humankind and nature coexist on earth but they are controlled by heaven.

Some of Wright's haiku portray nature as a model of humanity. In these, humanity emulates nature and, in the manner of Zen admonition, nature teaches humanity:

> As my anger ebbs,
> The spring stars grow again
>   And the wind returns.
> (*HTOW*, 721)

> Why did this spring wood
> Grow so silent when I came?
>   What was happening?
> (*HTOW*, 809)

Did somebody call?
Looking over my shoulder:
   Massive spring mountains.
(*HTOW*, 203)

In the first haiku, as "anger," a negative human attribute, subsides, "spring stars," a beautiful image of nature, grow brighter. Nature teaches Wright how to control his temper. The second haiku, "Why Did This Spring Wood," resembles a Zen mondo (question and answer). Wright asks the spring wood why it becomes so silent. The answer the spring wood gives him is that silence is a human virtue. This admonition reminds one of Benjamin Franklin's discussion of the thirteen virtues that represent the American national character. In his *Autobiography*, Franklin lists "Silence" as the second virtue among the thirteen virtues.[30] For the third haiku, Wright draws an analogy between the "massive spring mountains," a representation of nature, and his "shoulders," a representation of humanity. The haiku sounds as though Wright is receiving an epiphany from nature.

In many of his haiku, Wright contrasts the plight of humanity with the beauty of nature. The following haiku display a contrast between the poverty of humanity and the richness of nature:

I am paying rent
For the lice in my cold room
   And the moonlight too.
(*HTOW*, 459)

My decrepit barn
Sags full of self-consciousness
   In this autumn sun.
(*HTOW*, 695)

That abandoned house,
With its yard of fallen leaves,
   In the setting sun.
(*HTOW*, 38)

These haiku are characteristic of the aesthetic sensibility of *wabi*. In the first two, the poet's physical poverty is rewarded with the spiritual richness of nature. The beauty of the moonlight compensates for his cold, lice-infested rented room in the first haiku as does the beauty of the autumn sun for his decrepit barn. Similarly, in the third haiku, a beautiful scene where the setting sun shines on fallen leaves compensates for the abandoned house.

In the following two haiku, Wright depicts his own feelings of loneliness and isolation:

> Walking home alone
> From the sporting arena
>   A curve of spring moon.
> (*HTOW*, 475)

> This tenement room
> In which I sweat this August
>   Has one buzzing fly.
> (*HTOW*, 421)

In the first selection, the poet is lonely as he walks home, but he is accompanied by a beautifully curved spring moon. In the second haiku, he is confined in a hot, humid tenement room but is accompanied by a buzzing fly. To a modernist poet, the twin problems of humanity are loneliness and boredom. Wright sees the same problems exist in nature as "one buzzing fly" in the second haiku implies. As the first haiku shows, the aesthetic sensibility of *sabi* is evoked by the private world of the poet, the situation others cannot envision. The poet's capturing an image of beauty in nature compensates for his loneliness and boredom.

The two haiku below depict some of humanity's negative features:

> On a bayonet,
> And beyond the barbs of wire,—
>   A spring moon at dawn.
> (*HTOW*, 477)

> In this rented room
> One more winter stand outside
>   My dirty window pane.
> (*HTOW*, 412)

In the first example, "a bayonet"—an image of one of the most negative features of humanity—is contrasted with "a spring moon at dawn," a beautiful image of nature. In the second haiku, "my dirty window pane," an unpleasant, ugly image of humanity, is pitted against "one more winter . . . outside," an image of nature that compensates for the dirty windowpane. Both haiku illustrate the transcendence of materialism and the creation of beauty, as do Wright's other modernist haiku of *wabi* and *sabi*.

As Wright's and Pound's modernist haiku demonstrate, subjectivity in such haiku is expressed through the use of a personal pronoun, and the subject's desire is evoked in an image that reflects subjectivity. Subjectivity and desire, its dominant construct, are both expressed through pronominal language rather than through an image in nature that embodies the real or the unconscious. Wright's haiku were strongly influenced by classic Japanese haiku from the seventeenth and eighteenth centuries, and perhaps two-thirds of his haiku can be categorized as traditionalist haiku; in these an image of nature is the focus of the poem, and subjectivity is absent. The rest, a third of his haiku, might be called modernist. Some of Wright's haiku, however, can be read as both traditional and modernist.

8

JACK KEROUAC'S HAIKU,
BEAT POETICS, AND *ON THE ROAD*

1

Jack Kerouac (1922–1969), whose first novel, *On the Road* (1957), captured a huge audience, played a central role in the literary movement he named the Beat Generation. His second novel, *The Dharma Bums* (1958), gave an intimate biographical account of himself in search of the truth in life. In San Francisco he met Gary Snyder (1930–), and the two dharma bums explored the thoughts and practices of Buddhism. As Snyder left for Japan to study at a Zen monastery, Kerouac's search reached an apogee on a desolate mountaintop in the Sierras.

The uninhibited story of Kerouac and Snyder on the West Coast also coincided with the birth of the San Francisco Poetry Renaissance. Kerouac called the event "the whole gang of howling poets" gathered at Gallery Six on October 7, 1955. In the beginning of *The Dharma Bums*, Kerouac described the poetry reading:

> Everyone was there. It was a mad night. And I was the one who got things jumping by going around collecting dimes and quarters from the rather stiff audience standing around in the gallery and coming back with three huge gallon jugs of California Burgundy and getting them all piffed so that by eleven o'clock when Alvah Goldbook [Allen Ginsberg] was reading his, wailing his poem "Wail" [Howl] drunk with arms outspread everybody was yelling "Go! Go! Go!" (like a jam session) and old Rheinhold Cacoethes the father of the Frisco poetry scene was wiping his tears in gladness. Japhy [Gary Snyder] himself read his fine poems about Coyote the God of the North American Plateau Indians (I think), at least the God of the Northwest Indians, Kwakiutl and what-all. "Fuck you! sang Coyote, and ran away!" read

Japhy to the distinguished audience, making them all howl with joy, it was so pure, fuck being a dirty word that comes out clean. And he had his tender lyrical lines, like the ones about bears eating berries, showing his love of animals, and great mystery lines about oxen on the Mongolian road showing his knowledge of Oriental literature even on to Hsuan Tsung the great Chinese monk who walked from China to Tibet, Lanchow to Kashgar and Mongolia carrying a stick of incense in his hand. (13–14)

Not only did this inaugural meeting of the Beat Generation feature the three well-known writers Kerouac, Snyder, and Ginsberg (1926–1997), their subsequent interactions among them revealed their backgrounds and worldviews. Snyder, born in San Francisco, followed Ginsberg's first reading of *Howl* at this gathering with his own lyrical poems, as mentioned above. Later in *The Dharma Bums* Snyder observed, "East'll meet West anyway. Think what a great world revolution will take place when East meets West finally, and it'll be guys like us that can start the thing. Think of millions of guys all over the world with rucksacks on their backs tramping around the back country and hitchhiking and bringing the word down to everybody." Kerouac responded by referring to a Christian tradition he remembered as he grew up a Catholic in a French American family in Massachusetts: "That's a lot like the early days of the Crusades, Walter the Penniless and Peter the Hermit leading ragged bands of believers to the Holy Land." Snyder, admonishing Kerouac against believing in his Western legacy, said, "Yeah but that was all such European gloom and crap, I want my Dharma Bums to have springtime in their hearts when the blooms are girling and the birds are dropping little fresh turds surprising cats who wanted to eat them a moment ago" (203–4).

Discussing Buddhism and Zen philosophy, in particular, with Snyder, as well as reading books on Buddhism in the local libraries, Kerouac realized that Buddhism, rather than denying suffering and death, confronted both. For him, Buddhism taught one to transcend the origin of suffering and death: desire and ignorance. Most impressively, Buddhism taught Kerouac that the phenomenal world was like a dream and an illusion and that happiness consisted in achieving that strange vision in the mind—enlightenment. *The Dharma Bums* also informs that while Snyder was continuously fascinated with Zen, Kerouac was inspired by Mahayana Buddhism. To Kerouac, Zen, which teaches spontaneous, realistic action for human beings, compromises with active, worldly existence. Consequently, Zen admonished against existing in a world of temptation and evil. On the contrary, Kerouac was impressed with Mahayana Buddhism, for one's goal of life is to achieve Buddhahood, a celestial state of enlightenment and acceptance of all forms of life.

The genesis of the Beat movement goes back to the meeting of Kerouac and Ginsberg at Columbia University in the early 1940s. Kerouac and Ginsberg, who grew up in New Jersey of Russian Jewish immigrant parents, also shared their literary interests with William Burroughs (1914–1997), who hailed from Missouri. During this period, Kerouac, immersed in American transcendentalism, read Emerson, Thoreau, and Whitman. Kerouac was influenced by Emerson's concept of self-reliance as he learned of Whitman's singular, stubborn independence and refusal to subscribe to society's materialistic, commercial demands. At the same time, it was Thoreau's writings, such as *Walden, A Week on the Concord and Merrimack Rivers*, and "Civil Disobedience," that introduced Kerouac to Confucianism and Buddhism.[1]

Learning about Buddhism from Thoreau, Kerouac became seriously interested in studying its philosophy. His study of Buddhism, then, led to writing *The Dharma Bums*. For Kerouac, Mahayana Buddhism served to change the state of defeat in the world that the Beat movement represented to the beatific acceptance of life the Buddhist texts described. For Gary Snyder, Zen Buddhism transformed the Beats to the "Zen Lunatics" who refused

> to subscribe to the general demand that they consume production and therefore have to work for the privilege of consuming, all that crap they didn't really want anyway such as refrigerators, TV sets, cars . . . I see a vision of . . . Zen Lunatics who go about writing poems that happen to appear in their heads for no reason and also by being kind and also by strange unexpected acts keep giving visions of eternal freedom to everybody and to all living creatures. (*DB*, 97–98)

Kerouac responded, as did Snyder, to the Zen principle to establish authority in one's spontaneous and intuitive insights and actions. Kerouac took pains to see things as they existed, without commentary, interpretation, and judgment. For Kerouac, and for the Beat Generation, the Zen perspective made art conform to life itself. A Zen-inspired poet must see whatever happens in life—order and disorder, permanence and change. This Zen principle partly accounts for Kerouac's rejection of the idea of revision.[2] With respect to spontaneous prose, Kerouac stated, "And, Not 'selectivity' of expression but following free deviation (association) of mind into limitless blow-on-subject seas of thought, . . . write as deeply, fish down as far as you want, satisfy yourself first, then reader cannot fail to receive telepathic shock and meaning—excitement by same laws operating in his own human mind" ("Essentials of Spontaneous Prose," 73).

Upon publication of *On the Road*, Kerouac was writing haiku. Thanks to Regina Weinreich's edition, *Book of Haikus* by Jack Kerouac (2003), we have a well-detailed account of Kerouac's writing of those several hundred haiku. As mentioned in *The Dharma Bums*, Kerouac, while reading a number of books on Buddhism, also consulted the four-volume book on Japanese haiku by R. H. Blyth, especially the first volume, subtitled *Eastern Culture*. "Kerouac's pocket notebooks," as Weinreich notes, contained "haiku entries written in New York City, Tangier, Aix-en-Provence, London, New York City again, Berkeley, Mexico, and Orlando. As the notebooks and letters of this period show, Kerouac exhorted himself to write haiku, mindful of the traditional methods" (*BOH*, 106).

2

As Kerouac's *Book of Haikus* indicates, Kerouac continuously wrote haiku to render the Beats' worldview. "For a new generation of poets," Weinreich has observed, "Kerouac ended up breaking ground at a pioneering stage of an American haiku movement" (*BOH*, xv). Allen Ginsberg celebrated Kerouac's haiku:

> Kerouac has the one sign of being a great poet, which is he's the only one in the United States who knows how to write haikus. The only one who's written any good haikus. And everybody's been writing haikus. There are all these dreary haikus written by people who think for weeks trying to write a haiku, and finally come up with some dull little thing or something. Whereas Kerouac thinks in haikus, every time he writes anything—talks that way and thinks that way. So it's just natural for him. It's something Snyder noticed. Snyder has to labor for years in a Zen monastery to produce one haiku about shitting off a log! And actually does get one or two good ones. Snyder was always astounded by Kerouac's facility.[3]

There were, however, some poets who were not enthusiastic about Kerouac's haiku. Lawrence Ferlinghetti, who was associated with the Beat writers and the San Francisco Renaissance poets and who, founding his own press, published his friend Allen Ginsberg's work, said that Kerouac "was a better novel writer than a poem writer."[4]

As many of the classic haiku poets in Japan, like Basho, were influenced by Confucian thought, so was Kerouac. In the first volume, *Haiku: Eastern Culture*, which Kerouac studied in earnest, Blyth explains that, according to Confucius, the universe consists of heaven, earth, and human beings. *The Analects*, a collection of Confucian maxims and parables, contains Confucius's thoughts and observations on the relationships among heaven, human beings, and God. For Confucius, God is not a living being like a human being; God is a concept that originated from a human being. The individual living in society must formulate this concept by apprehending the ways of nature in heaven and on earth. One is conscious of the supremacy of heaven over earth and human beings.

Several of Kerouac's haiku reflect a Confucian perspective that all things in the universe are related and united:

> The tree looks
>   like a dog
> Barking at Heaven
> (*BOH*, 3)

Not only does this piece show the relatedness of a tree, a dog, and heaven, it intimates the sense that the dog and the tree, the animate and the inanimate, are united. This haiku recalls an illusion expressed in Moritake's haiku, which Ezra Pound quoted in his "Vorticism" essay:[5]

> The fallen blossom flies back to its branch:
>   A butterfly
> ("Vorticism," 467)

Another haiku by Kerouac on the same subject,

> Shooting star!—no,
>   lightning bug!—
> ah well, June night
> (*BOH*, 151)

also depicts an illusion, as does Kerouac's haiku above, "The Tree Looks," both haiku illustrating the Confucian thought that all things in the universe are related.

Some other haiku convey the conflated vision of Confucianism and Buddhism that all the living on earth are related and united:

Frozen
    in the birdbath,
A leaf
(*BOH*, 5)

This piece conveys the Buddhist doctrine that all things, even the inanimate, have the Buddha nature. The reason for Kerouac's stronger attraction to Buddhism than to Christianity was his realization that Buddhists believed in the existence and transmigration of the soul in animals as well as in human beings as Christians did not.[6] Not only are the bird and a leaf in this haiku, "Frozen," related, but water and ice also unite them as if their souls transmigrate between them.

Still other haiku, while illustrating the Confucian and Buddhist perspective of the world that the animate and the inanimate are united, express irony and humor:

After the shower,
    among the drenched roses,
The bird thrashing in the bath
(*BOH*, 14)

In "After the Shower," while the roses are benefiting from rainwater, the bird, thrashing in the water, appears uncomfortable. But from a human point of view, the bird also is benefiting from the rain water, which cleans it as if the bird were taking a bath. In the following piece,

Bee, why are you
    staring at me?
I'm not a flower!
(*BOH*, 15)

Kerouac is expressing the bee's perspective: a flower and a human being are the same, the difference being that a flower might provide a bee with honey whereas a human being might be the bee's enemy.

As a Beat writer, Kerouac was inspired by the Zen doctrine that to attain enlightenment is to reach the state of nothingness. Not only is this state of mind free of human subjectivity and egotism, it is even free of religious conception. The Rinzai Zen, as noted in the introduction, teaches its followers that if they see Buddha in their meditations, they must "kill" him. At the same time, Kerouac was deeply influenced by Mahayana Buddhism, which teaches that one can achieve Buddhahood in life or death and that the human soul, buttressed by the virtues of mercy and compassion, transmigrates from one living being to another.

In *The Dharma Bums*, Gary Snyder, a Zen Buddhist, had a dialogue with Kerouac, a Mahayana Buddhist, that revealed the two different religiosities the two branches of Buddhism represented. Snyder said to Kerouac, "I appreciate your sadness about the world. 'Tis indeed. Look at that party the other night. Everybody wanted to have a good time and tried real hard but we all woke up the next day feeling sorta sad and separate. What do you think about death . . . ?" Kerouac responded, "I think death is our reward. When we die we go straight to nirvana Heaven and that's that" (202). In "On the Beat Generation," an unpublished scroll manuscript, Kerouac wrote, "Beat Generation means a generation passed over into eternity. . . . The last trembling of a leaf, at being one with all time, a sudden brilliance of redness in the fall . . . The beat generation knows all about haikus" (*BOH*, 127). Kerouac's observations of the Beat Generation suggest that Beat poetics is not to describe the life of the beaten but to celebrate the life of the beatific.

For Kerouac, and for the Beat Generation, the state of beatitude can be attained in life or death. In the following piece,

Glow worms
   brightly sleeping
On my flowers
(*BOH*, 137)

Kerouac is envious of the glowworms sleeping on his flowers, which are oblivious of the chaotic society of which he is a member. The image of glowworms sleeping on flowers represents the life of the beatific. The worms, unlike humans, have reached their nirvana; it thrives on flowers, an image of natural beauty, in a garden, a space Kerouac and the worms, humanity and nature, share. This haiku has an affinity with Frost's "After Apple-Picking," in which Frost is envious of the woodchuck's peaceful hibernation as he is afraid of a nightmare caused by the chaotic world.[7]

Wandering in the fields and the woods, as Kerouac describes in *The Dharma Bums*, he thought that "the substance of my bones and their bones and the bones of dead men in the earth of rain at night is the common individual substance that is everlastingly tranquil and blissful?" It occurred to him, "Raindrops are ecstasy, raindrops are not different from ecstasy, neither is ecstasy different from raindrops, yea, ecstasy is raindrops, rain on, O cloud!" (110). Many of the haiku collected in his notebooks, "V. 1958–1959: Beat Generation Haikus / Autumn," and "VI. 1960–1966: Northport Haikus / Winter," describe what he called "ecstasy":

> The droopy constellation
>   on the grassy hill—
> Emily Dickinson's Tomb
> (*BOH*, 154)

> In enormous blizzard
>   burying everything
> My cat's out mating
> (*BOH*, 164)

Because the aim of a Beat poet is to reach eternity, the first haiku, "The Droopy Constellation," is reminiscent of Emily Dickinson's poetry. In such a poem as "I Died for Beauty" and "Because I Could Not Stop for Death," Dickinson describes her journey to eternity.[8] In the second haiku, "In Enormous Blizzard," an image of a powerful blizzard burying everything on earth suggests death and eternity, but it is juxtaposed to an image of lovemaking that suggests life and ecstasy. This piece bears a resemblance to Basho's "The Love of the Cats":

> The love of the cats;
> When it was over, the hazy moon
>   Over the bed-chamber.
> (Blyth, *Haiku: Eastern Culture*, 264)

Both of Kerouac's haiku suggest there is ecstasy in life and death, love and eternity.

Kerouac's Beat poetics, based on Zen doctrine, led to his concept of individual freedom. Lying on his bag smoking, as Kerouac describes his experience in *The Dharma Bums*, he thought, "Everything is possible. I am God,

I am Buddha, I am imperfect Ray Smith, all at the same time, I am empty space, I am all things. I have all the time in the world from life to life to do what is to do, to do what is done, to do the timeless doing, in finitely perfect within, why cry, why worry, perfect like mind essence and the minds of banana peels" (97). Later, envisioning "the bliss of the Buddha-fields," he wrote, "I saw that my life was a vast glowing empty page and I could do anything I wanted" (117). Earlier in the novel, he also recounts the life of a truck driver who gave him a ride when he was hitchhiking to visit his mother in North Carolina. He found that the driver "had a nice home in Ohio with wife, daughter, Christmas tree, two cars, garage, lawn, lawn-mower, but he couldn't enjoy any of it because he really wasn't free" (102).

In his notebook collection, "Beat Generation Haikus, 1958–1959," Kerouac included the following piece, which deals with individual freedom:

Jack reads his book
aloud at nite
—the stars come out.
(*BOH*, 133)

This haiku challenges the Zen concept of *mu* and asserts human subjectivity. Declaring his own ideas, Kerouac is able to find his audience. His call and the stars' response suggest that his vision of the world is as objective as the world's vision of him is subjective. Such a haiku is reminiscent of Robert Frost's poem "The Road Not Taken."[9] Like Frost, Kerouac takes pride in being free and being a nonconformist. The next two pieces also reflect individual freedom and autonomy:

On Desolation
    I was the alonest man
in the world
(*BOH*, 136)

High noon
    in Northport
—Alien shore
(*BOH*, 137)

"On Desolation" and "High Noon" both cherish Kerouac's state of mind dictated by no one but himself. To him, alienation from a corrupt society will

MODERNISTS

lead him to nirvana. Both haiku recall Langston Hughes's "The Weary Blues," in which a blues musician takes pride in his alienation and autonomy.[10] The following piece, "Reading the Sutra," recounts that the Buddhist scripture inspired Kerouac to attain enlightenment by decisive action on his part:

> Reading the sutra
>   I decided
> To go straight
> (*BOH*, 143)

This haiku has an affinity with Gwendolyn Brooks's "We Real Cool," in which the African American pool players are portrayed as daring individuals who enjoyed living freely on their instincts as did the beatniks.[11]

Not only are Kerouac's Beat Generation haiku poignant expressions of freedom and individualism, but many of them can also be read as direct indictments against materialistic society:

> Perfect moonlit night
>   marred
> By family squabble
> (*BOH*, 17)

This haiku depicts an image of celestial beauty. The image of the universe in harmony, however, is juxtaposed to the image of society in conflict. Such a haiku above is in contrast to another Beat Generation haiku:

> Ah, the crickets
>   are screaming
> at the moon
> (*BOH*, 140)

In this piece, the crickets, as they scream at the moon, the preeminent object in the sky, do not quarrel among them. This haiku suggests that human beings, by contrast, at times scream to one another rather than talk about beautiful things on earth and in the sky.

3

On the Road, Kerouac's first novel, as noted earlier, captured a huge audience and played a central role in the Beast Generation. This autobiographical

novel features himself, named Sal Paradise, as the protagonist and narrator. The story is developed as a quest taken by a young literary aspirant in
search of the truths in human life. He has a chief companion on his journey
named Dean Moriarty, whose prototype was Neal Cassady (1926–1968), a
major figure of the Beat Generation along with Allen Ginsberg.

For Kerouac, the central mission of *On the Road* is not to describe the
life of the beaten but to celebrate the life of the beatific. The narrative turns
out to be an experimental novel, for Kerouac himself wants to determine
whether he succeeds in achieving that ideal life he has imagined. At the
same time, he is intent upon finding out whether Dean also succeeds in
capturing the life of the beatific. Much like Tom Sawyer in Mark Twin's *Adventures of Huckleberry Finn*, Dean is Sal's friend as well as foil. Kerouac is
attracted to him as he is repulsed by him. *On the Road* begins with Kerouac's
initial portrait of Dean as a young jailbird who is interested in Nietzsche:

> I first met Dean not long after my wife and I split up. I had just gotten over a
> serious illness that I won't bother to talk about, except that it had something
> to do with the miserably weary split-up and my feeling that everything was
> dead. With the coming of Dean Moriarty began the part of my life you could
> call my life on the road. Before that I'd often dreamed of going West to see the
> country, always vaguely planning and never taking off. Dean is the perfect
> guy for the road because he actually was born on the road, when his parents
> were passing through Salt Lake City in 1926, in a jalopy, on their way to
> Los Angeles. First reports of him came to me through Chad King, who'd
> shown me a few letters from him written in a New Mexico reform school.
> I was tremendously interested in the letters because they so naïvely and
> sweetly asked Chad to teach him all about Nietzsche and all the wonderful
> intellectual things that Chad knew. At one point Carlo [Allen Ginsberg] and
> I talked about the letters and wondered if we would ever meet the strange
> Dean Moriarty. (*OTR*, 1)

The mysterious character of Dean Moriarty, unrevealed in the novel, is
compounded by the fact that Neal Cassady was married many times and
had children, but also had a long sexual relationship with Allen Ginsberg.

At the end of the road on the final journey, Kerouac describes his parting
with Dean with sadness and compassion:

> Dean took out other pictures. I realized these were all the snapshots which
> our children would look at some day with wonder, thinking their parents

had lived smooth, well-ordered, stabilized-within-the-photo lives and got up in the morning to walk proudly on the side walks of life, never dreaming the raggedy madness and riot of our actual lives, or actual night, the hell of it, the senseless nightmare road. All of it inside endless and beginningless emptiness. Pitiful forms of ignorance. "Good-by, good-by." Dean walked off in the long red dusk. Locomotives smoked and reeled above him. His shadow followed him, it aped his walk and thoughts and very being. He turned and waved coyly, bashfully. He gave me the boomer's high ball, he jumped up and down, he yelled something I didn't catch. He ran around in a circle. All the time he came closer to the concrete corner of the railroad overpass. He made one last signal. I waved back. Suddenly he bent to his life and walked quickly out of sight. (*OTR*, 253–54)

This passage is concluded with a brief description of Kerouac himself: "I gaped into the bleakness of my own days. I had an awful long way to go too" (*OTR*, 254). Such a self-criticism intimates that, although he himself is able to envision the beatific life, his ideal life is beyond reach.

Kerouac's description of the beatific vision of life intensifies because of a contrast drawn between the narrator and his companion. Kerouac introduces himself as Sal Paradise. The word "Paradise" resonates with the Christian heaven, the Garden of Eden. Although Dean is often called "An Angel," he acts like a lost archangel or a devil. "I suddenly realized," Kerouac remarks, "that Dean, by virtue of his enormous series of sins, was becoming the Idiot, the Imbecile, the Saint of the lot." Kerouac gives Dean an admonition:

You have absolutely no regard for anybody but yourself and your damned kicks. All you think about is what's hanging between your legs and how much money or fun you can get out of people and then you just throw them aside. Not only that but you're silly about it. It never occurs to you that life is serious and there are people trying to make something decent out of it instead of just goofing all the time. (*OTR*, 194)

"That's," utters the narrator, "what Dean was, the HOLY GOOF" (*OTR*, 194). To Kerouac, Dean has transgressed the Christian doctrine of compassion. Dean is antithetical to Kerouac, who tries to achieve a saintly, beatific, and compassionate human life.

In 1957, when Kerouac published *On the Road*, revealing to the literary public his adventures with Neal Cassady and epitomizing the Beat

Generation, he wrote many haiku, what Regina Weinreich calls "a fertile group of haiku."[12] While many of these haiku were written in Philip Whalen's cabin in Berkeley, California,[13] they reverberate with *On the Road*. As Kerouac was phrasing the images and ideas for the haiku, he must have been reflecting on his observations of the similar images and ideas that appear in *On the Road*.

Kerouac believed that the central theme of the novel is a spiritual quest of these characters. He was convinced, though his critics did not agree, that the Beat Generation was "basically a religious generation."[14] Some of the *Road* haiku are expressions of religious thoughts with religious references. Raised by his parents, devout French Catholics, Kerouac makes frequent references to Christianity in general and biblical words in particular.

While, to Kerouac, Dean seems to fail in his spiritual quest, he believes Kerouac will succeed in his quest. Envisioning Kerouac's success at the end of the road on the journey, Dean tells Kerouac:

> You spend a whole life of noninterference with the wishes of others, including politicians and the rich, and nobody bothers you and you cut along and make it your own way. . . . What's your road, man?—holyboy road, madman road, rainbow road, guppy road, any road. It's an anywhere road for anybody anyhow. Where body how? (*OTR*, 251)

Dean's listing of "holyboy road" at the top of the various roads suggests that Keouac will succeed in his spiritual quest because he has strong faith in God. Earlier in the story, Kerouac gives an intimation that his growing up in the East made him a genuine Christian and that his life in the West Coast converted him to a Buddhist. "There is something brown and holy about the East," he says, "and California is white like washlines and emptyheaded—at least that's what I thought then" (*OTR*, 79).[15]

Krouac's strong faith in Christianity is expressed in several of the group of haiku, "Road Haiku." The following haiku have direct references to Christianity:

> Shall I heed God's commandment?
>   —wave breaking
>   On the rocks—
> (*BOH*, 109)

A bottle of wine,
    a bishop—
Everything is God
(*BOH*, 108)

The focus of the first haiku is on Christian doctrine, whereas the emphasis in the second haiku is on the concept of pantheism. The second haiku thrives on concrete images—"a bottle of wine" and "a bishop." The following haiku that depicts a priest pays respect not only to the benevolent individual but also to Christianity as an institution devoted to the welfare of the people:

The vigorous bell-ringing priest
    the catch in the harbor
(*BOH*, 110)

This haiku expresses religious thought, represented by an image of "the vigorous bell-ringing priest," portraying the messenger of God and his demeanor as robust and joyful.

At the end of the road in the novel, Kerouac dwells on Christian legend and mythology. During his travels to Mexico, he becomes infatuated with Mexican women with Indian heritage. These women are depicted with biblical references:

"Look at those eyes!" breathed Dean. They were like the eyes of the Virgin Mother when she was a child. We saw in them the tender and forgiving gaze of Jesus. And they stared unflinching into ours. We rubbed our nervous blue eyes and looked again. Still they penetrated us with sorrowful and hypnotic gleam. . . . He stood among them with his ragged face to the sky, looking for the next and highest and final pass, and seemed like the Prophet that had come to them. (*OTR*, 297–98)

The background of this episode is described with biblical images:

The end of our journey impended. Great fields on both sides of us; a noble wind blew across the occasional immense tree groves and over old missions turning salmon pink in the late sun. The clouds were close and huge and rose. "Mexico City by dusk!: We'd made it, a total of nineteen hundred miles from the afternoon yards of Denver to these vast and Biblical areas of the world, and now we were about to reach the end of the road. (*OTR*, 299)

This portrayal of the Mexican landscape leads to Kerouac's speculation on the origin of Adam and Eve:

The waves are Chinese, but the earth is an Indian thing. As essential as rocks in the desert are they in the desert of "history." And they knew this when we passed, ostensibly self-important moneybag Americans on a lark in their land; they knew who was the father and who was the son of antique life on earth, and made no comment. For when destruction comes to the world of "history" and the Apocalypse of the Fellahin returns once more as so many times before, people will still stare with the same eyes from the caves of Mexico as well as from the caves of Bali, where it all began and where Adam was suckled and taught to know. These were my growing thoughts as I drove the car into the hot, sunbaked town of Gregoria. (*OTR*, 280)

From time to time, Kerouac's description of people and their lives on the road are highlighted by biblical words and expressions, such as "angel," "lamb," and "shepherd." In applauding the jazz performances in Chicago that give him his best times on the road, Kerouac portrays the black musician with a biblical expression:

Strange flowers yet—for as the Negro alto mused over every one's head with dignity, the young, tall, slender, blond kid from Curtis Street, Denver, jeans and studded belt, sucked on his mouthpiece while waiting for the others to finish; and when they did he started, and you had to look around to see where the solo was coming from, for it came from angelical smiling lips upon the mouthpiece and it was a soft, sweet, fairy-tale solo on an alto. Lonely as America, a throatpierced sound in the night. (*OTR*, 241)

Back in Colorado, Kerouac falls in love with a young girl he calls "the prairie angel." "She was about sixteen," he remarks, "and had Plains complexion like wild roses, and the bluest eyes. . . . She stood there with the immense winds that blew clear down from Saskatchewan knocking her hair about her lovely head like shrouds, living curls of them. She blushed and blushed" (*OTR*, 227–28).

On the road to New York from California, Kerouac meets a poor Mexican girl and consummates their love. "We had long, serious talks," he writes, "and took baths and discussed things with the light on and then with the light out. Something was being proved, I was convincing her of something, which she accepted, and we concluded the pact in the dark, breathless, then pleased, like little *lambs*" (*OTR*, 90, emphasis added).

Kerouac's description of the landscape in Mexico as he approaches the end of his journey is reminiscent of the Bible:

> We had reached the approaches of the last plateau. Now the sun was golden, the air keen blue, and the desert with its occasional rivers a riot of sandy, hot space and sudden Biblical tree shade. Now Dean was sleeping and Stan driving. The shepherds appeared, dressed as in first times, in long flowing robes, the women carrying golden bundles of flax, the men staves. Under great trees on the shimmering desert the shepherds sat and convened, and the sheep moiled in the sun and raised dust beyond. (*OTR*, 299)

Kerouac composed some of his *Road* haiku with biblical words and expressions:

> The Angel's hair
>   Trailed on my chin
> Like a cobweb
> (*BOH*, 138)

> The bottoms of my shoes
>   Are clean
> From walking in the rain
> (*BOH*, 8)

Kerouac's use of biblical language is indirect and subtle, as in the second haiku. The word "clean" might resonate with biblical words and expressions, such as "clear as crystal," "clear as glass," and "nothing unclean shall enter it."[16] The second haiku can be read as Kerouac's depiction of the state of beatitude that can be attained in human life. Another *Road* haiku, as the following one shows, has a direct reference to a Christian saint and martyr:[17]

> O Sebastian, where art thou?
>> Pa, watch over us!
> Saints, thank you!
> (*BOH*, 112)

Whereas Kerouac's vision of the beatific is influenced by Christianity, Dean's is not. Midway on their journey, the two men have a serious discussion on God:

> Dean was tremendously excited about everything he saw, everything he talked about, every detail of every moment that passed. He was out of his mind with real belief. "And of course now, no one can tell us that there is no God. We've passed through all forms. You remember, Sal, when I first came to New York and I wanted Chad King to teach me about Nietzsche. You see how long ago? Everything is fine, God exists, we know time. Everything since the Greeks has been predicted wrong. You can't make it with geometry and geometrical systems of thinking. It's all *this*! (*OTR*, 120)

Dean gives an illustration for his observation that God exists: driving on the road, for example, takes place by itself. "As we roll along this way," Dean tells Kerouac, "I am positive beyond doubt that everything will be taken care of for us . . . the thing will go along of itself and you won't go off the road and I can sleep" (*OTR*, 121). Although Kerouac finds it difficult to follow Dean's argument, he is nevertheless persuaded of Dean's observation that God exists.

Toward the end of the journey, Kerouac begins to have a pantheistic vision of the world. Traveling in the Western states with Dean, he finds himself in the midst of an open space at night under a cloudless sky:

> At night in this part of the West the stars, as I had seen them in Wyoming, are big as roman candles and as lonely as the Prince of the Dharma who's lost his ancestral grave and journeys across the spaces between points in the handle of the Big Dipper, trying to find it again. So they slowly wheeled the night, and then long before actual sunrise the great red light appeared far over the dun bleak land toward West Kansas and the birds took up their trill above Denver. (*OTR*, 223)

That Kerouac calls "the Seven Stars," a biblical terminology, "Big Dipper," a cosmological one, suggests that he is envisioning the universe as a pantheist.

At the end of the road on their final journey, Kerouac and Dean are elated to see a group of ranchers engaged in their daily activities in a border town in Mexico. They witness the lives of the ranchers protected by God under the bright sky. They come to see human life in harmony with the vast, infinite universe:

> Schooled in the raw road night, Dean was come into the world to see it. He bent over the wheel and looked both ways and rolled along slowly. We stopped for gas the other side of Sabinas Hidalgo. Here a congregation of local straw-hatted ranchers with handlebar mustaches growled and joked in front of antique gas-pumps. Across the fields an old man plodded with a burro in front of his switch stick. The sun rose pure on pure and ancient activities of human life. (*OTR*, 278)

As Kerouac is creating in his mind beatific images with biblical expressions, he is also seeing human life from the perspective of cosmology. At the end of the journey, Kerouac's effort to envision the beatific state of human life is intensified not only by his strong faith in Christianity but also by his latent interest in pantheism.

In the *Road* haiku, Kerouac composed several haiku that depict the infinite, immutable universe. As the following haiku show, the depiction of the world conveys the philosophical concepts of cosmology rather than the religious doctrine of All Mighty:

> The microscopic red bugs
> In the sea-side sand
> Do they meet and greet?
> (*BOH*, 111)

> Hand in hand in a red valley
> With the universal schoolteacher—
> the first morning
> (*BOH*, 111)

In the first haiku, focused on the microscopic world, Kerouac is able to imagine the beatific state of life. In the second haiku, the landscape of the mountain range is depicted by analogy with human life. Kerouac's vision is widened in the second haiku as it is narrowed in the first. One cannot physically see the insect world, nor can one the universe, but one can imagine such spaces in the universe. Both haiku not only thrive on the depiction of beatific state of life, but also the images, "red bugs" and "a red valley," are beautiful to look at. The first haiku features the cordial, friendly relationships of the bugs as the second express the warm, respectful relationships between teacher and pupil.

In the following haiku Kerouac depicts the immutable state of the universe, represented by nature on earth:

> Who cares about the pop-off trees
>> Of Provence?—
> A road's a road
> (*BOH*, 112)

> The backyard I tried to draw
>> —It still looks
> The same
> (*BOH*, 117)

In the first haiku, as he sees dead trees by the road, Kerouac envisions the state of nature beyond human control. Similarly, the second haiku expresses the immutable state of nature. He gives an admonition that humans must abide by the law and order of the universe to attain the beatific state of life for them.

The second haiku above, "The Backyard I Tried to Draw," is reminiscent of Basho's haiku, "The Mountains and Garden Also Move" in its expression of the state of nature:

> The mountains and garden also move;
> The summer drawing-room
>> Includes them.[18]
> (Basho)

The garden in Basho's haiku represents a space shared by human beings and the earth. So does the backyard in Kerouac's haiku. Both images suggest that, despite the human creation of the spaces, they still belong to the earth, a permanent, immutable space in the universe.

Both haiku by Basho and Kerouac can be read as expressions of Confucianism. As many of the classic haiku poets like Basho were influenced by Confucian thought, so was Kerouac. In *Haiku: Eastern Culture*, which Kerouac studied in earnest, R. H. Blyth explains that, according to Confucius, the universe consists of heaven, earth, and humans. *The Analects*, a collection of Confucian maxims and parables, contains Confucius's thoughts and observations on the relationships among heaven, earth, and God. For Confucius, God is not a living being like a human being; God is a concept that originates from a human being. The individual living in society must formulate this concept by understanding the ways of nature in heaven and on earth. One is conscious of the supremacy of heaven over earth and humans.

The following haiku by Kerouac also expresses the Confucian worldview:

> Reflected upside down
> > In the sunset lake, pines
> Pointing to infinity
> (*BOH*, 101)

This haiku focuses on an image of the universe that makes human existence infinitesimal in contrast to an infinite space that represents the universe. The image of pines reflected in the lake bears a resemblance to that of "the sacred pine-tree" in Emerson's famous poem, "The Problem":[19]

> Or how the sacred pine-tree adds
> To her old leaves new myriads?

Kerouac is impressed, as is Emerson, with the infinity of the universe. Emerson's argument is that divinity, which represents the universe, is proven by nature, not by the church or by human achievements like huge pyramids in Egypt and ancient temples in Greece. Similarly, Kerouac envisions the scope of the universe by looking at the pines reflected upside down in the sunset lake.[20]

Similarly, Kerouac's haiku, "Dust—the Blizzard," and Emerson's, "The Snow-Storm," both express the Confucian worldview:

> Dusk—The Blizzard
> > Hides everything,
> Even the night
> (*BOH*, 38)

Announced by all the trumpets of the sky,
Arrives the snow, and, driving o'er the fields,
Seems nowhere to alight: the whited air
Hides hills and woods, the river, and the heaven,
And veils the farm-house at the garden's end.[21]
(Emerson, "The Snow-Storm")

Both poems depict the supremacy of heaven over the earth and human beings.

The following haiku by Kerouac also depict the control the universe has over the earth and humanity:

Following each other,
    My cats stop
When it thunders
(*BOH*, 27)

The summer chair
    rocking by itself
In the blizzard
(*BOH*, 36)

In these haiku, the phenomena above the earth and humans have control over them. The first haiku, "Following Each Other," captures the moment when the thunderstorm halts the cats' movement. In the second haiku, "The Summer Chair," the blizzard rather than a human being is rocking the chair. Another haiku,

THE LIGHT BULB
    SUDDENLY WENT OUT—
STOPPED READING
(*BOH*, 64)

suggests that human law and action must follow the law and order of the universe. At night, without light from the sun, humans cannot see.

Confucianism, as Blyth shows, teaches "the sense of something that feeds the life of man, which can be absorbed into our own life and yet have a life of its own, which is organic and growing" (Blyth, *Haiku: Eastern*

Culture, 71). Some of Kerouac's haiku convey the Confucian thought that life in whatever form it exists is organic and generative. For example,

> May grass—
>   Nothing much
> To do
> (*BOH*, 118)

illustrates a phenomenon in nature with which humans have little to do. Another haiku by Kerouac,

> Waiting for the leaves
>   to fall;—
> There goes one!
> (*BOH*, 32)

not only illustrates an organic phenomenon but also captures a moment of change in nature. In the following haiku,

> No telegram today
>   —Only more
> Leaves fell
> (*BOH*, 5)

juxtaposing humanity to nature, Kerouac observes that nature is far more organic and far less isolated than humanity.

In his quest for the beatific in human life, Kerouac is always thinking about sex. From time to time he reflects on the subject, thinking what sex means to him, as well as to others. To Dean, sex represents the physical desire of a male. Kerouac tells Dean, as quoted earlier, "You have absolutely no regard for anybody but yourself and your damned kicks. All you think about is what's hanging between your legs" (*OTR*, 194). *On the Road* begins with the first impression Kerouac had of Dean when they first met in New York. "Dean," remarks Kerouac, "had dispatched the occupant of the apartment to the kitchen, probably to make coffee, while he proceeded with his love-problems, for to him sex was the one and only holy and important thing in life" (*OTR*, 2).

Kerouac, on the other hand, agrees with Dean that sex is holy. But observing Dean's unstable relationships with his wives has convinced Kerouac that Dean's view of sex is the least spiritual. In the first chapter of the novel, Kerouac characterizes Dean as if he were an animal:

> Dean just raced in society, eager for bread and love; he didn't care one way or the other, "so long's I can get that lil ole gal with that lil sumpin down there tween her legs, boy," and "so long's we can *eat*, son, y'ear me? I'm *hungry*, I'm *starving*, let's *eat right now!*"—and off we'd rush to *eat*, whereof, as saith Ecclesiastes, "It is your portion under the sun." (*OTR*, 8)

To Kerouac, sex is a centerpiece of the beatific state of life. "Somewhere along the line," remarks Kerouac, "I knew there'd be girls, visions, everything; somewhere along the line the pearl would be handed to me" (*OTR*, 8). In his mind, sex is not the physical act itself, but, surrounded and protected by "visions, everything," it constitutes a beautiful, precious experience signified by "the pearl."

Early in the novel Kerouac describes the first experience of sex he had with a young girl Dean introduced to him. "She was a nice little girl, simple and true," writes Kerouac, "and tremendously frightened of sex. I told her it was beautiful. I wanted to prove this to her. She let me prove it, but I was too impatient and proved nothing" (*OTR*, 57). Reflecting on his sexual relationships with Rita and others, Kerouac remarks:

> Boys and girls in America have such a sad time together; sophistication demands that they submit to sex immediately without proper preliminary talk. Not courting talk—real straight talk about souls, for life is holy and every moment is precious. (*OTR*, 58)

At the end of the road in Mexico City, Kerouac continues to view sex as a gift from God, in contrast to Dean, who believes that sex is a purely physical experience and something that appears "in a pornographic hasheesh daydream in heaven" (*OTR*, 289).

In the following haiku, Kerouac expresses his observation and belief that sex is holy:

> Sex—shaking to breed
>   as
> Providence permits
> (*BOH*, 91)

Kerouac views human sexuality as organic as the first line suggests and divine as the third line points out. This haiku recalls Whitman's lines in "Song of Myself":

> Urge and urge and urge,
> Always the procreant urge of the world.

> Out of the dimness opposite equal advance, always substance
>   and increase, always sex,
> Always a knit of identity, always distinction, always a breed of
>   life.[22]

Throughout "Song of Myself" Whitman demonstrates his observation and belief that sex is a divine gift. To him, as well as to Kerouac, sex is a representation of God.

On the Road was the most popular book Kerouac ever wrote. As an autobiography it thrives on the sentient, passionate self-portrait of an open-minded individual in quest of the truths in mid-twentieth-century American life. As his journey progresses, his vision of the world widens. As a devout Catholic, Kerouac's spiritual vision is influenced by Christian doctrine, but at the end of the journey it is also influenced by Pantheism. Many of Kerouac's haiku, derived from the observations and ideas conveyed in *On the Road*, succinctly and poignantly express them.

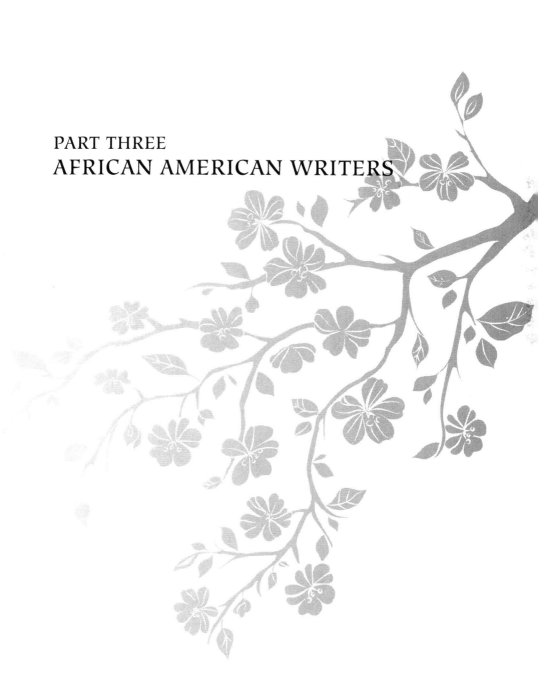

PART THREE
AFRICAN AMERICAN WRITERS

9

THE WESTERN AND EASTERN
THOUGHTS OF RALPH ELLISON'S *INVISIBLE MAN*

Among the well-known twentieth-century African American novels, *Invisible Man* (1952) has distinguished itself as a unique racial discourse. As a novel of racial prejudice, Richard Wright's *Native Son* awoke the conscience of the nation as its predecessors had failed to do. Toni Morrison's celebrated novel *Beloved* (1987) is perhaps one of the most poignant re-creations of the legacy of slavery. For the expression of an African American woman's love and suffering, Alice Walker's *The Color Purple* (1982) excels in its use of a vernacular, as does *Adventures of Huckleberry Finn*, told by an innocent, uneducated youth. Such novelists as Wright, Morrison, and Walker have succeeded in recording the ineffable agonies and rages of the racial victims, because their works are solidly based on fact and history. None of these novels, however, concerns the mindset of an individual more subtly than does *Invisible Man*. And this novel, unlike other African American novels, features the complexity of the protagonist's mind thoroughly foregrounded with a cross-cultural heritage. *Invisible Man*, then, represents the confluence and hybridity of Western and Eastern thoughts.

The different styles of writing notwithstanding, *Invisible Man* and *Native Son* both capture the plight of an African American trapped in a racist society at midcentury. While the social and economic backgrounds of the two novels remain similar, Ellison's technique is more modernistic and Wright's is more realistic. As a result, Ellison's protagonist is by far more articulate and subtle than Wright's. To defend the racial victim, Wright as a literary realist can rely on authentic court records, like those of the Robert Nixon murder trial and conviction in Chicago in the late 1930s. Ellison, on the other hand, as a psychological and highly imaginative realist, vividly recalls his personal experiences with an evocation of the social realities and cultural myths.

When such experiences, facts, and memories are presented in the novel, they become metaphoric rather than realistic. *Invisible Man* reads like a cross-cultural rather than a social discourse. Little wonder that when Ellison's protagonist-narrator revisits these historical, cultural sites and moments in the novel, he becomes invisible to those, in particular, who have excluded the existence of African Americans from their lives.

1

In "The World and the Jug," Ellison writes, "More important, perhaps, being a Negro American involves a *willed* (who wills to be a Negro? *I* do!) affirmation of self as against all outside pressures—an identification with the group as extended through the individual self which rejects all possibilities of escape that do not involve a basic resuscitation of the original American ideals of social and political justice" (*SA*, 132). Throughout *Invisible Man*, as Ellison reminds white Americans of their blindness to the true identity of their fellow citizens, Ellison proves how invisible an African American is to white American society at midcentury. To help white Americans better understand black life, Ellison is urging black Americans to re-create themselves instead of accommodating white Americans' superiority complex and allowing their condescension. To Ellison, then, making African Americans' invisibility visible means "a *willed* affirmation of self," the ultimate achievement of freedom and equality guaranteed in the Constitution.

Ellison's argument for the invisibility of the African American identity also suggests that black life in America constitutes not only the lives of African Americans but those of all Americans. Ellison's observation bears a strong resemblance to Wright's, as shown in *12 Million Black Voices*, published in 1941.[1] This well-documented work demonstrates that the principal motive African Americans had for their exodus from the rural South to the industrial North was their quest for freedom and equality. Wright himself, a victim of racial prejudice and hatred, fled to Chicago in search of the kind of freedom and dialogue he had never experienced in the South. "For the first time in our lives," he wrote, "we feel human bodies, strangers whose lives and thoughts are unknown to us, pressing always close about us." In stark contrast to the situation in the South, where African Americans were not allowed to communicate freely with white citizens, the crowded and noisy apartments in the northern cities became hubs of interracial mingling and communication, places where the migrant African

Americans came in close contact with "the brisk, clipped men of the North, the Bosses of the Buildings." Unlike the southern landlords, the city businessmen, Wright discovered, were not "at all *indifferent*. They are deeply concerned about us, but in a new way" (*12M*, 100).

In the industrial city, as Wright observed, an African American functioned as part of a "machine." Unlike his or her life in the rural South, which depended upon "the soil, the sun, the rain, or the wind," the life in the North was controlled by what Wright called "the grace of jobs and the brutal logic of jobs" (*12M*, 100). By living and working ever so closely with the white bourgeoisie, the minority workers in the city strove to learn their techniques. Consequently, Wright noted, African American workers "display a greater freedom and initiative in pushing their claims upon civilization than even do the petty bourgeoisie."[2] The harsh conditions under which African American workers had to produce and compete with white workers became an incentive to achieve a higher social and economic status. The interaction, dialogue, and competition involved in the activities yielded their initial consciousness of self-reliance. In short, the African Americans of the industrial North were given a chance to shape their own lives. Economically, an individual was a machine, and his or her production was measured not by his or her race but by his or her merit.

White citizens who worked in close contact with African Americans, in turn, viewed them with respect and friendliness. When white workers realized that they shared with African Americans the same working conditions and worldview, they became curious about African Americans' cultural legacy and, in particular, their musical heritage. In *12 Million Black Voices*, Wright traces the cross-racial and cross-cultural dialogue that took place in the industrial North:

> Alone together with our black folk in the towering tenements, we play our guitars, trumpets, and pianos, beating out rough and infectious rhythms that create an instant appeal among all classes of people. Why is our music so contagious? On the plantations our songs carried a strain of other-worldly yearning which people called "spiritual"; but now our blues, jazz, swing, and boogie-woogie are our "spirituals" of the city pavements, our longing for freedom and opportunity, an expression of our bewilderment and despair in a world whose meaning eludes us. (*12M*, 127–28)

To Wright, and to Ellison as well, the contribution of African American music to American life and culture served as a catalyst to developing affinities between African and European Americans. To today's Americans, jazz and the blues have become national music as much as they remain the African American legacy. More recently, Toni Morrison has also observed that the presence of African Americans enriched American life and culture; what she calls "Africanism" was the yoke of American culture. "Black slavery," she argues in *Playing in the Dark*, "enriched the country's creative possibilities" (38).

While Ellison shows in *Invisible Man* that African American freedom and identity can be achieved through genuinely autonomous cultural voices such as jazz and the blues, he also evokes Yeats, Joyce, and O'Casey because the contribution of these writers to British culture is similar to the influences of African American music on American culture.[3] To envision the latent consciousness of the invisible man, Ellison relies on the techniques of French writers like André Malraux and Paul Valéry. Among the European existential works, Malraux's *Man's Fate* had an influence on Ellison's characterization of the invisible man.[4] In commenting on the psychological makeup of Wright's *Black Boy*, Ellison points out that "all men possess the tendency to dream and the compulsion to make their dreams reality . . . and that all men are the victims and the beneficiaries of the goading, tormenting, commanding and informing activity of that imperious process known as the Mind—the Mind, as Valéry describes it, 'armed with its inexhaustible questions'" (*SA*, 81). Ellison considers *Black Boy* and *Invisible Man* not merely accurate representations of African American life but typical twentieth-century works that poignantly reflect humanity's quest of meaning for its existence.

As Ellison amply acknowledges in his essays, collected in *Shadow and Act* and *Going to the Territory*, he was also influenced by American writers, including Melville, Twain, Stephen Crane, Henry James, T. S. Eliot, Hemingway, and Faulkner. Although Ellison was more hesitant to express his closer ties with his African American predecessors such as Hughes and Wright than he was aware, he frequently discussed their works in the light of his own ideas and techniques underlying *Invisible Man*. All in all, what makes *Invisible Man* a unique modernist novel is its various cultural strands that have gone into its composition.[5]

2

Many of his essays suggest that Ellison underplayed the concept of self-creation, a major ideology inherited from national character, whether the ideology was ingrained in the African American or the European American tradition. The treatment of this theme in *Invisible Man*, however, strongly suggests that Ellison was highly conscious of the theories and practices of self-creation advocated by his American predecessors, such as Wright and Emerson. Wright and Emerson both taught Ellison that it is essential for African Americans to create themselves rather than be given identity by society. Wright's and Emerson's writings alike provide Ellison with an admonition that if a writer does not find needed theories, techniques, and representations to exist, the writer must invent them.

Wright's conception of self-creation is shown in *Black Boy*, the book Ellison admired the most among Wright's works. In that autobiography Wright enabled the narrator to convey the truth about African American experience as did Ellison in *Invisible Man*. What distinguishes *Black Boy* from Wright's other narratives was not an application of literary naturalism but a creation of perspective. This concept of perspective, which Wright finds most difficult to represent in a narrative, has an affinity with Ellison's concept of invisibility in his novel. The intellectual space Wright theorizes comprises, on the one hand, an African American writer's complex consciousness deeply involved in his or her experience and, on the other, a detachment from it. By a detachment Wright means a reflection accomplished in isolation, in a space like the underground hideout in *Invisible Man*, where neither those afflicted, such as Trueblood, Wheatstraw, and Mary, nor those sympathetic to their plight, such as Jack, Ras, and Sybil, are allowed to enter. Writing, though foregrounded in the clashing dialogue between the protagonist and others in society, as Wright argued in *American Hunger*, "had to be done in loneliness" (123).

Wright's attempt to establish perspective and provide it with intellectual space accounts for his lifelong commitment to a narrative by which he is able to express his own vision of life. Wright's determination to bring home such a narrative is similar to Ellison's dedication to writing *Invisible Man*. Wright's entire work has shown that Wright, like Ellison, was a remarkably resilient thinker and writer. At the outset of his career, his writing was as deeply influenced by Marxism as those of some other American writers, including Ellison. But later, as Wright became independent of the Marxist manifesto, he considered only the theory of class struggle valid and applicable to African American life but rejected, as did Ellison's invisible man, much of the Marxist practice, which suppressed freedom and individualism.

Whether Ellison attempted to draw an analogy between his concept of self-creation and Emerson's or wished to subvert Emerson's political ideology,[6] the reader is reminded of Ellison's creation of a fictional character named Emerson in *Invisible Man*. In his essay "The Negro and the Second World War," a 1943 editorial in *Negro Quarterly*, Ellison declared, "As long as Negroes fail to centralize their power they will always play the role of a sacrificial goat, they will always be 'expendable.' Freedom, after all, cannot be imported or acquired through an act of philanthropy, it must be won" (238). Ellison's admonition for African Americans' self-creation and autonomy in this editorial echoes Ralph Waldo Emerson's, stated in an 1844 journal entry:

> When at last in a race a new principle appears an idea, that conserves it. Ideas only save races. If the black man is feeble & not important to the existing races, not on a par with the best race, the black man must serve & be sold & exterminated. But if the black man carries in his bosom an indispensable element of a new and coming civilization, for the sake of that element no wrong nor strength nor circumstance can hurt him, he will survive & play his part. . . . The intellect, that is miraculous, who has it has the talisman, his skin & bones are transparent, he is a statue of the living God, him I must love & serve & perpetually seek & desire & dream on: and who has it not is superfluous. . . . I esteem the occasion of this jubilee to be that proud discovery that the black race can begin to contend with the white. . . . The negro has saved himself, and the white man very patronizingly says, I have saved you. If the negro is a fool all the white men in the world cannot save him though they should die. (*Selected Writings*, 123–24)

Although Emerson's statement on the antislavery issue betrays his condescension to African Americans, his argument for self-help and self-creation concerns humanity as a whole. Emerson, moreover, bases his argument on transcendentalism, his own observation that intellect, individualism, is a divine gift. "Days," Emerson's most favorite poem, written six years after the journal entry above, reads:

> Daughters of Time, the hypocritic Days,
> Muffled and dumb like barefoot dervishes,
> And marching single in an endless file,
> Bring diadems and fagots in their hands.
> To each they offer gifts after his will,
> Bread, kingdoms, stars, and sky that holds them all.
> I, in my pleached garden, watched the pomp,
> Forgot my morning wishes, hastily

Took a few herbs and apples, and the Day
Turned and departed silent. I, too late,
Under her solemn fillet saw the scorn.
(*Selected Writings*, 481)

This poem expresses Emerson's condescension to himself as a mere human being just as does his earlier journal entry to African American slaves. Emerson, however, places greater emphasis on human beings' tendency to be remiss in heeding God and rely on others than he does on the issues of race and gender.

In *Invisible Man*, self-reliance and self-creation function as Ellison's central theme. As Ellison's protagonist begins to doubt the import of Marxism in achieving African American individualism and independence, he reminisces about his college professor, who once discussed James Joyce's hero. "Stephen's problem, like ours," the invisible man heard his professor say, "was not actually one of creating the uncreated conscience of his race, but of creating the *uncreated features of his face*. Our task is that of making ourselves individuals" (354). To Ellison, Stephen's achievement is not the Irishman's success in transcending the oppression of the Irish by the English but his creation of an individual capable of seeing himself not as a member of a race, class, and gender, but a member of the human race. "[If] you have man," Emerson asserts, "black or white is insignificance. . . . I say to you, you must save yourself, black or white, man or woman. Other help is none" (*Selected Writings*, 123).

Ellison and Emerson not only agree on the principles of self-help and individualism, but both also share the vision that the achievement of African American individualism leads to the creation of a culture worthy of universal respect and admiration. Emerson projected in the journal entry quoted earlier that "if the black man carries in his bosom an indispensable element of a new & coming civilization . . . he will survive & play his part" (*Selected Writings*, 123). In the same journal entry, Emerson recognized that African Americans were on the verge of creating a culture worthy of his respect. In *Invisible Man*, on the other hand, Ellison draws an analogy between the creation of Irish culture conceived by Joyce's hero Stephen and the creation of African American culture seen by the invisible man. For Ellison, creating a culture for African Americans means creating "something far more important" than a race. "For the first time, lying there in the dark," the invisible man says, "I could glimpse the possibility of being more than a member of a race" (*IM*, 354–55).

Throughout the novel the Emersonian concept of self-reliance underlies the development of the invisible man's character. Even at the outset of his search for identity, Ellison's hero suspects that fighting a battle royal might lure him away from finding himself. "In those pre-invisible days," he ponders, "I visualized myself as a potential Booker T. Washington" (18). In his subsequent search and ordeal, various personages he encounters serve as a catalyst to making him less invisible to himself and others. Mr. Emerson's secretary gives the invisible man an advice: "But I want to help you do what is best. . . . What's *best*, mind you. Do you wish to do what's best for yourself?" (188). "Oh, God!" the secretary finally utters, "Don't you see that it's best that you do *not* see him?" (189).

Later in the novel, other figures likewise play the role of a catalyst for the invisible man's self-realization. The vet the invisible man meets urges him to be self-reliant and independent.[7] Wheatstraw serves as a model of the ideal African American—independent, self-reliant, and compassionate. As he comes in contact with his Marxist comrades like Brother Jack and Ras the Exhorter, he slowly realizes his own identity: "For one thing," he says, "they seldom know where their personalities end and yours begins; they usually think in terms of 'we' while I have always tended to think in terms of 'me'—and that has caused some friction, even with my own family" (316). It is this concept that Ellison finds lacking and hence invisible in American life.

3

Commenting on the essays collected in *Shadow and Act*, Ellison writes:

> The very least I can say about their value is that they performed the grateful function of making it unnecessary to clutter up my fiction with half-formed or outrageously wrong-headed ideas. At best they are an embodiment of a conscious attempt to confront, to peer into, the shadow of my past and to remind myself of the complex resources for imaginative creation which are my heritage. (xxii-xxiii)

Ellison sounds modest in calling some of his ideas "half-formed or outrageously wrong-headed." But when he calls these essays "an attempt to transform some of the themes, the problems, the enigmas, the contradictions of character and culture native to my predicament, into what André Malraux has described as 'conscious thought'" (xix), Ellison is acknowledging the import of existentialism, an ideology that underlies *Invisible Man* as equally as do other philosophies of life.

Ellison also remarks in the same introduction:

> When I began writing in earnest I was forced, thus, to relate myself consciously and imaginatively to my mixed background as American, as Negro American, and as a Negro from what in its own belated way was a pioneer background. More important and inseparable from this particular effort, was the necessity of determining my true relationship to that body of American literature to which I was most attracted and through which, aided by what I could learn from the literatures of Europe, I would find my own voice, and to which I was challenged, by way of achieving myself, to make some small contribution, and to whose composite picture of reality I was obligated to offer some necessary modifications. (xix)

Indeed, *Invisible Man* reverberates various voices heard in some of the well-known existential works of fiction by Ellison's contemporaries in America as well as in Europe. But what is interesting and significant to Ellison's novel as a representation of modern African American culture is that the protagonist's existential outlook is subtly tempered and modified by other related and yet different kinds of experience and thought Ellison cherished as an African American.

One of the existential works of fiction to which *Invisible Man* bears a striking resemblance is Wright's novella "The Man Who Lived Underground" (1945). In both stories the protagonist's identity is withheld throughout: the invisible man is anonymous just as Wright's protagonist is not clearly identified. Wright's underground man once spells his name on a typewriter in lower case as "freddaniels" (55). Alienation from society, a dominant theme in existential writing, is also characteristic of both works; initially the invisible man is convinced, as is Daniels, that being an African American is responsible for his alienation from society at large. The two men, who try to be good, law-abiding citizens, both suffer from the oppression that stems from what they consider a lawless, amoral, corrupt, and chaotic world with little human value and little hope for renewal.

Despite their anonymity, both protagonists are portrayed as highly realistic characters. Throughout the story, Fred Daniels is not an African American man in name only. Not only is his plight real, but all the major incidents and characters he is involved with, which at times appear to be

clumsily constructed representations, nevertheless reflect the racial struggle and oppression from which an African American like him suffers. Ellison's novel, on the other hand, is replete with such realistic personages as
Dr. Bledsoe, Norton, Wheatstraw, the vet, Mary, Sybil, Ras, and Jack. Once
confined in the sewers, Daniels is completely isolated from the white world,
and the only group of people he encounters is an African American congregation in a basement church. Even though they are African Americans,
he feels completely alienated from them. "After a long time," the narrator
says, "he grew numb and dropped to the dirt. Pain throbbed in his legs and
a deeper pain, induced by the sight of those black people groveling and
begging for something they could never get, churned in him" (*EM*, 33).

Similarly, once the invisible man settles down in his Harlem underground, he loses interest in returning to "Mary's, or to the campus, or to the
Brotherhood, or home" (*IM*, 571). The invisible man, finding the members
of the Brotherhood a group of deluded Marxists, becomes disenchanted
with their activities just as Daniels, seeing the black congregation, a group
of fanatic Christians, comes to despise them. Such scenes in both stories
are not inserted as symbols but serve as graphic details of the futility and
oppression of modern life. Such episodes not only make for depth but also
are subtle representations of existential ideology and protest.

Despite such similarities, however, there remain considerable differences in outlook between the two works. Wright's vision of society is far more
deterministic than Ellison's; unlike a typical antihero of the modernist novel that the invisible man is, Daniels, a racial victim, has no choice but to
flee to the underground world. He has no choice as well but to confess to a
crime he did not commit. The narrator at once intimates that Daniels "was
tired of running and dodging" (*EM*, 27), a case history of oppression and
persecution. The reader learns later that Daniels has falsely been accused
of the murder of one Mrs. Peabody. Her identity as a white woman is not
suggested until the midpoint of the story. Immediately after the episode
in the grocery, as Daniels steps into the world above, the narrator says, "A
few shy stars trembled about him. The look of things was beautiful, yet he
felt a lurking threat." Walking toward a deserted newsstand, Daniels sees
"a headline: HUNT NEGRO FOR MURDER" (49). At the end of the story
the racial theme is once again intensified. Unable to comprehend Daniels's
vision of the underworld, Lawson, one of the policemen, shoots him down,
insisting, "You've got to shoot his kind. They'd wreck things" (92). Unlike
Daniels's motive for living underground, the invisible man's is to hibernate

and re-create himself. "Here, at least," the invisible man says, "I could try to think things out in peace, or, if not in peace, in quiet. I would take up residence underground. The end was in the beginning" (*IM*, 571).

In contrast to Ellison's existential view of African American life, Wright's idea of the universal human condition is expressed in terms of a dialectic. Daniels, now settled in the underground cave, argues, "Maybe *any*thing's right, he mumbled. Yes, if the world as men had made it was right, then anything else was right, any act a man took to satisfy himself, murder, theft, torture" (*EM*, 64). What Daniels calls "the world as men had made it" is precisely the fact of human history, not a utopia, philosophy, or religion. For him, of course, it constitutes a world of racism and oppression. If such a world were deemed right, then, it would follow that any one person's offense—"murder, theft, torture"—would be right. What Daniels is saying rings true because one person's offense, however serious it may be, can scarcely compare with even a fraction of the past, not to mention the future, injustices in American society.

The ambiguity in Daniels's judgment of human behavior and the conflict between the personal and societal judgments lead to a nihilistic spirit which Wright, unlike Ellison, attempted to express in this story. For Daniels, at least, a human action, whether it is well intended or not, has no meaning. For a person to find value in his or her act or in a society that has victimized the person is sheer futility. If such value should exist, Daniels asserts, it should be annihilated.

On the contrary, the invisible man's worldview is not nihilistic. A series of epiphanies given underground provide the invisible man with an uplifting, congenial expression for human existence. He now realizes that he should be able to emulate an African American like Trueblood, an existential hero, who has created himself and now has his own life and destiny under control. Upon severing his lingering ties with the Brotherhood, the invisible man now begins to conceive a more compassionate worldview than before with a concept of brotherhood quite different from what Marxists and Communists believe in. He now wonders:

If only I could turn around and drop my arms and say, "Look, men, give me a break, we're all black folks together . . . Nobody cares." Though now I knew *we* cared, they at last cared enough to act—so I thought. If only I could say, "Look, they've played a trick on us, the same old trick with new variations— let's stop running and respect and love one another." (*IM*, 560)

The attitude he now takes toward his fellow African Americans is in singular contrast to the one he used to have at the beginning of the novel. Living under the tutelage of Dr. Bledsoe, he was pretentious and condescending to his peers, just as was Norton to Dr. Bledsoe and to him.

The invisible man's having compassion upon others is reminiscent of the vision that Cross Damon in Wright's existential novel has as he lies dying on a New York street. Wright presents Damon's worldview with some contradiction. Early in the novel Damon considers himself a nihilist, but at the end of his life he becomes a man of compassion. In *The Outsider*, Wright seems to have taken the risk of contradicting himself not only because of the realistic accumulation of detail but also because of his insistence that Damon judges life inherently meaningful, as does Ellison's invisible man. What is common between the two African American intellectuals is their constant compulsion to take action in search of the meaning of their lives. Unlike Daniels, they are endowed with what Emerson called "[the] intellect, that is miraculous" and God-given (*Selected Writings*, 123), as well as with the spirit of freedom to create an essence. Their actions result in something, whether it is love or hatred, happiness or tragedy. In the end, they create their existence and achieve their identity.

4

Some of the modernist novelists in Europe and America who produced existential works were also interested in Eastern thoughts and religions and in Zen Buddhism, in particular. Camus's *The Stranger*, as noted in a previous chapter, presents Meursault as an antihero who finds no meaning in life. Using crime as a thematic device, Camus focuses on the psychological effect of Meursault's crime on his vision of existence. After Meursault is sentenced to death, however, he realizes for the first time that his life has been enveloped in the elusive beauty of the world. Despite his death sentence, he remains calm and happy, for he has cleansed his mind of materialistic desire and fear. The prisoner, though alone and trapped by a society without human values, is freed from within. Meursault's state of mind at the end of his life is akin to Zen enlightenment.

Like Meursault, Daniels in Wright's story is also liberated from desire, greed, and hatred. In fact, Daniels is free of self-centered thought. It is difficult to determine whether Wright had Zen philosophy in mind when he wrote "The Man Who Lived Underground." But there is much evidence to indicate that, at least toward the end of his life, Wright was interested in

Zen philosophy and aesthetics, especially in haiku, as noted in the introduction and discussed in chapter 11 on Wright's haiku.[8]

The visions of human life Meursault and Daniels have at the end of their lives also resemble the outlook on life Ellison's invisible man gains underground. Early in the novel the invisible man, coming in contact with Trueblood, receives a revelation about African American life and identity. The invisible man learns that Trueblood, encountering the hardship of his life, "looks up and sees the stars and I starts singin'." "I don't mean to," Trueblood says, "I didn't think 'bout it, just start singin'. I don't know what it was, some kinda church song, I guess. All I know is I *ends up* singin' the blues" (*IM*, 66).

Like Wright's haiku, "It Is September," Trueblood's observation of human life is not based on thought but upon his spontaneous response to natural spirituality. In Zen-inspired art, nature is the mirror of humanity. Zen practice calls for self-effacement; one should not allow oneself to control action. "Drink tea when you are thirsty," writes Yone Noguchi, "eat food in your hunger. Rise with dawn, and sleep when the sun sets. But your trouble will begin when you let desire act freely; you have to soar above all personal desire" (*Story*, 242). This tenet of Zen, which teaches the followers to emulate nature, was one of the Taoist influences on Zen. Lao Tze said, "Man takes his law from the earth; the Earth its law from Heaven; Heaven its law from *Tao*; but the law of Tao in its own spontaneity" (*SJP*, 43). The twin deeds—naturalness and spontaneity—are in Zen the means by which human beings can be connected with the absolute, the achievement of satori. From a Zen point of view, such a vision of life as Trueblood attains is devoid of much thought and emotion. Trueblood thus enlightens himself by looking up and seeing stars and expresses his satori by singing the blues. For him, natural spirituality and the blues are the means by which he attains his enlightenment.

At the outset of the novel, the invisible man is also aware of various means by which he may be able to achieve his enlightenment. "Perhaps," he says, "I like Louis Armstrong because he's made poetry out of being invisible" (*IM*, 8). To make his invisibility visible, Ellison's protagonist literally and figuratively uses the electricity stolen from Monopolated Light & Power. "And I love light," he says. "Perhaps you'll think it strange that an invisible man should need light, desire light, love light. But maybe it is exactly because I *am* invisible. Light confirms any reality, gives birth to my form." The invisible man's form, then, is analogous to the state of nothingness in Zen. The hole in his Harlem underground has nothing in it and is dark, but now it is lit up like Broadway and the Empire State Building, the two brightest spots, which he satirically remarks, "are among the darkest of our whole civilization—pardon me, our whole *culture* (an important distinction, I've heard)." Ellison is treating this hole as a trope, for the invisible man says, "The point is now that I found a home—or a hole in the ground, as you will. Now don't jump to the conclusion that because I call my home a 'hole' it is damp and cold like a grave; there are cold holes and warm holes. Mine is a warm hole" (6).

Trueblood is also conscious of this state of mind when he sings the blues: "I sings me some blues that night ain't never been sang before, and while I'm singin' them blues I makes up my mind that I ain't nobody but myself and ain't *nothin'* I can do but let whatever is gonna happen, happen" (66, emphasis added). Not only is Trueblood's state of mind devoid of desire, egotism, and untruth, it is also capable of destroying any false social, political convention, tradition, and belief. Like Trueblood, a Zen Buddhist must purge his or her mind and heart of any materialistic thoughts and feelings and appreciate the wonder of the world here and now.

As does Trueblood, the invisible man gradually realizes that he has followed false conventions and beliefs. When the invisible man is handed over yams and called "one of these old-fashioned yam eaters," he nonchalantly responds, "They're my birthmark. . . . I yam what I am" (266). But at the same time it occurs to him, "What and how much had I lost by trying to do only what was expected of me instead of what I myself had wished to do? . . . I had accepted the accepted attitudes and it had made life seem simple" (266–67). Once he has settled down in his Harlem underground, however, he redeems himself. He finally realizes that, unlike Robert Frost as portrayed in his poem "The Road Not Taken," the invisible man has been a conformist all his life. "So after years of trying to adopt the opinions of others," he declared, "I finally rebelled. I am an *invisible* man. Thus I have come a long way and returned and boomeranged a long way from the point in society toward which I originally aspired" (573).

While the invisible man's rebellion against convention leads to his embracement of Emersonian self-reliance and individualism, his resolution at the end of the novel suggests that he is not entirely satisfied with his view of himself. The difference in the concept of individualism between Emersonian transcendentalism and Zen philosophy lies in one's view of self. Emerson defines enlightenment as self's consciousness of the over-soul, God, while Zen calls it self's achievement of relating self to the spirit of nature, a state of nothingness, where neither the ego of an individual nor the over-soul of God exists.

In contrast to Emerson, Zen, as noted earlier, is strikingly similar to Lacan's concept of human subjectivity.[9] In particular, the primacy of natural spirituality over human subjectivity, which Zen stresses, has a closer resemblance to Lacan's critique of subjectivity, which posits the human subject's inability to attain the real of natural experience. In *The Seminar of Jacques Lacan: Book I*, Lacan as a Zen master challenges his students to undermine their subjectivity. Because the emergence of the unconscious for Lacan constitutes reaching "the real Other," the conscious self, which is corrupted by male-oriented language and society, must be undermined.[10] For Emerson, on the other hand, the conscious self identifies its individuality with God, the over-soul, but this subjectivity is still emphasized in terms of the self.

Ellison's concept of individualism, represented by the invisible man, seems more closely allied with the concept of human subjectivity in Zen and Lacan than it is with Emerson. In fact, *Invisible Man* has few references in which the word of God or the over-soul is heeded. Earlier in the novel, the invisible man describes Dr. Bledsoe: "He stood before us relaxed, his white collar gleaming like a band between his black face and his dark garments, dividing his head from his body; his short arms crossed before his barrel, like a black little Buddha's" (118). The invisible man, seeking an interview with Mr. Emerson, sees in his office, which looks like a museum, "an ugly ebony African god that seemed to sneer (presented to the school by some traveling millionaire)" (181). It looks as though, while Emerson wishes to rely on the self as much as on God, Ellison and Lacan refuse to rely on Him. Zen's doctrine of self calls for the follower to annihilate self in reaching the state of nothingness so as to liberate self from the habitual way of life. In Zen, one must destroy, just as must the invisible man and Lacan, not only the self contaminated by society, but also God, Buddha, Christ, any prophet, or any idol, because it is only the true self, the self without the ego, that can deliver the person enlightenment.

It is this state of mind, a state of nothingness, that Ellison's protagonist is trying to achieve. At the end of the novel he calls the Zen-like state of mind "the *mind*": "So I took to the cellar; I hibernated. I got away from it all. But that wasn't enough. I couldn't be still even in hibernation. Because, damn it, there's the mind, the *mind*" (573). Later in the epilogue Ellison again intensifies his fascination with this state of mind (580). The invisible man's definition of "the *mind*" is neither his mind in the past nor the Emersonian conception of self. It is remindful of the Zen conception of the "here and now," as well as of Lacan's notion of the real. "It [*the mind*] wouldn't let me rest," the invisible man says. "Gin, jazz and dreams were not enough. Books were not enough. My belated appreciation of the crude joke that had kept me running, was not enough" (573). Dismissing from his mind his past endeavors, he wonders, "But what do *I* really want, I've asked myself. Certainly not the freedom of a Rinehart or the power of a Jack, nor simply the freedom not to run. No, but the next step I couldn't make, so I've remained in the hole" (575).

What the invisible man means by "the next step" is the real step, which is neither imaginary nor guided by anyone. In Zen Buddhism, life is endowed with spontaneity and natural spirituality. "Life is to be lived," he says, "not controlled" (577). In the tradition of Zen instruction, the attainment of satori is as practical as is actual human life. When the young Bassui, who later became a celebrated Zen priest in Japan in the fourteenth century, asked his master, "What's the highway to self-elevation?" the master replied, "It's *never stop*." Failing to understand, Bassui persisted: "Is there some higher place to go on to?" The master finally answered, "It's just underneath your standpoint."[11]

At the end of the novel, the invisible man, without a Zen master, meditates underground, awaiting the answer to his own question. Later in the epilogue, Ellison intensifies the invisible man's preoccupation with this answer:

> In going underground, I whipped it all except the mind, the *mind*. And the mind that has conceived a plan of living must never lose sight of the chaos against which that pattern was conceived. That goes for societies as well as for individuals. Thus, having tried to give pattern to the chaos which lives within the pattern of your certainties, I must come out, I must emerge. (580–81)

This vision of life offers "infinite possibilities," one of which he says he has now taken. "What a phrase—still it's a good phrase," he says, "and a good view of life, and a man shouldn't accept any other; that much I've learned underground" (576). While his view of life looks like Melville's symbolization of the whiteness of the whale, in which the universe appears indefinite, void, and invisible,[12] his outlook on his own life also has a strong affinity with the principle of the "here and now" in Zen philosophy.

10

PAGAN SPAIN: RICHARD WRIGHT'S
DISCOURSE ON RELIGION, POLITICS, AND CULTURE

Upon its publication, *Pagan Spain* (1957) appeared to signal a departure from Wright's earlier nonfiction and from *Black Power* (1954) and *The Color Curtain* (1956) in particular. While the two previous travelogues are focused on the non-Western world, African and Asian cultures, respectively, *Pagan Spain* is primarily concerned with a Western culture. But what is common among the three works is, as *Black Power* and *The Color Curtain* have shown, that the narrator is distinctly an American. Although Wright claims the African heritage, in *The Color Curtain* he does not speak like an African. Even though he speaks in *Pagan Spain* as a European resident, he still remains an American. If these works are read as travelogues, commentaries on foreign cultures, his perspectives of vision strike one as realistic, impartial, and critical.

That *Pagan Spain* contains many disparaging remarks about Spanish culture is partly responsible for the fact that the book has been published in such European countries as Germany, Holland, Sweden, and Italy, but not in Spain. Wright's aim at achieving objectivity is indicated by his interview with a magazine reporter in 1959: "*Pagan Spain* is about a journey—or rather it's a descriptive account of three automobile trips I made in Spain, the Spanish people I met, the fiestas, flamencos, bullfights, the feeling of the country, the warmth of the people and the incredible poverty."[1] As this statement suggests, his intention for the book—unlike *The Color Curtain*, in which the informants are predominantly intellectuals, what he calls "Asian elites"—was to deal with all classes of the Spanish people, including aristocrats and gypsies, businessmen and workers, dancers and prostitutes, matadors and pimps, priests and shop clerks. As a result, *Pagan Spain* turns out to be not only a vivid portrayal of Spain after World War II but also an acute cultural criticism just as *Black Power* and *The Color Curtain* served as highly insightful cultural criticisms of Africa and Asia, respectively. Because Wright had established his reputation by the end of World War II, his later works, as Paul Gilroy has observed, attracted little critical attention.[2]

As Hemingway in the 1920s took Gertrude Stein's advice, which partly led to writing such books on Spain as *The Sun Also Rises* (1926) and *For Whom the Bell Tolls* (1940), Wright eagerly listened to the legendary authoress when he arrived in Paris in 1946. "You'll see the past there," she told him. "You'll see what the Western world is made of. Spain is primitive, but lovely. And the people! There are no people such as the Spanish anywhere. I've spent days in Spain that I'll never forget. See those bullfights, see that wonderful landscape" (*PS*, 1–2). Despite Stein's urging, however, he had postponed his journey for nearly a decade. In the summer of 1954, at the urgings of his friends Alva and Gunnar Myrdal, the well-respected Swedish sociologists, he finally drove past the Pyrenees to Barcelona. In contrast to Gertrude Stein's romanticized, traditional, and ritualistic view of Spanish culture, *Pagan Spain* is dedicated to Myrdals, *"who suggested this book and whose compassionate hearts have long brooded upon the degradation of human life in Spain."*

This dedication intimates that his immediate motive for the book was to explore the fate of Spanish exiles and victims under Franco's totalitarian regime. Reflecting on his own experience in America, he says, "I had never been able to stifle a hunger to understand what had happened there and why. . . . An uneasy question kept floating in my mind: How did one live after the death of the hope for freedom?" (2). What Myrdal called "the degradation of human life in Spain" reminded him of his birth under a racist government in Mississippi, of his formative twelve years under the dictatorship of the American Communist Party, and of a year of his intellectual life under the terror of Argentine dictator Perón. "The author," as a reviewer noted, "gives his reader bitter, stark facts at the same time that he unwittingly reveals his own bitter, hurt self."[3] His avowed opposition to Franco's totalitarianism, evident throughout the text, contributed to the better reviews *Pagan Spain* received in the United States than did *Black Power* or *The Color Curtain*.

But some American readers "were shocked to see" a black writer discuss a white culture. Before Wright, a usual pattern had been for a Western anthropologist or a Western writer like Joseph Conrad to comment on Asian or African life. If Wright considered himself an African, his situation would have been the opposite of that of a Western writer. He declared, "I was reversing roles."[4] If, on the other hand, he regarded himself as an American writer, commenting on Europe as he did, indeed, signaled a reversal of commenting on America as did Alexis de Tocqueville and D. H. Lawrence, whose views of American culture remain classic. Similarly, from today's vantage point, Wright's view of Spain remains a unique cultural criticism.

Three years after the publication of *Pagan Spain*, *L'Express*, in its interview with him, posed this question: "Is there in the United States an important output of Negro literature, and do you number many friends among these writers?" In response he stated:

> Yes, many. Negro literature in the United States is actually so important that it even preoccupies our government. American blacks are testifying against the most modern of Western countries. . . . In the United State, the tendency is to tell black writers: "Don't be preoccupied with your experience as Negroes. Don't be polarized by it. You are people. Write exactly as any other people would do on any other subject." I would be inclined to tell them, "On the contrary, take your ghetto experience as a theme, for this precisely is a *universal* topic."[5] (emphasis added)

Wright is suggesting that one's racial experience is a representation of universal experience. By analogy, a Spaniard's experience represents not only Spanish culture but also universal experience. Not surprisingly, Wright's observations in *Pagan Spain* are closely related to those of African American experience.

1

What underlies Wright's cultural discourse in *Pagan Spain* is a notion that Spain, despite its history, was not nearly as Christian as it looked. His chief interest lies not in the Catholic Church as it became entangled with Franco's totalitarian regime, but in an exploration of the intriguing boundaries of Spanish religiosity. Initially he was puzzled by the Falangists, made up of "*half monks, half soldiers*" (60). He saw all of them worship the Virgin Mary, whose statue had been carved by St. Luke. "It is further claimed," Wright recounts, "that it was brought to Spain by St. Peter himself in A. D. 30." He was also told, "Hermán Cortés came here to ask blessings from the Black Virgin. Even Columbus made a pilgrimage here" (60). As his exploration of Spain's religious character delves into the past against the present political situation, and into the interior against the Catholic Church as a modern institution, his expressions become increasingly flexible, fluid, and dynamic. An anonymous reviewer interpreted *Pagan Spain* primarily as Wright's indictment against the machinations of the church and the state: "It is the Spain of the ready thumb of the church and the state, the thumb which twists and turns the lives of the poor mortals beneath it, shaping and moving the poor mortals in a way repugnant to much of the world."[6] While he relies on conventional metaphor, symbolism, and imagery in describing religious practices, he is bent on creating representations that strike the reader as unconventional, metonymical, and psychoanalytical.

Anyone commenting on the political situation of Spain in the 1950s could not help seeing the exploitation of the Catholic Church by the politicians. Their strategy was to equate Spanish Catholicism with Spain's glorious past; Catholicism was pitted against Protestantism, what the majority of Spaniards perceived as a decadent, materialistic religion. "The average Spaniard," Wright says, "knows nothing of Protestantism." Even Spanish intellectuals feel "uneasy when the subject of Protestantism is mentioned" (137). Juan Perrone, S. J., in his catechism in 1950, asserted that Protestantism came into its existence in Spain to propagate Socialism and Communism. But from Wright's point of view, Spanish Protestantism was far more concerned with the lives of the poor and socially oppressed than was Catholicism. Reflecting on his own Protestant background, he sympathized with the Spanish Protestants for "the needless, unnatural, and utterly barbarous nature of the psychological suffering" they had undergone at the hands of the religious and political officials. What interested him was a psychological, uncanny affinity that existed between the Protestants in Spain and African Americans, Jews, and other oppressed minorities in the United States. "It is another proof, if any is needed today," he argues, "that the main and decisive aspects of human reactions are conditioned and are not inborn" (138).

Economically, Catholicism in Spain fared worse than Protestantism. The Protestants were known for their ability to cope with reality, while the Catholics were slow in adapting themselves to change in life in general and industrialization in particular. To Wright, Protestantism, however suitable for industrialism and modernism, was rejected in Spain, just as was "the murderous rationalism of sacrificial Communism . . . in favor of an archaic collective consciousness based on family symbols: One Father, One Mother, One Spirit" (240). This definition of Spanish Catholicism as archaic, unrealistic, and impractical, however, is only attributed to a superficial characteristic of Spanish religiosity. Although Ferdinand and Isabel had driven the Moors out of Spain in 1492 under the banner of Catholicism,

Spanish culture kept intact, as Wright notes, "all the muddy residue of an irrational paganism that lurked at the bottom of the Spanish heart" (240). He is convinced that the Spanish people would turn back the clock of history and cling to paganism. In this old, predominantly Catholic nation, its social, religious, and familial customs and rituals, as he shows throughout the book, reflect a religious philosophy that is not Catholic but primitive and primeval.

As for the sources of paganism in Spain, he relies on the commonly held view: "the pagan streams of influence flowing from the Goths, the Greeks, the Jews, the Romans, the Iberians, and the Moors lingered strongly and vitally on, flourishing under the draperies of the twentieth century" (193). From time to time, he also implies that paganism in Spain had also come from Asia through Buddhism and possibly Confucianism, both of which antedate Christianity by five hundred years or more. Spanish paganism, he speculates, was related to the Egyptian divinity and the Akan god, which fascinated him when he traveled to West Africa.

But the most convincing argument for Spanish paganism is derived from his examination of the Black Virgin at Montserrat, one of the famous tourist attractions in Spain. "The ascent to Montserrat," he describes his own sensation, "was breath-taking. We climbed, spinning and circling slowly round the naked mountain peaks on tiny roads that skirted the sheer edges of cloud-filled chasms whose depths made the head swim" (60–61). The representations such a passage creates are avowedly Freudian, though Wright de-emphasizes it, and his approach to Spanish national character is unmistakably psychoanalytical:

> More and more nations of seriated granite phalluses, tumefied and turgid, heaved into sight, each rocky republic of erections rising higher than its predecessor, the whole stone empire of them frozen into stances of eternal distensions, until at last they became a kind of universe haunted by phallic images—images that were massive, scornful, shameless, confoundingly bristling, precariously floating in air, obscenely bare and devoid of all vegetation, filling the vision with vistas of a non- or superhuman order of reality. (61)

The phallic images that dominate the geological environment of the Black Virgin do not allude to what Saunders Redding called "a paganism as gross and a venality as vulgar as the temples of Baal."[7] To Wright, such images represent not *prurience*—a physical, as opposed to psychological, emotion—but *procreation*, "a non- or superhuman order of reality."

Wright indeed defines the genesis of the Virgin as non-Western. The Virgin in Spain is "a perhaps never-to-be-unraveled amalgamation of Eastern and African religions with their endless gods who were sacrificed and their virgins who gave birth perennially" (240). In portraying the statue of the Virgin, he seized upon the Virgin's black face exhibiting "a kind of quiet, expectant tension" (62). Her facial feature recalled a mixture of the Roman and the Oriental. Moreover, the infant Christ seated on her lap, possessing "that same attitude of quiet, tense expectancy," resembled her (63). Wright continued to speculate: "Maya, the mother of Buddha, was supposed to have been a virgin. Chinese temples have long had their images of the Holy Mother sitting with the Child on her lap. The Egyptians worshiped Isis, mother of Horus, as a virgin, and she was called Our Lady, the Queen of Heaven, Mother of God" (65).[8] In all these religions, then, the image of the mother symbolizes how human beings feel about their birth. Divinity or superhumanity, as he maintains, "is inescapably bound up with sex." As human beings throughout history have worshiped the mother, "the female principle in life," Spaniards have worshiped the Black Virgin (65). A reviewer of *Pagan Spain*, an American Catholic priest, called Wright's interpretation of paganism in Spain heretic: "Montserrat, for him, can be accounted for according to the categories of Freud's pan-sexual theories. This attempt to explain religious phenomena in the crude terms of sexual sublimation has well been described as a type of Machiavellian denigration. There is no space here to expose the fallacy."[9]

Viewing religion in Spain, as Wright does, from the perspective of superhumanism reveals that Spaniards were scarcely conscious of class and racial differences. Rather than staying at a hotel, he chose to spend the first night with a Spanish family in a village. To his surprise, the family took him into their Christian fellowship even before they knew his name. "To these boys," he remarks, "it was unthinkable that there was no God and that we were not all His sons" (9). Even the Falangists' book of political catechism includes such a dialogue:

ARE THERE THEN PEOPLE WHO WITHOUT BEING BORN IN SPAIN ARE SPANIARDS?

Yes; all who feel themselves to be incorporated in the destiny of Spain.

AND CAN THERE BE PEOPLE BORN IN SPAIN WHO ARE NOT SPANIARDS?

Yes; children of foreigners and those who disassociate themselves from the destiny of the Motherland.

THEN, DO YOU SEE CLEARLY THAT FOR US THE MOTHERLAND IS NOT THE LAND IN WHICH WE ARE BORN BUT THE FEELING OF FORMING PART OF THE DESTINY OR AIMS WHICH THE MOTHERLAND MUST FULFILL IN THE WORLD?

Yes.

WHAT IS THIS DESTINY?

To include all men in a common movement for salvation.

WHAT DOES THIS MEAN?

Ensure that all men place spiritual values before material. (23)

To the western industrialized world, the primacy of the spiritual over the materialistic looked irrational and primitive. Wright calls Spanish paganism "an infantile insistence upon one's own feelings as the only guide and rule of living . . . to sustain their lives by being overlords to the 'morally' less pure, to the 'spiritually' inferior" (151). It was not class and race but faith in universal superhumanism that determined one's superiority or inferiority in Spain.

2

Pagan Spain ends with Wright's lasting impression of the Virgin, made during his third and final visit to Seville. The hooded penitents in the procession were upholding the Virgin as if the Ku Klux Klan in the South were trying to protect white womanhood. But he says, "Some underlying reality more powerful than the glittering Virgin or southern white women had gripped these undeniably primitive minds. They were following some ancient pattern of behavior and were justifying their actions in terms that had nothing whatever to do with that pattern" (237). By "some ancient pattern of behavior," he means Spanish paganism, which has its psychological origin in the female principle of life. Though the Virgin in Spain was an established symbol of Catholicism, she was, in reality, a representation of paganism, the principle of eternal procreation: "A God died that man might live again, and the Virgin stood eternally ready to give birth to the God that was to die, that is, the Man-God" (238). Just as Wright was awed by the procreating image of the Virgin at Montserrat, he was struck again by what he witnessed in Seville: "The cross was held high and on it was the bloody, bruised figure of a Dying Man. . . . But behind the Dying Man was the Virgin ready to replenish the earth again so that Life could go on" (239), a spectacle remindful of the matriarchalism of the Ashanti, or the sun goddess in Japanese Shintoism.

Spanish religiosity, based as it was on sexuality, betrays another paradox. Toward the end of his travels, Wright met a naturalized Spanish woman who told him, "The Church here will tell you that the people here love God so much that sex has been conquered. But all that you hear about here is sex. When I first came here, I thought that the Spanish had just discovered sex—they talked so much about it, and they still do. Sometimes they act as if they invented sex" (212–13). To her, life was "upside down here" (213). Spaniards were obsessed with sex as much as with the Virgin; they were overly concerned with innocence as much as with sex. Such a contradiction revealed itself in all aspects of Spanish life. "Even the prostitution, the corruption, the economics, the politics," Wright observed, "had about them a sacred aura. *All was religion in Spain*" (192).

Although the preeminence of religion over sexuality suggests sexual repression on the part of Spanish men, it took a heavier toll on Spanish women. Antifeminism was rampant in all segments of Spanish society. At home men dominated women: "The women ate silently with one eye cocked in the direction of their men, ready at a moment's notice to drop their knives and forks and refill the half-empty masculine plates" (90). In public, men tended to move away from women and vice versa, a common scene indicating the separation of sexes. Young women, Wright saw, were always protected from contact with men so that virginity was guarded till marriage. At a hotel he found an American woman intimidated by the manager, who claimed that she had refused to pay for baths she did not take. The Spaniard "smiled and explained . . . that men were not, perhaps, superior to women, but they were certainly more intelligent. His air was one of cynicism and his manner asked me to join him in his masculine game of domination" (74). As a fellow traveler, Wright admonished her not to be hysterical: "You are acting like a Negro. . . . Negroes do that when they are persecuted because of their accident of color. The accident of sex is just as bad. And crying is senseless" (76).

Not surprisingly, Franco's Falangists were bent on brainwashing young women. The government officials imposed a "moral" position on Spanish women. While women were protected, men were allowed to exploit prostitutes, a blatant antifeminist contradiction. Under the Falangist doctrine, feminine heroism was defined as subservience to men: "*though for* [*women*] *heroism consists more in doing well what they have to do every day than in dying heroically.*" Women's temperament, the catechism continued, "*tends more to constant abnegation than to heroic deeds*" (77). Women under the Franco regime were called heroic if they sacrificed the pleasures of life for the sake of the dictatorship.

For Wright, the Falangist concept of the state, which denied the liberal doctrines of Jean Jacques Rousseau and the right of universal suffrage, was in direct opposition to superhumanism. This political repression, in turn, resulted in a sexual repression evident in the Flamenco dance. During his visit to the legendary Granada, Wright met an accomplished Flamenco dancer. He was deeply impressed by her performance as well as by the audience. "I pantomimed," he says, "what I wanted to say and they were willing to take time to imagine, to guess, and, in the end, to understand; and they were patiently determined to make others know and feel what they thought and felt." The dancer "began a sensual dance that made a kind of animal heat invade the room" (171). Even before the performance, he was keenly aware of the frustration of the people. He assured the dancer, whose husband had died in the civil war fighting for the republic against Franco, "I shall tell [Americans] that the people of Spain are suffering" (170). Wright was also a witness to the orgiastic ecstasy of the gypsy dance, the emotion that Western culture in general and modern Spanish culture in particular had long suppressed. Though a tourist himself, he watched the audience: "The Germans, Swiss, Americans, Englishmen gazed open-mouthed at an exhibition of sexual animality their world had taught them to repress" (167), a spectacle that suggests Carl Jung's collective, unconscious repression.[10]

Whether sexual repression in Spain was viewed collectively or individually, its chief culprit was the church. The church, which condemned sex, made Spaniards more conscious of it. In Europe, Spain had the highest rates of prostitution in the city as well as in the village. "To be a prostitute was bad," Wright quips at the church, "but to be a prostitute who was not Catholic was worse" (21). This collective, almost unconscious sexual repression that permeated Spanish society manifested itself in a vicious circle of prostitution and the church. Spanish Catholicism was "a religion whose outlook upon the universe almost legitimizes prostitution" (151). The Spanish people largely acquiesced in a circular argument the church had maintained over the centuries: "Sin exists, so declares this concept. Prostitution is sin, and proof of sin. So prostitution exists." This universal prostitution, then, was not regarded as something that must be eradicated, a cynical sign that "the work of salvation is not yet complete" and that the church must make "a more strenuous effort" to save men as well as women in the name of God (152).

From a sociological perspective, the church and prostitution helped each other. The church took great pride in its generosity by accepting fallen women under any circumstances with open arms: "a prostitute can at any time enter a church and gain absolution" (152). Such generosity, however, was not always considered a genuinely religious endeavor by Spanish men. Rumor ran rampant throughout the country that some priests openly took advantage of "lonely" women, let alone prostitutes who sought salvation in the church. Since sexual freedom was condoned by the church, Spanish laymen were jealous of the sexual lives of the priests. A Spanish man felt that "if they can do it and get away with it, so can I." Wright reflects, "I, for one, feel it naïve in our Freudian, twentieth-century world even to allude to the bruited sexual lives of priests and nuns. I do not know nor am I interested in whether they have sexual lives or not. I hope that they do, for their own sake; and I'm sure that God does not mind" (154). Given paganism and superhumanism that characterized Spanish religion and culture, Wright's reflection emphasizes a conviction that human sexuality, as exhibited at Montserrat, as well as in the Spanish Catholic Church, was the best and absolute proof of the existence of God.

From an economic point of view, prostitution and poverty were intertwined in Spain. In the middle of the twentieth century, Spain was the poorest nation in Western Europe. As an American, Wright paid homage to Seville, where Christopher Columbus's body was held in the cathedral. Despite the surrounding lands rich with orange groves, olive gardens, and wheat and rice farms, "the impression of poverty was so all-pervading, touching so many levels of life that, after an hour, poverty seemed to be the normal lot of man." Recollecting the fertile southern landscape and the teeming city life in America he had left behind, and Paris and the peaceful southern provinces of France, Wright comments, "I had to make an effort to remember that people lived better lives elsewhere" (178). Seville, a capital of "white slave" trade, was not only a glaring metonym but also the whole nation "seemed one vast brothel" (187). In Spain, poverty and sexuality indeed went hand in hand.

Spanish sexuality begins in childhood. "No people on earth," Wright stresses, "so pet and spoil their young as do the Spanish" (152). A Spanish woman at an early age is trained to be a "seductress." Once married to a poor man, she can justify selling her body if it is for feeding her children. On a national level, sex is regarded as a medium of exchange for goods and services. Significantly as well, "white slavery between Spain and the bristling brothels of North Africa is a wide-scale, well-organized, and genially conducted business—prostitution being perhaps the biggest business in the Mediterranean world" (150). Just as a poor young mother in the village is tempted to become a prostitute for the sake of feeding her hungry children, a young domestic earning low wages in a coastal city is enticed to travel to North Africa as a prostitute rather than "to be an ill-clad, half-starved slave to some spoiled, bourgeois Spanish wench" (151). Prostitution flourished in Spain, for there was behind this indigenous poverty a persistent pagan outlook upon life, a love of ritual, dance, sex, and nightlife.

3

Among the rituals, customs, and social activities Wright saw in Spain, bullfighting created a profound impression on his understanding of Spanish culture and religion. On the surface, a bullfight was a representation of the Spaniard's love for ritual and ceremony, "a delight in color and movement and sound and harmony" (151). But underneath, this cruel ritual smacks of the central paradox of Spanish religion. On the one hand, bullfighting as a religious ritual found its sanction and justification in the canons and practices of Spanish Catholicism. On the other, however, it was antithetical to Spanish paganism, what Wright calls superhumanism, as represented by the Black Virgin at Montserrat, as noted earlier. Whereas Spanish Catholics believed in the sanctity of saving the human soul over protecting the nonhuman life, pagans, such as Buddhists and Hindus, made no distinction between human beings and the rest of the animate because they believed that the soul resides in them as well as in animals.

The paradox of bullfighting is also apparent in the expression of "*Ole!*" when the matador incites the bull. The expression means "For God's sake," the pagan religious phrases of the Moors, but the audience, as Wright points out, were not aware of the pagan origin of the expression. It is ambivalent that the matador and the audience were invoking the name of God in keeping with the Christian as well as pagan tradition. Wright makes a reference in the footnote to Américo Castro's *The Structure of Spanish History* (*PS*, 90).

As the opening section of *Pagan Spain*, "Life after Death," reaches its apogee with the concept of eternal procreation, the female principle in life, as represented by the Black Virgin of Montserrat, the following section,

"Death and Exaltation," is dramatized with the portrayal of a bullfight Wright attended in Barcelona. At the beginning of the journey into Spain he befriended a Catalan family with whom he stayed for a short period. They told him that Spaniards, and Catalans in particular, "don't shrink from dark skins" and that they were traditionally miscegenational (80). But once he went into a village, he was constantly stared at as if he were a total stranger, one who did not belong to Europe. "Amidst these naïve yokels," he felt, "I became something that I had never been before, an object that was neither *human* nor *animal*, my dark skin and city clothes attracting more attention than even the bullfighters" (emphasis added, 131–32). While some Spaniards would consider him neither human nor animal, it seemed as though bullfighting was a religious ritual which reflected both Catholicism, a religion eminently concerned with the human soul, and paganism, a superhuman and pantheistic philosophy of life encompassing all forms of life on earth.

From this ambivalent point of view, Wright's description of the bullfight is a unique achievement. Above all, he was able to describe not only how the bullfighter faced death but also how the bull himself felt:

Chamaco's left hand now grasped the muleta firmly; he turned away from the bull, looking at him sideways, letting the red cloth drop below his left knee. He now lifted his gleaming sword chin high and sighted along the length of it, pointing its sharp, steel tip at the tormented and bloody mound of wounds on the bull's back. . . . The bull's horns rushed past his stomach as Chamaco tiptoed, leaning in and over the driving horns, and sent the sword to its hilt into the correct spot in the bull's body.

The bull halted, swayed. Chamaco stood watching him, gazing gently, sadly it seemed, into the bull's glazed and shocked eyes. . . .

I watched the bull. He sagged, his eyes on his tormentor. He took an uncertain, hesitant step forward, and then was still. Chamaco lifted his right hand high above the bull's dying head; it was a gesture that had in it a mixture of triumph and compassion. The bull now advanced a few feet more on tottering legs, then his back legs folded and his hind part sank to the sand, his forelegs bent at the knees. And you saw the split second when death gripped him, for his head nodded violently and dropped forward, still. A heave shook his body as he gave up his breath and his eyes went blank. He slid slowly forward, resting on his stomach in the sand, his legs stretching straight out. He rolled over on his back, his four legs already stiffening in death, shot up into the air. (111–12)

Although Wright vividly describes human's battle against beast, the triumph of human's will over nature's power, as sanctioned by Catholicism, his implication is unmistakable: the bullfight is a crime against life, nature, and God. Viewed from any religious vantage point, it is a blatant representation of the depravity of the human soul. At the conclusion of the bullfight, he says, "The man-made agony to assuage the emotional needs of men was over" (112).

What agonized Wright the most about this ritual, as it would perhaps have agonized any humanist, was the behavior of the audience in the bullring in the aftermath of the slaughter. He was appalled to see the spectators wildly rush to the dead bull, kick its testicles, stomp them, spit at them, and grind them under their feet, "while their eyes held a glazed and excited look of sadism" (134). Even though the bull was dead, they looked as though they were venting their long-repressed feelings. Such a behavior reflected one that occurred during the performance as well: "The peak of muscle back of his neck gushed blood. That was the way it had been planned. The means were cruel; the ends were cruel; the beast was cruel; and the men who authored the bloody drama were cruel. The whirlpool of discordant instincts out of which this sodden but dazzling drama had been projected hinted at terrible torments of the heart" (102). As noted earlier, the cruelty of a bullfight is a reflection of the human-centered Catholicism, in which beast, part of nature, is regarded as human's adversary. In a pagan religion, the followers are taught to respect man as well as beast. Wright was quick to point out that, though the predominant sentiment of the crowd was sadistic, there were some who had compassion upon the bull: "The crowd began to howl, protesting, disapproving, fearing that the bull was being punished too much, would be too weak to fight well" (104–5). This sentiment of the spectators was a sign not only of paganism but also of universal humanism.

The sadism displayed on the part of the spectators also involved the bullfighter. One Whitney, an American, who lived in Spain to become a bullfighter, informed Wright that the bullfight "has the intensity of religious emotion" and that the bullfighter is expected to offer his life to the bull. "Without that, there is no bullfight," Whitney explained (130). "More and more, when you're in the ring, you're not fighting the bull; you're trying to live up to the legend the public has built up about you. They ask for risks and they boo you when you refuse to take them. When the bullfighter believes in his legend and tries to obey the crowd, he's on his way to the graveyard" (131). Such a testimony suggests that Spaniards were fascinated by the cruelty perpetrated not only on the bull but on the bullfighter, a perverted psychology akin to one often seen among the spectators who enjoy watching race car accidents.

In Wright's description of the bullfight, the cruel treatment of the dead bull by the spectators is suggestive of the lynch victims he had witnessed in the South. In his poignant portrayal of a lynching in "Big Boy Leaves Home," the victim is hanged on a tree and burned alive as the white mob chants in an ecstasy of joy.[11] In *The Long Dream*, Wright's last novel, Chris, the protagonist's friend, is lynched for having had sexual relations with a white girl; consequently he is castrated and white women are fascinated by his genitals.[12] Watching the bullfight, Wright was filled with horror at the sadism the ritual created: "It had been beautiful and awful and horrible and glorious," he thought, "and ought to have been forbidden." When he confessed, "I was revolted, but hungry for more . . . indignant, but bewitched, utterly" (109), he was also expressing the paradox of Spanish character.

This sadism, a sign of human selfishness, to which he thought Spaniards were prone, was in contrast to the African primal outlook upon life he saw among the Ashanti. As reported in *Black Power*, he was enormously impressed by the African reverence for the nonhuman life, an innate faith in nature that was absent in Christianity in general and Catholicism in particular. In his journey into Africa, Wright also found a strong resemblance between the Akan religion and a pagan religion such as Buddhism. Africans, as he saw in Ghana, would not cut down a live tree without first appeasing its spirit; they identified its livelihood with theirs. Both the Akan religion and Buddhism share the faith that humankind occupies a mere fraction of the universe. Small wonder that Wright, as he watched the bull being slaughtered, poured out his deepest sympathy for it; he was genuinely concerned about how it felt, as most of the Spaniards were ecstatic about its tragic death.

If the bullfight was viewed as a uniquely Christian ritual, it was nothing more than a religious practice in which the followers were taught not only how to accept the inevitability of death but also how to create death, a means of sacrificing animal life for the benefit of human life. This human selfishness, egotism, once more manifested itself in the drama enacted in the bullring: "*There was no doubt but that this beast had to be killed!* He could be allowed to linger along; he could be played with, teased even, but he had to go, for there was no possibility of coming to terms with him. . . . This beast had not only to be slain, but *ceremoniously* slain—slain in a manner that would be unforgettable" (97). For Wright, the drama signified the mystery and miracle of human life. The mystery rested upon "why the human heart hungered for this strange need"; the miracle involved "the heart's finding that a rampaging bull so amply satisfied that need" (98).

As the Catholic priest offered faithful prostitutes absolution, the matador as a lay priest offered a mass in front of a huge audience in the bullring, the guilty penitents. What the priest and the matador shared was a common practice in which they themselves gained salvation in their work. But Wright realized that the matador's work was far more disciplined than the priest's. Whitney, the American bullfighter, told him that bullfighters in Spain "are not supposed to touch women or liquor. This is not to help you in fighting the bull; it is to keep you in condition to recuperate when you are gored. And make no mistake, you will be gored" (130). When the lives of the priest and the matador were compared, Whitney's observation that the bullfight, buttressed as it was by intensely religious emotion, always took risk of one's life seemed an ironic understatement.

Relying on Whitney's experience and understanding, Wright was fascinated by the emotional aspect of the bullfight. Whitney told him, "The essence of the bullfight is not in moving around, but in standing still. And that's a hard thing to do. When you're holding that muleta and facing a bull, your instinct prompts you to run. And if you do, you're dead, for the bull can outrun you. You must plant your feet in the sand and face death" (129). Whitney's understanding was derived from Juan Belmonte, the most celebrated matador in Spain. Wright was interested in Belmonte's characterization of bullfighting as, in Belmonte's words, "a spiritual exercise and not merely a sport. Physical strength is not enough." Wright interpreted this exercise as "the conquering of fear, the making of a religion of the conquering of fear. Any man with enough courage to stand perfectly still in front of a bull will not be attacked or killed by that bull" (113). Wright was told the local legend of a matador who stood sill reading a newspaper and of a bull that ignored him. But Wright thought it humanly impossible and inconceivable for a man to remain still against a surging beast that weighs ten times as much as he does.

While Juan Belmonte's concept of bullfighting was concerned with the emotional aspect of the sport, the test of courage in the face of death, Hemingway was interested in portraying the technical and artistic aspects of the rite. Hemingway describes Romero's bullfight in *The Sun Also Rises* as though he were drawing a painting:

The bull did not insist under the iron. He did not really want to get at the horse. He turned and the group broke apart and Romero was taking him out with his cape. He took him out softly and smoothly, and then stopped and, standing squarely in front of the bull, offered him the cape. The bull's tail went up and he charged, and Romero moved his arms ahead of the bull, wheeling, his feet firmed. The dampened, mud-weighted cape swung open and full as a sail fills, and Romero pivoted with it just ahead of the bull. At the end of the pass they were facing each other again. Romero smiled. The bull wanted it again, and Romero's cape filled again, this time on the other side. Each time he let the bull pass so close that the man and the bull and the cape that filled and pivoted ahead of the bull were all one sharply etched mass. It was all so slow and so controlled. It was as though he were rocking the bull to sleep. He made four veronicas like that, and finished with a half-veronica that turned his back on the bull and came away toward the applause, his hand on his hip, his cape on his arm, and the bull watching his back going away. (216–17)

As Wright in *Pagan Spain* discusses the concept of Belmonte, who, fighting the bull closely, displayed his courage in facing death, Hemingway in *The Sun Also Rises* also refers to Belmonte's principle of always working close to the bull. "This way," Jake Barnes, Hemingway's mouthpiece, says, "gave the sensation of coming tragedy. People went to the corrida to see Belmonte, to be given tragic sensations, and perhaps to see the death of Belmonte" (214). Because Belmonte in the novel is neither a major character nor a representation of bullfighting as a religious rite, Hemingway underplays Belmonte's role and underscores Romero's bullfight as a central image of lovemaking:

The bull was squared on all four feet to be killed, and Romero killed directly below us. He killed not as he had been forced to by the last bull, but as he wanted to. He profited directly in front of the bull, drew the sword out of the folds of the muleta and sighted along the blade. The bull watched him. Romero spoke to the bull and tapped one of his feet. The bull charged and Romero waited for the charge, the muleta held low, sighting along the blade, his feet firm. Then without taking a step forward, he became one with the bull, the sword was in high between the shoulders, the bull had followed the low-swung flannel, that disappeared as Romero lurched clear to the left, and it was over. The bull tried to go forward, his legs commenced to settle, he swung from side to side, hesitated, then went down on his knees, and Romero's older brother leaned forward behind him and drove a short knife into the bull's neck at the base of the horns. The first time he missed. He drove the knife in again, and the bull went over, twitching and rigid. (220)

Wright, on the other hand, describes the bullfight as a test of one's courage in the face of death. He watched this drama of life for man, or death for beast, as it unfolded in the bullring. "Man and beast," he writes, "had now become fused into one plastic, slow-moving, terrible, delicate waltz of death, the outcome of which hung upon the breath of a split second" (*PS*, 109).

In contrast to Hemingway's treatment of the matador, Wright was interested in bullfighting as a profession. Compassionate as he was, Wright was troubled to see that a young bullfighter was too young to risk his life, but Wright was told by a Spanish informant that the boy, coming from a poor family, had become rich: "Pain caused by a bull's horn is far less awful than pain caused by hunger" (107). Such a fact of poverty recalls a social and economic environment that bred prostitutes for the sake of feeding hungry children. Observing the young matador's performance, Wright also felt that the young man "did not quite believe in the value of what he had done . . . and harbored some rejection or doubt about the Niagara of applause that deafened his ears" (113). The boy, in fact, regarded the bullfight as nothing more than his livelihood; neither emotionally nor philosophically was he concerned with his profession.

4

Despite the deeply religious tradition, whether Catholic or pagan, that buttressed its culture, Spain in modern times revealed degradation at all levels of society. Before Wright begins his discourse, he quotes two lines from Carl Sandburg:

> *I tell you the past is a bucket of ashes.*
> *I tell you yesterday is a wind gone down,*
>   *a sun dropped in the west.*

Wright is alluding to his own observation that the vestiges of the glorious past were scarcely visible in modern Spain. Not only did Spain lose its political influences in the modern world, but its spiritual tradition also fell victim to materialism and a decadent commercialism. Even though Spain remained a vital part of the capitalist world, its development was hampered by its outdated social and economic policies and practices. *Pagan Spain* begins with a quotation from Nietzsche, "*How poor indeed is man*," and ends with Wright's own statement "How poor indeed he is." By "he" Wright means the twentieth-century Spaniard, modern Spanish national character, that had lost touch with "the *rich* infinities of possibility looming before the eyes of men," the "hearts responding to the call of a high courage," and "the will's desire for a new wisdom" (emphasis added, 241). For Wright, the Spanish people were indeed economically poor, but more importantly they seemed *poor* at adapting themselves to a modern progressive culture.

Throughout the text Wright tries to demonstrate the conservatism that gripped Spanish life individually as well as collectively. He saw, for instance, a Spanish Communist leader carry a statue of the Virgin on his back in an Easter procession because the statue was from his own neighborhood. To Wright's informant, this was a glaring contradiction. "I cannot support that kind of nonsense," the man uttered. "That man had sworn that he did not believe in God. Yet there he was carrying the Virgin. How can you fight with men who twist and turn like that?" (215).

Conservatism and traditionalism in Spain, on the other hand, had little effect on its race relations. Surprisingly, Wright found most Spaniards free of racial prejudice. None of them he met during his travels showed a trace of racism, with which he was so accustomed in America and by which he was on occasion disturbed in France. Not only was he welcomed by Spaniards personally and affectionately wherever he visited, but he found them, and young intellectuals in particular, invariably antiracist, anti–anti-Semitic, anti-Franco, anti-imperialist, anti-Russian, and anti-American.

For Wright, Spaniards as a whole possessed an innate virtue that enabled them to relate to their fellow human beings on a personal and spiritual basis rather than in terms of a social and political relationship, a human-made trait that plagued race relations in America. Such a virtue notwithstanding, Spaniards were found as pecuniarily greedy as Americans, with a materialistic outlook on life that also degraded their culture. Historically, Spanish colonialists had been regarded as less resistant to miscegenation than other Europeans, and yet, as a Spanish informant told Wright, "We gave them our culture in a way that no other European nation ever did, and we meant it. But we were greedy; we were after gold. And that ruined us" (213).

One of the culprits responsible for Spain's cultural stagnation was the church. Spanish intellectuals were all in agreement that reforming the archaic tradition must begin "at the cradle" and with "a new generation"

(204). But the church, in collaboration with Franco, the Falange, and the army, was always in the way of change. Earlier in his discussion of Spanish character Wright has posed this question:

> But why was Spain a dictatorship? I had long believed that where you found tyranny, such as exists in Russia, you would also find a confounding freedom secreted somewhere; that where you had a stifling bureaucracy, such as in France, there was a redeeming element of personal liberty; that where you had a police state, such as was in Argentina, you had under it, disguised, a warm comradeship; and that where you had a restrained and reserved attitude, such as is in England, you had, somewhere nearby, equalizing it, a licentious impulse to expression. *Did that principle hold true in Spain?* (12)

Wright's subsequent observation confirmed that a sense of freedom and open-mindedness existed in Spain only on the surface of its daily living.

Otherwise, as Wright recognized, the Spanish mind was stifled by its own uniquely religious and irrational consciousness. Indeed, Spanish culture was irrational as Akan culture was irrational. And the sacredness and irrationality of Spain was in contrast to the secular that had liberated the rest of Europe from its past. Even compared with some part of Africa, and most of Asia, Spain lagged behind in its progress toward modernism. "The African," Wright remarks, "though thrashing about in a void, was free to create a future, but the pagan traditions of Spain had sustained no such mortal wound" (193). Africa and Asia, as he saw, were endowed with seeds of modernism, while Spain sadly was locked in tradition and religion.

Such a critical view of Spain notwithstanding, Wright was nevertheless sympathetic to the energetic maternal instinct of the Spanish woman, without which Spanish culture would not have survived after World War II. He discovered, for example, a strong affinity between the indigenous matriarchalism in the Ashanti, as discussed in *Black Power*, and the stalwart womanhood in Spain. Spain, beleaguered as it seemed by modernism and multiculturalism, withdrew into the past to regain its usable elements, however irrational and primeval they might have appeared in the eyes of the world. Over the centuries, Spanish men had built a state but never a society, a fact of history that betrayed another paradox of Spanish culture. Wright was convinced above all that Spanish women, not Spanish men, had borne the burdens of an economically poor nation. As women worked and reared children, men idled away their time talking abstract nonsense in the countless establishments of entertainment that flooded an otherwise chaotic landscape. If there was a semblance of society, it was based only on the hearts and minds of women whose devotion to life stabilized Spain. This apotheosis of Spanish womanhood is derived from the female principle in life, a salient characteristic of pagan Spain.

11

PRIVATE VOICE AND BUDDHIST ENLIGHTENMENT IN ALICE WALKER'S *THE COLOR PURPLE*

Nineteenth-century American writers such as Emerson, Thoreau, and Whitman expressed their profound interest in Eastern philosophies and religions. When Emerson declared, "The Buddhist . . . is a Transcendental-ist" (*CEOE*, 91–92), he meant that Buddhism, unlike a religion, is a philos-ophy that emphasizes the primacy of the spiritual and transcendental over the material and empirical. Zen Buddhism in particular, unlike other sects in the same religion, teaches its believer how to achieve Buddhahood with-in the self, a precept that sounds much like the one given by Emerson, who urges the reader to think not for the sake of accomplishing things but for the sake of realizing one's own world. The achievement of godhead within, rather than its discovery elsewhere, is echoed by Thoreau and Whitman as well. *Walden* shows the reader how to attain one's enlightenment through natural objects like trees, birds, and sands. In "Song of Myself" Whitman admonishes the reader, "Not I, not any one else can travel that road for you, / You must travel it for yourself" (64).[1]

In twentieth-century American literature, the influences of Eastern thought and poetics on Ezra Pound and William Carlos Williams in the 1910s and 1920s are well-known,[2] as is the fascination of the writers of the Beat Movement in midcentury, such as Jack Kerouac, Allen Ginsberg, and Gary Snyder, with Zen Buddhism, as noted earlier. Since the late fif-ties, not only have a number of African American writers—including Richard Wright, Charles Johnson, Ishmael Reed, Alice Walker, and Toni Morrison—all paid their homage to African philosophies and religions, but they have also expressed their strong interest in cross-culturalism. Among these writers, Wright, as shown in a previous chapter, was deeply influenced by Zen philosophy and aesthetics.

Although much of the contemporary African American literature focuses, as does Wright's later work, on African American cultural traditions, it is also drawn from, or meant to reflect on, cross-cultural and multicultural traditions and ideologies. *The Color Purple* (1982) serves as a prime example of such a text. While the novel reads distinctly contemporary because it concerns the gender conflicts and racial issues of the African American tradition, as well as of the more recent American cultural dialogue, it also reflects as strongly the philosophical and religious traditions of other cultures. In particular, I would like to demonstrate that, in establishing herself, the central character, Celie, acquires her own voice through Buddhist enlightenment. Walker has recently stated publicly that she considers herself a Buddhist, but it is unknown whether she had, in fact, an affinity with Buddhist thought when she wrote the novel over two decades ago. My primary aim is not to try to find the sources for Walker's interest in Buddhism but, through intertextuality, interauthoriality, and cross-culturalism, to show a reading of the Buddhist enlightenment behind Celie's self-creation, the novel's central theme.

1

At the outset of her story, Celie is deprived of her own voice. Finding herself at a loss, she is unable to express herself. *The Color Purple* begins with a letter to God so that He may provide her with voice:

> Dear God,
> I am fourteen years old. ~~I am~~ I have always been a good girl.
> Maybe you can give me a sign letting me know what is happening to me.
> (1)

Although she is able to hear the public voice that describes her pregnancy, for example, she does not understand what that description means, nor is she able to express her feelings about the traumatic event that has befallen her: "A girl at church say," Celie writes to God, "you git big if you bleed every month. I don't bleed no more" (6).

Despite her repeated appeal to God, He has failed to grant her a voice. As late as the midpoint of the story, when a series of other disasters have taken place, she continues to complain:

Dear God,

....

But I feels daze.

My daddy lynch. My mama crazy. All my little half-brothers and sisters no kin to me. My children not my sister and brother. Pa not pa. (183)

One of the difficulties Celie faces in her quest for voice is the concept of God she had inherited from Christian doctrine: God and Christ are both male figures. To dramatize this dilemma, a gulf between His voice and hers, Walker develops a dialectic discourse. Her sister Nettie, who works for a Christian missionary stationed in the Olinka community in Africa, continues to communicate with Celie in the language Nettie has learned. Whereas Nettie's language is stilted, wordy, and lengthy, Celie's is ungrammatical, terse, and choppy. But Celie's language, like Huck Finn's, is vernacular and sounds more natural than Nettie's. Just as Huck's language subverts Tom's, so does Celie's "outsmart" Nettie's, which smacks of patriarchy, sexism, and political correctness.

The most important characteristic of Celie's language is poetry. Even at the outset of the story, the reader is impressed that Celie has potential to become a poet; she is indeed endowed with poetic inspiration like a young boy whose "tongue's use sleeping," in Whitman's "Out of the Cradle Endlessly Rocking."[3] In *In Search of Our Mothers' Gardens* (1983), Walker discusses Celie's prototype: those ancestral "grand mothers and mothers of ours . . . not Saints, but Artists; driven to a numb and bleeding madness by the springs of creativity in them for which there was no release. . . . Perhaps she sang . . . perhaps she wove the most stunning mats or told the most ingenious stories of all the village storytellers. Perhaps she was herself a poet–though only her daughter's name is signed to the poems we know" (233–43). A young African American's potentiality to become a poet is also reminiscent of the young Richard Wright's lyricism, vividly described in *Black Boy*. One of Wright's haiku, "Don't they make you sad, / Those wild geese winging southward, / O lonely scarecrow?" (*HTOW*, 146), originates from a passage in *Black Boy*: "There were the echoes of nostalgia I heard in the crying strings of wild geese winging south against a bleak, autumn sky" (*BB*, 14).[4]

The most serious obstacle that stands in the way of her search for voice is the fact that the public voice, the language of society, is dominated by males. As the story begins, Celie is forced to identify the public voice with the voice of Alphonso, who she supposes is her father but turns out to be her stepfather. Since God fails to answer her letters, she cannot help accepting Alphonso's voice as the voice of so powerful earthly authority. She is always at the mercy of Alphonso's language and action; during his first rape, Alphonso starts to choke her, saying, "You better shut up and git used to it" (2). When her mother asks her who is her newborn baby, Alphonso's, she gives an ambiguous reply: "I say God took it. He took it. He took it while I was sleeping. Kilt it out there in the woods. Kill this one too, if he can" (3). In Celie's voice, God and Alphonso are merged into the almighty patriarchal figure.

As the story unfolds, however, Walker's use of patriarchal discourse becomes less direct and pervasive and at times reads subtle. For example, Albert's family and his father, in particular, are portrayed as conventional and conservative. Albert's father tries to forbid Albert to marry the flamboyant blues singer Shug Avery for fear that her unknown paternity and her erotic behavior will ruin the family reputation. Albert's brother Tobias also tries to dissuade Albert from living with Shug so as to set up a rivalry between Celie and Shug, known as "Queen Honeybee," a patriarchal, antifeminist putdown. Such episodes suggest that even a man like Albert falls victim to the oppressive patriarchal family system as does Celie. Besides Shug, another blues singer, Mary Agnes, also challenges the patriarchal, racist convention; Mary creates her own songs:

> They calls me yellow
> like yellow be my name
>
> They calls me yellow
> like yellow be my name
>
> But if yellow is a name
> Why ain't black the same
>
> Well, if I say Hey black girl
> Lord, she try to ruin my game (104)

By denying her nickname and the categorization of color and sexual attraction made up by a racist society, Mary is able to express herself through her own voice.

Celie learns from Shug and Mary that the first step in creating her own voice is to make male language female. If Celie's "text, her creation of selfhood, is to proceed," Lindsay Tucker points out, "the male text of the deity must be overturned and rewritten in female terms."[5] All the male figures Celie is associated with in the beginning are called by their generic male titles: her father by "Him," Albert by "Mr.—," Samuel by "the Rev. Mr.—." Little wonder Nellie tries to make Celie acquainted with the deity of the Olinka. In her letter to Celie, Nettie writes, "We know a roofleaf is not Jesus Christ, but in its own humble way, is it not God? So there we sat, Celie, face to face with the Olinka God. And Celie, I was so tired and sleepy and full of chicken and groundnut stew, my ears ringing with song, that all that Joseph said made perfect sense to me. I wonder what you will make of all this?" (160).

This letter clearly indicates that Nettie understands the Olinka god to be male. In this connection it would be significant to contrast the Olinka god with the Akan god, the divinity of the Ashanti in West Africa, a central theme of Wright's *Black Power*.[6] The Akan god, as Wright learned, is female, and, as he expounds its history and doctrine, the religion has over the centuries supported the survival of their life and culture. If Nettie's letter about the Olinka intimates some forms of female oppression in that society, Wright's observation vindicates the absence of such oppression in the Ashanti.[7]

2

To acquire a voice of her own, as Celie soon realizes, must be accompanied by a treatment of her own body as a precious being. As Albert's wife, she is treated as if she were a commodity like a cow and her body is used like a toilet. She has no pleasure but pain in their sexual relations, and he always demands that she keep his house clean and take care of his unruly children. "He beat me like he beat the children," Celie complains. "Cept he don't never hardly beat them. He say, Celie, git the belt. The children be outside the room peeking through the cracks. It all I can do not to cry. I make myself wood" (23). Regarding her body as a piece of wood is equating a living being with a material thing. Buddhism teaches its believer that the soul exists not only in human beings but in all living beings. At this point of her self-creation and search for voice, she says to herself, "Celie, you a tree. That's how come I know trees fear man" (23).

A few scenes later, Walker, through Celie's mouth, gives a parable of Buddhist enlightenment with a pair of lucid signifiers, a living tree and a table:

Everybody say how good I is to Mr.— children. I be good to them. But I don't feel nothing for them. Patting Harpo back not even like patting a dog. It more like patting another piece of wood. Not a living tree, but a table, a chifferobe. Anyhow, they don't love me neither, no matter how good I is. (31)

Her quest for voice and identity reaches its apogee when Shug Avery discusses with her the meaning of God. Shug says, "God is inside you and inside everybody else. You come into the world with God. But only them that search for it inside find it" (202). Upon hearing this definition of God, Celie applies it to her own life: "She say, My first step from the old white man was trees. Then air. Then birds. Then other people. But one day when I was sitting quiet and feeling like a motherless child, which I was, it come to me: that feeling of being part of everything, not separate at all. I knew that if I cut a tree, my arm would bleed" (203).

Shug's epiphany that God resides inside Celie and inside everybody else is akin to Emersonian and Whitmanesque transcendentalism. But Shug's further observation that only those who search for God inside them find it and Celie's knowledge that cutting a living tree is the same as cutting her arm suggest that Walker's belief bears a strong resemblance to Zen Buddhism. Zen teaches that divinity exists in nature only if the person is intuitively conscious of divinity in the self. To Emerson and Whitman, on the other hand, God exists in nature regardless of whether the person is capable of such intuition.

When Celie asks Shug whether God is male or female, Shug answers, "Yeah, It. God ain't a he or a she, but a It." To Celie's persistence, "But what do it look like?" Shug says, "Don't look like nothing. . . . It ain't a picture show. It ain't something you can look at apart from anything else, including yourself. . . . Everything that is or ever was or ever will be. And when you can feel that, and be happy to feel that, you've found It" (202–3). Shug's use of the word "nothing" is remindful of the Zen doctrine of *mu* and satori. This state of mind is absolutely free of materialistic and egotistic thought and emotion; it is so completely free that such a consciousness corresponds to that of nature. This state of mind is what postmodern psychoanalysts like Lacan call the unconscious and the real, the truth that is neither imaginary nor symbolizable.

Shug's and Celie's Zen-like enlightenment also has a striking affinity with what Wright calls in *Black Power* "his [the African's] primal outlook upon life" (266).[8] Just as enlightened Celie sees herself and trees, Wright saw in African life a closer relationship between human beings and nature than he did between human beings and their social and political environment. In his haiku, as well as in *Black Power*, Wright takes great pains to express a Zen-like enlightenment in which human beings must learn the conscious or unconscious truth of human existence from the spirit of nature.

The primacy of the spirit of nature over the strife of humanity is what Walker and Wright share. This primal vision of life, which has its genesis in *Black Boy* and its further pronouncement in much of Wright's later work, does underlie Walker's characterization of Celie and Shug in *The Color Purple*. In Wright's "Blueprint for Negro Writing" (1937), as pointed out earlier, one of the theoretical principles calls for the African American writer to explore universal humanism. Wright's explanation of the Ashanti convinced him that the defense of African culture meant renewal of Africans' faith in themselves. He realized that African culture was based upon universal human values—such as awe of nature, family kinship and love, faith in religion, and honor—that had made the African survival possible.

Before discussing Ashanti culture in *Black Power*, Wright quotes a passage from Edmund Husserl's *Ideas* that suggests that the world of nature is preeminent over the scientific vision of that world, that intuition is preeminent over knowledge in search of truth. Similarly, Wright's interpretation of African philosophy and Walker's demonstration of that philosophy in *The Color Purple* both recall a teaching in Zen Buddhism. Zen's emphasis on self-enlightenment is indeed reflected in Walker's characterization of Celie in *The Color Purple*. At the climactic moment of the novel, Shug, like a Zen master, gives her disciple, Celie, an admonition on the doctrine of *mu*: "You can just relax, go with everything that's going" (203). With a senryu-like sense of humor, Shug continues her admonition: "I think it pisses God off if you walk by the color purple in a field somewhere and don't notice it" (203).[9] "The color purple," as a free signifier, may mean many things, but I would like to read it as Zen enlightenment.

3

If Shug played the role of a Zen master, she would urge Celie to be self-reliant and find her own path in search of truth and happiness. This is what happens in the story after Shug gives Celie a lesson on the color purple. In the tradition of Zen instruction, the attainment of satori is as practical as it is in actual human life. When the young Bassui, a celebrated Zen priest in medieval Japan, asked his master, "What's the highway to self-elevation?" The master replied, "It's *never stop*." Bassui failed to understand what the master meant; the master told him, "It's just underneath your standpoint."[10]

The master's point about *"never stop"* is reminiscent of the spirit's reply to Whitman in "Song of Myself":

> This day before dawn I ascended a hill and look'd at the
> crowded heaven.
> And I said to my spirit *When we become the enfolders of those*
> *orbs, and the pleasure and knowledge of every thing in*
> *them, shall we be fill'd and satisfied then?*
> And my spirit said, *No, we but level that lift to pass and*
> *continue beyond*
> (*CPOW*, 64)

The Zen master's pronouncement also recalls the last passage in "Song of Myself": "If you want me again look for me under your boot-soles. / . . . / . . . / . . . / Failing to fetch me at first keep encouraged, / Missing me one place search another," (*CPOW*, 68).

Shug's admonition of self-enlightenment and self-reliance is described with sorrow and stoicism:

> Dearest Nettie,
> Sometimes I think Shug never loved me. I stand looking at my naked self in the looking glass. What would she love? I ast myself. My hair is short and kinky because I don't straighten it anymore. . . . Nothing young and fresh. My heart must be young and fresh though, it feel like it blooming blood.
> I talk to myself a lot, standing in front the mirror. Celie, I say, happiness was just a trick in your case. Just cause you never had any before Shug, you thought it was time to have some, and that it was gon last. Even thought you had the trees with you. The whole earth. The stars. But look at you. When Shug left, happiness desert. (*CP*, 266)

This letter is reminiscent of Emerson's poem "Give All to Love," which is an admonition that stoical self-reliance must be kept alive underneath one's passion: "Heartily know / When half-gods go, / The gods arrive" (*PRWE*, 65). As long as one relies on others, "half-gods," one cannot attain enlightenment.

Celie's self-creation, inspired by self-enlightenment, depends upon annihilating the patriarchal and racist view of African American women and accepting her own body as beautiful and worthy of love and happiness.

Although Celie thinks Shug's desertion of her is a sign for lack of love, perhaps mistakenly, she feels her heart is still "young and fresh" and is "blooming blood" (266). Earlier in the story, Shug has taught Celie that what Celie felt beautiful and happy was exactly what God felt: "God love all them feelings. That's some of the best stuff God did. And when you know God loves 'em you enjoys 'em a lot more" (203). Such a revelation has also made Celie realize that a female body is a beautiful reflection of nature and divinity. She has learned from Nettie that both the Olinka and Christians have a worldview just opposite to Celie's newly experienced outlook. Like the Ashanti, Celie is convinced that human beings are not the center of the universe. Nettie, on the other hand, writes, "I think Africans are very much like white people back home, in that they think they are the center of the universe and that everything that is done is done for them. The Olinka definitely hold this view. And so they naturally thought the road being built was for them" (174). *Black Power* demonstrated that the Ashanti were conscious of the unimportance of human beings in the universe.[11] Celie thus shares her worldview with the Ashanti as Nettie does not.

Celie's change of heart about human life has now led to a more tolerant attitude toward others. Celie no longer hates Albert as she used to, for she now realizes that he is genuinely in love with Shug, who used to love him as well. Celie also observes that, like herself, he listens to her as if he were a disciple receiving admonition from a Zen master:

> Plus, look like he trying to make something out of himself. I don't mean just that he work and he clean up after himself and he appreciate some of the things God was playful enough to make. I mean when you talk to him now he really listen, and one time, out of nowhere in the conversation us was having, he said Celie, I'm satisfied this the first time I ever lived on Earth as a *natural* man. It feel like a *new* experience. (267, emphasis added)

Albert's recognition of himself being "a natural man" suggests that, like a true Buddhist, he adheres more to the spirit of nature than to the egotism of humanity. His life as "a new experience" suggests that it is based on Zen doctrine. Zen is not considered a religion that teaches the follower to have faith in a monolithic deity. Like Thoreauvian transcendentalism, Zen teaches one a way of life completely different from what one has been conditioned to lead.

As her worldview changes in the course of her story, Celie also learns under Shug's guidance that one must experience sexuality with the spirit of nature. A consummation of love she experiences with Shug is portrayed as a natural maternal experience of love: both make love not only without guilt and repression but without egotism and oppression. Indeed, annihilation of egotism and oppression is one of the cardinal principles of life taught in Buddhism. "Then," Celie says to God, "I feels something real soft and wet on my breast, feel like one of my little lost babies mouth. Way after while, I act like a little lost baby too" (118). Evoking "heaven," the supreme spirit of nature, or nirvana, Celie tells God, "I feel Shug's big tits sorta flop over my arms like suds. It feel like heaven is what it feel like, not like sleeping with Mr.— at all" (119). Referring to the sexual relationship between Celie and Shug, Linda Abbandonato argues that sexuality is able to "resist the ideological laws that operate through its very terrain, to survive and flourish in 'aberrant' forms despite the cultural imposition of a norm." She also considers this kind of sexuality "highly disruptive potential."[12] In the context of the novel, however, the sexuality of Celie and Shug seems far from "aberrant" and disruptive; rather it reads natural and peaceful.

Not only is this sexuality depicted as an innate maternal act of love, it reads as an ideal act of love between two individuals. It is concentric, as opposed to phallocentric; Shug and, in particular, Celie have both been victimized by the patriarchal and racist convention. Even Shug, a seemingly liberated woman, has fallen victim to the antifeminist prejudice that Albert's family perpetuates. Most importantly, these two individuals' sexuality is consensual; their motive is an enactment of genuine, requited love. Their sexuality transcends all elements of materialistic desire in society that stand in the way of the search for love and happiness. Shug as a fictional character is not used for what Henry James calls *ficelle*, a functional character.[13] She appears in the story not merely as what Lindsey Tucker calls "an image, an objectification of the female to counter the victim-figures."[14] Like Celie, whose heart "feel like it blooming blood" (266) and whose "arm would bleed" if she "cut a tree" (203), Shug also feels her heart pounding and feels her arm would bleed if she cut a live tree; both share the spirit of nature, upon which Buddhist doctrine is based.

In this novel, Celie's and Shug's sexuality as drawn with Zen-like spontaneity and naturalness, is diametrically opposed to that fundamentally flawed human relationship, the rape of a woman by a man, which destroys love and tenderness, the most universal and precious human values. Some readers may call the two women's sexuality lesbian. Julia Kristeva has observed that "to believe that one 'is a woman' is almost as absurd and obscurantist as to believe that one 'is a man.'"[15] I agree with Kristeva and would like to say further that to call Celie and Shug lesbians is to grossly misread their sexual relationship. In *The Color Purple* Celie and Shug are *hito* or *ningen*, human beings, as they are called in Buddhist texts.

12

TONI MORRISON, RICHARD WRIGHT, AND AFRICAN CULTURE

What Wright's travelogues and Morrison's *Beloved* (1987) have in common is to reconsider Western discourse, which is characterized by imperialism and a male-centered worldview. Schoolteacher in *Beloved*, for example, functions as an agent representing the most treacherous kind of institutional evil. Such a figure operates with the approval of a hegemonic culture under the guise of reason and enlightenment. This figure represents European imperialists and Christian missionaries in Wright's *Black Power* as it does the Falange and the Catholic Church in his *Pagan Spain*. The expedition that Sethe, Schoolteacher's pupil, makes outside school teaches her to refute lessons given by her teacher. In a similar vein, Wright, who had left America, where he was born and schooled, made an expedition into Africa and Spain. As a result, *Black Power* and *Pagan Spain* turn out to be not merely portrayals of African and Spanish cultures but, more importantly, a penetrating cultural criticism of the West. Wright's travelogues and *Beloved* both examine the tradition-bound Western myths as enshrined in religious, political, and legal discourses and as reflected in such institutions as Christianity, slavery, and marriage.

In their efforts to displace Western discourse, Wright and Morrison try to reinstate what Wright calls "his [the African's] primal outlook upon life" (*BP*, 266). "If my work," Morrison remarks, "is to confront a reality unlike the received reality of the West, it must centralize and animate information discredited by the West . . . because it is information described as 'lore' or 'gossip' or 'magic' or 'sentiment'" ("Memory," 388). Though fiction, *Beloved*—clearly informed by the tenor of the postmodern—thrives on protesting voices in challenging political consensus and expanding concepts of history. Morrison, in fact, takes pride in the political nature of her work. "The work," she has argued, "must be political. . . . The best art is political and you ought to be able to make it unquestionably political and irrevocably beautiful at the same time" ("Rootedness," 344–45). She is in agreement with Wright, who told James Baldwin, "*All* literature is protest. You can't name a single novel that isn't protest."[1]

In *Black Power*, Wright repeatedly shows that the primal outlook in African culture is buttressed by the African's "basically poetic apprehension of existence" (266) and "poetic humanity" (dedication). The vision Wright and Morrison come to share is postmodern in its recognition not only of political and historical situatedness but also of aesthetic discourse in order to contest and disrupt from within. In his journey into Africa, Wright discovered that in the face of European imperialism, the Ashanti had survived on the strength of familial and tribal kinship and love. His travels to Spain, as discussed in chapter 10, revealed that Spanish religiosity was more pagan than Christian and that the pillar of Spanish culture was the Spanish womanhood represented by the Black Virgin of Montserrat. The communal kinship in Africa, epitomized by matriarchal society and symbolized by the Black Virgin, is also embodied in Sethe's enduring relationship with Beloved in Morrison's novel. The African's primal outlook indeed underlies the theme of *Beloved*. "Critics of my work," Morrison notes, "have often left something to be desired because they don't always evolve out of the culture, the world, the given quality out of which I write."[2]

1

When Wright traveled to West Africa to write *Black Power*, he was struck by a culture in transition. The profound myths, traditions, and customs underlying African culture were in conflict with its modernization. In the eyes of Western anthropologists and imperialists, African culture looked primitive and irrational. Wright, however, realized that the African always seems a "savage" to the Westerner just as the modern developments in the west are "fantastic" to the African. To Wright, the Western definition of the inferiority of the African race had derived from the hegemonic assumptions of academicians, assumptions that were scarcely related to the fundamental African beliefs. In short, African culture looks irrational to Westerners just as Western culture does to Africans.

One of the African beliefs Westerners find it difficult to comprehend is the African concept of time, the time that is not chronological and linear but cyclical. Believing in a circular movement of time, the African wishes what happened in the past to happen again. Africans, Wright thought, were capable of adapting to Western technology and industrialization, but their concept of time would be detrimental to the modernization of an old culture. Accra, the first city in Africa Wright visited en route to Kumasi, the Ashanti capital, reflected such a concept of time. The houses in Accra had no street numbers, a lack that not only indicated a chaotic urban development but also suggested a circular concept of time and space. Having no numbers assigned to individual houses meant that they had come to their existence regardless of order and location and that the city functioned like a maze.[3]

Unlike the traditional journey motif, mainly concerned with the male narrator's worldview, Morrison's quest in *Beloved* is to acquire what Wright calls in *Black Power* the African's "primal outlook upon life" (266). Just as Wright in his journey into pagan Spain witnessed the energetic maternal instinct of the Spanish woman and the female principle in life represented by the Black Virgin of Montserrat, Sethe in her journey from slavery to freedom seizes upon the maternal love of child innate in African culture. In stark contrast to the traditional slave narrative, *Beloved* features the heroic slave mother to replace the figure of the heroic male fugitive.

Morrison's technique in *Beloved* is also innovative and strikingly postmodern. In the traditional gothic tale, the movement is either from the present to the past or from the past to the present; in Edgar Allan Poe's "Ligeia," for example, the first half of the story takes place as the narrator contemplates past events and the latter half elaborates Ligeia's gradual return to the present. In *Beloved* the movement in time is extremely fluid; the story begins one day in 1873 at 124 Bluestone Road in Cincinnati and goes back not only to Sethe's slavery in Kentucky and the Middle Passage, but also to her ancestors in Africa. Throughout the text, the story constantly goes back and forth between the present and the past. In *Black Power* Wright speaks of the African's concept of time: "His was a circular kind of time; the past had to be made like the present" (175). To Africans, time is cyclic rather than linear as in Western discourse. In *Beloved* Morrison uses this concept of time: the past and the present are intermingled to form one continuum. The movement in time, then, enables their "dead" ancestors to return to the present with their primal outlook intact as guiding forces.[4]

For Morrison as narrator, this concept of time allows her to convert the past to the present through memory. "Because so much in public and scholarly life," she has complained, "forbids us to take seriously the milieu of buried stimuli, it is often extremely hard to seek out both the stimulus and its galaxy and to recognize their value when they arrive." The value of

Sethe's vision in the present, then, is determined by the intensity and quality of memory, the memory generated not only by one individual but by her race and culture. "Memory," Morrison underscores, "is for me always fresh, in spite of the fact that the object being remembered is done and past" ("Memory," 385).

Unlike the traditional journey narrative, *Beloved* does not make the identity of the two women, "the join" on their travel, its ultimate goal. Morrison's quest for that memory is open-ended; as Beloved reappears, Sethe disappears, and the thrust of the story in the end is toward the future, suggesting that the story must not "pass on," must not die, must continue. Morrison's concept of time allows the characters not only to reflect on the past but also to plan on the future. At the end of the novel, Paul D reminds Sethe of their future. Their experiences suggest that African American life in the future must be strengthened by the African primal view of existence: communal and familial kinship.

Time in *Beloved* is not only cyclic as it is in African culture but also fluid and mysterious. Beloved's appearance at the beginning of the novel is contrasted to her disappearance in the end: "By and by all trace is gone, and what is forgotten is not only the footprints but the water too and what it is down there. The rest is weather. Not the breath of the disremembered and unaccounted for, but wind in the eaves, or spring ice thawing too quickly. Just weather" (275). Not only are such images as "wind in the eaves" and "spring ice thawing too quickly" signs of the future, but Morrison also brings home her worldview: the primacy of spirit over flesh, humanism over materialism, harmony over disruption. Her attainment of such vision is a nebulous affair; however, Beloved's appearance and disappearance, in particular, can be interpreted psychoanalytically.[5] "Appearance/disappearance," Jacques Lacan theorizes, "takes place between two points, the initial and the terminal of this logical time—between the instant of seeing, when something of the intuition itself is always elided, not to say lost, and that elusive moment when the apprehension of the unconscious is not, in fact, concluded, when it is always a question of an 'absorption' fraught with false trails" (*Four Fundamental Concepts*, 32).

Wright, on the other hand, appreciated the ancestral worship not only characteristic of the African religion but also typical of other religions such as Hinduism, Buddhism, and Shintoism; even so, he was unable to penetrate the detail and symbolism of its mystery. He had no difficulty understanding, for example, the dedication of an African woman's life to preparing and serving food to the bones of the dead king, a ritual analogous to Buddhist woman's service in offering food to statues of the Buddha. Just as a menstruating woman is feared in Ashanti life, a Shintoist woman in the same condition abstains from consecrating the food to be presented at the household shrine. But Wright found it difficult to appreciate the symbolism of the Golden Stool, shrouded in mystery. To him the stool represented the collected souls of a million people. Ashanti appeared Oriental, for a soul hidden behind the dark face "shrinks from revealing itself" (*BP*, 273). Indeed, Western discourse is incapable of explaining the depth of the tribal culture. Africans, conscious of the unwritten history, have created methods of representation to cast doubt to the Westerners attempting to understand them.

The African primal outlook of life, in which a person's consciousness, as Wright and Morrison both believe, corresponds to the spirit of nature, bears a strong resemblance to the concept of enlightenment in Buddhism. To the African mind and to Buddhism, divinity exists in nature only if the person is intuitively conscious of divinity in the self. Wright's discussion of the African concept of life is also suggestive of Zen's emphasis on transcending the dualism of life and death. Zen master Dogen taught that life and death both constitute human experience and that there is no need to avoid death.[6] The funeral service Wright saw in an Ashanti tribe showed him that "the 'dead' live side by side with the living; they eat, breathe, laugh, hate, love, and continue doing in the world of ghostly shadows exactly what they had been doing in the world of flesh and blood" (*BP*, 213).

Like a Buddhist text, Dr. J. B. Danquah's *The Akan Doctrine of God* persuaded Wright of the African belief that spirits reside in inanimate objects like trees, stones, and rivers, an innate African philosophy on which Morrison's narrative in *Beloved* is based. Wright also witnessed Africans' belief in ghosts and in the spirits of the dead as Morrison used the concept in her fiction. Just as, in Zen, a tree contains satori only when the viewer can see it through his or her enlightened eyes, Wright saw in African life a closer relationship between human beings and nature than between human beings and their social and political environment:

Africa, with its high rain forest, with its stifling heat and lush vegetation, might well be mankind's queerest laboratory. Here instinct ruled and flowered without being concerned with the nature of the physical structure of the world; man lived without too much effort; there was nothing to distract him from concentrating upon the currents and countercurrents of his heart. He was thus free to project out of himself what he thought he was. Man has lived here in a waking dream, and, to some extent, he still lives here in that dream. (*BP*, 159)

Wright created here an image of the noble black man; Africa evokes in one "a total attitude toward life, calling into question the basic assumptions of existence," just as Zen teaches one a way of life completely independent of what one has been socially and politically conditioned to lead. As if echoing the enlightenment of Zen, Wright says, "Africa is the world of man; if you are wild, Africa's wild; if you are empty, so's Africa" (159).

Wright was moreover fascinated by the African reverence for nonhuman beings, a primal African attitude that corresponds to Buddhist belief:

The pre-Christian African was impressed with the littleness of himself and he walked the earth warily, lest he disturb the presence of invisible gods. When he wanted to disrupt the terrible majesty of the ocean in order to fish, he first made sacrifices to its crashing and rolling waves; he dared not cut down a tree without first propitiating its spirit so that it would not haunt him; he loved his fragile life and he was convinced that the tree loved its life also. (*BP*, 261–62)

The concept of unity, continuity, and infinity underlying that of life and death is what the Akan religion and Buddhism share.[7] When Wright was among the Ashanti, he was not conscious of an affinity between the two religions, but as he later read R. H. Blyth's explanation of Zen and its influence on haiku, he found both religious philosophies fundamentally alike.

This unity and continuity that exist between life and death, a quintessential African outlook, is fictionalized in *Beloved* with much intricacy and in depth. At times Morrison freely lets time elapse for generations and centuries. Sethe remembers the dancing feet of her dead mother as she feels the kicking legs of Denver in her womb. The pain caused by Denver's movement makes her feel as if she were rammed by an antelope, a wild animal roaming in Africa centuries earlier. Even though she has not seen an antelope before, the creation of this image bridges the gap between the occurrences of the present and those of the past. "Oh but when they sang," Morrison writes. "And oh but when they danced and sometimes they danced the antelope. . . . They shifted shapes and became something other. Some unchained, demanding other whose feet knew her pulse better than she did. Just like this one in her stomach" (31). Morrison bridges the gap between Denver's generation and her grandmother's, as well as that between American history and African history, by merging the images of the antelope, the grandmother's dancing, and Denver's kicking into a unified image. Later in the story Beloved recalls her traumatic experiences on a slave ship in which the captured Africans were herded into a crammed space: "All of it is now it is always now there will never be a time when I am not crouching and watching others who are crouching too I am always crouching the man on my face is dead" (210). A slave woman's crouching in the confined space immediately evokes the image of a free woman's crouching in an open field on the African continent, "where a woman takes flowers away from their leaves and puts them in a round basket before the clouds she is crouching near us but I do not see her until he locks his eyes and dies on my face" (211–12). This image unifies Beloved's stream-of-consciousness rememberings of the two women from the different centuries.

On the surface of the story, the distinction of present and past reflects that of outside and inside, the outer world and the character's mind. But the story cannot distinguish the present from the past. Denver, for example, views the present in terms of the past because she is obsessed with the premonition that Beloved is her ghost sister. The character's inability to distinguish between his or her inner mind and the outer world, the past and the present, manifests itself in Sethe's relationship with Beloved, Morrison's central theme. At a climactic moment, Morrison depicts the mother and daughter's reunion:

> I have to have my face I go in the grass opens she opens it I am in the water and she is coming there is no round basket no iron circle around her neck she goes up where the diamonds are I follow her we are in the diamonds which are her earrings now my face is coming I have to have it I am looking for the join I am loving my face so much my dark face is close to me I want to join (213)

As Beloved sees her own face reflected in the water, she at once identifies with her mother.

2

The primacy of kinship over individualism, a social practice based on the African primal outlook of human existence, is also conveyed in Morrison's fiction. Morrison takes pains to express this African idealism in terms of place as well as of time. As time plays a crucial role in unifying various planes of existence in *Beloved*, so does the word "place." Morrison's use of such a word is so powerful that it imbues the text with a postmodern sense of situatedness. As Wright explains the Akan doctrine of God, in which the deceased live exactly as do the living, Morrison portrays spirits and ghosts as if they were alive. Sethe's smile at Beloved, for instance, is reflected on Beloved's face: "I see her face which is mine it is the face that was going to smile at me in the *place* where we crouched" (212–13, emphasis added). Beloved's use of the words "face" and "place" suggests her inability to separate her own body from that of her mother. Earlier in the story, Sethe reminisces about a woman named Nan who "used different words," the same language her own mother spoke. Although she does not remember the language, "the messages—that was and had been there all along" (62) link her back to her mother and to her mother's land, the place where women picked flowers in freedom before the slave traders invaded their place.

As the function of time in *Beloved* is fluid, so is Morrison's use of the word "place." The characters journey from place to place freely and abruptly as they please. They constantly traverse the boundary between the visible and the invisible, the physical and the spiritual, the conscious and the unconscious. Baby Suggs, for example, expresses primal human sensations:

> "Here," she said, "in this here place, we flesh; flesh that weeps, laughs; flesh that dances on bare feet in grass. Love it. Love it hard.... Love your hands!... Touch others with them, pat them together, stroke them on your face.... The dark, dark liver—love it, love it, and the beat and beating heart, love that too. More than eyes or feet. More than lungs that have yet to draw free air. More than your life-holding womb and your life-giving private parts, hear me now, love your heart. For this is the prize." (88–89)

In her exhortations with emphasis on this place and this time, Baby Suggs is calling not only for self-love but also for communal kinship. In her use of words, she is remindful of a transcendental poet like Whitman in "Song of Myself."[8]

Morrison's use of "place" varies from character to character, from the dead to the living in particular. The referents of a place for Baby Suggs are characterized by their concrete and contemporaneous existence: "flesh," "feet," "grass," "hands," "face," "backs," "shoulders," "arms," "womb," "lungs," "heart." By contrast, Beloved's referent for a place is not only abstract but elusive as a dialogue between Beloved and Denver illustrates:

"What is it?" asks Denver.

"Look," she points to the sunlit cracks.

"What? I don't see nothing." Denver follows the pointing finger

....

Beloved focuses her eyes. "Over there. Her face."

Denver looks where Beloved's eyes go; there is nothing but darkness there.

"Whose face? Who is it?"

"Me. It's me."

She is smiling again. (124)

Moreover, Morrison's language in *Beloved* is strikingly postmodern in its use of contestatory voices and ironic, parodic modes of expression. It challenges Western discourse and expands concepts of history. Stamp Paid, for example, parodies the anthropological observation, as Wright in *Black Power* assails Western anthropologists, that the "jungle" life of black people originated from African culture: "Whitepeople believed that whatever the manners, under every dark skin was a jungle." He challenges such a notion by articulating fact and history:

> The more coloredpeople spent their strength trying to convince them how gentle they were, how clever and loving, how human, the more they used themselves up to persuade whites of something Negroes believed could not be questioned, the deeper and more tangled the jungle grew inside. But it wasn't the jungle blacks brought with them to this *place* from the other (livable) *place*. It was the jungle whitefolks planted in them. (*B*, 198, emphasis added)

The most poignant use of "place" is reserved for Morrison's expression of the central theme. Her aim in this narrative is to deconstruct and reconstruct history about an incident in which, out of her innate love of child, what Stamp Paid calls "how gentle . . . and loving, how human . . . something Negroes believed could not be questioned," a slave mother ran away to Cincinnati in 1855 by attempting to kill her four children when chased by her owner.[9] Sethe, faced with this genuinely human dilemma, opts for murdering Beloved. The text Morrison creates to dramatize Sethe's dilemma and action reverberates the morally unquestionable ideology that, for human beings, the place of death is better than that of slavery. From the beginning of the story, Morrison is intent upon creating a parody to drive home the meaning of slavery. Early in the story, Sethe reminisces about her experiences at Sweet Home. "After choosing Halle for her husband," she wonders about their wedding: "Mrs. Garner," Morrison describes the scene, "put down her cooking spoon. Laughing a little, she touched Sethe on the head, saying, 'You are one sweet child.' And then no more" (26). It is utterly ironic that the kinship of Sethe and Beloved, the mother-daughter relationship that has overcome slavery, is inherently stable and permanent whereas the mother-daughter relationship Mrs. Garner and Sethe forged at Sweet Home is not.

What motivates the African American characters in *Beloved* is their primal outlook on life: spiritualism and kinship. Searching for their "beloved," Sethe and Denver try to reconnect their kinship with all sixty million women and deny any boundary between the individual and the group. Such action disrupts the Western and American character: individualism and self-reliance. Sethe's and Denver's quest is further intensified by Paul D's appearance on the scene. Trying to revive Sethe with the words and images both remembered, Paul D reconnects her with the community. In Morrison's fiction, alienation from community and kinship leads to tragic consequences; the reassertion of this bondage makes possible the recovery of order and wholeness.

As pointed out earlier, Wright discovered in Ashanti tribal culture the primacy of kinship and community over individualism. For the Ashanti, this solidarity, a defense mechanism to fend off industrialism and imperialism, was a form of African nationalism that challenged the cross-cultural politics in modern Africa. Wright's Marxist stories in *Uncle Tom's Children* are endowed with this communal spirit. In "Long Black Song," Silas's individualistic spirit in competing with white farmers is negated by the lack of solidarity with his black community; one individual's liberation is not accomplished until all oppressed people are liberated. In a similar vein, Morrison has stated that African American communal kinship is rooted in African culture. "The contemporary autobiography," she says, "tends to be 'how I got over—look at me—alone—let me show you how I did it.' . . . I want to point out the dangers, to show that nice things don't always happen to the totally self-reliant if there is no conscious historical connection" ("Rootedness," 339–40, 344).

Contrary to Morrison's view of self-reliance, however, Wright's is ambivalent. In *Black Power*, while Wright admired close relationships that bonded the Ashanti family and tribe, he was troubled by the denial of individualism. All his life he believed in the twin values of American life:

individualism and freedom. Not only did he remain ambivalent on the subject, but to him the tribal solidarity and the lack of individualism in African life signified the African paradox in modern times. The open letter he wrote Nkrumah on his way home reflects his ambivalent feelings about African culture in general and this African pioneer's political strategy in particular.[10]

In fact, Paul D's advice to Sethe bears a striking resemblance to Wright's to Nkrumah. Reviewing Sethe's ordeal in slavery, Sethe and Paul D are engaged in this dialogue:

> "It ain't my job to know what's worse. It's my job to know what is and to keep them away from what I know is terrible. I did that."
> "What you did was wrong, Sethe."
> "I should have gone on back there? Taken my babies back there?"
> "There could have been a way. Some other way."
> "What way?"
> "You got two feet, Sethe, not four," he said, and right then a forest sprang up between them; trackless and quiet. (165)

Reminding Sethe of having two feet rather than four, Paul D admonishes her against reliance on others. At the end of the novel, however, he abandons his earlier doctrine of individualism and self-reliance and comes to believe in communality as the most powerful weapon in the battle of life. "Look," he calls her attention, "Denver be here in the day. I be here in the night. I'm a take care of you, you hear? Starting now. First off, you don't smell right. Stay there. Don't move. Let me heat up some water . . . Is it all right, Sethe, if I heat up some water?" Quipping at him for the conversion, she asks him, "And count my feet?" (272).

3

As the title of Morrison's novel suggests, this insistence on communal kinship, the African primal view of existence, permeates the entire text. It is mother's love of child that constitutes the deepest layer of human relationship. As Sethe's story unfolds, Denver gradually comes to understand the paradox that compelled her mother to kill Beloved. Sethe convinces Denver that her act of murder was justified because it came from spiritual love.[11] Pitted against the male-female relationship such as that of Paul D and Sethe, how strong and deep this mother-child bond remains becomes evident as the narrative develops. From time to time Morrison emphasizes the depth and permanence of mother-child kinship with such images as baby blood, mother's milk, and growing trees. At the end of the novel Paul D tries to negotiate his future with Sethe, but his attempt fails because spiritual love does not exist between them. By the time Beloved has chased Paul D out of Sethe's house and lured him into spiritless sex in the coldhouse, she deals the relationship of Paul D and Sethe permanent separation. When he goes to live in the cellar of the church, Stamp Paid tries vainly to rectify the situation by pleading with him: "She ain't crazy. She love those children. She was trying to outhurt the hurter" (234).

The mother-daughter kinship that dominates Sethe's story is remindful of the female principle in life represented by the Black Virgin in Wright's *Pagan Spain*. Instead of applying Freudian psychoanalysis,[12] which overemphasizes male sexual desire, Wright views the Black Virgin in terms of what he calls "superhuman order of reality" (*PS*, 61). Contrary to the male principle of life, which smacks of Christianity,[13] he defines the genesis of the Virgin in Spain as pagan, for in Eastern and African religions, the Holy Mother, the perennial life-giver, is a representation of nature. In *Beloved*, mother's irresistible urge to feed milk, child's insatiable sucking of mother's nipple, "no stopping water breaking from a breaking womb" (51)—all such natural actions establish the strongest, most undeniable nexus between mother and child. At the triumphant moment of her maternal quest, Sethe declares, "I was big, Paul D, and deep and wide and when I stretched out my arms all my children could get in between. I was *that* wide" (162).

As shown in *Black Power*, the African concept of society is derived from kinship and love in the family. As the Akan god is a woman, the state is owned by a female king and a child is under the custody of its mother, while the state is ruled by a male king and a family is managed by a father. Because the state is supported by women, the family is matrilineal in its inheritance. The supremacy of woman in the African state and family reflects the universal idea of Mother Nature. Womanhood in *Black Power* constitutes an innate representation of African character. Just as Wright in his journey into pagan Spain witnessed the energetic maternal instinct of the Spanish woman and the female principle in life represented by the Black Virgin of Montserrat, Sethe in her journey from slavery to freedom seizes upon the maternal love of child innate in African culture. In contrast to the traditional slave narrative, *Beloved* features the heroic slave mother to replace the figure of the heroic male fugitive.

The mother-daughter bondage in *Beloved*, representative of superhumanism, originated in African religiosity. According to the Akan doctrine of God, as reported in *Black Power*, Africans believed in reincarnation just as do Buddhists: ancestors freely return to the present and their spirits reside in nonhuman objects. Africans indeed denied the Western dichotomy of life and death. For them, life in the spiritual world exactly reflects that in this world: the dead carry on their lives exactly as do the living in the present world. Given this vision of existence, not only can we understand a slave mother's infanticide in *Beloved*, but we are painfully reminded of humankind's worst crime, slavery.

13

AFRICAN AMERICAN HAIKU: RICHARD WRIGHT, SONIA SANCHEZ, AND JAMES EMANUEL

1

During the early decades of the twentieth century, few books had been published on haiku. The end of World War II, however, provoked an outpouring of interest in Japanese haiku. In the late 1940s and 1950s, a number of important books in English on haiku were published. Among them, R. H. Blyth's four volumes of Japanese haiku with his translations and analyses inspired many Americans to write haiku in English. Many of the poets of the Beat Generation—most notably Allen Ginsberg, Jack Kerouac, and Gary Snyder—tried their hand at composing haiku. Among them, Jack Kerouac, who captured a huge audience when his first book, *On the Road*, appeared in 1958, wrote numerous haiku throughout his career and played a central role in the literary movement he named the Beat Generation.

The most influential East-West artistic, cultural, and literary exchange that has taken place in modern and postmodern times was reading and writing of haiku in the West. As noted earlier, among others in the West, Richard Wright, the most influential African American writer, distinguished himself as a haiku poet by writing over four thousand haiku in the last eighteen months of his life while in exile in Paris.

When Wright turned to writing haiku, he was certainly not working in an artistic vacuum. Artists in the Western world had been interested in haiku, its history and meaning, and had been writing haiku since early in the twentieth century. As a result of visits to Japan, French writers Julien Vocance, Paul-Louis Couchoud, and others began to write haiku in French. In 1910 a translation of a Japanese anthology of literature was made by Michel Revon, who referred to Basho's hokku as "haikai." Then

241

in 1915 Vocance wrote a group of poems called *Cent Visions de Guerre* in the haiku form. By 1920 at least a dozen poets were writing haiku for the *Nouvelle Revue Française*. In London at the end of 1910, Basil Hall Chamberlain's second edition of Japanese poetry was published, with his essay "Basho and the Japanese Poetical Epigram."[1]

Soon American poets began to write haiku. As pointed out earlier, the most famous was Ezra Pound, who wrote "In a Station of the Metro" in 1914. Some might consider this poem to be the first published haiku written in English in the West. Other Americans rapidly followed Pound's lead: Wallace Stevens in 1917, William Carlos Williams in 1919, and Amy Lowell in the same year. As early as 1909, the imagist group of poets were influenced by both the tanka (a short verse form of five lines with five, seven, five, seven, seven syllables, respectively) and the haiku forms. The group included Ezra Pound, Amy Lowell, and John Gould Fletcher.[2] In 1915 in Boston, Lafcadio Hearn's translations of hokku and tanka were collected and published as *Japanese Lyrics*.[3] By the mid-1930s, Georges Bonneau began to publish a series of books, with his translation into French, of Japanese poetry, *Le Haiku*. English translations of Japanese haiku by Harold G. Henderson came out in 1934 as *The Bamboo Broom*.

The Second World War temporarily sidetracked the Western world's interest in haiku. But after the war, British writers in Tokyo began to renew Western interest in haiku. The most important of these writers were Harold G. Henderson and R. H. Blyth. Their interest in haiku and subsequent books and translations once again made haiku a viable literary art form for Western poets. As noted earlier, Blyth showed with numerous classic haiku that the Buddhist ontologies and Zen philosophy, in particular, underlie haiku composition. His *Haiku: Eastern Culture*, the first of the four volumes, came out in 1949 and later was reissued in 1952 under the title *Haiku*.

John Gould Fletcher introduced the West to Kenneth Yasuda's *A Pepper-Pod*, a translation of Japanese haiku with selections of original haiku written in English in 1946. Gary Snyder wrote haiku in his diary, published in 1952 under the title *Earth House Hold*. Allen Ginsberg read Blyth's work on haiku and started to write haiku himself. An entry in his journal reads as follows: "Haiku composed in the backyard cottage at . . . Berkeley 1955, while reading R. H. Blyth's 4 volumes *Haiku*." In 1958 Harold G. Henderson's revised 1930 work, retitled *An Introduction to Haiku*, appeared in America and generated more interest in haiku. Another influential work that year was Jack Kerouac's *The Dharma Bums*, mentioned earlier. Kerouac's character Japhy Ryder writes haiku and had read a four-volume work on Japanese haiku. This was a reference to Blyth's four volumes on haiku. In fact, hundreds of Americans, some Canadians and Britishers began to write haiku.[4]

Harold G. Henderson, in *An Introduction to Haiku*, gives thanks to R. H. Blyth, with whom he had had personal contact, and refers to Blyth's "monumental four-volume work on haiku."[5] And William J. Higginson, in *The Haiku Handbook*, refers to the African American writer Richard Wright and says that he had studied R. H. Blyth's books and "wrote several hundred [sic] haiku during the last year and a half of his life."[6]

In 1953 Wright traveled to Africa, and published *Black Power* the following year. In 1955 he attended the Bandung Conference of the Third World; two years later he was a member of the First Congress of Negro Artists and Writers, which met in Paris in September. During that same period, he liked to work in his garden on his Normandy farm,[7] an activity that supplied many themes for his haiku.

The decade of the 1950s was rich in possibilities for Wright. The Third World was coming into its own artistically, socially, and politically, and Wright was gradually shedding his romantic belief that in denying men the chance to act on the basis of their feelings, social institutions cause the individual to destroy such feelings. But set against this positive mood were the effects of his financial and personal problems. His works were not bringing in much money, nor had he written anything in the previous few years that was financially successful. In addition, by the beginning of 1959 he was ill and often confined to his bed. He was approaching the end of the decade in an ambivalent mood, ready for union with that which lies beyond the artist, a theme appropriate for haiku. Exhausted by his financial problems, sickness, and the polemics surrounding him that were a drain on his rational powers, Wright was mentally and emotionally receptive to the ideas, beauty, and form of haiku. Under these conditions he seemed to be liberated from the restrictions of rationality and to enjoy his intuitive responses to other powers and images latent within him.

Sometime during the summer of 1959, he had been introduced to haiku by a young South African friend who loved its form.[8] Wright borrowed from him, as noted earlier, R. H. Blyth's four volumes on the art of haiku and its relationship to Zen and settled down to rediscover his old dream of oneness with all life. By March 1960 he was so captivated by its beauty that he was already in the midst of composing what was to turn out to be almost four thousand separate haiku. In response to a letter from his friend and Dutch translator, Margrit de Sablonière, he said that he had returned to poetry and added, "During my illness I experimented with the Japanese form of poetry called haiku; I wrote some 4,000 of them and am now sifting them out to see if they are any good."[9]

In his discussion of this event, Michel Fabre notes that Wright's interest in haiku involved his research into the great Japanese masters, Buson, Basho, and Issa. Wright ignored the European and American forms that were then becoming popular. Fabre notes further that Wright made "an effort to respect the exact form of the poem," and adds that it was curious for Wright to become interested in haiku at a time when he was fighting his illness. As Fabre reasons, "Logically he should have been tempted to turn away from 'pure' literature and to use his pen instead as a weapon."[10] Just as curiously, Wright's biographer, Constance Webb, refers to none of this material. She merely says that Wright had lost his physical energy and that "while lying against the pillows one afternoon he picked up the small book of Japanese poetry and began to read it again." Apparently it had been given to him earlier, and he read and reread it, excited by its style. She comments that Wright "had to study it and study to find out why it struck his ear with such a modern note." Then she adds that Wright "would try to bring the life and consciousness of a black American" to its form. Again, according to Webb, the haiku "seemed to answer the rawness he felt, which had, in turn, created a sensitivity that ached. Never had he been so sensitive, as if his nervous system had been exposed to rough air." In a letter to Paul Reynolds, his friend and editor, Wright said that he had sent to William Targ of the World Publishing Company a manuscript of his haiku.[11] In that same letter he commented that "these poems are the results of my being in bed a great deal."[12] Until we read the poems in *Haiku: This Other World* and his 3,183 unpublished haiku, we will probably never know the other reasons why Wright turned to haiku during the last years of his life.[13] But that knowledge, while helpful, is not necessary to reread and enjoy these newly published haiku. What is necessary, both for enjoyment and understanding of Wright's haiku, is some knowledge about haiku as the great Japanese poets developed the genre.

Wright's travel to the newly independent Ghana in West Africa in 1953 had a great impact on his writing of haiku. The African philosophy of life Wright witnessed among the Ashanti, "the African primal outlook upon life," as he called it, served as an inspiration for his poetic sensibility.

Ezra Pound's theory that the poet's use of an image is not to support "some system of ethics or economics" coincides with a theory that haiku expresses the poet's intuitive worldview. Wright, then, found the haiku poet's intuitive worldview akin to that of the African.

2

Since 1998, when Wright's posthumous *Haiku: This Other World* was published, Wright's haiku have made an immediate impact on some of the contemporary American poets, most notably Robert Hass (1941-), Sonia Sanchez (1935-), James A. Emanuel (1921-2013), and Lenard D. Moore (1958-). Hass, US Poet Laureate 1995-1997, wrote in *The Washington Post*:

> Here's a surprise, a book of haiku written in his last years by the fierce and original American novelist Richard Wright. Wright changed American literature by writing books—"Native Son," "Black Boy"—about the fact that poverty, discrimination and hopelessness are not necessarily a formula for producing virtuous citizens. He wrote (especially in "Native Son," the novel that brought him to public attention and became an unexpected bestseller in 1940) about the consequences of racism with an angry exactness that took readers—black and white —by surprise. . . . What an outpouring! Wright's way with the form was to keep strictly to the syllable count of the Japanese tradition—five syllables, seven syllables, five syllables.[14]

Not only was Hass deeply impressed by Wright's haiku, but his commentary on them also reveals how Wright had learned the theory and practice of haiku composition and applied them to the subtexts of his haiku, whether they were the French countryside, the rural Mississippi of his childhood, or the urban environments in Chicago, New York, Paris, and other cities. Among other subtexts, Hass considered "the pulse of his own life" the most original. He chose five haiku for his comments:

The first poem in the book suggests why the form was so useful to him:

> I am nobody:
> A red sinking autumn sun
> Took my name away.

It lifted away from him for a moment his writer's vita, his radical's dossier, the fury of a life of literary controversy, and gave him permission to be, to look:

> I give permission
> For this slow spring rain to soak
> The violet beds.

Many of the poems seem to be about paying attention, what the haiku form is so much about:

> With a twitching nose
> A dog reads a telegram
> On a wet tree trunk.

Some of them look back on his own life and also seem to absorb into him his own mortality:

> Burning autumn leaves,
> I yearn to make the bonfire
> Bigger and bigger.

That poem must be about aging, but it also has to pun on the angry black man Bigger Thomas, the protagonist of "Native Son." Enough commentary. Here is one more:

> A sleepless spring night:
> Yearning for what I never had
> And for what never was.[15]

Among the initial reviews *Haiku: This Other World* received, one by William J. Higginson, author of *The Haiku Handbook* (1985), was most thorough and discerning. While Higginson considers some of Wright's haiku mediocre, he reads many of them as excellent haiku. To Higginson, not only was this edition the largest collection of haiku written in English, but it was the best haiku collection to come out of the 1950s and 1960s. Higginson, a haiku critic deeply impressed by Wright's works of prose, such as *Native Son* and *Black Boy*, is as deeply impressed by his haiku. In this review he points out that Wright's early poems focused mainly on the social and political environments and that his poetry turned out to be merely timely poems of protest. "Once his fiction and other prose writings made him famous," Higginson remarks, "his involvement with poetry diminished—until the last 18 months of his life."[16]

Higginson also points out, as noted earlier, that Wright acquired the theory and technique of haiku composition from R. H. Blyth, as did the writers of the Beat Generation, such as Gary Snyder, Allen Ginsberg, and Jack Kerouac. Higginson also notes that Wright adhered to the traditional Japanese syllabic measure of five-seven-five, as well as to the requirement of *kigo* (seasonal reference) in many of his haiku.

With respect to the content and style of Wright's haiku, Higginson's comments on several of his favorite haiku by Wright are insightful. His reading and impression of these haiku is based on Wright's subtexts:

A somber tone pervades much of Wright's Haiku; he was ill while writing these haiku, and some of his closest friends and his mother died during this same period. Nonetheless, the collection shows a wider range of subject and tone than any other body of haiku in English from the period—a range fully justified by the range of Japanese haiku. The best poems among Wright's haiku exhibit the pure, significant observation, the delicate sensitivity, or the mysterious narrative fragment that characterize many of the best Japanese haiku, from an American perspective. Here are a few of my personal favorites:

The sound of the rain,
Blotted out now and then
By a sticky cough.

The first day of spring:
A servant's hips shake as she
Wipes a mirror clean.

Standing in the field,
I hear the whispering of
Snowflake to snowflake.[17]

Higginson is critical of some of Wright's haiku that "fall flat" because they sound like reports on social events. Wright is a master haiku poet, as Higgins shows, when his haiku reflect "the human comedy or give us a peek at an apparent mystery."[18] Higginson quotes these haiku as examples:

He hesitated
Before hanging up his coat
On the scarecrow's arm.

One autumn evening
A stranger enters a village
And passes on through.

In my sleep at night,
I keep pounding an anvil
Heard during the day.

This last is one of the very few poems in Wright's haiku that does not contain a seasonal reference, an element thought essential by most Japanese haiku poets. And this is one contribution the book makes, for American poets from the first have only somewhat paid lip service to the seasons in their attempts at haiku; many ignore the seasons altogether. Some of Wright's haiku echo themes and even the language of poems found in Blyth's volumes. Here are two, with what may have been their unconscious models in Blyth's translations.

The sound of a rat
Scampering over cold tin
Is heard in the bowels.

The sound
Of a rat on a plate,—
How cold it is!
(Buson)

A shaggy brown dog
Squatting under winter trees,
Shitting in the rain.

A stray cat
Excreting
In the winter garden.
(Shiki)

Of Shiki's poem, Blyth says, "This is an extraordinarily good haiku." Wright's language is as direct as Shiki's, which Blyth's is not. "There are many poems of stark, harsh reality in Wright's collection, and many more that simply don't make the grade. But, poem for poem, Wright's haiku is the best large American haiku collection . . . and the only full collection of haiku by a major American writer to remotely suggest both the range and depth possible in the genre."[19]

Leza Lowitz, another reviewer, wrote, "*Haiku: This Other World* is an outstanding addition to Wright's literary and humanist achievements and stands as a beacon to this other world, masterful and free."[20] She found the nexus between Wright's haiku and the illness Wright was battling in his last years in Paris. "As his illness worsened," Lowitz observes,

Wright reflected on another world beyond race or politics—this other world just beneath the surface of everyday perception—and magnified its moments with humor, joy, dignity and a kind of imagistic delicacy, while touching on those broader themes. And where his writing was once forceful and direct, here it is gentle and suggestive:

In the falling snow
A laughing boy holds out his palms
Until they are white.

While nature plays a large role in Wright's haiku, and humor can be found in the many "senryu" collected here, the themes of loss, betrayal, exile, wandering, mourning and longing surface over and over again. Yet, haiku seems to have offered Wright a kind of nurturing in the face of his own death, a spiritual home in exile. It's almost as if by accepting the cyclical spirit of nature rather than struggling against it, one can accept the human spirit with all of its inherent contradictions and losses. Ultimately, one finds a kind of home.[21]

Lowitz's reading of some of Wright's haiku as reflections of his illness echoes that of Julia Wright. Julia Wright, "an immature eighteen-year-old" as she called herself, was gravely concerned about her father's deteriorating health as she watched her father hang, on metal rods in his narrow studio, hundreds of sheets on which the haiku were typed. She read this haiku at his memorial service:

> Burning out its time,
> And timing its own burning,
> One lonely candle.

Lowitz also remarks that many of Wright's haiku reflect his thoughts about human mortality. In 1958 Edward Aswell, his trusted editor and friend, died, and a year later, another close friend, George Padmore, with whom Wright was planning another travel to Africa, also died. In the same year Wright was deeply shocked as he heard Camus, whom he had admired, was killed in a car accident. Julia Wright was also a witness to her father's long mourning over his mother's death. These haiku are, she felt, "Wright's poetry of loss and retrieval, of temperate joy and wistful humor, of exile and fragments of a dreamed return" ("Introduction" to *Haiku: This Other World*, xii).

3

The publication of Wright's haiku, some of which appeared in 1978, has inspired several African American poets to write haiku, not to mention numerous haiku enthusiasts in the English-speaking world. Among them Sonia Sanchez (1934–) has published two collections of haiku: *Like the Singing Coming Off the Drums* (1998) and *Morning Haiku* (2010). While Sanchez is known as an activist poet, much of her poetic impulse in *Like the Singing Coming Off the Drums* (1998) derives from the tradition of Japanese haiku, in which a poet pays the utmost attention to the beauty inherent in nature. A great majority of Sanchez's first collection of poems are entitled haiku, tanka, or *sonku*. Reading such poems indicates that Sanchez, turning away from the moral, intellectual, social, and political problems dealt with in her other work, found in nature her latent poetic sensibility. Above all, her fine pieces of poetry show, as do classic Japanese haiku and tanka (short song), the unity and harmony of all things, the sensibility that nature and humanity are one and inseparable. In this collection, much of her poetry poignantly expresses a desire to transcend social and racial differences and a need to find union and harmony with nature.

Both Sanchez and classic Japanese haiku poets are always inspired by the visual beauty in which nature presents itself. Buson was well-known in his time as a professional painter as he is today, and many of his haiku reflect his singular attention to color and its intensification. One of Sanchez's haiku included in the middle section, "Shake Loose My Skin," and one of the longer poems entitled "A Poem for Ella Fitzgerald" both thrive on colorful imagery. The haiku reads:

i am you loving
my own shadow watching
this noontime butterfly.
(61)

"A Poem for Ella Fitzgerald," the longest poem in this collection, is focused on these lines:

the moon turned red in the sky,

....

nightingales in her throat

....

an apollo stage amid high-stepping
yellow legs

....

i remember it was april
and the flowers ran yellow
the sun downpoured yellow butterflies
(104–7)

"Shake Loose My Skin" and "A Poem for Ella Fitzgerald" are both reminiscent of Buson's "Also Stepping On," a haiku that can be compared to Wright's haiku "A butterfly makes / The sunshine even brighter / With fluttering wings," discussed in chapter 7:

Also stepping on
The mountain pheasant's tail is
The spring setting sun.[22]

For a seasonal reference to spring, Buson links an image of the bird with spring sunset, because both are highly colorful. As a painter he is also fascinated by an ambiguous impression the scene he has drawn gives him; it is not clear whether the setting sun is treading on the pheasant's tail or the tail on the setting sun. In any event, Buson has made both pictures beautiful to behold. In Sanchez's haiku "I Am You Loving," it is ambivalent whether the focus is on "my own shadow" or "this noontime butterfly"; both constitute beautiful images of nature. Likewise, "A Poem for Ella Fitzgerald" juxtaposes the image of the red moon with that of nightingales. Sanchez in these poems creates, as does Buson in his, a pair of counterimages, themselves highly colorful and bright, which in turn intensify each other.

The predilection to portray human life in close association with nature means that the poet is more interested in genuinely natural sentiments than in moral, ethical, or political problems. Looking at the wind as a primal signifier of nature, Sanchez composed two poems in "Naked in the Streets," one entitled "Haiku" and the other "Blues Haiku":

Haiku

how fast is the wind
sailing? how fast did i go
to become slow?
(38)

Blues Haiku

let me be yo wil
derness let me be yo wind
blowing you all day.
(39)

Traditionally, another singular, awe-inspiring signifier of nature in haiku is silence. Besides "The Old Pond," Basho is also known for another haiku that concerns nature's silence, "How Quiet It Is," another well-known haiku that was earlier compared to Wright's haiku on a similar subject:

How quiet it is!
Piercing into the rocks
The cicada's voice.[23]

In the middle section, "Shake Loose My Skin," Sanchez wrote this haiku:

how still the morning sea
how still this morning skin
anointing the day.
(50)

Just as Basho was awed by the silence pervading the backdrop of the scene in contrast to "the shrill of cicada," Sanchez is struck by the equation between the stillness of "the morning sea" and that of "this morning skin." As pointed out earlier, Richard Wright, perhaps influenced by Basho, composed the following pair of haiku in which he focused on nature's silence:

> In the silent forest
> A woodpecker hammers at
> The sound of silence.
> (*HTOW*, 79)

> A thin waterfall
> Dribbles the whole autumn night,—
> How lonely it is.[24]
> (*HTOW*, 143)

What is common in these haiku by the three poets is that the scene is drawn with little detail and the mood is provided by a simple, reserved description of fact. These haiku create the kind of beauty associated with the aesthetic sensibility of *sabi* that suggests loneliness and quietude as opposed to overexcitement and loudness.[25]

Traditionally as well, the haiku in its portrayal of human beings' association with nature expresses the poet's enlightenment, a new way of looking at humanity and nature. In some of her poems in *Like the Singing Coming Off the Drums*, Sanchez follows this tradition. The second stanza in "Love Poem [*for Tupac*]," the following lines,

> the old ones
> say we don't
> die we are
> just passing
> through into
> another space
> (111)

suggests Sanchez's fascination with the Buddhist theory of transmigration. The Buddhist concept of reincarnation, as discussed in my reading of Wright's *Black Power*, has a striking affinity with the Akan concept of life and death. Buddhism and the Akan religion share the belief, as does

Lacan, that death is not the opposite of life but that death is a continuation of life.[26]

The following haiku expresses not only the concept of reincarnation but also an enlightenment in Zen philosophy:

> what is done is done
> what is not done is not done
> let it go . . . like the wind.
> (27)

The last line "let it go . . . like the wind" spontaneously expresses the truth about nature and humanity. Some of Sanchez's haiku like this one have an affinity with the Zen concept of *mu*. This state of nothingness, as discussed earlier, is devoid of all thoughts and emotions that are derived from human subjectivity and egotism and contrary to the conscious or unconscious truth represented by nature. An enlightened person is liberated from the self-centered worldview, convention, or received opinion that lacks fairness and justice. While Sanchez, in the first two lines of this haiku, describes facts in human life, she, in the last line, gives an admonition as a Zen master that one must emulate the principles of nature in molding one's conduct and action.

Not only do many of Sanchez's haiku follow Zen doctrine, but they also share the aesthetic principles that underlie classic haiku. One of the most delicate principles of Eastern art is called *yugen*, mentioned earlier. Originally, *yugen* in Japanese art was an element of style pervasive in the language of noh. It was also a philosophical principle originated in Zen metaphysics. In Zen, every individual possesses Buddhahood and must realize it. *Yugen*, as applied to art, designates the mysterious and dark, what underlies the surface. The mode of expression, as noted earlier, is subtle as opposed to obvious, suggestive rather than declarative. *Yugen* functions in art as a means by which human beings can comprehend the course of nature. Although *yugen* seems allied with a sense of resignation, it has a far different effect upon the human psyche. The style of *yugen* can express either happiness or sorrow.

The sense of loss also underlies the principle of *yugen*. Sanchez's first tanka in "Naked in the Street" expresses such a sentiment:

> i thought about you
> the pain of not having

you cruising my bones.
no morning saliva smiles this
frantic fugue about no you.
(18)

A pair of blues haiku, included in the same section, figure a brightened
sense of *yugen*:

when we say good-bye
i want yo tongue inside my
mouth dancing hello.
(16)

you too slippery
for me. can't hold you long or
hard. not enough nites.
(17)

As aesthetic principles, *yugen* and the blues share the sentiments derived
from private and personal feelings. As modes of expression, the blues stylistically differs from *yugen* since, as Amiri Baraka has observed, the blues
"issued directly out of the shout and of course the spiritual" (62). Whereas
yugen is characterized by reservation and modesty, the blues tradition calls
for a worldly excitement and love. Unlike *yugen*, the blues confines its attention solely to the immediate and celebrates the bodily expression; both
"When We Say Good-Bye" and "You Too Slippery" convey direct, unre-
served sexual manifestations. Most importantly, Sanchez tries to link the
blues message with sexually charged language so as to liberate black bodies
from the distorted images slavery inflicted.

That the blues tradition has a greater impact on Sanchez's poetry than
does the aesthetics of *yugen* can be seen in how Sanchez constructs her imagery. If imagery in classic haiku is regarded as indirect and suggestive, the
imagery in Sanchez's poetry has the directness and clarity of good prose as
opposed to the suggestiveness and vagueness of symbolist poetry. The first
poem in "Naked in the Streets" has an extremely sensuous image: dancing
is described in terms of "corpuscles sliding in blood" (3). In the second
poem of the same section, a haiku quoted earlier, the central image of running "naked in the streets" does not suggest anything other than what it
describes:

you ask me to run
naked in the streets with you
i am holding your pulse.
(4)

In another poem, a blues haiku, in "Shake Loose My Skin," a series of images consist of instantaneous actions:

legs wrapped around you
camera. action. tightshot.
this is not a rerun.
(68)

Both poems have an affinity with imagistic poems in the expression of love, such as Pound's "Alba," as discussed earlier:

As cool as the pale wet leaves
of lily-of-the-valley
She lay beside me in the dawn.
(*Personae*, 109)

In this haiku-like poem, what Pound expressed was not the personal feeling he had about the woman lying beside him at dawn but his spontaneous sensation of the coolness of "the pale wet leaves / of lily-of-the-valley." Likewise, the actions themselves of running "naked in the streets" and "legs wrapped around you" were Sanchez's subjects in the poems.

Such poems as "You Ask Me to Run" and "Legs Wrapped Around You" bear a structural resemblance as well to Pound's famous imagistic haiku "In a Station of the Metro," quoted earlier. Unlike Sanchez's haiku, Pound's "In a Station of the Metro" is constructed in two lines simply because Pound had in mind "a form of super-position" in which the poem was to be composed. "In a poem of this sort," he explained, "one is trying to record the precise instant when a thing outward and objective transforms itself, or darts into a thing inward and subjective" ("Vorticism," 467). Compared to Pound's "In a Station of the Metro," Sanchez's "You Ask Me to Run" has a similar structure in imagery. Just as in the other haiku, "Legs Wrapped Around You," Sanchez in this poem is trying to record the precise instant when a thing outward and objective, that is, running "naked in the streets," transforms itself or darts into a thing inward and subjective, that is, the image of "i am holding your pulse." The image of running "naked in the streets" is based in immediate experience, whether real or imagined since Sanchez lived in Philadelphia. Not only did she see the "thing," but it also must have generated such a sensation that she could not shake it out of her mind.

Although most of the short poems collected in *Like the Singing Coming Off the Drums* are stylistically influenced by the poetics of haiku as well as by the aesthetics of modernist poetry, much of Sanchez's ideological concern is postmodern, postcolonial, and African American. Many of her poems aim at teaching African Americans to achieve individualism and value their heritage. Even such a haiku as

> mixed with day and sun
> i crouched in the earth carry
> you like a dark river.
> (36)

succinctly expresses what Langston Hughes does in "The Negro Speaks of Rivers":

> I've known rivers:
> I've known rivers ancient as the world and older than
>   the flow of human blood in human veins.
>
> My soul has grown deep like the rivers.

Hughes reminds readers of the ancient rivers such as the Euphrates, the Congo, and the Nile, and then leads them to the most important river for African Americans, the Mississippi:

> I bathed in the Euphrates when dawns were young.
> I built my hut near the Congo and it lulled me to sleep.
> I looked upon the Nile and raised the pyramids above it.
> I heard the singing of the Mississippi when Abe Lincoln
>   went down to New Orleans, and I've seen its muddy
>   bosom turn all golden in the sunset.
> (*SPLH*, 4)

Sanchez and Hughes are both portraying how the African American soul, a symbol of humanity, is deeply embedded in the earth. The soul, as Hughes sees, "has grown deep like the rivers"; anyone endowed with it, like Sanchez, carries anyone else "like a dark river."

Hughes's signifying thrives on a chain of signs, signifiers, and signifieds. While "the Euphrates," "the Congo," "the Nile," and "the Mississippi" are all signs of great rivers, they also signify different human histories. All the signifieds in turn signify yet other historical events. For African Americans, "the Mississippi" signifies its "singing . . . when Abe Lincoln went down to New Orleans"; not only does it signify "its muddy bosom," but its signified in turn signifies a beautiful image, the golden river under sunset. Sanchez's haiku, on the other hand, is comprised of fewer but nonetheless equally powerful signs, signifiers, and signifieds: the words "mixed," "day," "sun," "i," "crouched," "earth," "carry," "you," "dark," and "river." These words express natural, spontaneous human sentiments, as do those in classic haiku, rather than emotional, personal feelings. In fact, an epiphany given in Sanchez's haiku, "Mixed with Day and Sun," bears a strong resemblance to a cross-cultural vision captured in Hughes's "The Negro Speaks of Rivers."

Sanchez's most important thematic concern is love of humanity, an act of faith that must begin with self-love. The last poem in the collection, dedicated to Gwendolyn Brooks, is a response and rejoinder to such a poem as Brooks's "The Mother." Not only is Brooks portrayed as "a holy one," but she has also become a universal symbol of the mother with enduring love and humanity:

> restringing her words
> from city to city
> so that we live and
> breathe and smile and
> breathe and love and
> breath her . . .
> this Gwensister called life.
> (133)

The sign that Sanchez's "For Sister Gwen Brooks" shares with Brooks's "The Mother" signifies the universal vision that love emanates from mother. Sanchez's refrain "for she is a holy one" further signifies the goddess worshiped among the Ashanti and the female king who owns her children, as described in Richard Wright's *Black Power*. In *Pagan Spain*, as Wright speculates, the universal motherhood has derived from the Virgin Mary, "Maya, the mother of Buddha," and "Isis, mother of Horus." As Wright remarks, "Egyptians worshiped Isis . . . and she was called Our Lady, the Queen of Heaven, Mother of God" (*PS*, 65).

The penultimate poem in *Like the Singing Coming Off the Drums* is dedicated to Cornel West. In contrast to the rest of the poems, it is a prose poem like Whitman's "Song of Myself." Cornel West, a Harvard professor, is not presented as a spokesman of the academia but characterized as a cultural activist like Whitman, Hughes, and Brooks, each of whom in a unique way sought to apotheosize the humanity of the land. Sanchez sees West as a foremost individual at the dawn of the twenty-first century, a spokesperson always "questioning a country that denies the sanctity, the holiness of children, people, rivers, sky, trees, earth" (130). Sanchez urges the reader to "look at the father in him. The husband in him. The activist in him. The teacher in him. The lover in him. The truth seeker in him. The James Brown dancer in him. The reformer in him. The defender of people in him. The intellectual in him" (130–31). West is

> This man. Born into history. This humanist. This twenty-first-century traveler pulling us screaming against our will towards a future that will hold all of humankind in an embrace. He acknowledges us all. The poor. Blacks and whites. Asians and Native Americans. Jews and Muslims. Latinos and Africans. Gays and Lesbians. (131)[27]

Rather than dwelling on the racial conflict and oppression the country has suffered, Sanchez admonishes the reader to see cross-pollination in the various cultures brought together to the land.

Whether *Like the Singing Coming Off the Drums* is Sanchez's best work remains to be seen in the generations to come, but an effort to use diverse principles of aesthetics in molding her poetry has few precedents in American literature. Thematically, nineteenth-century American writers like Emerson, Poe, Dickinson, and Whitman were partly influenced by various cultural and religious thoughts, as twentieth-century American writers like Ezra Pound, Wallace Stevens, Richard Wright, Allen Ginsberg, Jack Kerouac, and Gary Snyder at some points in their careers emulated Eastern poetics. Sanchez, on the other hand, remains one of the accomplished contemporary American poets writing from the perspective of cross-cultural visions for the form and content of her poetry.

4

The posthumous publication of Richard Wright's haiku also inspired James Emanuel (1921–2013), an African American poet, to write haiku as it had an impact on Sonia Sanchez. Like Wright and Sanchez, Emanuel became frustrated with the state of racism in America. Like Wright, Emanuel went into exile in Europe and died in Paris. Like Wright, Emanuel wrote haiku in France. As Sanchez related the aesthetic of haiku with that of blues music, Emanuel found a strong affinity between haiku and jazz. With the publication of *Jazz from the Haiku King* (1999), he created a new literary genre, jazz haiku, often read with musical accompaniment throughout Europe and Africa.

Even on the surface there is much in common between jazz and haiku. As jazz performance thrives on an endless improvisation the composer makes out of traditional materials, so does haiku composition on an infinite improvisation upon beautiful objects in nature and humanity. Because of improvisation, the composer in both genres must efface his or her identity. In jazz, play changes on ideas as well as on sounds so as to create unexpected sensations. In haiku, the poet spares no pains to capture unexpected sensations. In both genres, the composer and the composed, subject and object, coalesce as the identity of the composer disappears in the wake of creation.

Jazz also shares many of the philosophical principles that underlie haiku. As noted earlier, haiku since Basho has traditionally been associated with Zen philosophy. Zen teaches the follower to attain enlightenment, a new way of looking at humanity and nature. Just as Zen stresses self-reliance, not egotism, and nature, not materialism, so does jazz. Like haiku, jazz, characterized by innovation, seeks a new way of looking at ourselves and the world around us. As jazz challenges us to hear the sounds and rhythms we have not heard before, so does haiku to see the images of humanity and nature we have not seen before. Jazz and haiku enable us to open our minds and imagine ways of reaching a higher ground in our present lives.

In contrast to the blues and the spirituals, jazz is well-known for improvisation and syncopation. Individualism, which also distinguishes jazz, aside, another salient feature of jazz is the anonymity of jazz artists, as Ralph Ellison observes:

Some of the most brilliant of jazzmen made no records; their names appeared in print only in announcements of some local dance or remote "battles of music" against equally uncelebrated bands. Being devoted to an art which traditionally thrives on improvisation, these unrecorded artists very often have their most original ideas enter the public domain almost as rapidly as they are conceived to be quickly absorbed into the thought and technique of their fellows. Thus the riffs which swung the dancers and the band on some transcendent evening, and which inspired others to competitive flights of invention, become all too swiftly a part of the general style, leaving the originator as anonymous as the creators of the architecture called Gothic. (*SA*, 234)

The anonymity of jazz musicians has an affinity with that of noh dramatists. W. B. Yeats, inspired by noh drama, wrote such a play as *At the Hawk's Well*. In the performance of the play, Yeats used masks to present anonymous, time-honored expressions just as the Roman theatre used the mask instead of makeup (*SJP*, 60). Yeats clearly implied in his letter to Yone Noguchi that contemporary arts in the West were infected with egotism, while classical works of art in Japan were created as if anonymously (SE-WOYN, 2:14).

What seemed to have inspired Yeats was the "simplicity" of the artists, an ancient form of beauty that transcends time, place, and personality. Irked by modern ingenuity and science, he was adamantly opposed to realism in art and literature. For him realism failed to uncover the deeply ingrained human spirit and character. He later discovered that noble spirits and profound emotions are expressed with simplicity in the noh play. Noguchi observed, "It was the time when nobody asked who wrote them, if the plays themselves were worthy. What a difference from this day of advertisement and personal ambition! . . . I mean that they are not the creation of one time or one age; it is not far wrong to say that they wrote themselves, as if flowers or trees rising from the rich soil of tradition and Buddhistic faith" (*SJP*, 63). In its simplicity and appeal, jazz has much in common with noh drama.

Unlike the blues, jazz is characterized by its flexibility and creativity. As the blues emphasizes individuality and personality, does jazz anonymity and impersonality. While both individuality and communal affirmation are central to the blues, their relationship and importance to jazz are different from those to the blues. "Seen in relation to the blues impulse," Craig Werner observes, "the jazz impulse provides a way of exploring implications of realizing the relational possibilities of the (blues) self, and of expanding the consciousness of self and community through a process of continual improvisation."[28] Involving both self-expression and community affirmation, jazz is a genre of ambivalence and of what Ellison calls "a cruel contradiction." He remarks:

> For true jazz is an art of individual assertion within and against the group. Each true jazz moment (as distinct from the uninspired commercial performance) springs from a contest in which each artist challenges all the rest; each solo flight, or improvisation, represents (like the successive canvasses of a painter) a definition of his identity: as individual, as member of the collectivity and as a link in the chain of tradition. (*SA*, 234)

In light of the relation of self and community, jazz also bears a strong resemblance to *renga*, the Japanese linked song, from which haiku evolved, as noted earlier. *Renga*, which flourished in the beginnings as comic poetry, was a continuous chain of fourteen- (seven-seven) and seventeen- (five-seven-five) syllable verses, each independently composed but connected as one poem, a communal composition.[29]

In practice, however, jazz in the early 1950s emphasized individuality, in technical virtuosity and theoretical knowledge, rather than community and its involvement with jazz. "In response," Werner notes, "jazz musicians such as Miles Davis, Ornette Coleman, and John Coltrane established the contours of the multifaceted 'free jazz' movement, which includes most AACM [the Association for the Advancement of Creative Musicians] work."[30] As Gayl Jones has also remarked, jazz, rendered through nonchronological syncopation and tempo, thrives on the essence of jazz, "the jam session," that "emerges from an interplay of voices improvising on the basic themes or motifs of the text in keywords and phrases." This interplay of self and other and self and community, what Jones calls "seemingly nonlogical and associational," makes the jazz text more complex, flexible, and fluid than the blues text.[31] Jazz, as Louis Armstrong said, is a genre of music that should never be played in the same way as before.[32]

Jazz and haiku both convey spontaneously created expressions that are free from any economic, social, or political impulses. "Jazz," he writes in his preface, "I knew—like the Caruso I heard on the same phonograph—had no boundaries; but its immense international magnetism seemed inadequately explored in poetry" (iv–v). In haiku, despite its brevity, he found much of the height and depth of vision as he did in jazz.

In the haiku "Dizzy's Bellows Pumps," under the title "Dizzy Gillespie (News of His Death)," placed in the middle of the collection,

Dizzy's bellows pumps.
Jazz balloon inflates, floats high.
Earth listens, stands by.
(44)

Emanuel hears Gillespie's music reverberate in the sky and on earth. Traditionally haiku express and celebrate the unity of humanity and nature; a part of a haiku usually has a *kigo* (seasonal word). Even though Emanuel's "Dizzy's Bellows Pumps" lacks a seasonal reference, it displays the nexus of humanity and nature: Gillespie and sky and earth. This haiku is an elegy as Whitman's "When Lilacs Last in the Dooryard Bloom'd" is an elegy for Lincoln. In celebrating the lives of the great men, both poems express the immortality of their spirits. As Lincoln will return with lilacs in the spring and the northern star at night, Gillespie will be remembered for his jazz.

Emanuel's haiku on Gillespie is also remindful of Zen philosophy, which emphasizes the fusion of humanity and nature. Zen teaches its followers to transcend the dualism of life and death. Zen master Dogen observed that life and death are not separated as they seem and that there is no need to avoid death. Similarly, Emanuel and Whitman both seek a reconciliation of life and death. Whitman's feat of turning the national bereavement in the elegy into a celebration of death is well-known, but less known is his idea of death given in "A Sight in Camp in the Daybreak Gray and Dim." To Whitman, the dead soldier in this poem appears no less divine than the savior Christ; they both represent the living godhead. In a similar vein, as Gillespie's jazz balloon floats high in the sky and the earth stands by and listens, this jazz master is vividly alive.

Emanuel captures the affinity of jazz and haiku in many of the poems in the collection. The first chapter, "Page One," features various types of jazz haiku with translations into other languages: "The Haiku King," "Jazzanatomy," "Jazzroads," "Jazzactions," "Bojangles and Jo." The first of the four poems under the group title "Jazzanatomy" reads:

EVERYTHING is jazz:
snails, jails, rails, tails, males, females,
snow-white cotton bales.
(2)

To Emanuel, jazz represents all walks of life, human and nonhuman alike. Human life is represented by "males" and "females," animal life by "snails" and "tails," and inanimate life by "snow-white." "My haiku," Emanuel remarks in his preface, "added the toughness of poverty and racial injustice" (iv). The images of "jails" and "cotton bales," signifying the unjustified imprisonment of African Americans and their immoral slave labor, represent the twin evils in American life: racism and poverty. "Song of Myself," a narrative and autobiographical poem, also concerns all walks of American life. Focusing on human life, Whitman declares, "I am the poet of the Body and I am the poet of the Soul," and "I am the poet of the woman the same as the man." About the problems of good and evil, he writes, "The pleasures of heaven are with me and the pains of hell are with me" (*CPOW*, 39).

Emanuel's view of humanity and nature is shared by his American predecessors, such as Whitman, Countee Cullen, and Wright. The opening pages of Wright's *Black Power* has a passage addressed "To the Unknown African" and two quotations from Cullen and Whitman. "To the Unknown African" records an observation derived from Wright's view that the African was victimized by slave trades because of the African's primal outlook on human existence. The quotations from both Cullen and Whitman suggest that Africans, the inheritors and products of nature, have been exploited by a materialistic civilization. Before Europeans appeared with their machines, the continent had thrived on its pastoral idylls. Now it exists at the services of Western traders who exploit African products. Whitman's line *Not till the sun excludes you do I exclude you*," quoted in *Black Power*, expresses not merely his compassion for African Americans but also strongly, as do Cullen's lines, their natural and divine heritage.[33]

From a philosophical perspective, Emanuel's jazz haiku has an affinity with the Zen concept of *mu*. A series of ten haiku in the chapter "Jazz Meets the Abstract (Engravings)," for example, describe various human actions in which Emanuel is in search of space, a Zen-like state of nothingness. This space is devoid of egotism and artificiality; it transcends human reasoning and personal vision. In the first haiku,

Space moves, contours grow
as wood, web, damp, dust. Points turn,
Corners follow. JAZZ!
(87)

Jazz creates a space that moves as its contours "grow / as wood, web, damp, dust," their points "turn," and their corners "follow." Neither intellectuality nor emotion such as hatred and anger is able to occupy such a space.

Emanuel further shows, in his jazz haiku, the state of nothingness that jazz is able to achieve:

> No meaning at birth:
> just screams, squirms, frowns without sight,
> fists clenched against light.
> (88)

Jazz is like a newborn child with its "fists clenched against light." The child just "screams, squirms, frowns without sight"; all this has "no meaning at birth," a state of nothingness. In the next pair of jazz haiku,

> Abstract, I try you
> (walk, sit, stretch). You say nothing.
> Good fit; to wit: JAZZ
> (90)

> No dust, rust, no guilt
> in home JAZZ built; it cheers, STANDS,
> charms guests from ALL lands
> (93)

Emanuel tries jazz, as he does an infant, "(walk, sit, stretch)." Like the infant, jazz says "nothing," *mu*, but is a good fit. Such a space has "no dust, rust," and such a state of mind has "no guilt." Whereas jazz was born and reared in America, it has attracted "guests from ALL lands." To Emanuel, jazz and Zen, characteristic of their respective cultures, have a common, universal appeal.

In other jazz haiku, he also envisions the world in which the state of *mu* can be attained. In this haiku, for example,

> Soars, leapfrogs, yells: JAZZ!
> But don't expect no tantrums,
> no crazyman spells
> (6)

height and intensity define jazz: it "soars, leapfrogs, yells." Emanuel cautions, however, that soaring sounds and "yells" do not signal "tantrums" and "crazyman spells." The sound of jazz, like the sound of the water made by a leaping frog in Basho's haiku, signifies enlightenment, the state of *mu*. Just as Basho is impressed with the depth and silence of the universe, so is Emanuel with the height and intensity of jazz. This state of consciousness jazz creates has the effect of cleansing the human mind of impurity. The Haiku on Louis Armstrong,

Jazz-rainbow: skywash
his trumpet blew, cleansing air,
his wonderworld there
(56)

captures Armstrong's ability to create his utopia, a "wonderworld," purified of social ills and racial conflicts.

Armstrong's utopia is, in turn, buttressed by individualism. The last four haiku under the title "Steppin' Out on the Promise" in chapter 5, "Jazzmix," urge on African Americans the imperative of individualism. The first pair of jazz haiku address "Brother" and "Sister":

Step out, Brother. Blow.
Just pretend you plantin' corn,
gold seeds from your horn.

Step out, Sister. Blow.
Must be Lord told you to play,
gifted you that way.

Emanuel impels each of the African Americans, brothers and sisters, sons and daughters, to be individualistic, self-reliant in their efforts to realize the Promised Land. He tells his brother to blow his horn and plant "gold seeds" from it; he tells his sister to blow her horn and play the way God told her. The second pair then address "Daughter" and "Son":

Step out, Daughter. Shine.
Make 'em switch their lights on, chile.
Make 'em jazzophile.

Step out, Sonny. Blow.
Tell 'em all they need to know.
Lay it on 'em. GO!
(84)

Emanuel urges his daughter to shine in her performance and make her audience "jazzophile," as he tells his son to blow his horn and enlighten his audience with "all they need to know." Emanuel's command "Step out," which begins each of the jazz haiku, emphasizes the principles of subjectivity and individuality in jazz performance. Each of the jazz haiku above, unlike a classic haiku, is united in its rhythm and meaning by a rhyme between the last two lines: "corn" and "horn," "play" and "way," "chile" and "jazzophile," "know " and "GO!"

Adding rhyme to haiku, much like deleting seasonal reference, is an innovation Emanuel has made in his haiku. He has attempted to widen the sensory impact of haiku beyond the effect of the single impression given in a traditional haiku. Jazz is not only an expression of African American individualism, but it also inspires African Americans into cooperation and dialogue. A series of haiku under the title "Jazz as Chopsticks" feature the unity and cooperation of two individuals:

If Twin's the arrow,
Chops plays bow. No JAZZ fallin'
if they both don't go.

Chops makes drum sounds SPIN.
Twin coaxes them, herds them in,
JAZZ their next of kin.
....
When stuck on his lick,
Chops runs the scale. Twin slides loose,
then harpoons the whale.
"Chops, whatcha doin'?"
"Waitin' for Twin. It's my bass
his melody's in."
(82)

The four haiku quoted above describe jazz performance in terms of a pair of chopsticks. In his notes Emanuel remarks, "Chops and Twin are names given to the chopsticks (Chops the slower, sturdier one, Twin the roaming, more imaginative one)" (82). The pair play the roles of bow and arrow; if they do not work together, they fall and fail to capture what they desire. The pair are in unison with the music, Chops making "drum sounds SPIN" and Twin "coax[ing] them, herd[ing] them in." Jazz would not be inspirational if only one individual played the music; Chops's role is as important as Twin's. Jazz captures life as though the pair "harpoons the whale"; while "Chops runs the scale," "Twin slides loose." And jazz music intensifies with a coordination of bass and melody, a pair of chopsticks.

Emanuel's admonition for African Americans to be individualistic in their lives is remindful of Zen doctrine. The concept of subjectivity in Zen, however, goes a step further, for it calls for a severe critique of self. The doctrine of satori calls for the follower to annihilate self to reach the higher state of *mu* so as to liberate self from the habitual way of life. In Zen, one must destroy not only self-centeredness and intellectualism but also God, Buddha, Christ, any prophet, or any idol, because it is only the self, no one else, that can deliver the individual to the state of *mu*. Emanuel urges the liberation of self and the destruction of injustice in such jazz haiku as "Jackhammer," and "Ammunition," and "Impressionist":

Jackhammer

Jackhammer Jazz POUNDS—
just breathes—on your door. Message:
don't lock it no more.

Ammunition

Weapons ready-y-y. JAZZ!
People fall, rise hypnotized,
maybe civilized.

Impressionist

Impressionist pipe
puffs JAZZ where pigments solo,
brightsoapbubbling air.
(70)

Each poem focuses on the sound of jazz that inspires the liberation of self from the ways one has been conditioned to lead. Jazz pounds away the door of racism. Jazz is an ammunition to destroy barbarism; people will "fall, rise hypnotized, / maybe civilized." Through its impressionist pipe, jazz creates "brightsoapbubbling air," a colorful, exciting new world.

The liberation of self that jazz inspires is akin to the concept of liberation in Zen. Zen teaches its followers to liberate themselves from human laws, rules, and authorities. For jazz, as for Zen, liberation results from one's desire to adhere to the law and spirit of nature. In a haiku on "The Rabbit Capers," which resembles a senryu,[34]

> White Bugsy Rabbit
> went scratch-scratch-scratch: jailed for theft
> from The Old Jazz Patch
> (78)

the jazz caper is portrayed as a work of art that is created for its own sake; the jazzrabbit, in another haiku, "aims his gun, shoots / . . . just for fun" (78). For Emanuel, jazz inspires one, as does Zen, with a new way of life; jazz and Zen admonish one to purge one's mind and heart of any materialistic thoughts and feelings, and appreciate the wonder of life here and now.

Jazz, as Emanuel remarks in his preface, "has crossed oceans and continents to spread its gospel of survival through joy and artistic imagination" (v). Throughout *Jazz from the Haiku King* he is intent upon composing haiku on the basis of its well-established philosophical and aesthetic principles. Philosophically, his finely wrought haiku enlighten the reader as inspiring jazz does the listener. Aesthetically as well, Emanuel's haiku, sharing the devices of both haiku and jazz by which to seize the moments of revelation, express natural, spontaneous sentiments. His haiku, with sharp, compressed images, strongly reflect the syncopated sounds and rhythms of African American jazz.

NOTES

INTRODUCTION

1. Arthur Versluis, *American Transcendentalism and Asian Religions* (New York and Oxford: Oxford University Press, 1993), 10.

2. Ibid., 52.

3. Walter Harding, *A Thoreau Handbook* (New York: New York University Press, 1959), 98.

4. Donald Keene, *World within Walls: Japanese Literature of the Pre-Modern Era, 1600–1868* (New York: Grove, 1976), 93.

5. Martin Heidegger, *Poetry, Language, Thought,* trans. A. Hofstadter (New York: Harper and Row, 1975), 46.

6. Ernest Fenollosa, *The Chinese Written Character as a Medium for Poetry*, ed. Ezra Pound (New York: Arrow, 1936), 8.

7. McKay Jenkins, "Womb with a View: Proust's Magical Mindfulness," in *Modernity in East-West Literary Criticism: New Readings*, ed. Yoshinobu Hakutani (Madison, NJ: Fairleigh Dickinson University Press / London: Associated University Presses, 2001), 166.

8. Leza Lowitz, "Haiku as a Tether to Life and Emotional Safety Net," *Japan Times*, April 27, 1999.

9. William J. Higginson, "His Last Poems: Haiku," *Santa Fe New Mexican*, February 21, 1999.

10. Roland Barthes, *Empire of Signs*, trans. Richard Howard (New York: Hill and Wang, 1982), 78–79.

11. McKay Jenkins, "Rushdie's *Midnight's Children*, Meditation, and the Postmodern Conception of History," in *Postmodernity and Cross-Culturalism*, ed. Yoshinobu Hakutani (Madison, NJ: Fairleigh Dickinson University Press/London: Associated University Presses, 2002), 62.

12. Shawn St. Jean, "'Three Meals a Day and the Fun of It': Existential Hunger and the Magnificent Seven/Samurai," in Hakutani, *Postmodernity and Cross-Culturalism*, 76.

13. Nicole Cooley, "'Japan Has Become the Sign': Identity and History in Theresa Hak Kyung Cha's *Dictee*," in Hakutani, *Postmodernity and Cross-Culturalism*, 117.

14. Bruce Ross, "North American Versions of Haibun and Postmodern American Culture," in Hakutani, *Postmodernity and Cross-Culturalism*, 168–70.

CHAPTER 1

1. Robert D. Richardson Jr. cautions that Thoreau's "running quarrel with Christianity should not be read as the mark of an irreligious or scoffing nature, and his feelings toward the natural world frequently compelled him to use sacred terminology" (*Henry Thoreau: A Life of the Mind* [Berkeley: University of California Press, 1986], 50).

2. Shoji Goto, in *The Philosophy of Emerson and Thoreau: Orientals Meet Occidentals* (Lewiston, NY: Edwin Mellen, 2007), remarks that Frederic Ives Carpenter and Arthur Christy both failed to recognize Emerson and Thoreau's fascination with Confucian philosophy. Goto quotes Christy as asserting, "It is fruitless to attempt finding in him [Thoreau] a resemblance to the ethics of Confucius" (6–8).

3. This analect is remindful of John Keats's line "Beauty is truth, truth beauty" in "Ode on a Grecian Urn" (1819). Emily Dickinson personifies beauty and truth in her poem "I died for Beauty—but was scarce." Dickinson sees beauty and truth united in life and death:

> He questioned softly, "Why I failed"?
> "For Beauty," I replied—
> "And I—for Truth—Themself are One—
> We Brethren, are," He said—
>
> And so, as Kinsmen, met a Night—
> We talked between the Rooms—
> Until the Moss had reached our lips—
> And covered up—our names—
> (*CPOED*, 216)

4. Goto, *Philosophy*, 113.
5. Ibid.
6. Ibid., 126–27.
7. Ibid., 127.

8. Thoreau, Robert D. Richardson Jr. argues, "believed with Kant and Emerson that the mind possesses structures that are prior to our experience and that in fact help shape that experience. The world we live in, the phenomenal world, is a collaboration between the actual material stuff of the world and the individual active mind." Richardson, "Thoreau, Henry David," in *Encyclopedia of American Literature*, ed. by Steven R. Serafin, (New York: Continuum, 1999), 1144–45.

9. Goto, *Philosophy*, 145.

10. Emerson, in his poem "The Problem," in *Selections from Ralph Waldo Emerson*, ed. Stephen E. Whicher (Boston: Houghton Mifflin, 1960), was fascinated by how a pine tree expands its life:

> Or how the sacred pine-tree adds
> To her old leaves near myriads?
> Such and so grew these holy piles,
> Whilst love and terror laid the titles
> (418)

11. "Thoreau," Robert D. Richardson Jr. notes, "recognizes wildness or wilderness not as the enemy or opposite of civilization, but as the essential raw material out of which all civilization and culture is created" ("Thoreau, Henry David," 1145).

12. In the Far East countries such as China, Korea, and Japan, a teacher or a professional such as a physician is often addressed as 先生 (Previously Born), a traditional custom that reflects Confucian ethics. Such an individual is supposed to have not only more experience but also more knowledge.

13. Benjamin Franklin in *The Autobiography*, ed. Max Farrand (Berkeley: University of California Press, 1949), names thirteen virtues. "12. Chastity" is defined: "Rarely use venery but for health or offspring—never to dullness, weakness, or the injury of your own or another's peace or reputation" (103).

CHAPTER 2

1. Frederic Ives Carpenter, *Emerson and Asia* (Cambridge: Harvard University Press, 1930), 150.

2. Robert Samuels quotes this passage from Jacque Lacan's first published version of *The Seminar of Jacques Lacan*. See Samuels, "Emerson, Lacan, and Zen: Transcendental and Postmodern Conceptions of the Eastern Subject," in *Postmodernity and Cross-Culturalism*, ed. Yoshinobu Hakutani (Madison, NJ: Fairleigh Dickinson University Press / London: Associated University Presses, 2002); and *The Seminar of Jacques Lacan*, bk. 2, *The Ego in Freud's Theory and in the Techniques of Psychoanalysis, 1954-1955*, ed. Jacques-Alain Miller, trans. Sylvana Tomaselli (New York: Norton, 1988), 1.

3. For a further discussion of Lacan as the master of psychoanalysis, see Samuels, "Emerson, Lacan, and Zen," and Mikkel Borch-Jacobsen, *Lacan: The Absolute Master*, trans. Douglas Brick (Stanford: Stanford University Press, 1991).

4. Roland Barthes, *Empire of Signs*, trans. Richard Howard (New York: Hill and Wang, 1982), found an empty center in signs of traditional Japanese culture, such as its food, its landscapes, and its quintessential poetic form, haiku (3–37).

5. In a haiku, as Blyth argues, the poet, the subject, tries to liberate self from the confines of language, just as Lacan theorizes that the subject, conditioned by language, must escape the control of language in order to achieve freedom and independence. For Blyth, unlike a typical art that "tends from life to artificiality, from the simple to the complex, the penny plain to the tuppence coloured," haiku is an art that proceeds just in reverse; R. H. Blyth, *A History of Haiku* (Tokyo: Hokuseido, 1963), 1:1.

6. Emerson's exploration of the Indian wilderness is reminiscent of Philip Freneau's "The Indian Burying Ground," in which, contrary to common belief, the poet describes the life-like sprints of the dead:

> In spite of all the learned have said,
>   I still my old opinion keeps;
> The posture, that we give the dead,
>   Points out the soul's eternal sleep.
> Not so the ancients of these lands—
>   The Indian, when from life released,
> Again is seated with his friends,
>   And shares again the joyous feast.
> (2:369)

The North American Indians, Freneau realizes, bury their dead in a sitting posture. The buried Indian continues to thrive on his life activity after death: "His imaged birds, and painted bowl, / And venison, for a journey dressed, / Bespeak the nature of the soul, / Activity, that knows no rest" (2:369). In contrast to Emerson's poem, Freneau's depicts the continuity of life after death; the dead Indian after death is as active as when he was alive. Freneau's poem demonstrates, as Lacan theorizes, that death, to Native American Indians, is not separate from life but is part of life.

7. For Dogen's teaching on death, see Kodo Kurebayashi, *Introduction to Dogen Zen* [in Japanese], (Tokyo: Daihorinkaku, 1983), 44–50.

CHAPTER 3

1. The Hokke sect is known for the practice in which the believers recite *Namu Amida Butsu* (Praise to Amida Buddha); the Shingon sect, founded by the priest

Kukai, seeks salvation by means of charms and spells, popularized and corrupted forms of Sanskrit sayings; the Tendai sect is a fusion of Buddhism and Shintoism, the indigenous and national religion in Japan.

2. "Zazen" literally means "kneeling on the floor"; it is a formalized and stylized ritual in Zen Buddhism by which the follower kneels down on the hard floor and meditates for hours till he or she achieves enlightenment.

3. In "Experience" Emerson explains that each individual has an ability to develop the "great and crescive self" and that he should reflect on his accomplishment. "Life," writes Emerson, "is not intellectual or critical, but sturdy. . . . Nature hates peeping, and our mothers speak her very sense when they say, 'Children, eat your victuals, and say no more of it.' To fill the hour—that is happiness; to fill the hour and leave no crevice for a repentance or an approval" (*CEOE*, 350).

4. The best-known interpreter of Zen Buddhism in the West is Daisetz T. Suzuki, *An Introduction to Zen Buddhism*. New York: Philosophical Library, 1949. "The object of Zen discipline," Suzuki writes,

> consists in acquiring a new viewpoint for looking into the essence of things. If you have been in the habit of thinking logically according to the rules of dualism, rid yourself of it and you may come around somewhat to the viewpoint of Zen. . . . *Satori* may be defined as intuitive looking-into, in contradiction to intellectual and logical understanding. Whatever the definition, satori means the unfolding of a new world hitherto unperceived in the confusion of a dualistic mind. (88)

5. One of the most perceptive Western interpreters of Eastern thought is Lafcadio Hearn. "For Buddhism," writes Hearn, "the sole reality is the Absolute,— Buddha as unconditioned and Infinite Being. There is no other veritable existence, whether of Matter or of Mind; there is no real individuality or personality; the 'I' and the 'Not-I' are essentially nowise different . . . 'Very true,' the Buddhist metaphysician would reply; 'we cannot know the sole Reality while consciousness lasts. *But destroy consciousness, and the Reality becomes cognizable.* Annihilate the illusion of Mind, and the light will come.' This destruction of consciousness signifies Nirvana,—the extinction of all that we call Self. Self is blindness: destroy it, and the Reality will be revealed as infinite vision and infinite peace." See Hearn, *Japan: An Attempt at Interpretation* (New York: Grosset & Dunlap, 1904), 234–35.

6. According to Arthur Waley, the noh plays were influenced more strongly by the other sects of Buddhism than by the Zen sect. Because Zen Buddhism was not concerned with good and evil, a murderer's interest in Zen doctrine was considered a weakness in his character and was portrayed as the cause of his undoing. See Waley, *The Nō Plays of Japan* (New York: Grove, 1920), 58–59.

7. Although its origin is obscure, haiku flourished in the seventeenth century with such an eminent poet as Matsuo Basho (1644-1694).

8. See Noguchi, *The Story of Yone Noguchi Told by Himself* (London: Chatto and Windus, 1914), 231–32. Noguchi discusses elsewhere the true meaning of abstraction as opposed to reality: "While I admit the art of some artist which has the detail of beauty, I must tell him that reality, even when true, is not the whole thing; he should learn the art of escaping from it. That art is, in my opinion, the greatest of all arts; without it, art will never bring us the eternal and the mysterious" (*The Spirit of Japanese Art* [London: John Murray / New York: Dutton, 1915], 103). Yone Noguchi (1875–1947), father of the sculptor Isamu Noguchi, is the earliest Japanese American poet who published in America, England, and Japan six volumes of poetry originally written in English. Besides well over fifty books in Japanese, he also wrote several books in English of literary and art criticism, and of autobiography.

9. Shoei Ando, *Zen and American Transcendentalism* (Tokyo: Hokusei Press, 1970), 164.

10. Max Loehr, *The Great Paintings of China* (New York: Harper and Row, 1980), 216.

11. Hugo Musterberg, *The Arts of Japan: An Illustrated History* (Rutland, VT; Tokyo: Tuttle, 1957), 110.

12. Earl Miner, *The Japanese Tradition in British and American Literature* (Princeton, NJ: Princeton University Press, 1958), 140.

13. Lian Kai's Buddha is an emaciated figure with an unevenly shaped head, eyes, ears, nose, mouth, arms, and feet, standing diagonally. By contrast, Buddha's picture shown in the temples other than those of the Zen sect is usually a figure with a round face, arms, and hands, and with a symmetrically shaped head, eyes, eyebrows, nose, ears, mouth, and round mark on the forehead, sitting straight with a halo around the head and with a round hat.

14. Emerson's flower, found in a dark, subdued atmosphere, can be compared to a Zen painting in which a dark color is dominant but is the kind of darkness that settles one's heart. This calm and "enlightened" darkness is pervasive in a Zen-inspired teahouse, since bright light would distract one's mind. The dim light that permeates the teahouse is reminiscent of the moonlit chamber described in Hawthorne's "Custom House," for in each case such an atmosphere is said to be conducive to a deeper concentration of the human soul and thus a greater creativity for the artist.

15. Unlike zazen, Whitman's prayer for Columbus resembles the prayer practiced by the Shingon sect of Buddhism in Japan. Its followers recite a sutra, *Saddharma Pundarika Sutra* in Sanskrit, as an important means of salvation. Whitman's "Prayer of Columbus" ends in this passage:

And these things I see suddenly, what mean they?
As if some miracle, some hand divine unseal'd my eyes,
Shadowy vast shapes smile through the air and sky,

And on the distant waves sail countless ships,
And anthems in new tongues I hear saluting me.
(*CPOW*, 296)

The "anthems in new tongues" Whitman hears "saluting" him suggest his reliance on God for his salvation rather than his self-enlightenment, Zen's supreme doctrine.

16. A tanka, also known as a *waka*, is a highly stylized Japanese syllabic verse of five vertical lines arranged in a sequence of five-seven-five-seven-seven syllables. Much older than the haiku, the tanka dates back to *Manyoshu*, a poetry anthology published in the eighth century.

CHAPTER 4

1. Earl Miner, in *The Japanese Tradition in British and American Literature* (Princeton, NJ: Princeton University Press, 1958), closely examines Yeats's relationship to the noh play and also discusses Yeats's association with Ezra Pound with respect to East-West literary relations. But Miner does not consider Yone Noguchi in this context. Makoto Ueda's *Zeami, Basho, Yeats, Pound: A Study in Japanese and English Poetics* (The Hague: Mouton, 1965), does not mention Noguchi. Nor does Liam Miller's *The Noble Drama of W. B. Yeats* (Dublin: Dolmen, 1977), which includes well-annotated analyses of Yeats's noh plays in comparison with the Japanese model, mention Noguchi.

2. Among the East-West comparative critics, Roy E. Teele is the one who demonstrates Fenollosa's failure to understand the Japanese language, particularly the essential rhythm of the noh text Fenollosa translated. See Teele's "The Japanese Translations," *Texas Quarterly* 10 (1967): 61-66.

3. For a discussion of Noguchi's English poetry and literary criticism, see Yoshinobu Hakutani, "Yone Noguchi's Poetry: From Whitman to Zen," *Comparative Literature Studies* 22 (1985): 67-79.

4. *The Egoist* was one of the prestigious literary magazines published in London in the 1910s. When Noguchi contributed two of his articles to the magazine, its assistant editor was T. S. Eliot.

5. This lecture was published as "Chapter II: The Japanese Hokku Poetry" in Noguchi's *The Spirit of Japanese Poetry* (London: John Murray / New York: Dutton, 1914), 33–53.

6. This lecture was published as "Japanese Poetry" in *The Transactions of the Japan Society of London* 12 (1914): 86–109.

7. See *Hiroshige*. This book was followed by other books on Japanese painting: *Korin, Utamaro, Hokusai, Harunobu,* and *Ukiyoye Primitives*.

8. Kodo Kurebayashi, *Introduction to Dogen Zen* [in Japanese], (Tokyo: Daihorinkaku, 1983), 121–29.

9. E. A. Sharp, *William Sharp: A Memoir* (London: Heinemann, 1910), 280–81.

10. A unifying image or action appears frequently in Yeats's noh plays as it does in Japanese noh plays. The well choked up with leaves in *At the Hawk's Well* is represented by a piece of cloth that remains throughout the performance just as the bed-ridden lady Aoi no Ue, the heroine of the noh play *Aoi no Ue*, is symbolized by a sleeve laid on the stage during the performance. In Yeats's *The Dreaming of the Bones*, the young girl's spirit speaks impersonally of herself as the old man and the old woman in the noh play *Nishikigi*, in Pound's version, speak in unison. The climactic dance of the Rainbow Skirt and Feather Jacket performed in Noguchi's noh play "The Everlasting Sorrow" is also a unified image since it symbolizes the flight of two birds with one wing.

11. See Noguchi's "The Everlasting Sorrow: A Japanese Noh Play," *Egoist* 4 (1917):141–43, in which the Sovereign Ming Huang longs for the earthly return of his mistress Yang Kue-fei, who has long departed for heaven. A Taoist priest is commanded by the Sovereign to find the Lady Bang's lost soul. Upon finding her the priest asks her to give a token as proof of his meeting with her. Though she offers her hairpin to take back with him, he declines it as too common and asks her to present something special that Ming Huang would remember as belonging to her alone. "In deep," Yang Kuei-fei responds, "I now happen to recall to my mind how on the seventh day of the seventh moon, in the Hall of Immortality, at midnight when no one was anear,—" Then the chorus sings: "—the Sovereign whispered in my ears, after pledging the two stars in the sky:

In heaven we will ever fly like one-winged birds;
On earth grow joined like a tree with branches twining
    tight."

At the climax of the play, Yang Kuei-fei performs for the priest a dance of the Rainbow Skirt and Feather Jacket to convey Ming Huang "the dancer's heart." Noguchi adds a note: "Each bird must fly with a mate, since it has only one wing" (142).

12. One of the players who made an indispensable contribution to Yeats's understanding of noh performance was a Japanese dancer, Michio Itoh. He came from a distinguished family of theatre artists. Two of his brothers, Kensaku Itoh and Koreya Senda, who also distinguished themselves in the theatre in Japan as late as after World War II, are both famous for their work as stage designers and as dancers. The papier-mâché mask Itoh wore for the performance of *At the Hawk's Well* in 1926 was made by Isamu Noguchi, the son of Yone Noguchi and his American wife Leonie Gilmour (Isamu Noguchi, *A Sculptor's World* [New York: Harper & Row, 1968], 123). The performance of the play demanded in its music, movement, and visual effect first-hand knowledge of the noh theatre. It was Pound who introduced Itoh to Yeats, who thought Itoh's "minute intensity of movement in the dance of the hawk so well suited our small room and private art" (*POY*, 417).

13. In the play a fisherman finds on a pine tree a feather robe that belongs to a fair angel. She begs him to return the robe and offers to dance for him in return. He insists on keeping the robe with him until she completes her dance. She assures him that angels never break promises, saying that falsehood exists only among mortals. The fisherman, deeply ashamed, hands back the robe to her. The angel, completing her performance, vanishes into the air.

14. For Pound's and Fenollosa's version, see Pound and Fenollosa, *CNT*, 98–104.

15. In the play, the mountain elf during the night circles round the mountain, a symbol of life. At the climax, a famous dancer, another elf, who has lost her way in the Hill of Shadow on her way to the Holy Buddhist Temple, appears and inquires the right road of the mountain elf "with large star-like eyes and fearful snow-white hair." The mountain elf then shows the dancer how to encircle the mountain (*SJP*, 66–67).

CHAPTER 5

1. Much of Yone Noguchi's biographical information is found in the autobiographical essays written in English and in Japanese. The most useful is a collection of such essays titled *The Story of Yone Noguchi Told by Himself* (London: Chatto and Windus, 1914).

2. Yone Noguchi, *Seen and Unseen, or, Monologues of a Homeless Snail*, (San Francisco: Gelett Burgess and Porter Garnett, 1897); *The Voice of the Valley* (San Francisco: Doxey, 1897).

3. Willa Cather, "Two Poets: Yone Noguchi and Bliss Carman," in *The World and the Parish: Willa Cather's Articles and Reviews, 1893–1902*, ed. William M. Curtin (Lincoln: University of Nebraska Press, 1970), 2:579.

4. The most comprehensive, though often inaccurate, bibliography of Yone Noguchi's writings in Japanese and in English is included in Usaburo Toyama, ed., *Essays on Yone Noguchi*, vol. 1, Tokyo: Zokei Bijutsu Kyokai, 1963.

5. Sanehide Kodama, ed., *Ezra Pound and Japan: Letters and Essays* (Redding Ridge, CT: Black Swan, 1987), 4.

6. Yone Noguchi, *Collected English Letters*, ed. Ikuko Atsumi (Tokyo: Yone Noguchi Society, 1975), 210–11.

7. Noguchi, *The Spirit of Japanese Poetry* (London: John Murray / New York: Dutton, 1914); *Through the Torii* (Boston: Four Seas, 1922); *The Spirit of Japanese Art* (London: John Murray / New York: Dutton, 1915).

8. See Yone Noguchi, "The Everlasting Sorrow: A Japanese Noh Play," *Egoist* 4 (October 1917), 141–43; and "The Japanese Noh Play," *Egoist* 5 (August 1918), 99.

9. See K. L. Goodwin, *The Influence of Ezra Pound* (London: Oxford University Press, 1966), 32.

10. Noguchi first met Yeats in 1903 as indicated in a letter Noguchi wrote to Leonie Gilmour, his first wife: "I made many a nice young, lovely, kind friend

among literary genius (attention!) W. B. Yeats or Laurence Binyon, Moore and Bridges. They are so good; they invite me almost every day" (Noguchi, *Collected English Letters*, 106). In 1921 Yeats, who was in Oxford, England, sent a long letter to Noguchi, who was in Japan: "Though I have been so long in writing your 'Hiroshige' has given me the greatest pleasure. I take more and more pleasure from oriental art; find more and more that it accords with what I aim at in my own work. The European painter of the last two or three hundred years grows strange to me as I grow older, begins to speak as with a foreign tongue. . . . The old French poets were simple as the modern are not, & I find in Francois Villon the same thoughts, with more intellectual power, that I find in the Gaelic poet [Raftery]. I would be simple myself but I do not know how. I am always turning over pages like those you have sent me, hoping that in my old age I may discover how. . . . A form of beauty scarcely lasts a generation with us, but it lasts with you for centuries. You no more want to change it than a pious man wants to change the Lord's Prayer, or the Crucifix on the wall [blurred] at least not unless we have infected you with our egotism" (Noguchi, *Collected English Letters*, 220–21).

11. Goodwin, *Influence of Ezra Pound*, 32.

12. The translation of this verse and others quoted in this chapter, unless otherwise noted, is by Yoshinobu Hakutani.

13. See Donald Keene, *World within Walls: Japanese Literature of the Pre-Modern Era, 1600–1868* (New York: Grove, 1976), 13.

14. A certain group of poets, including Ito Shintoku (1634–1698) and Ikenishi Gonsui (1650–1722) of the Teitoku school, and Uejima Onitsura (1661–1738), Konishi Raizan (1654–1716), and Shiinomoto Saimaro (1656–1738), of the Danrin school, each contributed to refining Basho's style (Keene, *World within Walls*, 56–70).

15. A detailed historical account of haikai poetry is given in Keene, *World within Walls*, 337–55.

16. The translation of this haiku is by Yone Noguchi. See *SEWOYN*, 2:73–74.

17. The original of this haiku is quoted from Harold Henderson, *An Introduction to Haiku: An Anthology of Poems and Poets from Basho to Shiki* (New York: Doubleday/Anchor, 1958), 49.

18. The original of "A Morning-Glory" is quoted from Fujio Akimoto, *Haiku Nyumon [Introduction to Haiku]* (Tokyo: Kodansha, 1971), 23.

19. The original of "Autumn is Deepening" is quoted from Noichi Imoto, *Basho: Sono Jinsei to Geijitsu [Basho: His Life and Art]* (Tokyo: Kodansha, 1968), 231.

20. The original of "A Crow" is quoted from Imoto, *Basho*, 86. The English version is quoted from R. H. Blyth, *A History of Haiku* (Tokyo: Hokuseido, 1964), 2:xxix. The middle line in a later version of the poem reads: "Karasu no tomari keri" (Henderson, *Introduction to Haiku*, 18). The earlier version has a syllabic measure of five-ten-five, while the later one has five-nine-five syllables, both in an unusual pattern.

21. The original of "Sunset on the Sea" is quoted from Imoto, *Basho*, 117.

22. The original of "Were My Wife Alive" is quoted from Akimoto, *Haiku Nyumon*, 200.

23. The original of "The Harvest Moon" is quoted from "Meigetsu • ya • tatami-no ue • ni • matsu-no-kage" (Henderson, *Introduction to Haiku*, 58).

24. The impact of hokku on Pound was apparently greater and more beneficial than that on his fellow imagists. Regarding the form of super-position as ideal for expressing instantaneous perception, Pound wrote in a footnote, "Mr. Flint and Mr. Rodker have made longer poems depending on a similar presentation of matter. So also have Richard Aldington, in his In Via Sestina, and 'H. D.' in her Oread, which latter poems express much stronger emotions than that in my lines here given" ("Vorticism," *Fortnightly Review*, n.s., 573 [1914]: 467). Pound's argument here suggests that hokku and Pound's hokku-like poems can express instantaneous and spontaneous perception better than can the longer poems and the poems with stronger emotions.

25. E. A. Sharp, *William Sharp: A Memoir* (London: Heinemann, 1910), 280–81.

26. See Noguchi, "What Is a Hokku Poem?" *Rhythm* 11, no. 10 (1913): 354–59. The essay was reprinted in Noguchi's *Through the Torii*, 126–39. The page numbers cited hereafter refer to the *Rhythm* version.

27. See William Pratt, *The Imagist Poem* (New York: Dutton, 1963), 14–15; J. B. Harmer, *Victory in Limbo: Imagism 1908–1917* (New York: St. Martin's, 1975), 17; Humphrey Carpenter, *A Serious Character: The Life of Ezra Pound* (Boston: Houghton Mifflin, 1988), 115.

28. It is speculative, of course, but quite possible that Aldington, fascinated by Japanese visual arts, might have read the three articles about the subject Noguchi published in this period: "Utamaro," *Rhythm* 11, no. 10 (November 1912), 257–60; "Koyetsu," *Rhythm* 11, no. 11 (December 1912), 302–5; "The Last Master [Yoshitoshi] of the Ukiyoye School," *Transactions of the Japan Society of London* 12 (April 1914), 144–56. Moreover, Noguchi, *Spirit of Japanese Art* (1915), includes chapters on major Japanese painters such as Koyetsu, Kenzan, Kyosai, Busho Hara, besides Utamaro and Hiroshige. If Aldington had read these essays, he would very well have been acquainted with Noguchi's writings about Japanese poetics.

29. Aldington's poem reads:
    The apparition of these poems in a crowd:
    White faces in a black dead faint.

See Richard Aldington, "Penultimate Poetry," *Egoist* 1, no. 2 (January 1914). This poem sounds more like senryu, a humorous haiku, than the hokku Pound was advocating. Senryu originated from Karai Senryu, an eighteenth-century Japanese haiku poet.

30. See Donald Davie, *Ezra Pound* (New York: Viking, 1975), 42; and Carpenter, *Serious Character*, 247.

31. Harmer, *Victory in Limbo*, 38.

32. Earl Miner, "Pound, Haiku and the Image," *Hudson Review* 9 (Winter 1957): 572.

33. See Toyama, *Essays on Yone Noguchi* (mostly in Japanese), 1:327.

34. See A. R. Jones, *The Life and Opinions of Thomas Ernest Hulme* (Boston: Beacon, 1960), 122. Neither Noel Stock in *Poet in Exile: Ezra Pound* (Manchester: Manchester University Press, 1964), nor Humphrey Carpenter in *Serious Character* mentions Pound's activities at the Quest Society, let alone Pound's possible interactions with Noguchi.

35. See T. S. Eliot's introduction to *Literary Essays of Ezra Pound* (New York: New Directions, 1954), 23.

36. Alan Durant tries to show that Pound's metro poem linguistically contains a number of metaphors and associations, and that it is not as imagistic as critics say. While Durant's interpretation is valid as far as the various elements in the poem appear to the reader as metaphors and associations, Pound's intention does differ from the reader's interpretation. The same thing may occur in the interpretation of a Japanese hokku, but traditionally the language of the hokku, as Noguchi demonstrates throughout *Spirit of Japanese Poetry*, shuns metaphor and symbolism. See Alan Durant, "Pound, Modernism and Literary Criticism: A Reply to Donald Davie," *Critical Quarterly* 28 (Spring-Summer 1986): 154-66.

37. To the Japanese, such expressions as "the light of passion" and "the cicada's song" immediately evoke images of hot summer. These phrases in Japanese are attributed to or closely associated with summer.

CHAPTER 6

1. See Charles I. Glicksberg, "Existentialism in *The Outsider*," *Four Quarters* 7 (January 1958): 17-26; and "The God of Fiction," *Colorado Quarterly* 7 (Autumn 1958): 207-20. Michel Fabre has shown in some detail that Wright's composition of *The Outsider* was influenced by Camus's *The Stranger*. See Fabre, "Richard Wright, French Existentialism, and *The Outsider*," in *Critical Essays on Richard Wright*, ed. Yoshinobu Hakutani (Boston: G. K. Hall, 1982), 191.

2. See James N. Rhea, *Providence Sunday Journal*, March 22, 1953.

3. See Saunders Redding, review of *The Outsider*, by Richard Wright, *Baltimore Afro-American*, May 19, 1953; Lloyd Brown, "Outside and Low," *Masses and Mainstream* 6 (May 1953): 62-64.

4. See Glicksberg, "Existentialism in *The Outsider*"; "The God of Fiction."

5. Fabre, "Richard Wright, French Existentialism, and *The Outsider*," 191.

6. Margolies, *The Art of Richard Wright* (Carbondale: Southern Illinois University Press, 1969), 135.

7. Fabre, "Richard Wright, French Existentialism, and *The Outsider*," 186.

8. See Albert Camus, *Lyrical and Critical Essays*, ed. Philip Thody, trans. Ellen C. Kennedy (New York: Knopf, 1968), 335–37.

9. See, for instance, Robert de Luppe, *Albert Camus* (Paris: Temps Present, 1951) 46–47.

10. Stropher B. Purdy, "*An American Tragedy* and *L'Étranger*," *Comparative Literature* 19 (Summer 1967): 261.

11. The most precise analysis of Camus's concept of time is presented in Ignace Feuerlicht, "Camus's *L'Étranger* Reconsidered," *PMLA* 78 (December 1963): 606-21.

12. See Redding's review of *The Outsider*, by Richard Wright, in *Baltimore Afro-American*, repr., John M. Reilly, *Richard Wright: The Critical Reception* (New York: Franklin, 1978), 225–27; and Melvin Altschuler, "An Important, but Exasperating Book," review of *The Outsider*, by Richard Wright, *Washington Post*, repr., Reilly, *Richard Wright*, 203–4.

CHAPTER 7

1. Both manuscripts are among the Richard Wright manuscripts and papers, housed in the Beinecke Rare Book and Manuscript Library, Yale University, New Haven, Connecticut.

2. Richard Wright, *Haiku: This Other World*, ed. with notes and afterword by Yoshinobu Hakutani and Robert L. Tener (New York: Arcade, 1998; repr., New York: Random House, 2000; repr., *Haiku: The Last Poems of an American Icon*, New York: Arcade, 2012).

3. R. H. Blyth, *Haiku*, 4 vols. (Tokyo: Hokuseido, 1949). Volume 1 was reprinted as *Haiku: Eastern Culture* (Tokyo: Hokuseido, 1981).

4. Waley further shows with Zeami's works that the aesthetic principle of *yugen* originated from Zen Buddhism. "It is obvious," Whaley writes, "that Seami [Zeami] was deeply imbued with the teachings of Zen, in which cult Yoshimitsu may have been his master." See Arthur Waley, *The Nō Plays of Japan* (New York: Grove, 1920), 21–22.

5. The translation is by Hakutani.

6. See Max Loehr, *The Great Paintings of China* (New York: Harper and Row, 1980), 216.

7. R. H. Blyth, *A History of Haiku* (Tokyo: Hokuseido, 1949), 2:xxix. The translation is by Blyth.

8. The original is quoted from Fujio Akimoto, *Haiku Nyumon* [*Introduction to Haiku*] (Tokyo: Kodansha, 1971), 222. The translation of the haiku is by Hakutani.

9. The translation of the haiku is by Hakutani.

10. T. S. Eliot, *Selected Essays, 1917–1932* (New York: Harcourt, 1932), 247.

11. The original is quoted from Harold G. Henderson, *An Introduction to Haiku: An Anthology of Poems and Poets from Basho to Shiki* (New York: Doubleday/Anchor, 1958), 164. The translation is by Hakutani.

12. The original is quoted from Henderson, *Introduction to Haiku*, 160. The translation is by Hakutani.

13. Blyth, *Haiku: Eastern Culture*, 262. The translation is by Blyth.

14. Ibid., 262. The translation is by Blyth.

15. Ibid., 308–9. The translation is by Blyth.

16. Nathaniel Hawthorne, *The Scarlet Letter*, ed. Ross C. Murfin (Boston: St. Martins, 1991), 53–54.

17. The original of the haiku is in Henderson, *Introduction to Haiku*, 18. The translation is from Blyth, *History of Haiku*, 2:xxix.

18. The original of Buson's haiku is in Henderson, *Introduction to Haiku*, 104. The translation is by Hakutani.

19. The original of Buson's haiku is in Henderson, *Introduction to Haiku*, 102. The translation is by Hakutani.

20. The original of Kikaku's haiku is in Henderson, *Introduction to Haiku*, 58. The translation is by Hakutani.

21. Jacques Lacan, *The Four Fundamental Concepts of Psychoanalysis*, ed. Jacques-Alain Miller, trans. Alan Sheridan (New York: Norton, 1881), 188.

22. Jacques Lacan, *The Seminar of Jacques Lacan*, bk. 2, *The Ego in Freud's Theory and in the Techniques of Psychoanalysis, 1954–1955*, ed. Jacques-Alain Miller, trans. Sylvana Tomaselli (New York: Norton, 1988), 285.

23. Ibid., 302.

24. Ezra Pound, "Vorticism," *Fortnightly Review*, n.s., 573 (September 1914), 463.

25. Lacan, *Seminar*, 176–77, 31.

26. Ibid., 308.

27. The translator of Moritake's haiku is unknown. Pound might have quoted the translation of this haiku from a book, or he himself might have translated the original in Japanese. As seen in R. H. Blyth, *A History of Haiku* (Tokyo: Hokuseido, 1949), the original has three phrases:

Rak-ka eda ni kaeru to mireba kocho-o kana
(2:56)

A literal translation in three lines reads:

A fallen petal
Seems to return to the branch—
It's a butterfly!

28. Ezra Pound, *Ezra Pound: Selected Poems* (New York: New Directions, 1957), 36.

29. Lacan, *Seminar*, 234.

30. Franklin's precept for the virtue of silence reads, "Speak not but what may benefit others or yourself. Avoid trifling Conversation." See Benjamin Franklin, *The Autobiography*, in *Anthology of American Literature*, vol. 1, *Colonial through Romantic*, 6th ed., ed. George McMichael (Upper Saddle River, NJ: Prentice Hall, 1997), 384.

CHAPTER 8

1. In *A Week on the Concord and Merrimack Rivers* (1849), Thoreau wrote, "We can tolerate all philosophies, Atomists, Pneumatologists, Atheists, Theoists,— Plato, Aristotle, Leucippus, Democritus, Pythagoras, Zoroaster and Confucius. It is the attitude of these men, more than any communication which they make, that attracts us" (152). In the conclusion of "Civil Disobedience," Thoreau evoked Confucius: "The progress from an absolute to a limited monarchy, from a limited monarchy to a democracy, is a progress toward a true respect for the individual. Even the Chinese philosopher was wise enough to regard the individual as the basis of the empire" (*The Variorum Civil Disobedience*, ed. Walter Harding [New York: Twayne, 1967], 55).

2. John Tytell observes, "Kerouac . . . attacked the concept of revision sacred to most writers as a kind of secondary moral censorship imposed by the unconscious" (*Naked Angels: The Lives & Literature of the Beat Generation* [New York: McGraw-Hill, 1977], 17).

3. Tom Lynch, "Intersecting Influences in American Haiku," in *Modernity in East-West Literary Criticism: New Readings*, ed. Yoshinobu Hakutani (Madison, NJ: Fairleigh Dickinson University Press, 2001), 123–24.

4. Barry Gifford and Lawrence Lee, *Jack's Book: An Oral Biography of Jack Kerouac* (New York: St. Martin's, 1978), 271.

5. As noted earlier, Pound quoted Moritake's haiku just before discussing the often-quoted poem "In a Station of the Metro": "The apparition of these faces in the crowd: / Petals, on a wet, black bough" ("Vorticism," *Fortnightly Review*, n.s., 573 [September 1914]: 48). A literal translation of Moritake's first two lines, "Rakka eda ni / Kaeru to mireba," would read, "The fallen blossom appears to come back to its branch." Pound tried to apply the principle of terseness and intensity in Moritake's haiku to the construction of a single image in his poetry. "The 'one image poem,'" Pound noted, "is a form of superposition, that is to say it is one idea set on top of another. I found it useful in getting out of the impasse in which I had been left by my metro emotion" ("Vorticism," 467).

6. Like Thoreau, Kerouac grew up a Christian and was well versed in the Bible but became fascinated with Buddhism. "It is necessary not to be Christian," Thoreau argued, "to appreciate the beauty and significance of the life of Christ. I know

that some will have hard thoughts of me, when they hear their Christ named be-side my Buddha, yet I am sure that I am willing they should love their Christ more than my Buddha" (*AW*, 67).

7. "After Apple-Picking," in Robert Frost, *Robert Frost's Poems*, ed. Louis Unter-meyer (New York: Pocket Books, 1971), ends with these lines:

> This sleep of mine, whatever sleep it is.
> Were he not gone,
> The woodchuck could say whether it's like his
> Long sleep, as I describe its coming on,
> Or just some human sleep.
> (229)

8. See the last stanza in each poem. The last stanza of Dickinson's poem 449, "I died for Beauty," reads:

> And so, as Kinsmen, met a Night—
> We talked between the Rooms—
> Until the Moss had reached our lips—
> And covered up—our names—.

9. See the last stanza of "The Road Not Taken":

> I shall be telling this with a sigh
> Somewhere ages and ages hence:
> Two roads diverged in a wood, and I—
> I took the one less traveled by,
> And that has made all the difference.
> (Frost, *Frost's Poems*, 223)

10. See the lines in "The Weary Blues":

> In a deep song voice with a melancholy tone
> I heard that Negro sing, that old piano moan—
>   "Ain't got nobody in all this world,
>   Ain't got nobody but ma self.
> (*SPLH*, 33)

11. See the first two and last two lines in "We Real Cool," in Gwendolyn Brooks, *Selected Poems* (New York: Harper Perennial, 1999):

> We real cool. We

Left school. We

....

Jazz June. We
Die soon.
(73)

12. See Jack Kerouac, *Book of Haikus*, ed. and with an introduction by Regina Weinreich (New York: Penguin Books, 2003): 106. Editing this group of haiku, Weinreich places them as "Part IV. 1957: Road Haiku / Summer." She further notes, "Kerouac's pocket notebooks contain haiku entries written in New York City, Tangier, Aix-en-Province, London, New York City again, Berkeley, Mexico, and Orlando. As the notebooks and letters of this period show, Kerouac exhorted himself to write haiku, mindful of the traditional methods" (106).

13. See Regina Weinreich's comments about "Road Haiku," *Book of Haikus*, 106.

14. See Ann Charters, "Introduction," in *On the Road* (New York: Viking, 1958), xxix.

15. Kerouac's description of California as "white like washlines and emptyheaded" might mean the Buddhist doctrine of *mu*, the state of nothingness.

16. See New Testament, Revelation 21, verses 11, 18, and 27, respectively.

17. Saint Sebastian (died c. 288) is said to have been killed during the Roman Emperor Diocletian's persecution of Christians.

18. Basho's haiku is quoted from R. H. Blyth, *Haiku: Eastern Culture* (Tokyo: Hokuseido, 1981): 38. The translation of the haiku is by Blyth.

19. The lines are quoted from Ralph Waldo Emerson, *Selections from Ralph Waldo Emerson*, ed. Stephen E. Whicher (Boston: Houghton Mifflin, 1960): 418.

20. In *The Dharma Bums*, Kerouac sees human existence as a strange beetle when he climbs Mount Hozomeen: "Standing on my head before bedtime on that rock roof of the moonlight I could indeed see that the earth was truly upsidedown and man a weird vain beetle full of strange ideas walking around upsidedown and boasting, and I could realize that man remembered why this dream of planets and plants and Plantagenets was built out of the primordial essence." See *DB*, 238.

21. The lines are quoted from *Selections from Ralph Waldo Emerson*, 414.

22. See Walt Whitman, *CPOW*, 26.

CHAPTER 9

1. In his essay "Remembering Richard Wright," included in *Going to the Territory* (New York: Random House, 1986), Ellison expresses his indebtedness to the encouragement and advice Wright offered the young Ellison. Ellison, however, is somewhat critical of *Native Son*: "I feel that *Native Son* was one of the major literary events in the history of American literature. And I can say this even though at this point I have certain reservations concerning its view of reality" (*Going*, 210–11).

But among Wright's works, Ellison was most impressed by *12 Million Black Voices*, which he thought is Wright's "most lyrical work." While Ellison thought that this compelling work of literature "could move [Wright's] white readers to tears," he also realized that Wright forged "such hard, mechanical images and actions that no white reading them could afford the luxury of tears" (*Going*, 211).

2. Richard Wright, "Blueprint for Negro Writing," in *Richard Wright Reader*, ed. Ellen Wright and Michel Fabre (New York: Harper, 1978), 38.

3. Wright similarly refers to the Irish tradition in *12 Million Black Voices*: "We lose ourselves in violent forms of dances in our ballrooms. The faces of the white world, looking on in wonder and curiosity, declare: '*Only* the negro can play!' But they are wrong. They misread us. We are able to play in this fashion because we have been excluded, left behind; we play in this manner because all excluded folk play. The English say of the Irish, just as America says of us, that only the Irish can play, that they laugh through their tears. But every powerful nation says this of the folk whom it oppresses in justification of that oppression" (128).

4. For a study of Malraux's influence on Ellison, see Pancho Savery, "'Not Like an Arrow, But a Boomerang': Ellison's Existential Blues," in *Approaches to Teaching Ellison's "Invisible Man*," ed. Susan Resneck Parr and Pancho Savery (New York: MLA, 1986), 65-74.

5. *Conversations with Richard Wright*, ed. Keneth Kinnamon and Michel Fabre (Jackson: University Press of Mississippi, 1993), also is witness to Ellison's alliance with modern European literatures and traditions. In an interview for *American Weekend*, published in Paris on January 24, 1959, Wright said, "Negro literature . . . is a good barometer of Negro reaction. As fields open up to Negroes, it will be reflected in Negro literature. There is a large group of Negro writers in Europe—Demby and Ellison in Rome, for instance. All of them are broadening their experiences in a European context" (*Conversations*, 185).

6. Kun Jong Lee, "Ellison's *Invisible Man*: Emersonianism Revised," *PMLA* 107 (March 1992): 331-44, demonstrates that while Ellison appropriates Emerson's condescending attitude toward the black race, he redirects this negative aspect of Emersonian self-reliance. Ellison, Lee argues, "both accepts and rejects Emersonianism" (342).

7. Robert Butler, "The City as Psychological Frontier in Ralph Ellison's *Invisible Man* and Charles Johnson's *Faith and the Good Thing*" in *The City in African-American Literature*, ed. Yoshinobu Hakutani and Robert Butler (London and Toronto: Associated University Presses, 1995), 127, reads as a trope the vet in *Invisible Man*, whose words admonish the protagonist to "learn to look beneath the surface" (*IM*, 153) and subvert the materialistic values of the Horatio Alger myth.

8. For recent discussions of Zen philosophy and aesthetics, see Hakutani, "Emerson, Whitman, and Zen Buddhism," *Midwest Quarterly* 31 (Summer 1990): 433-48, and "Ezra Pound, Yone Noguchi, and Imagism," *Modern Philology* 90 (August

1992): 46-69.

9. For a discussion of the relationship between Zen and Lacan, see Robert Samuels, "Emerson, Lacan, and Zen: Transcendental and Postmodern Conceptions of the Eastern Subject," in *Postmodernity and Cross-Culturalism*, ed. Yoshinobu Hakutani (Madison, NJ: Fairleigh Dickinson University Press / London: Associated University Presses, 2002).

10. Most modern works on Zen stress the importance of genderlessness in their discussions of Zen. See, for example, Kodo Kurebayashi, *Introduction to Dogen Zen* [in Japanese], (Tokyo: Daihorinkaku, 1983), 142–49.

11. The Zen master's pronouncement "*never stop,*" noted earlier, recalls Whitman's last passage in "Song of Myself": "Failing to fetch me at first keep encouraged, / Missing me one place search another" (68), or the last lines in "Passage to India": "O my brave soul! / O farther farther sail! / O daring joy, but safe! are they not all the seas of God? / O farther, farther, farther sail!" (294). Whitman's final statement in "Song of Myself"—"If you want me again look for me under your boot-soles" (68)— echoes the Zen master's: "It's just underneath your standpoint." Shoei Ando, *Zen and American Transcendentalism* (Tokyo: Hokusei Press, 1970), 164.

12. In the chapter "The Whiteness of the Whale" in *Moby-Dick*, ed. Harrison Hayford and Hershel Parker (New York: Norton, 1967), Melville writes, "Is it that by its indefiniteness it shadows forth the heartless voids and immensities of the universe, and thus stabs us from behind with the thought of annihilation, when beholding the white depths of the milky way? Or is it, that as in essence whiteness is not so much a color as the visible absence of color, and at the same time the concrete of all colors; is it for these reasons that there is such a dumb blankness, full of meaning, in a wide landscape of snows—a colorless all-color of atheism from which we shrink?" (169).

CHAPTER 10

1. Barry Learned, "U. S. Lets Negro Explain Race Ills, Wright Declares," in *Conversations with Richard Wright*, ed. Keneth Kinnamon and Michel Fabre (Jackson: University Press of Mississippi, 1993), 185.

2. Paul Gilroy, in *The Black Atlantic: Modernity and Double Consciousness* (Cambridge: Harvard University Press, 1993), has defended Wright's later works, such as *Black Power*, *Pagan Spain*, and *The Color Curtain*, against "those tendencies in African-American literary criticism which argue that the work he produced while living in Europe was worthless when compared to his supposedly authentic earlier writings" (x).

3. See Mary Ellen Stephenson, "Spain Gets Bitter Barks from Visitor," in *Richard Wright: The Critical Reception*, ed. John M. Reilly (New York: Burt Franklin, 1978),

307.

4. See Wright, "Interview with Richard Wright by Peter Schmid/1946," in Kinnamon and Fabre, *Conversations with Richard Wright*, 203.

5. Kinnamon and Fabre, *Conversations with Richard Wright*, 204–05.

6. See "No Castles in Spain," *Charlotte News*, repr., Reilly, *Richard Wright*, 290.

7. See Redding, *Baltimore Afro-American*, repr., Reilly, *Richard Wright*, 299.

8. The supreme, pantheistic divinity in Shintoism, the Japanese state religion, is the goddess *Ama-Terasu Ohmi Kami*, literally translated as "Heaven-Shining Great God."

9. See Francis E. McMahon, S. J., "Spain through Secularist Spectacles," *America* 96 (March 1957): 648, 653, repr., Reilly, *Richard Wright*, 300.

10. Instead of emphasizing sexuality for the cause of repression, Carl Jung theorized that the primal, universal, collective unconsciousness has a sexual as well as nonsexual component. According to Jungian psychology, personality consists of the *persona*, which is consciously presented to the world, and the *anima*, which is unconsciously repressed. When Wright explored the Black Virgin at Montserrat, he seemed to be more impressed by the collective, racial unconsciousness akin to Jungianism than by the sexual repression in Freudianism. To his Spanish companion Wright said, "Pardo, don't you see that conglomeration of erect stone penises? Open your eyes, man. You can't miss. I'm not preaching the doctrines of Freud. Let the facts you see speak to you" (*PS*, 66).

11. In Wright's *Uncle Tom's Children* (1940, repr., New York: Harper and Row, 1965), Big Boy, hiding in a kiln, watches Bobo lynched and burned:

"LES GIT SOURVINEERS!"

. . . .

"Everybody git back!"
"Look! He's gotta finger!"

. . . .

"He's got one of his ears, see?"

. . . .

"HURRY UP N BURN THE NIGGER FO IT RAINS!"

. . . .

Bobo was struggling, twisting; they were binding his arms and legs. . . . The flames leaped tall as the trees. The scream came again. Big Boy trembled and looked. The mob was running down the slopes, leaving the fire clear. Then he saw a writhing white mass cradled in yellow flame, and heard screams, one on top of the other, each shriller and shorter than the last. The mob was quiet now, standing still, looking up the slopes at the writhing white mass gradually growing black, growing black in a cradle of yellow flame. (49)

12. Wright describes the scene where a black physician examined Chris's body:

290

"He rolled the corpse upon its back and carefully parted the thighs. 'The *genitalia* are gone,' the doctor intoned. Fishbelly saw a dark, coagulated blot in a gaping hole between the thighs and, with defensive reflex, he lowered his hands nervously to his groin. 'I'd say that the genitals were pulled out by a pair of pliers or some like instrument,' the doctor inferred. 'Killing him wasn't enough. They had to *mutilate* 'im. You'd think that disgust would've made them leave *that* part of the boy alone. . . . No! To get a chance to *mutilate* 'im was part of why they killed 'im. And you can bet a lot of white women were watching eagerly when they did it. Perhaps they knew that that was the only opportunity they'd ever get to see a Negro's genitals—'" (*The Long Dream* [1958, repr., New York: Harper and Row, 1987], 78).

CHAPTER 11

1. For comparative studies of American transcendentalism and Zen, see, for example, Shoei Ando, *Zen and American Transcendentalism* (Tokyo: Hokusei Press, 1970), and Yoshinobu Hakutani, "Emerson, Whitman, and Zen Buddhism," *Midwest Quarterly* 31 (Summer 1990): 433-48.

2. For recent studies of the influences of Eastern poetics on Ezra Pound and William Carlos Williams, see, for example, Hakutani, "Ezra Pound, Yone Noguchi, and Imagism," *Modern Philology* 90 (August 1992): 46-69, and Charles Tomlinson, "Introduction to *Selected Poems* by William Carlos Williams," in *William Carlos Williams and Charles Tomlinson: A Transatlantic Connection*, ed. Barry Magid and Hugh Whitemeyer (New York: Peter Lang, 1999), 89–102.

3. Whitman in "Out of the Cradle Endlessly Rocking," endowing a young boy with a poetic inspiration, celebrates the birth of a poet:

> Demon or bird! (said the boy's soul,)
> Is it indeed toward your mate you sing? or is it really to
>   me?
> For I, that was a child, my tongue's use sleeping, now I
>   have heard you,
> Now in a moment I know what I am for, I awake,
> And already a thousand singers, a thousand songs, clearer,
>   louder and more sorrowful than yours,
> A thousand warbling echoes have started to life within me,
>   never to die.
> (183)

4. Wright's lyricism is evident in the early section of *Black Boy*, in which a young African American seeks a harmony between nature and society.

5. Lindsey Tucker, "Alice Walker's *The Color Purple*: Emergent Woman,

Emergent Text," *Black American Literature Forum* 22 (Spring 1988), 84.

6. As discussed earlier, after his journey into Africa to write *Black Power*, Wright traveled to Spain to write *Pagan Spain*. Even compared with some parts of Africa, and most of Asia, Spain to him lagged behind in its progress toward modernism. "The African," Wright notes in *Pagan Spain*, "though thrashing about in a void, was free to create a future, but the pagan traditions of Spain had sustained no such mortal wound" (193). Such a critical view of Spain notwithstanding, he was nevertheless sympathetic toward the energetic maternal instinct of the Spanish woman, without which Spanish culture would not have survived after World War II. Wright discovered, as noted earlier, a strong affinity between the indigenous matriarchalism in the Ashanti and the stalwart womanhood in Spain.

7. In his review of *The Color Purple*, Mel Watkins commented, "While Netti[e]'s letters broaden and reinforce the theme of female oppression by describing customs of the Olinka tribe that parallel some found in the American South, they are often mere monologues on African history. Appearing, as they do, after Celie's intensely subjective voice has been established, they seem lackluster and intrusive" (7).

8. Wright defines the African primal view of life in terms of the cultural differences between a person of African heritage and that of a European immigrant: "There is no reason why an African or a person of African descent—in America, England, or France—should abandon his primal outlook upon life if he finds that no other way of life is available, or if he is intimidated in his attempt to grasp the new way. . . . There is nothing mystical or biological about it. When one realizes that one is dealing with two distinct and separate worlds of psychological being, two conceptions of time even, the problem becomes clear; it is a clash between two systems of culture" (*BP*, 266).

9. During the eighteenth century, a satirical form of haiku called senryu was developed by Karai Senryu (1718–1790) as a kind of mock haiku with humor, moralizing nuances, and a philosophical tone, expressing "the incongruity of things" more than their oneness, dealing more often with distortions and failures, not just with the harmonious beauty of nature.

10. Ando, *Zen and American Transcendentalism*, 164.

11. Wright writes about the Ashanti's worldview: "The pre-Christian African was impressed with the littleness of himself and he walked the earth warily, lest he disturb the presence of invisible gods. When he wanted to disrupt the terrible majesty of the ocean in order to fish, he first made sacrifices to its crashing and rolling waves; he dared not cut down a tree without first propitiating its spirit so that it would not haunt him; he loved his fragile life and he was convinced that the tree loved its life also" (*BP*, 261–62).

12. Linda Abbandonato, "A View from 'Elsewhere': Subversive Sexuality and the Rewriting of the Heroine's Story in *The Color Purple*," *PMLA* 106 (October 1991):

1112.

13. In his preface to *The Ambassadors*, ed. S. P. Rosenbaum (New York: Norton, 1964), Henry James accounts for the function of a minor character like Maria Gostrey in his rendition of a major character, Lambert Strether: "The *'ficelle'* character of the subordinate party is as artfully dissimulated, throughout, as may be, and to that extent that, with the seams or joints of Maria Gostrey's ostensible connectedness taken particular care of, duly smoothed over, that is, and anxiously kept from showing as 'pieced on'; this figure doubtless achieves, after a fashion, something of the dignity of a prime idea" (13).

14. Shug plays the role of a functional character, Tucker maintains, so that Celie is able to "'write herself' . . . to counter the victim-figures like her mother, and the dominant male figures of Albert and her father" (Tucker, "Alice Walker's *The Color Purple*," 85).

15. Abbandonato, "A View from 'Elsewhere,'" 1113.

CHAPTER 12

1. James Baldwin, *Nobody Knows My Name* (New York: Dell, 1961), 157.

2. Nelie McKay, "An Interview with Toni Morrison," *Contemporary Literature* 24 (Winter 1983): 425.

3. Discussing Wright's impressions of a colonial city like Accra, which looked sordid and decaying, Jack B. Moore in "No Street Numbers in Accra," in *The City in African-American Literature,* ed. Yoshinobu Hakutani and Robert Butler (Madison, NJ: Fairleigh Dickinson University Press / London: Associated University Presses, 1995), remarks, "True, the Old Slave Market in Christianborg is crumbling, its walls rotting and columns broken into rubble . . . but that is made to seem not a symbol of the old life's death, but of the constant decay of matter in the city where Ghana's new life will soon be constructed and centered" (71).

4. Commenting on African American novelists' use of a journey motif, Trudier Harris in *Fiction and Folklore: The Novels of Toni Morrison* (Knoxville: University of Tennessee Press, 1991), observes, "Paule Marshall has consciously tried to reconnect African-American and African traditions by exploring those in the Caribbean; her *Praisesong for the Window* (1983) also incorporates a journey motif with a quest for ancestors through legends told about them and ceremonies performed for them" (191).

5. Iyunolu Osagie, in "Is Morrison Also among the Prophets?: 'Psychoanalytic' Strategies in *Beloved*," *African American Review* 28 (Fall 1994): 423-40, also intrigued by Beloved's appearance and disappearance, argues that "the stories about Beloved's identity, her appearance, and her leave-taking are actually left to the reader's imagination." Osagie further notes that the "multiple readings of *Beloved* echo the elusive nature of psychoanalysis and its tendency to recover itself

constantly; this tendency makes psychoanalysis an uncanny representation of literature" (435).

6. Dogen's teaching is a refutation of the assumption that life and death are entirely separate entities as are seasons; Kodo Kurebayashi, *Introduction to Dogen Zen* [in Japanese] (Tokyo: Daihorinkaku, 1983), 121–29.

7. Interviewed by *L'Express* in 1955 shortly after the publication of *Black Power*, Wright responded to a question, "*Why do you write?*": "The accident of race and color has placed me on both sides: the Western World and its enemies. If my writing has any aim, it is to try to reveal that which is human on both sides, to affirm the essential unity of man on earth" (*Conversations with Richard Wright*, ed. Keneth Kinnamon and Michel Fabre [Jackson: University Press of Mississippi, 1993], 163).

8. Baby Suggs's celebration of love and kinship bears a resemblance to the opening lines of Whitman's "Song of Myself":

> I celebrate myself, and sing myself,
> And what I assume you shall assume,
> For every atom belonging to me as good belongs to you.
>
> I loafe and invite my soul,
> I lean and loafe at my ease observing a spear of summer
> grass. (*CPOW*, 25)

Later in the story, Morrison, in describing Baby Suggs's self-creation, refers to "the roots of her tongue" (*B*, 141), with which Baby Suggs tries to fill "the desolated center where the self that was no self made its home" (140). Whitman's lines quoted above are followed by these lines:

> My tongue, every atom of my blood, form'd from this soil,
> this air,
> Born here of parents born here from parents the same, and
> their parents the same. (25)

9. Trudier Harris reads Sethe's infanticide in light of the love theme: "If, on the other hand, we understand, accept, and perhaps even approve of the dynamics that allowed a slave mother to kill rather than have her children remanded to slavery, would not the dominant theme be love?" (*Fiction and Folklore*, 159–60).

10. While Wright was emotionally attracted to the tribal life, he was critical of its mysterious elements. Although he was convinced of the inevitable industrialization capitalism would bring about in Africa, he was extremely apprehensive of the exploitation of human power, a new form of slavery, that industrialism would introduce into Africa. Whether his argument is concerned with people or politics,

his emphasis is placed on self-creation, the generation of confidence in Africans themselves individually and as a culture.

11. Sethe's paradox is remindful of the action of Roxy, a slave mother in Mark Twain's *Pudd'nhead Wilson*. What Roxy does in switching the babies is deemed morally just because her action comes from her heart, from a mother's genuine love for her child.

12. Osagie's observation seems to reflect Wright's: "Freudian psychoanalysis," Osagie argues, "has its foundation in the oedipus complex. African psychoanalysis has its roots in the social and cultural setting of its peoples—in their beliefs in concepts such as nature, the supernatural realm, reincarnation, and retribution" ("Is Morrison Also among the Prophets?," 424).

13. Wright also maintains that Freudian approach does not apply to paganism, which characterizes Spanish culture. In discussing the symbolism of the Black Virgin, he tells his Spanish companion, "I'm not preaching the doctrine of Freud. Let the facts you see speak to you" (*PS*, 66). Later in the book Wright observes that "to have attempted a psychological approach in a Freudian sense would have implied a much more intimate acquaintance with the daily family lives of the people than I had—an access to case histories and clinical material even. Otherwise my facts would have been forever wide of the theories. In the end I resolved to accept the brute facts and let the theories go" (195).

CHAPTER 13

1. See Higginson, *Haiku Handbook*, 49–51.

2. See Yasuda, *Japanese Haiku*, xvii.

3. Higginson, *Haiku Handbook*, 51.

4. Ibid., 63–64.

5. See Harold Henderson, *An Introduction to Haiku: An Anthology of Poems and Poets from Basho to Shiki* (New York: Doubleday/Anchor, 1958), x.

6. Higginson, *Haiku Handbook*, 65.

7. See Kiuchi and Hakutani, *Richard Wright: A Documented Chronology*, 1908–1960, 204.

8. Michel Fabre, *The Unfinished Quest of Richard Wright* (New York: Morrow, 1973), 505. This poet was later identified as Sinclair Beiles, a South African Beat poet who was living in Paris as was Wright.

9. Ibid., 505–6.

10. Ibid., 506.

11. See Constance Webb, *Richard Wright: A Biography* (New York: Putnam, 1968), 387, 393–94.

12. Richard Wright, "Blueprint for Negro Writing," in *Richard Wright Reader*, ed. Ellen Wright and Michel Fabre (New York: Harper, 1978), 46.

13. Eight hundred seventeen haiku were published in *HTOW*; 3,183 haiku, the rest of the four thousand in the posthumous manuscript "Four Thousand Haiku," remain unpublished.

14. Robert Hass, "Five Haikus by Richard Wright," *Washington Post*, April 11, 1999.

15. Ibid.

16. William J. Higginson, "His Last Poems: Haiku," *Santa Fe New Mexican*, February 21, 1999.

17. Ibid.

18. Ibid.

19. Ibid.

20. Leza Lowitz, "Haiku as a Tether to Life and Emotional Safety Net," *Japan Times*, April 27, 1999.

21. Ibid.

22. The original in Japanese reads "Yama-dori-no | o | wo | fumu | haru no | iri-hi | kana" (Henderson, *Introduction to Haiku*, 102). The English translation is by Hakutani.

23. The original of this haiku by Basho is in Henderson, *Introduction to Haiku*, 40. The translation is by Hakutani.

24. See *HTOW*. The 817 haiku are numbered consecutively, as noted earlier; "In the Silent Forest" is 316 and "A Thin Waterfall" 569.

25. The word *sabi* in Japanese, a noun, derives from the verb *sabiru*, to rust, implying that what is described is aged, as discussed in chapter 1. Buddha's portrait hung in Zen temples, the old man with a thin body, is nearer to his soul as the old tree with its skin and leaves fallen is nearer to the very origin and essence of nature. For a further discussion of Buddha's portrait, see Max Loehr, *The Great Paintings of China* (New York: Harper and Row, 1980), 216.

26. As discussed earlier, while Freud defines death as the opposite of life, meaning that death reduces all animate things to the inanimate, Lacan defines death as "human experience, human interchanges, intersubjectivity," suggesting that death is part of life (*The Seminar of Jacques Lacan*, bk. 2, *The Ego in Freud's Theory and in the Techniques of Psychoanalysis, 1954–1955*, ed. Jacques-Alain Miller, trans. Sylvana Tomaselli [New York: Norton, 1988], 80). To Lacan, the death instinct is not "an admission of impotence, it isn't a coming to a halt before an irreducible, an ineffable last thing, it is a concept" (*Seminar*, 70).

27. This stanza, filled with rather superficial racial and cultural labels, is reminiscent of the least inspiring stanza in Whitman's "Song of Myself":

Magnifying and applying come I,
Outbidding at the start the old cautious hucksters,
Taking myself the exact dimensions of Jehovah,

Lithographing Kronos, Zeus his son, and Hercules his
 grandson,
Buying drafts of Osiris, Isis, Belus, Brahma, Buddha,
In my portfolio placing Manito loose, Allah on a leaf, the
 crucifix engraved,
With Odin and the hedeous-faced Mexitli and every idol and
 image.
(*CPOW*, 58)

28. Craig Werner, *Playing the Changes: From Afro-Modernism to the Jazz Impulse* (Urbana: University of Illinois Press, 1994), xxii.

29. The first collection of *renga*, *Chikuba Kyogin Shu* (*Chikuba Singers' Collection*, 1499) includes over two hundred *tsukeku* (adding verses) linked with the first verses of another poet. As the title of the collection suggests, the salient characteristic of *renga* was a display of ingenuity and coarse humor.

30. Werner, 247.

31. Gayl Jones, *Liberating Voices: Oral Tradition in African-American Literature* (Cambridge: Harvard University Press, 1991), 200.

32. Craig Werner has provided an incisive account of the jazz impulse: "Jazz, observed Louis Armstrong, is music that's never played the same way once. The world changes, the music changes. Jazz imagines the transitions, distills the deepest meanings of the moment we're in, how it developed from the ones that came before, how it opens up into the multiple possibilities of the ones to come" (*Change*, 132).

33. In "A Sight in Camp in the Daybreak Gray and Dim" (*CPOW*, 219), an elegy for the dead soldiers, Whitman, as noted earlier, celebrates their death and alludes to their natural and divine heritage.

34. Senryu, as noted earlier, is a humorous haiku. Senryu as a poetic genre thrives on moralizing nuances and a philosophical tone that expresses the incongruity of things rather than their oneness. Because senryu tend to appeal more to one's sense of the logical than to intuition, this jazz haiku can be read as a senryu.

WORKS CITED

Abbandonato, Linda. "A View from 'Elsewhere': Subversive Sexuality and the Rewriting of the Heroine's Story in *The Color Purple*." *PMLA* 106 (October 1991): 1106-15.

Akimoto, Fujio. *Haiku Nyumon* [*Introduction to Haiku*]. Tokyo: Kodansha, 1971.

Alcott, Bronson. "The Ideal Church." *Concord Days*. Boston: Roberts, 1872.

Aldington, Richard. "Penultimate Poetry." *Egoist* 1, no. 2 (January 1914).

Altschuler, Melvin. "An Important, but Exasperating Book." Review of *The Outsider*, by Richard Wright, *Washington Post*. Reprinted in Reilly, *Richard Wright*, 203–4.

Ando, Shoei. *Zen and American Transcendentalism*. Tokyo: Hokusei Press, 1970.

Anon. "No Castles in Spain." *Charlotte News*. Reprinted in Reilly, *Richard Wright*, 290.

Baldwin, James. *Nobody Knows My Name*. New York: Dell, 1961.

Barthes, Roland. *Empire of Signs*. Translated by Richard Howard. New York: Hill and Wang, 1982.

Blyth, R. H. *Haiku*. 4 vols. Tokyo: Hokuseido, 1949.

———. *Haiku: Eastern Culture*. Tokyo: Hokuseido, 1981.

———. *A History of Haiku*. 2 vols. Tokyo: Hokuseido, 1963, 1964.

Bontemps, Arna. Review of *The Outsider*, by Richard Wright. *Saturday Review* 36 (March 1953): 15-16.

Borch-Jacobsen, Mikkel. *Lacan: The Absolute Master*. Translated by Douglas Brick. Stanford: Stanford University Press, 1991.

Brooks, Gwendolyn. *Selected Poems*. 1963. Reprint, New York: Harper Perennial, 1999.

Brown, Lloyd. "Outside and Low." *Masses and Mainstream* 6 (May 1953): 62-64.

Butler, Robert. "The City as Psychological Frontier in Ralph Ellison's *Invisible Man* and Charles Johnson's *Faith and the Good Thing*." In *The City in*

African-American Literature, edited by Yoshinobu Hakutani and Robert Butler, 123-37. London and Toronto: Associated University Presses, 1995.

Camus, Albert. *Lyrical and Critical Essays*. Edited by Philip Thody. Translated by Ellen C. Kennedy. New York: Knopf, 1968.

———. *The Stranger*. Translated by Stuart Gilbert. 1942. Reprint, New York: Vintage, 1946.

Carpenter, Frederic Ives. *Emerson and Asia*. Cambridge: Harvard University Press, 1930.

Carpenter, Humphrey. *A Serious Character: The Life of Ezra Pound*. Boston: Houghton Mifflin, 1988.

Cather, Willa. "Two Poets: Yone Noguchi and Bliss Carman." In *The World and the Parish: Willa Cather's Articles and Reviews, 1893-1902*, edited by William M. Curtin. Vol. 2. Lincoln: University of Nebraska Press, 1970.

Christy, Arthur. *The Orient in American Transcendentalism*. New York: Columbia University Press, 1932.

Cooley, Nicole. "'Japan Has Become the Sign': Identity and History in Theresa Hak Kyung Cha's *Dictee*." In *Postmodernity and Cross-Culturalism*, edited by Yoshinobu Hakutani, 117-43. Madison, NJ: Fairleigh Dickinson University Press / London: Associated University Presses, 2002.

Crane, Stephen. *Great Short Works of Stephen Crane*. Edited by James B. Colvert. New York: Harper and Row, 1965.

Danquah, J. B. *The Akan Doctrine of God: A Fragment of Gold Coast Ethics and Religion*. London: Frank Cass, 1944.

Davie, Donald. *Ezra Pound*. New York: Viking, 1975.

de Luppe, Robert. *Albert Camus*. Paris: Temps Present, 1951.

Derrida, Jacques. *Writing and Difference*. Translated by Alan Bass. 1967 [in French]. Reprint, Chicago: University of Chicago Press, 1978.

Dickinson, Emily. *The Complete Poems of Emily Dickinson*. Edited by Thomas H. Johnson. Boston: Little, Brown, 1960.

———. *The Poems of Emily Dickinson*. 3 vols. 1951. Edited by Thomas H. Johnson. Cambridge: Harvard University Press, 1963.

Dimock, Wai Chee. *Through Other Continents: American Literature across Deep Time*. Princeton, NJ: Princeton University Press, 2006.

Dreiser, Theodore. *Sister Carrie*. New York: Doubleday, 1900.

Durant, Alan. "Pound, Modernism and Literary Criticism: A Reply to Donald Davie." *Critical Quarterly* 28 (Spring-Summer 1986): 154-66.

Eliot, T. S. *Selected Essays, 1917-1932*. New York: Harcourt, 1932.

Ellison, Ralph. *Going to the Territory*. New York: Random House, 1986.

———. *Invisible Man*. 1952. Reprint, New York: Vintage, 1995.

———. "The Negro and the Second World War." *Negro Quarterly* (1943). Reprinted in *Cultural Contexts for Ralph Ellison's "Invisible Man*,*"* edited by Eric J. Sundquist, 233-40. Boston: Bedford, 1995.

———. "Richard Wright's Blues." *Antioch Review* 5 (June 1945): 198-211.

———. *Shadow and Act.* New York: Random House, 1964.

Emanuel, James A. *Jazz from the Haiku King.* Detroit: Broadside, 1999.

Emerson, Ralph Waldo. *The Complete Essays and Other Writings of Ralph Waldo Emerson.* Edited by Brooks Atkinson. New York: Modern Library, 1940.

———. *Journals of Ralph Waldo Emerson, 1821-1872.* Vol. 1. Edited by E. W. Emerson and W. E. Forbes. Boston: Houghton Mifflin, 1911.

———. *The Poems of Ralph Waldo Emerson.* Edited by Louis Untermeyer. New York: Heritage, 1945.

———. *Selected Writings of Ralph Waldo Emerson.* Edited by William H. Gilman. New York: New American Library, 1965.

———. *Selections from Ralph Waldo Emerson.* Edited by Stephen E. Whicher. Boston: Houghton Mifflin, 1960.

———. *The Works of Emerson.* 4 vols. New York: Tudor, 1900.

Fabre, Michel. "The Poetry of Richard Wright." In *Critical Essays of Richard Wright*, edited by Yoshinobu Hakutani, 252-72. Boston: G. K. Hall, 1975.

———. *Richard Wright: Books and Writers.* Jackson: University Press of Mississippi, 1990.

———. "Richard Wright, French Existentialism, and *The Outsider*." In *Critical Essays on Richard Wright*, edited by Yoshinobu Hakutani, 182-98. Boston: G. K. Hall, 1982.

———. *The Unfinished Quest of Richard Wright.* New York: Morrow, 1973.

Fenollosa, Ernest. *The Chinese Written Character as a Medium for Poetry.* Edited by Ezra Pound. New York: Arrow, 1936.

Feuerlicht, Ignace. "Camus's *L'Étranger* Reconsidered." *PMLA* 78 (December 1963): 606-21.

Franklin, Benjamin. *The Autobiography.* Edited by Max Farrand. Berkeley: University of California Press, 1949.

———. *The Autobiography.* In *Anthology of American Literature.* Vol. 1, *Colonial through Romantic*, 6th ed., edited by George McMichael. Upper Saddle River, NJ: Prentice Hall, 1997.

Freneau, Philip. "The Indian Burying Ground." In *The Poems of Philip Freneau*, edited by Fred Lewis Pattee. New York: Russell and Russell, 1963.

Frost, Robert. *Robert Frost's Poems.* Edited by Louis Untermeyer. New York: Pocket Books, 1971.

Gifford, Barry, and Lawrence Lee. *Jack's Book: An Oral Biography of Jack Kerouac.* New York: St. Martin's, 1978.

Gilroy, Paul. *The Black Atlantic: Modernity and Double Consciousness.* Cambridge: Harvard University Press, 1993.

Glicksberg, Charles I. "Existentialism in *The Outsider*." *Four Quarters* 7 (January 1958): 17-26.

———. "The God of Fiction." *Colorado Quarterly* 7 (Autumn 1958): 207-20.

Goodwin, K. L. *The Influence of Ezra Pound.* London: Oxford University Press, 1966.

Goto, Shoji. *The Philosophy of Emerson and Thoreau: Orientals Meet Occidentals.* Lewiston, NY: Edwin Mellen, 2007.

Graham, Don B. "Yone Noguchi's 'Poe Mania.'" *Markham Review* 4 (1974): 58-60.

Hakutani, Yoshinobu. "Emerson, Whitman, and Zen Buddhism." *Midwest Quarterly* 31 (Summer 1990): 433-48.

———. "Ezra Pound, Yone Noguchi, and Imagism." *Modern Philology* 90 (August 1992): 46-69.

———. "Father and Son: A Conversation with Isamu Noguchi." *Journal of Modern Literature* 42 (Summer 1990): 13-33.

———. *Richard Wright and Racial Discourse.* Columbia: University of Missouri Press, 1996.

———. "Richard Wright's Haiku, Zen, and the African 'Primal Outlook upon Life.'" *Modern Philology* 104 (May 2007): 510-28.

———. "Yone Noguchi's Poetry: From Whitman to Zen." *Comparative Literature Studies* 22 (1985): 67-79.

Harding, Walter. *A Thoreau Handbook.* New York: New York University Press, 1959.

Harmer, J. B. *Victory in Limbo: Imagism 1908-1917.* New York: St. Martin's, 1975.

Harris, Trudier. *Fiction and Folklore: The Novels of Toni Morrison.* Knoxville: University of Tennessee Press, 1991.

Hawthorne, Nathaniel. *The Scarlet Letter.* Edited by Ross C. Murfin. Boston: St. Martin's, 1991.

Hearn, Lafcadio. *Japan: An Attempt at Interpretation.* New York: Grosset & Dunlap, 1904.

Heidegger, Martin. *Poetry, Language, Thought.* Translated by A. Hofstadter. New York: Harper and Row, 1975.

Hemingway, Ernest. *The Sun Also Rises.* New York: Charles Scribner's Sons, 1926.

Henderson, Harold G. *An Introduction to Haiku: An Anthology of Poems and Poets from Basho to Shiki.* New York: Doubleday/Anchor, 1958.

Hisamatsu, Hoseki Shin'ichi. *Zen and Fine Arts.* Kyoto: Bokushi-sha, 1958.

Hughes, Langston. *Selected Poems of Langston Hughes.* New York: Knopf, 1959.

Imoto, Noichi. *Basho: Son Jinsei to Geijitsu [Basho: His Life and Art].* Tokyo: Kodansha, 1968.

James, Henry. "Preface to *The Ambassadors.*" In *The Ambassadors,* edited by S. P. Rosenbaum, 1-15. New York: Norton, 1964.

Jefferson, Thomas. *Notes on the State of Virginia.* Edited by William Peden. Chapel Hill: University of North Carolina Press, 1955.

Jenkins, McKay. "Rushdie's *Midnight's Children,* Meditation, and the Postmodern Conception of History." In *Postmodernity and Cross-Culturalism,* edited by

Yoshinobu Hakutani. Madison, NJ: Fairleigh Dickinson University Press / London: Associated University Presses, 2002.

———. "Womb with a View: Proust's Magical Mindfulness." In *Modernity in East-West Literary Criticism: New Readings*, edited by Yoshinobu Hakutani, 158-68. Madison, NJ: Fairleigh Dickinson University Press / London: Associated University Presses, 2001.

Jones, A. R. *The Life and Opinions of Thomas Ernest Hulme*. Boston: Beacon, 1960.

Jones, Gayl. *Liberating Voices: Oral Tradition in African-American Literature*. Cambridge: Harvard University Press, 1991.

Keene, Donald. *World within Walls: Japanese Literature of the Pre-Modern Era, 1600-1868*. New York: Grove, 1976.

Kenner, Hugh. *The Poetry of Ezra Pound*. Millwood, NY: Kraus, 1947.

Kerouac, Jack. *Book of Haikus*. Edited and with an introduction by Regina Weinreich. New York: Penguin Books, 2003.

———. *The Dharma Bums*. New York: Viking, 1958.

———. "Essentials of Spontaneous Prose." *Evergreen Review* 2 (Summer 1958): 72-73.

———. *On the Road*. New York: Viking, 1957.

Kiuchi, Toru. Letter to Yoshinobu Hakutani on Sinclair Beiles. August 7, 2005.

Kiuchi, Toru, and Yoshinobu Hakutani. *Richard Wright: A Documented Chronology, 1908–1960*. Jefferson, NC: McFarland, 2014.

Kodama, Sanehide, ed. *Ezra Pound and Japan: Letters and Essays*. Redding Ridge, CT: Black Swan, 1987.

Kurebayashi, Kodo. *Introduction to Dogen Zen* [in Japanese]. Tokyo: Daihorinka-ku, 1983.

Lacan, Jacques. *The Four Fundamental Concepts of Psychoanalysis*. Edited by Jacques-Alain Miller. Translated by Alan Sheridan. New York: Norton, 1881.

———. *The Seminar of Jacques Lacan*, bk. 2, *The Ego in Freud's Theory and in the Techniques of Psychoanalysis, 1954-1955*. Edited by Jacques-Alain Miller. Translated by Sylvana Tomaselli. New York: Norton, 1988.

Learned, Barry. "U. S. Lets Negro Explain Race Ills, Wright Declares." In Kinnamon and Fabre, *Conversations with Richard Wright*, 184-86.

Lee, Kun Jong. "Ellison's *Invisible Man*: Emersonianism Revised." *PMLA* 107 (March 1992): 331-44.

Loehr, Max. *The Great Paintings of China*. New York: Harper and Row, 1980.

Lynch, Tom. "Intersecting Influences in American Haiku." In *Modernity in East-West Literary Criticism: New Readings*, edited by Yoshinobu Hakutani. Madison, NJ: Fairleigh Dickinson University Press / London: Associated University Presses, 2001.

McKay, Nelie. "An Interview with Toni Morrison." *Contemporary Literature* 24 (Winter 1983): 413-29.

McMahon, Francis E., S. J. "Spain through Secularist Spectacles." *America* 96 (March 1957): 648, 653. Reprinted in Reilly, *Richard Wright*, 300.

Melville, Herman. *Moby-Dick*. Edited by Harrison Hayford and Hershel Parker. New York: Norton, 1967.

Miller, Liam. *The Noble Drama of W. B. Yeats*. Dublin: Dolmen, 1977.

Miner, Earl. *The Japanese Tradition in British and American Literature*. Princeton, NJ: Princeton University Press, 1958.

——. "Pound, Haiku and the Image." *Hudson Review* 9 (Winter 1957): 570-84.

Moore, Jack B. "No Street Numbers in Accra." In *The City in African-American Literature*, edited by Yoshinobu Hakutani and Robert Butler, 64-78. Madison, NJ: Fairleigh Dickinson University Press / London: Associated University Presses, 1995.

Morrison, Toni. *Beloved*. New York: Knopf, 1987.

——. *Jazz*. New York: Plume, 1993.

——. "Memory, Creation, and Writing." *Thought* 59 (1984): 385-90.

——. "Rootedness: The Ancestor as Foundation." In *Black Women Writers (1950-1980): A Critical Evaluation*, edited by Mari Evans, 339-45. Garden City, NY: Doubleday, 1984.

Myrdal, Gunnar. *An American Dilemma: The Negro Problems and American Democracy*. 2 vols. 1944. Reprint, New York: McGraw Hill, 1962.

Noguchi, Isamu. *A Sculptor's World*. New York: Harper and Row, 1968.

Noguchi, Yone. *Collected English Letters*. Edited by Ikuko Atsumi. Tokyo: Yone Noguchi Society, 1975.

——. "The Everlasting Sorrow: A Japanese Noh Play." *Egoist* 4 (October 1917): 141-43.

——. *Japan and America*. Tokyo: Keio University Press, 1921.

——. *Japanese Hokkus*. Boston: Four Seas, 1920.

——. "The Japanese Noh Play." *Egoist* 5 (August 1918): 99.

——. "Japanese Poetry." *The Transactions of the Japan Society of London* 12 (1914): 86-109.

——. "Koyetsu." *Rhythm* 11, no. 11 (December 1912): 302-5.

——. "The Last Master [Yoshitoshi] of the Ukiyoye School." *Transactions of the Japan Society of London* 12 (April 1914): 144-56.

——. *The Pilgrimage*. 2 vols. Tokyo: Kyobunkan, 1909.

——. *Seen and Unseen, or, Monologues of a Homeless Snail*. San Francisco: Gelett Burgess and Porter Garnett, 1897.

——. *Selected English Writings of Yone Noguchi: An East-West Literary Assimilation*. Edited by Yoshinobu Hakutani. 2 vols. Rutherford, NJ: Fairleigh Dickinson University Press / London: Associated University Presses, 1990, 1992.

——. *The Spirit of Japanese Art*. London: John Murray / New York: Dutton, 1915.

———. *The Spirit of Japanese Poetry*. London: John Murray / New York: Dutton, 1914.

———. "The Spirit of Japanese Poetry," in Noguchi, *Selected English Writings of Yone Noguchi*, 2:73-74.

———. *The Story of Yone Noguchi Told by Himself*. London: Chatto and Windus, 1914.

———. *Through the Torii*. Boston: Four Seas, 1922.

———. *Utamaro*. London: Elkin Mathews, 1923.

———. "Utamaro." *Rhythm* 11, no. 10 (November 1912): 257–60.

———. *The Voice of the Valley*. San Francisco: Doxey, 1897.

———. "What Is a Hokku Poem?" *Rhythm* 11, no. 10 (January 1913): 354-59.

Orwell, George. "Inside the Whale." In *Collected Essays, Journalism and Letters*. London: Penguin, 1970.

Osagie, Iyunolu. "Is Morrison Also among the Prophets?: 'Psychoanalytic' Strategies in *Beloved*." *African American Review* 28 (Fall 1994): 423-40.

Poe, Edgar Allan. *The Complete Works of Edgar Allan Poe*. Edited by James Albert Harrison. New York: Crowell, 1902.

———. *Selected Writings of Edgar Allan Poe*. Edited by Edward H. Davidson. Boston: Houghton Mifflin, 1956.

Pound, Ezra. "As for Imagisme." *New Age* 14 (1915): 349.

———. *Ezra Pound: Selected Poems*. New York: New Directions, 1957.

———. *Gaudier-Brzeska: A Memoir*. 1916. Reprint, New York: New Directions, 1970.

———. *Literary Essays of Ezra Pound*. Edited and introduced by T. S. Eliot. New York: New Directions, 1954.

———. *Personae*. New York: New Directions, 1926.

———. *The Spirit of Romance*. New York: New Directions, 1968.

———. "Vorticism." *Fortnightly Review*, n.s., 573 (September 1914): 461-71.

Pound, Ezra, and Ernest Fenollosa. *The Classic Noh Theatre of Japan*. New York: New Directions, 1959.

Pratt, William. *The Imagist Poem*. New York: Dutton, 1963.

Prescott, Orville. Review of Richard Wright, *The Outsider*. *New York Times*, March 10, 1953.

Proust, Marcel. *Remembrance of Things Past*, vol. 1. Translated by C. K. Scott Moncrief and Terence Kilmartin. New York: Random House, 1981.

Purdy, Stropher B. "*An American Tragedy* and *L'Étranger*." *Comparative Literature* 19 (Summer 1967): 252-68.

Redding, Saunders. "Reflections on Richard Wright: A Symposium on an Exiled Native Son." In *Anger and Beyond: The Negro Writer in the United States*, edited by Herbert Hill. New York: Harper, 1966.

———. Review of *The Outsider*, by Richard Wright. *Baltimore Afro-American*, May 19, 1953, 15-16.

———. Review of *Pagan Spain*, by Richard Wright. *Baltimore Afro-American*. Reprinted in Reilly, *Richard Wright*, 299.

Reilly, John M., ed. *Richard Wright: The Critical Reception*. New York: Franklin, 1978.

Rhea, James N. *Providence Sunday Journal*, March 22, 1953.

Richardson, Robert D., Jr. *Henry Thoreau: A Life of the Mind*. Berkeley: University of California Press, 1986.

———. "Thoreau, Henry David." In *Encyclopedia of American Literature*, edited by Steven R. Serafin, 1142-46. New York: Continuum, 1999.

Ross, Bruce. "North American Versions of Haibun and Postmodern American Culture." In *Postmodernity and Cross-Culturalism*, edited by Yoshinobu Hakutani, 168-200. Madison, NJ: Fairleigh Dickinson University Press / London: Associated University Presses, 2002.

Rushdie, Salman. *Shame*. London: Picador, 1983.

Samuels, Robert. "Emerson, Lacan, and Zen: Transcendental and Postmodern Conceptions of the Eastern Subject." In *Postmodernity and Cross-Culturalism*, edited by Yoshinobu Hakutani, 157-67. Madison, NJ: Fairleigh Dickinson University Press / London: Associated University Presses, 2002.

Sanchez, Sonia. *Like the Singing Coming Off the Drums*. Boston: Beacon , 1998.

———. *Morning Haiku*. Boston: Beacon, 2010.

Savery, Pancho. "'Not like an arrow, but a boomerang': Ellison's Existential Blues." In *Approaches to Teaching Ellison's "Invisible Man,"* edited by Susan Resneck Parr and Pancho Savery, 65-74. New York: MLA, 1986.

Sharp, E. A. *William Sharp: A Memoir*. London: Heinemann, 1910.

Shirane, Haruo. *Traces of Dreams: Landscape, Cultural Memory, and the Poetry of Bashō*. Stanford, CA: Stanford University Press, 1998.

Stephenson, Mary Ellen. "Spain Gets Bitter Barks from Visitor." In Reilly, *Richard Wright*, 307.

Stepto, Robert. *From behind the Veil: A Study of Afro-American Narrative*. Urbana: University of Illinois Press, 1979.

St. Jean, Shawn. "'Three Meals a Day and the Fun of It': Existential Hunger and the Magnificent Seven/Samurai." In *Postmodernity and Cross-Culturalism*, edited by Yoshinobu Hakutani. Madison, NJ: Fairleigh Dickinson University Press / London: Associated University Presses, 2002.

Stock, Noel. *Poet in Exile: Ezra Pound*. Manchester: Manchester University Press, 1964.

Suzuki, Daisetz T. *An Introduction to Zen Buddhism*. New York: Philosophical Library, 1949.

Teele, Roy E. "The Japanese Translations." *Texas Quarterly* 10 (1967): 61-66.

Thoreau, Henry David. *Early Essays and Miscellanies*. Edited by Joseph J. Moldenhauer et al. Princeton, NJ: Princeton University Press, 1975.

———. *Journal: The Writings of Henry D. Thoreau*. Edited by Elizabeth Hall Whitherell et al. 10 vols. Princeton, NJ: Princeton University Press, 1981.

———. *The Portable Thoreau*. Edited by Carl Bode. Revised Edition. New York: Viking, 1964.

———. *Reform Papers: The Writings of Henry D. Thoreau*. Edited by Wendell Glick. Princeton, NJ: Princeton University Press, 1973.

———. "Sayings of Confucius." In *Early Essays and Miscellanies*, edited by Joseph J. Moldenhauer et al, 140-42. Princeton, NJ: Princeton University Press, 1975.

———. *The Variorum Civil Disobedience*. Edited by Walter Harding. New York: Twayne, 1967.

———. *Walden*. Edited by J. Lyndon Shanley. Princeton, NJ: Princeton University Press, 1971.

———. *A Week on the Concord and Merrimack Rivers*. Edited by Carl F. Hovde et al. Princeton, NJ: Princeton University Press, 1980.

Tomlinson, Charles. "Introduction to *Selected Poems* by William Carlos Williams." In *William Carlos Williams and Charles Tomlinson: A Transatlantic Connection*, edited by Barry Magid and Hugh Witemeyer, 89-102. New York: Peter Lang, 1999.

Tonkinson, Carol, ed. *Big Sky Mind: Buddhism and the Beat Generation*. New York: Riverhead, 1995.

Toyama, Usaburo, ed. *Essays on Yone Noguchi*. 3 vols. Tokyo: Zokei Bijutsu Kyokai, 1963.

Tucker, Lindsey. "Alice Walker's *The Color Purple*: Emergent Woman, Emergent Text." *Black American Literature Forum* 22 (Spring 1988): 81-95.

Twain, Mark. *Adventures of Huckleberry Finn*. Edited by Sculley Bradley et al. New York: Norton, 1977.

Tytell, John. *Naked Angels: The Lives & Literature of the Beat Generation*. New York: McGraw-Hill, 1977.

Ueda, Makoto. *Zeami, Basho, Yeats, Pound: A Study in Japanese and English Poetics*. The Hague: Mouton, 1965.

Versluis, Arthur. *American Transcendentalism and Asian Religions*. New York and Oxford: Oxford University Press, 1993.

Waley, Arthur. *The Nō Plays of Japan*. New York: Grove, 1920.

Walker, Alice. *The Color Purple*. 1982. Reprint, New York: Pocket Books, 1985.

———. *In Search of Our Mothers' Gardens*. New York: Harcourt, 1983.

Walker, Margaret. *Richard Wright: Daemonic Genius*. New York: Warner Books, 1988.

Webb, Constance. *Richard Wright: A Biography*. New York: Putnam, 1968.

Werner, Craig. *A Change Is Gonna Come: Music, Race & the Soul of America*. New York: Plume, 1999.

———. *Playing the Changes: From Afro-Modernism to the Jazz Impulse*. Urbana: University of Illinois Press, 1994.

Whitman, Walt. *Complete Poetry and Selected Prose*. Edited by James E. Miller Jr. Boston: Houghton Mifflin, 1959.

———. *Democratic Vistas and Other Papers*. Edited by Richard Maurice Bucke et al. London: Routledge & Kegan Paul, 1906.

———. *Leaves of Grass*. Edited by Sculley Bradley et al. New York: New York University Press, 1980.

Wright, Julia. "Introduction." In *Haiku: This Other World* by Richard Wright, edited by Yoshinobu Hakutani and Robert L. Tener, vii-xii. New York: Arcade, 1998. Reprint, New York: Random House, 2000.

Wright, Richard. *American Hunger*. 1977. Reprint, New York: Harper and Row, 1979.

———. *Black Boy: A Record of Childhood and Youth*. 1945. Reprint, New York: Harper and Row, 1966.

———. *Black Power: A Record of Reactions in a Land of Pathos*. New York: Harper, 1954.

———. "Blueprint for Negro Writing." In *Richard Wright Reader*, edited by Ellen Wright and Michel Fabre, 36-49. New York: Harper, 1978.

———. *The Color Curtain: A Report on the Bandung Conference*. Cleveland: World, 1956.

———. *Conversations with Richard Wright*. Edited by Keneth Kinnamon and Michel Fabre. Jackson: University Press of Mississippi, 1993.

———. *Eight Men*. Cleveland: World, 1961.

———. "Four Thousand Haiku." Unpublished manuscript. New Haven: Beinecke Rare Book and Manuscript Library, Yale University, 1960.

———. *Haiku: This Other World*. Edited by Yoshinobu Hakutani and Robert L. Tener. New York: Arcade, 1998. Reprint, New York: Random House, 2000. Reprint, *Haiku: The Last Poems of an American Icon*. New York: Arcade, 2012.

———. "An Interview with Richard Wright by Peter Schmid/1946." In Kinnamon and Fabre, *Conversations with Richard Wright*, 106-10.

———. *Later Works*. Edited by Arnold Rampersad. New York: Library of America, 1991.

———. *The Long Dream*. 1958. Reprint, New York: Harper and Row, 1987.

———. "The Man Who Lived Underground." In Wright, *Eight Men*.

———. *Native Son*. 1940. Reprint, New York: Harper and Row, 1966.

———. *The Outsider*. 1953. Reprint, New York: Harper and Row, 1965.

———. *Pagan Spain*. New York: Harper and Brothers, 1957.

———. "This Other World: Projections in the Haiku Manner." Unpublished manuscript. New Haven: Beinecke Rare Book and Manuscript Library, Yale University, 1960.

————. *12 Million Black Voices: A Folk History of the Negro in the United States*. New York: Viking, 1941.

————. *Uncle Tom's Children*. 1940. Reprint, New York: Harper and Row, 1965.

Yeats, W. B. *Autobiography*. New York: Macmillan, 1938.

————. "Introduction to *Certain Noble Plays of Japan* by Pound & Fenollosa." In *The Classic Noh Theatre of Japan*, 151-63. New York: New Directions, 1959.

————. *The Poems of W. B. Yeats*. Edited by Richard J. Finneran. New York: Macmillan, 1983.

————. *Reveries over Childhood and Youth*. Dublin: Cuala, 1916.

————. *The Variorum Edition of the Plays of W. B. Yeats*. Edited by Russell K. Alspach. New York: Macmillan, 1966.

Youmans, Rich. "For My Wife on Our First Anniversary." *Brussels Sprout* 11, no. 3 (1994): 15.

Yu, Beongcheon. *The Great Circle: American Writers and the Orient*. Detroit: Wayne State University Press, 1983.

INDEX

Baraka, Amiri, 23, 255

Barthes, Roland, 19, 48, 271n10, 274n4

Basho, 7, 8, 28–29, 32, 40–43, 48, 52, 61, 64,
92–97, 106, 131–34, 136, 139–40, 157,
160, 171–72, 241–42, 244, 252–53, 260,
266, 275n7, 277n1, 280n14, 280nn17,
19–20, 281n21, 283n11, 287n18, 295n5,
296n23

*Basho: Sono Jinsei to Geijitsu [Basho: His Life
and Art]* (Imoto), 280n19

Bassui, 59, 194, 221

"Because I Could Not Stop for Death" (Dickinson), 160

Beethoven, Ludwig van, 38

Beiles, Sinclair, 16, 295n8

Beloved (Morrison), 179, 227–32, 234–36,
238–39, 293n5, 294n8

Bhagavad Gita, 4, 6

"Big Boy Leaves Home" (Wright), 208

Binyon, Laurence, 280n10

*Black Atlantic: Modernity and Double Con-
sciousness* (Gilroy), 289n2

Black Boy: A Record of Childhood and Youth
(Wright), 14–15, 131, 182–83, 217, 221,
246, 291n4

*Black Power: A Record of Reactions in a Land
of Pathos* (Wright), 20–21, 195–96,
208, 213, 219–21, 223, 227–29, 235–36,
238–39, 243, 253, 258, 264, 289n2,
292nn6, 8, 11, 294n7

"Blueprint for Negro Writing" (Wright), 221,
288n2, 295n12

"Blues Haiku" (Sanchez), 252

Blyth, R. H., 16–18, 28–32, 39–43, 48, 131,
134–36, 156–57, 160, 172–73, 232,
241–43, 247–49, 274n5, 280n20, 283nn3,
7, 284nn13–15, 17, 27, 287n18

"Bojangles and Jo" (Emanuel), 263

Bonneau, Georges, 242

Bontemps, Arna, 129

Book of Haikus (Kerouac), 156, 287nn12–13

Borch-Jacobsen, Mikkel, 274n3

"Brahma" (Emerson), 62, 65

Brancusi, Constantin, 110

Brick, Douglas, 274n3

Bridges, Robert, 72, 102, 280n10

"Bright Harvest Moon, The" (Kikaku), 142

Brooks, Gwendolyn, 162, 258–59, 286n11

Brown, James, 259

Brown, Lloyd, 282n3

Buddha Leaving the Mountains (Liang K'ai),
61, 65, 134

Burgess, Gelett, 89, 279n2

Burroughs, William, 16, 155

Buson, 48, 92, 94, 104, 106, 131, 140–41, 244,
248, 250–52, 284n18–19

Butler, Robert, 288n7, 293n3

"Butterfly Makes, A" (Wright), 140

Calvary (Yeats), 77, 83

Camus, Albert, 14, 16, 23, 111, 113, 115–21,
124–27, 129–30, 190, 250, 282nn1, 8,
283nn9, 11

"Camus's *L'Étranger* Reconsidered" (Feuerlicht), 283n11

Cantos (Pound), 81, 109

Carlyle, Thomas, 88

Carman, Bliss, 89, 279n3

Carpenter, Frederic Ives, 4, 45, 272n2, 273n1

Carpenter, Humphrey, 281nn27, 30, 282n34

Cassady, Neal, 163–64

Castro, Américo, 205

Cathay (Pound), 109

Cather, Willa, 89, 279n3

Cent Visions de Guerre (Vocance), 241

Certain Noble Plays of Japan (Yeats), 71

Cha, Theresa Hak Kyung, 22, 272n13

Chamberlain, Basil Hall, 242

Chap Book, The (journal), 89

Charters, Ann, 287n14

Chikuba Kyogin Shu (collection of *renga*),
92–93, 297n29

"Chinese Written Character as a Medium of
Poetry, The" (Fenollosa), 10

*Chinese Written Character as a Medium of
Poetry, The* (Fenollosa), 271n6

"Chiru Hana wo" (Sadaiye), 92

Christy, Arthur, 4, 272n2

"City as Psychological Frontier in Ralph Ellison's *Invisible Man* and Charles Johnson's
Faith and the Good Thing, The" (Butler),
288n7

ABOUT THE AUTHOR

Yoshinobu Hakutani is Professor of English and University Distinguished Scholar at Kent State University in Ohio. He is the author of several books, including *Richard Wright and Haiku* (University of Missouri Press). He lives in Kent, Ohio.